THE
LAST
MISSION

Jim B. Smith

For Vincent Di Gangi Sr. —
A Privilege To Share This
"Unknown" B-29 Saga
With You.   Blessings Always
Jim

J. B. SMITH ENTERPRISES, LTD.

Jim B. Smith
1996

2

Published by: J. B. SMITH ENTERPRISES, LTD.
                  111 N. Jefferson
                  Mt. Pleasant, IA 52641

All opinions contained herein are those of the author and in no way reflect the views of the publisher, either expressed or implied.

Assist
Cover Design,
Layout and
Typography: A.N.T. Publications

Printing: Dodd Printing & Stationery, Inc./Kimberley Press, Ltd.

TABLE OF CONTENTS

ACKNOWLEDGMENTS

I want to thank the 20th Air Force and all of its B-29 crew members for setting the standards of excellence that gave all of us the biggest punch with the least risk.

If it weren't for the teamwork and commitment of my crew I wouldn't be here to write this story. In my opinion, they were without equal: Carl Schahrer, Aircraft Commander; John Waltershausen, Pilot; Dick Marshall, Bombardier; Hank Gorder, Engineer; Tom Cosola, Navigator; Dick Ginster, Radar Navigator; Hank Leffler, Left Scanner; Henry Carlson, Right Scanner; Sid Siegel, Tail Gunner.

I also want to give my thanks and gratitude to our super-dedicated and miracle-working Crew Chief, Technical Sergeant Lloyd Jennings, and to his crew. They kept our bird "The Boomerang" at full fighting strength under always difficult and sometimes impossible circumstances.

A special thank you goes to the following people who so generously shared their photographs and their memories: Margaret Hubbard, widow of General Boyd Hubbard; Fred J. Williams; Rodger Jensen; Chuck Miller; William E. Cooper; John T. Nightingale and Suzanne M. Nightingale, son and daughter of Stanley W. Nightingale; other contributing members of the 315th Bomb Wing. I also want to thank Richard Zeke Cormier and Chris G. Patterakis for their generous participation. And I want to thank my friend, Arnold Moselle, W. W. II B-17 Commander and writer, for his meticulous editing.

A salute to A.N.T. Publications: Jim and Lani Muche, Bill and Dave Moyle, Jeff Williams. This top team of experts picked up The Last Mission project, dusted it off, and set it on its true course. My sincere gratitude to these individuals whose relentless dedication to aviation speaks loud and clear in their contributions to this book.

Mort Dodds, Audrey Dodds, and I brought back the beginning and our forever friendship as we harmonized to "Sioux City Sue" in Phoenix, Arizona. One thing led to another and Mort asked to take over the publishing of "The Last Mission" story. We all thank him and Audrey for making this remarkable story available to the world.

My sincere gratitude to the 20th Air Force Association President, John E. Jennings, for his support in the preparation of this story. As one of the youngest Aircraft Commanders, he flew a high number of combat missions including one of the final missions of W. W. II.

And finally, I dedicate The Last Mission story to Darin C. Maurer, the boy I proudly call my son. He lifted me, gave me purpose, and insisted that I write this eyewitness account myself. Without his persistence and encouragement, this book would have been a watered-down story by Jim B. Smith "as told to", or Jim B. Smith "with so and so."

PROLOGUE

World War II, 1945:

I was a radio operator on "The Boomerang", a B-29B Superfortress which was attached to the 315th Bombardment Wing. The 315th Wing and its four bomb groups conducted combat bombing missions from Northwest Field, Guam to the Japanese Empire. On August 14/15, 1945, we of the 315th flew the longest mission in history, striking a Japanese target that was located 277.8 miles northwest of Tokyo. Our bombs destroyed the mission target 9 days after the first atomic bomb devastated Hiroshima, and 6 days after the second atomic bomb had demolished Nagasaki. The B-29s we flew had been stripped of all armament with the exception of a tail turret which featured two fifty caliber machine guns and a 20 millimeter cannon. We carried a maximum bomb load and flew without the assistance of bomb bay fuel tanks. The official end of the war was announced while we were still airborne. The atomic bombs brought Japan to the peace table, but it took The Last Mission to end the war.

I suspected from the moment we were ordered to fly this last mission, that there was more to the operation than met the eye. The touchdown on our return to Northwest Field marked the end of the mission but the beginning of what became my unrelenting search for the truth of this event. The tactical mission report of the last mission was quietly declassified in 1985, but its explosive findings supported my initial feeling that this strike was vastly more important than anyone had first

believed. This information, along with a bountiful harvest of other hard evidence gathered over the years, shows how the last mission insured a Japanese surrender that was being seriously challenged by an Imperial Palace insurrection. Any extension of the war could have triggered the atomic bombing of Tokyo or a US invasion; either option carried the promise of unthinkable consequences, especially for Japan. For Japan, the last U.S. bombing mission was a monumental blessing in disguise.

We of the 315th Bomb Wing were chosen to fly all weather precision missions using the AN/APQ-7 Eagle radar system. This system was synchronized electrically to the optical Norden bombsight, facilitating a new bombing technique that was called synchronous radar bombing.

Our B-29s had been stripped of armament so we could fly higher, faster, farther, and carry a heavier bomb load. We flew by night to compensate for our lack of firepower, and to keep our stripped aircraft a secret. Daylight takeoffs and landings were ordered to further maximize safety. The Wing took off for mission targets in late afternoon and returned some 13 to 17 hours later.

An unexpected field order scheduled my crew, along with 143 other 315th Wing B-29's to fly the last mission on 14/15 August 1945. One hundred thirty two B-29s effectively bombed the primary target and it was the longest mission ever attempted from the Mariannas with a full bomb load and without bomb bay fuel tanks. The duration of the mission was 16 hours and 50 minutes.

HISTORY REVEALED

In March 1942, President Franklin D. Roosevelt wrote to the Director of the Bureau of the Budget and ordered each war agency to prepare an accurate and objective account of the agency's war experience. Lieutenant Colonel Wesley Frank Craven of New York University and Major James Lea Cate of the University of Chicago were selected as editors for the Army Air Forces historical accounts. Craven and Cate prepared seven volumes, The Army Air Forces in World War II, which were published between 1948 and 1958. In this prestigious work the authors state that all historical works a generation old suffer limitations from subsequent findings. Craven and Cate predicted that new information would supersede and change the emphasis of their historical accounts as well.

In the memoirs of Harry S. Truman, the late President states: "Occasionally, as we pore through the pages of history, we are struck by the fact that some incident, little noted at the time, profoundly affects the whole subsequent course of events."

The awesome destructive power of the atom bomb captured all the imagination and interest of the day. The true significance of the last B-29 mission was simply upstaged by the atom and lost to the mushrooming clouds of Hiroshima and Nagasaki.

It's been my passion to bring the last mission back into focus and show how this longest strike by the 315th Bomb Wing impacted history. I have opened up a time capsule of the last days of the Pacific War, and then connected our B-29B operation with the new facts that have now been revealed. By connecting the parts I have shown how the last mission could have changed human destiny. In this dissertation I feel that I have captured the true essence of the hearts and souls of the B-29 crews who flew with the 315th Wing. I have combined the human equation with the facts of history in order to give you the total truth and the excitement of those last days of war. In a real sense you are about to become crew member #11 on a B-29B we named "The Boomerang".

Chapter One

FAIRMONT AND THEN LAS VEGAS

I separated from the Air Corps 16 January 1946, and entered college that fall. After a year at the University of Texas, I moved to Los Angeles where I enrolled in a music and drama school and, in 1950, I earned my professional Screen Actor's Card at R.K.O. studios in a John Wayne/Janet Leigh movie, "Jet Pilot". The questions I had concerning the last mission were put on hold for a time, but a strange event happened in 1959 that re-kindled my curiosity concerning the whole affair.

I had driven from California through Arizona, New Mexico, Colorado and then proceeded across the state line into Nebraska, on my way to visit my step-mother and Dad in Iowa. It was February and I soon discovered that this was not the best time to be wheeling a car down a Nebraska highway. A snow storm was picking up from the Northwest, and the old #6 two-line highway was beginning to get a little icy. It was late afternoon and I had planned to stop overnight with friends, the Joe Patricks, in Omaha. Joe and I had attended the same junior high school and then we were classmates and buddies at North High in Des Moines, Iowa from 1939 to 1942.

JOE PATRICK

Patrick had become a well known sportscaster in Nebraska, and I knew that he would be calling a Creighton-University

of Nebraska game from the field house in Lincoln. I found the station and, in spite of the storm, old Joe was coming in loud and clear. R-5, S-5 as we used to say in the Army Air Corps (on a scale of five, that means readability five and signal strength five).

Joe has always been a fun-loving guy who likes to stretch out and tackle all the life he can get his hands on. He's a formidable type, standing well over 6 feet one and tipping the Toledos at 220 plus. After serving as a Navy pilot in World War II, he came back to Des Moines and enrolled in a radio broadcasting course at Drake University. Joe says he was looking for a snap course that wouldn't interfere with his playing football. (I've never known a more gentle person than Joe Patrick, but football inspired him to new dimensions; he used a gorge himself on running backs.)

Patrick had survived a couple of crashes during his military flying career, but undaunted, he still yearned to drill some holes into the wild blue. He found a surplus BT-13 Army basic trainer that had a reasonable price tag (just over a thousand dollars), and he couldn't resist. The Des Moines airport had some tie down space available that worked with J's finances and so he parked the BT there to await his prime pleasure.

In the meantime, I had been separated

1

out of the Air Corps and enrolled at the University of Texas for a serious bout with law or medicine. As soon as summer vacation rolled around, I hitchhiked to Des Moines and hooked up with my flying friend, Joe. We spent a month terrorizing farm houses and lakeshore residents with low level, high prop-pitch (makes a terrific noise) passes and, after getting that out of our systems, we decided to fly to California. Joe had some relatives in the Glendale area and my mother, who was divorced from my dad, was living in Hollywood.

The airplane had a weak battery, an inoperative intercom, and it was not licensed for night flying. (The BT was equipped with night lights but they were not operational.) We found a shop to slow-charge the battery, and my Dad, who had been an electrician at one time, patched up the intercom system.

JOE, THE BT-13 AND I HEAD FOR CALIFORNIA

I slipped into my old B-29 summer flight suit (the same one that I wore on the last mission) and took the rear cockpit position. Joe and I lifted off the Des Moines airport runway and headed for California via Oklahoma City, Albuquerque, New Mexico, and Prescott, Arizona. I had attempted to rent a parachute both in Des Moines and Oklahoma City but no luck. I didn't like flying in an Army trainer cross country without a 'chute, but I wasn't about to scuttle the opportunity to fly to California. Joe, sporting some hot, movie-star-type sun glasses and a baseball hat, kept giving me hand signals from the front cockpit that in case of emergency he was over the side, and it was up to me to save the BT. The W.W. II Uncle Sam slogan,

"Take her up alone Mister" flashed through my mind, but after sizing up the uninviting terrain below, I wasn't excited about the prospects of this Mister taking her down alone, especially when my log book showed only a handful of very light aircraft hours.

We arrived in Prescott in the late afternoon and, since we weren't flying a night bird, we decided that it would make good sense to rest overnight. Joe and I were running low of gas money so we planned to sack out in the airplane rather than to donate our dwindling dollar reserves to a motel. We advised the airport manager of our intentions but he suggested that we could make it to our destination, Glendale, California, before nightfall. "You can fly until 8:30, easy," the guy said. That was enough encouragement for us, so we cranked up our bird and full throttled to altitude. We navigated by dead reckoning (using visual references) until 7:00 p.m. at which time the sun fell down behind the mountains. We then attempted to navigate by the old "A" and "N" quadrant radio navigational system. The decrepit radio couldn't handle the demands over this mountainous, magnetic area and, in less than an hour, we were both totally disoriented. I glanced at my watch, and it showed 7:30 p.m. We were flying blind.

Joe was taking a lot of time and fuel circling left and right trying to establish a course from the radio range facilities, but it was useless. Now we were in a bad situation: lost, no lights, running low of fuel, and heading into some extremely rugged mountainous areas, a recipe for disaster guaranteed. I could feel my body intermittently shiver and shake to the tune of fear, frustration, and the bone chilling cold of night altitude. And through it all I was trying to recall emergency procedures on the radio. Someone was trying to answer, but the response was so broken up that neither Joe nor I could decipher the caller's transmission. We both pulled out a book of paper matches we'd pocketed from an Oklahoma City "pick and grin" palace the night before and tried to illuminate our light-dead instruments. We had decided to follow a westerly heading at our established altitude of 8,500 feet, figuring that we might have enough fuel to take us to the coast where, hopefully, one of us could spot an airport or a highway on which to land. The two of us were in the middle of a dilemma: if we climbed any higher to avoid possible mountain ranges, we'd be sacrificing precious fuel, but if we stayed at 8,500 feet the possibility loomed that our BT could hit a peak. If we were within a few miles of our navigational course the mountains wouldn't be a problem, so we gambled. The reality of the situation came in loud and clear however, and we knew our plight could be deadly.

Joe tried the "A" "N" system in one last desperate attempt and we chased faint signals north and then south, but the radio didn't happen; we were more disoriented than ever. We held our south bound heading for a few minutes figuring that we'd compensate for the distance we had chased radio signals north. J. P. tried to lighten up things again by reminding me once more that he was the only one who had a parachute, and he might be forced to abandon ship and leave the "driving" to me. I didn't respond to the pun this time; Joe took a beat to contemplate my uncharacteristic no response, and then asked me if I were scared? I gave him a fast and honest, "Roger", and he answered in a low voice, "I'm scared too." His response made me think of my first B-29

mission over Japan when I asked the engineer, Hank Gorder, the same question. Hearing fearless Joe confess that he was scared emphasized to me just how bad things really were.

THREE LIGHTS

As I was thinking over my misspent youth, and figuring that I might be introduced to my Maker at any moment, my eyes locked onto three distant lights at four o'clock horizon high. I screamed at Joe over the intercom! He banked hard right and aimed at the lights. In a little over ten minutes we were close enough to make out a very small town. J.P. put the BT into a right spiral dive. "There has to be a highway down there", he yelled over the intercom, "and we're going to land on it." I gave Joe a big resounding "Roger" on that one.

Miracles were still happening, though, because as we approached the lights we made out a landing strip just north of the small town. Warm desert air whistled by the canopy as we descended, giving us comforting assurance that we were once again returning to earth. The strip was lit up nicely and Joe kissed the bird in."This is the best landing I've ever made". "Yeah," I went for the old cliché, "Didn't crack an egg." "I don't mean that", said Joe, "I mean just to get this thing down in one piece has to stack up as my best landing. I never realized how much I loved terra firma, and I was beginning to wonder how we would re-enter it." I had never heard Joe admit to any close calls in flying before and so, to me, his statement was a whole book on the near disaster we had just survived.

As we taxied up to the operations area, two girls came running out to meet us, and for a moment we pondered whether we had crash landed in heaven. Instead of the traditional pearly gates, however, there was just a regular house that was apparently being used for airport operations. Actually, as we learned from the girls, the place had been leased by the Civil Aeronautics Administration for emergencies and for broadcasting weather reports. We had landed at the Silver Lake Airport, Baker, California, 90 plus miles southwest of Las Vegas. The two girls said that they had tried to call us but there had been no response. One of them, whom we soon discovered was a regular Powder Puff Derby participant, showed us on the map where they had triangulated us with radio: "We fixed you several times and you guys were just minutes away from the San Bernadino Mountain range. Gorgonio Mountain, which stands 11,485 feet high could have been a problem and if you missed that one you could have nailed Mt. San Antonio in the San Gabriel mountain range which is 10,090 feet. Some refer to this particular geographical area as the "The Graveyard for small airplanes'." The other girl added the chiller line, "We figured you two would be statistics in about twelve minutes." Joe and I fixed one another with grim looks-- "Well, we lucked out again, Smith. It's a good thing you spotted the lights." "And it's a good thing you can fly a BT by braille", I countered. "One of these days we've gotta have a little talk with the Prescott guy about what time it gets dark." Joe just grinned, "Maybe we ought to send him a Farmer's Almanac, and circle the section on sundowns."

The girls cooked up bacon and eggs, popped a couple of beers for us, and then tucked us into bunk beds. We had no trouble sleeping. We rose with the morning light, swallowed some orange juice and toast, thanked the girls for the "Waldorf" treatment, and then gave them a buzz job that we usually reserved for Iowa farm houses. Joe waggled our wings good-bye as we aimed the BT towards California. Our route took us directly to Palmdale and then into Glendale. Everything was in the green all the way.

Joe and I needed some fun money while we frolicked in L.A. so Joe thought he should peddle the BT. He ran an ad in the paper offering up the basic trainer for sixteen hundred bucks. An interested party offered fourteen fifty, but Joe turned it down, and finally ended up flying the old BT back to Des Moines by himself. (Joe held on to the BT too long, and finally unloaded it for something like three hundred fifty dollars.)

JOE'S P-51 CATCHES FIRE

Patrick later began flying P-51's in the Des Moines National Guard and, during a night exercise, the Mustang he was flying caught on fire. Joe hung in there until his chute started to scorch, and then hit the silk. One of his loafers flew off when his chute opened, and his shoe-less foot took some punishment on impact. He landed in a cornfield and survived with just scrapes and a slightly sprained ankle. J.P. found a farm house, and scared the wits out of an old lady who opened her door for him. He was bleeding a bit from the scratches and, to the horrified lady, he must have resembled a character straight out of a horror movie. Joe quickly explained his situation and then used the phone to get transportation back to the Des Moines airport base.

The P-51 accident took over the headlines and feature story of the Des Moines

Register the next morning. Drake students were doubly amazed at seeing Joe in class the following day, and even more astounded when they saw him playing football that Saturday. (If they had really known Joe, they wouldn't have been surprised at all.) Joe has always said that the P-51 episode was really a piece-of-cake compared to our BT-13 adventure. We both realize that if it hadn't been for luck and grace, we wouldn't be here today. Every time I drive to Las Vegas I stop at that Baker/Silver Lake airport and remind myself how fortunate I am to be still breathing in and out.

NEBRASKA AND THE BLIZZARD

Now here it was 12 years later and I was pushing my luck again--this time down Nebraska's old highway #6. The weather had turned suddenly, and my new Chevy and I were being progressively swallowed up by a raging old-fashioned Nebraska blizzard. The sound of Joe's voice on the radio was a good measure of comfort to me since we had always been a lucky combination. The blizzard was increasing in intensity and my Chevrolet was beginning to lose traction on the black ice that I couldn't see. I did a side slip, and muttered, "C'mon baby, easy, straight and level, straight and level."

I was too busy trying to handle the ice on the road to study my position on the map, but I figured there should be a small town coming up soon. I could reassess my situation at that point. Joe called a fast break play just as I made out an eighteen wheeler approaching from the opposite direction. As the huge truck blew by, the Venturi effect sucked me into another icy skid. I cranked the wheel in the direction of the slide, but this time I ended up on the right hand shoulder precariously close to a large drainage ditch. That did it. I made up my mind that I would hang up this nonsense at the next town and hopefully drive on to Omaha the following day.

I didn't see any town signs, but there appeared to be a gas station coming up on my right. I pulled in next to the pumps and the attendant timed it to meet me at the driver's side. I grabbed my top coat and opened the door. "Fill 'er up please", I said as I pulled my coat on, "I have to make a quick long distance call. I'll be back in a minute. "I trotted to a near-by phone booth which I had spotted as I drove in. I finally reached the field house in Lincoln after a couple of tries and some help from the local operator. I was handed over to Joe's spotter until the first commercial break. Joe got on the phone with a "Hey, what's happening, Smith?". I jumped in with a quick summary of events and then added, "I'll have to try and make it to Omaha tomorrow. "Where the heck are you?" Joe asked. (I hadn't mentioned the town because I didn't know the name of the place.) I popped the hinged door a crack and called out to the attendant, "What's the name of this town?" "Fairmont", he yelled, and I felt a shudder go through my body. "It's Fairmont Joe, I can't believe it". Joe remembered,: "Isn't that where you trained in B-29's?" "Affirmative," I said. "This is eerie." Practical Joe is not the type to be caught up with eerie things: "C'mon, Smith, you must have planned it that way. Okay, I'll see you tomorrow; drive carefully."

I followed the attendant through blowing snow back to the station office and handed him a credit card. He grinned, and asked, "You sure looked startled when I said Fairmont. Have you been here before?" I told him that I had been stationed in B-29's at the Fairmont Army Air Field, at Geneva, and I hadn't been back this way since 1945. "I was just trying to get out of the blizzard, and I didn't have a clue to what town I was in. "The guy shook his head, "Strange. There must be a reason. Always is." The fellow removed his cap, shook the snow off, brushed a shock of thick brown hair back with his hand and then put the cap back on, adjusting it with a quick double pull on the bill, "About all that's left of that old base site is one hangar and part of a runway. The county uses it to store equipment, and a light airplane or two. "Were you a pilot?" he asked. "I started out that way," I said, "in fact I began flying at the Creighton University Training Detachment in Omaha. I got bounced when they closed classification on me in Santa Ana, California. They decided all of a sudden that they had too many pilots and I ended up a radio operator. It wasn't a good day." "Oh,"the fellow said with some disappointment, "did you make it overseas?" "Yeah, that I did, I flew ten missions over Japan. As a matter of fact, I flew the last mission of the Pacific War." The fellow lit up, "You must have been one of them fellas that dropped the atomic bomb on Japan." "Not quite", I said, "Our bombing mission wasn't flown until five days after the second atomic bomb exploded on Nagasaki." The attendant shook his head incredulously, "But I thought the atom bombs ended the war." I shook my head, "Nope, but you're not alone. I think the whole world believes the atomic bombs ended it, but there was more to the end of the war than the history books tell you. Next time I get back this way I'll let you in on what really happened." The fellow opened his eyes in anticipation, and he waggled his finger as a friendly reminder, "I'm going to hold you to your word now." I smiled and nodded okay, and asked him to point me towards a motel. The fellow indicated that there was one a block and a half west on the same side of the road. I checked into one of the last vacancies.

It was tough falling asleep, and the Gideon Bible didn't seem to help. I kept thinking of the incredible coincidence of my ending up in this place--or was it a coincidence? The gas station attendant had reminded me again that everyone still believed that the atomic bombs ended the war--period. Maybe this freaky event was telling me that I was the one to set the record straight. One thing for sure, I had to drive out and see the old base site.

A whole litany of war time remembrances kept me turning under my blankets until a very late hour. Scraping road graders sounded reveille, and I pulled the double drapes back just enough to see a clear blue sky. I found a truck stop café close by and asked the waitress for directions to the old air base. "Turn right at the next intersection west, and about two miles south look for a big white silo on your right hand side; make a right turn at the very next road, and drive about a quarter of a mile; you'll see one of the old hangars standing there--can't miss it. The snow plows have been working all morning, so you shouldn't have any trouble getting out to the place."

THE OLD B-29 HANGAR

I spotted the white silo, cranked right and drove another quarter of a mile. Sure enough, there was the old B-29 hangar and a runway. I got out of the car and was instantly punished by a stinging north wind. I turned up my coat collar in defense, and carefully climbed over a sagging barbed wire fence to get a better look at things. A cotton-tailed rabbit startled me as it jumped up from a clump of snow laden grass that I had stepped on. I watched the rabbit in fascination as it made some quick broken field moves and zipped out of sight. The huge Fairmont Army Air Force Base had been replaced by pure country, but with the help of the hangar and partial runway, I could visualize where some of the other base facilities had been located.

I pictured the briefing building and relived the top secret meeting in which a Washington, D.C. general had delivered a stunning revelation to the crews: We were being sent to war in B-29's that had been stripped of all armament except a tail turret with two fifty caliber machine guns and a 20 millimeter cannon. We shouldn't worry, however, since we'd be using the newly developed AN/APQ-7 Eagle Radar system in a synchronous radar bombing technique that would permit us to drop our ordnance from thirty to forty thousand feet. The General told us that Japanese fighters and antiaircraft defenses were ineffective at those higher bombing altitudes.

I tried to figure out where my old barracks would have been, and I thought of Steveson, a fellow radio operator who had bunked above me. Steve was a super person, and I picked on him unfairly one day over a minor incident. I had carried some guilt feelings with me from that time on, and I was devastated when Steve and his crew crashed on Northwest Field, Guam. Steve's charred remains still haunt my memory.

I took one last look at the runway area and, in my mind's eye, I could see a B-29 roaring down its length. The Big Bird rotated majestically and lifted up and away toward the open arms of the infinite. It made its departure turn at five hundred feet catching the bright rays of morning, and became a shimmering diamond in an ocean of ice-blue sky.

That unbelievable Fairmont, Nebraska snow stop rekindled my curiosities concerning the unique 315th Bomb Wing, our B-29 campaign against the Japanese Empire, and particularly the last mission. I was also itching to learn more about the military's thinking behind our stripped aircraft, and why we were ordered to fly the last mission when everyone on both sides, with the possible exception of President Harry S. Truman, was proclaiming the end of the war. I wondered again if this amazing Fairmont coincidence was an accident or was it predestined. Was there a message somewhere in this experience for me?

CHRIS PATTERAKIS, THE THUNDERBIRD BOSS

The Fairmont incident happened in the late fifties. At the time I was involved in live television and film acting, both in New York City and Hollywood. Years slipped by but I often found myself thinking about the 315th Bomb Wing and our operation during the final days and hours of the Pacific War. Then came another jolting reminder of those days when an odd's-defying encounter took place in Las Vegas, Nevada in July 1976. I had been working as an actor in a Universal Studio's television episodic which was being filmed on location in

Former Thunderbirds Leader Chris Patterakis

Former Blue Angels Leader Zeke Cormier

Victorville, California. The famous Air Force Thunderbirds Air Demonstration Flying Team was involved in the show and I had the opportunity to meet the members. Years before I had met The Thunderbirds' Navy counterpart, The Blue Angels. I had performed the role of a pilot in a Navy training film at the Naval Air Station in Jacksonville, Florida; there I met and worked with Duke Ventimiglia, a future member of the Navy's Blue Angel Flight Demonstration team. Eventually I met all of the Blues through Duke, including Pacific War ace and Team Leader Zeke Cormier, and in July 1967 I was given a V.I.P. ride in a F9F-8T Cougar by Blue Angel pilot, Lieutenant Dave Rottgering, at Patuxent River, Maryland.

The Thunderbird leader, Major Chris Patterakis, who had flown left wing for the Thunderbirds from 1966 through 1967 and who rejoined the team in 1975 as Commander-Leader, knew some of my Blue Angel buddies. (Chris Patterakis, a man of uncommon talent, is now a captain flying for United Airlines out of San Francisco.) He kindly invited me to attend the team's end-of-season show at the Nellis Air Force Base, Las Vegas, and the Thunderbirds awards banquet that was to follow that evening.

BRIGADIER GENERAL BOYD HUBBARD

The Thunderbirds' award dinner and program took place in one of the Las Vegas casino banquet rooms, and I was seated with several other people at a stage-side table. An older gentleman on my right, without the formality of introduction, began conversing with me about the festivities, and questioning me about my association with the Thunderbirds: "How did you meet the Team? Were you in the service? Where did you serve?" I really wanted to button up the dialogue and concentrate on the upcoming presentations so I gave a two part answer that I thought would satisfy the gentleman's apparent interest in my presence there: "I met the Thunderbirds during the recent filming of a television episode; I was a flying cadet and later a crew member on a B-29. My Wing was assigned to Guam where we flew missions over the Japanese Empire. As a matter of fact, we flew the last mission of World War II." Apparently that was the wrong thing to say to satisfy this gent's curiosity, since my answers appeared only to stimulate his line of questioning. He seemed to be hung up on the last mission that I had mentioned. I was beginning to feel as if I were the center piece of a press conference; I finally took a deep breath and joked that he must be writing a book about the Pacific War. "Nope, he smiled, "I just wanted to see if you had your facts straight." I pondered his line for a moment, and then asked him good naturedly how he would know? The fellow grinned and said, "I would know all right, I was your Group commander, and I led the 501st on that last mission. My name is Boyd Hubbard. It was Colonel then, and I recently retired as a Brigadier General after commanding Nellis Air Force Base. I was made an honorary Thunderbird in 1963 and that's why I'm here."

I was stopped in my tracks, and when I recovered some of my composure I asked the General if I had been close to target in my accounts of the 315th? He laughed, "You were right on the money, Smith, and if you ever want anyone to back you up, just get in touch with me here in Las Vegas." I thanked him and assured him that I would. Then I added, "You did a great job, General." He clouded a little, "We all did a great job, Smith, but we've heard a lot of talk in the past years that our operation didn't amount to much. I guess we bombed a lot of empty oil storage tanks. Maybe we weren't as important as we thought we were." I nodded in agreement, "Yes sir, I've heard that also. All I can say is that everyone gave their best effort." General Hubbard paused for a moment and then he asked, "What did you think of that last mission?" "With all due respect," I answered, "I think it was overkill and unnecessary." Hubbard smiled and told me that there were still some very important questions to be answered about that strike. It appeared that the General didn't know a great deal more about the details than I, but he was just as curious about the reasons for flying it. I thought if Hubbard doesn't have this information, how far up the rank ladder would a person have to go to get any answers? The ceremonies began on that note and our conversation was abbreviated.

Someone at the table spread the word about the remarkable chance meeting between Hubbard and me, and as soon as the awards program was over, we were surrounded by animated Thunderbirds who wanted to know more about Smith and Hubbard's World War II background. I didn't have the opportunity to discuss any more details of the 315th Wing operation and the last mission with the General--only to say good bye, and tell him how honored I was to have met him. As General Hubbard and his wife were leaving, he looked back at me and smiled. "Remember what I said, Smith. If you need any corroboration of the facts, just call me." I gave him a half salute and grinned my appreciation. I hadn't mentioned to General Hubbard that I might write a story about our 315th Wing operation someday but, looking back, the man seemed to sense that I was going to take the last mission episode a bit further than present history.

Chapter Two

BASIC TRAINING AND BASIC GESTAPO

The Fairmont, Nebraska incident I experienced in the late 50s, and now this no-odds chance meeting with my former 501st Group Commander, General Boyd Hubbard, kept playing back in my mind as I drove the return leg to Los Angeles. Unbelievable! I was now convinced that something was pushing me to research and recount the curious last mission story. My thoughts turned back to those days on Guam, and the mission we were ordered to fly despite our understanding that Japan was already out of the ball game. The "false start and go" mission had left me with the feeling that there was more to this bombing raid than any of us had suspected, and now, after the Hubbard meeting, I was determined more than ever to get to the bottom of things.

Since I was a participating eye-witness in the 315th Bombardment Wing I had somewhat of a perspective from our side of the war, but all I knew about Japan was what I had gleaned from press releases. The atomic bombs ignited a fire storm of military and diplomatic processes in both the US and Japan that soon led to the end of World War II. Did the 315th, and particularly the last operational mission, play a significant role in drawing down the curtain on World War II? To me those were the crucial questions that I had to answer.

NO GOOD-BYES

Las Vegas had served me with two earth shaking events, the first one was just as traumatic as the General Hubbard meeting was uplifting. It was there in "sin city" that my mother walked out on me and my dad when I was only seven years old.

It was 1932. My dad had driven my mother, and me, and an old pregnant yellow dog named Suzy, from Leon, Iowa, to my mother's sister's place in Las Vegas. From the time my mother won first place in the State-of-Iowa high school Declamatory Drama Competition, she dreamed of an acting career in Hollywood. The dream became an obsession which continued even after she married my dad, and brought me onto the world scene. My appearance didn't change my mother's career goal one whit and she eventually talked my dad into leaving a good job in Iowa and making a temporary move to her sister's place. The plan was for my Dad to find a job in Los Angeles, and then bring my mother and me to Hollywood. Mother was convinced that she would be discovered by a studio talent scout, and signed to a long term career contract. From there she'd go on to stardom and glamour; we would all live happily forever after. What could be sweeter?

My Dad loaded us up in an old Model A Ford and, after a very long adventurous trip complicated by the "ever ready to deliver" Suzy (who had taken over the rumble seat), we arrived in the high desert city of Las Vegas. My Dad tried to find work in Los Angeles, but that effort turned out to be a dry run. The fact that the country was in the throes of "the great depression" didn't help matters. The timing couldn't have been worse. My Dad was convinced that we couldn't make it in the west. We packed up to drive back to Iowa and, at the last minute, my mother informed us that she wasn't going with us. There were no hugs or kisses; she just walked out of our lives.

DOW CITY, IOWA AND RESUME SPEED

My dad turned me over to his mother in Dow City, Iowa, and he moved on to Des Moines to live with his sister and brother-in-law until he found work.

Dow City boasted five hundred and sixty five occupants (I always suspected the census included a few old hound dogs). It would definitely qualify for the old joke: "The town was so small its name and "Resume Speed" were painted on the same sign." Dow City was a Huckleberry Finn town in reality and, as I look back, I'm convinced that the community imparted a healthy sense of traditional values to every one who lived there. A dependency on one another is one of the ingredients in a small town and that seems to have a leveling effect on folks. So it was in Dow City. If your ego got out of hand there were those who could take you back down a few pegs to the nuts and bolts of reality; if your self-esteem flagged a little, some of your friends would always be there to lift you to higher ground. Most of us had a pretty good balance when the time came for us to watch the city limits in the rear view mirror.

I seemed to choose buddies who were a few years older than myself; I suppose they fulfilled a parental need for me. One of my closest friends was Bob Moeller, who happened to be a mechanical genius and totally into airplanes. His enthusiasm for flying rubbed off on me quickly. I'm convinced that Bob could fly an airplane before he ever climbed into one. I saw him solo in an old Curtis Robin biplane after a hefty three hours of instruction, and he was as smooth as silk.

Shortly after Bob's solo accomplishment, the pilot of another biplane made a forced landing in a farmer's sweet clover field just north of town. I think the guy just ran out of gas, but then he damaged his landing gear when he set down on the rough ground. The pilot left the airplane in the farmer's care for a local mechanic to repair and Bob was called in to do the job.

Bob asked me join him as his assistant while he doctored the damaged plane and, of course, I was thrilled to oblige. It took Bob only an hour to fix the gear like new, after which he told me to climb into the rear cockpit and check out the dual controls. He showed me how to hold the brakes down and then he reached into the front cockpit, and turned the ignition on. Bob stepped confidently to the nose of the airplane, "Be sure to hold those brakes down now," he hollered. He flipped the prop down hard and the engine sputtered into action. Bob crawled into the front cockpit and teased the throttle forward a little. He pushed in a little more throttle, and the plane began to move forward. Slowly we picked up speed, and soon we were accelerating for take-off. Bob pushed the stick forward just enough to lift the tail, and my heart began beating a fast cadence in anticipation of lift off. I saw a barbed wire fence coming up and hoped we would clear it, but Bob chopped the throttle and braked the two winger to a smooth stop just short of the fence. He cut the engine and we both yelled and laughed with unrestrained enthusiasm. My feelings exploded into words, "I know what I'm going to be--I'm going to be a pilot!"

One of our pals was Harold Sharp and, although he wasn't outwardly interested in airplanes, he was destined to become a military pilot. Harold was smart, had the looks of a superstar, and was blessed with a great sense of humor. He had a healthy self-esteem which some mistakenly took for cockiness but, in spite of a few envious critics, Harold was an extremely popular fellow. Sharp was dedicated to fun and frivolity, but he never hesitated to defend himself when some jealous tough threatened to change his good looks. And for the record, I can't remember Harold ever losing a fight.

HAROLD AND THE SKUNK

On one occasion, all in the spirit of fun, Harold painted his Angora cat to look like a skunk and then paraded the animal in front of the assembly class. The gag was so well set up that everyone bought it. All hands cleared the area with fire drill speed and precision. Everyone laughed when they learned what Harold had done — everyone but the principal that is. That gentleman responded by giving Mr. Sharp a mountain of assignments and a three weeks leave. Of course, that gave Harold a chance to sharpen his game of rotation in Jim Pearsall's pool hall.

My Dad married again and I left Dow City to join him and my new step-mother in Des Moines. Moving from a town the size of Dow City into Des Moines required a tremendous adjustment. My self-esteem dipped a little. I looked down at my shoes for a while, but things got better with time.

I was a junior enrolled in North High School when the Japanese bombed Pearl Harbor December 7, 1941. Next day the United States declared war on Japan, and since Japan was a member of the Axis, we were also technically at war with Germany which made its own declaration of war against the United States on December 11, 1941. Everyone that I knew was itching to join up with Uncle Sam for the fight. Occasionally you might find a fellow who was looking for a way out, but that person would be rare. We were proud of America in those days. Our patriotism was fierce--and real.

THE CASE OF THE SHORT LEG

I received my classification and I wanted to join the Navy's V-5 program. I had one more year to complete high school and then I could go on to college providing that I qualified, under the Navy program which would allow me to get my degree, and at the same time become a flying officer. I ran to sign an application for the V-5 at the Naval recruitment office. They sure didn't waste any time calling me; I received my appointment two days later. I knew I could pass the physical with no sweat, but then something happened that I hadn't counted on. We were asked to undress, hold our hands out in front of us, and face the wall. The examining medical officer stopped in back of me, and then, with an over-officious voice that still echoes in my memory, told me to turn around. "You can't fly in the Navy young man, your right leg is an inch shorter than your left". As soon as I got my breath I blubbered that I was one of the fastest guys on my football team; I ran track; I played baseball. "My legs have never bothered me, ever! Sir, I'm fine; I don't have any problem with my legs. Why my legs are the strongest part of me." I have never lacked sensitivity, and I knew in my heart that this Doctor couldn't be turned around. He had a definite sadistic look when he told me: "You can't fly in the Navy--that's the end of it."

I don't remember dressing, I don't remember leaving the recruiting station. The next thing I did was to make an appointment with Doctor Benny Devine, a highly respected orthopedic surgeon, who was formerly an all-American football player at the University of Iowa. Doctor Benny was a charismatic individual who often led our pre-game football rallies. I spilled out my story to him and the more I spilled, the more I was overcome with emotion. I choked down my feelings until my throat ached. I didn't want Doctor Benny, the former All American, to see me cry. After all I pictured myself as a pretty tough football player and I was trying to keep that image. It didn't work. I just hung my head and sobbed. The Doctor put his arm around me and led me to an examination table. As Benny examined me, and measured my legs, he became almost as upset as I was. "There's not a damn thing wrong with your back or legs. I'm going to write a letter for you to take back to this Navy Doctor, and if that doesn't work, I'll take him out to dinner and soften him up with a steak. You'll be flying for the Navy, Jim. There's nothing wrong with you."

I hand-delivered Doctor Devine's letter to the Navy medical examination office, and waited for a response that never came. A few weeks later I was riding a trolley car and I spotted the Navy Doctor who had examined me. I walked over to where he was seated, reminded him who I was, and asked if he had received the letter from Doctor Devine? The Doc nodded affirmatively, and then with a cruel smile added, "I told you, you weren't going to fly for the Navy." I wanted to unload my pent up feelings on the guy, but I figured if there was any chance at all that this doctor would change his mind, I didn't want to blow it. It's sad that these kinds of military people exist, but if you've been in the service you've run into them. Thank God the bad guys don't constitute a majority, or we'd be in rough shape. The Doctor apparently had some kind of a hang up, and I guess his busting up my chances to fly made him feel better.

There was still the Army Air Corps and I decided that would be the way for me to go.

Note: Interestingly enough, with all the physical examinations I underwent in the Army Air Corps, not one examining doctor ever mentioned that one leg was shorter than the other. My Air Corps medical examinations, substantiated by my personal records, never indicated any kind of physical restriction in the 2 and 1/2 years that I served in the military.

FLAT FEET

Soon after "flunking" the Navy physical, I heard from Bob Moeller. He'd been rejected from the Army Air Corps pilot training program because of flat feet. Bob had a great body, but he inherited his flat walkers from his Dad. Bob was athletic and he never had any problems with his feet. They were just naturally flat, that's all. The Army Air Corps missed having one of the greatest natural flying talents of all time when they passed on Bob Moeller. With these kinds of screw ups I began to wonder how we would ever win the war. The air Corps told Bob that he'd still be inducted in the Air Corp, but that he would be classified as an aircraft ground mechanic. What an unfair break, I thought. I could visualize Bob as an enlisted man, supporting a flying officer who would no doubt have half the qualifications as himself. SNAFU and the fickle finger of fate all rolled into one. I had encountered those two booby traps in my quest to sign up for the Navy's V-5 Flying program. It was beginning to look like the whole military was one total SNAFU. I hoped I was wrong in my perceptions because we still had a couple of wars to win.

Our buddy, Harold Sharp, had been accepted into the Army Air Corps, and assigned to fly the B-17, Boeing's great four engine bomber. Harold would have been perfectly cast as a fighter pilot, but with his personality, ability to lead, and overall talent, there was no question in my mind but what he'd also make a great B-17 commander.

HAROLD'S B-17 SALUTE TO DOW CITY

Harold's practical jokes, including his famous "Skunk" stunt, were all dwarfed by a final Harold Sharp salute to Dow City. Without any forewarning or announcement, he flew his B-17 crew from the Army Air Base in Lincoln, Nebraska and buzzed the community for over an hour. Harold began his roof shaking air show with some low level passes over Dow City's outlying farms.

Farmers reportedly stopped their tractors in the fields, while others poured out of their farm houses to watch, in awe, as the bomber shook structures and scattered live stock. Then the B-17 skimmed over the town just above tree top level and buzzed main street.

It was Main Sreet where all the Dow City action always took place; especially on Wednesday and Saturday night when the farmers came to town. The big excitement for us kids was to watch cowboy movies at the local main street theatre, and then run the streets. We used to get pretty cranked up after watching Tom Mix, or Ken Maynard fight bad guys for two hours and then, using our first finger and thumb for a six shooter, we'd re-enact what we had seen as soon as we hit the side walks. Dow City's old German sheriff, Gus Shrader, used to chase us all over the place threatening to lock us up in the one tiny jail when we became a little too rowdy. Gus was really a lovable old soul, and he never once fulfilled his promise to incarcerate us. I don't know why we gave Gus such a going over. Perhaps it was just that natural kid desire to test the rules. It was all good clean fun in those days. We were mischievous but certainly not dangerous.

I know that my buddy, Harold, had Gus in mind when he rattled Main Street with one four engine pass after another. By this time the shocked citizenry were guessing that the air extravaganza taking place before their very eyes could only be coming from the hand that painted the Angora cat to look like a skunk—their own Harold Sharp. No one else had the flair and the nerve for such a performance. They laughed, they yelled, they took pictures, and they have been talking about it every since. You know who was as

Harold Sharp

Bob Moeller

Jim B. Smith with son
Darin B. Maurer,
receiving award at
Creighton University
1994

Joe Patrick and his BT-13

thrilled as anyone with Harold's show? Yep, none other than old Gus Shrader. Some of the eye-witnesses who watched the festivities with Gus out in front of Les Hansen's barber shop said Gus was grinning ear to ear.

Harold kept in touch with me, and steadily encouraged me to go all the way for the Army Air Corps pilot training program.

CALIFORNIA, HERE I COME

I graduated from high school and, like Bob Moeller, I was awaiting the military call. In the meantime Bob had heard that there were some good jobs available at Consolidated Aircraft Corporation located in San Diego, and so he packed up and headed for Southern California. He connected at Consolidated and then suggested to me that I join him. It didn't take any coaxing to get me packing. I met Bob and he helped me to hire on at the same aircraft corporation. Consolidated manufactured the two engine PBY-5 Catalina flying boat, the four engine PB-2Y3 flying boat Coronado, and the B-24 "Liberator" bomber.

Our work kept us close to airplanes and that made it all exciting for us. Consolidated was in full swing producing thousands of aircraft. The Navy began using the PBY Catalina flying boat in 1936. Consolidated built 3,290 of the aircraft for the United States and Canada and several hundred more for the U.S.S.R. The PB-2Y3 Coronado had its maiden flight December 17, 1937 and was pressed into service in 1941. Consolidated produced 216 of the Coronados.

The B-24 was designed in 1939 and entered service 1941. The Liberator was a multifunctional aircraft: bomber transport, Navy reconnaissance, and anti-submarine. Consolidated produced 18,188 of them, more than any other World War II American aircraft. The Liberator dropped 635,000 tons of bombs on enemy targets and shot down 4,189 enemy aircraft. It transported thousands of troops across the world and served as a long range bomber in the Pacific. The B-24 operated in the Army, Navy, the RAF, and with several Allied Air Forces.

The PBYs and the PB-2Y3s operated off our runways as air sea rescue aircraft. Seeing those aircraft along with an occasional B-24 always punched up a memory trip to San Diego's Consolidated Aircraft Corporation. I earned my "E" for excellence pin there as one small member of a very large team but, even so, I took pride in my job as a lowly tool chaser. After watching aircraft being assembled, it was a double thrill to see them at war.

HOLLYWOOD

I took the Air Corps written examination in San Diego, and passed with no problem. It was my desire to get that part of the process out of the way so that I could ensure my induction into the Army Air Corps. After a few months at Consolidated, Bob and I began to feel the hot breath of the Army so we decided to quit our jobs and go back home to await final orders. I boarded a train for Des Moines and Bob planned to go back to Dow City a few days later.

My first train stop was in Los Angeles, and I debated whether or not to call my mother. She was re-married and living in Hollywood. Mother hadn't had much luck finding work in the movie industry, and she had written in a Christmas card that she was working in a downtown Los Angeles department store. It was the weekend so I figured that my mother would be home and I finally decided to give her a call. She was excited to hear from me and asked me to stay over a few days. She said that she would take the "Red Car" (trolley transit) and come meet me. We hadn't seen one another for years so we both described what we would be wearing.

I waited for my mother with wet palms, but I had no trouble picking her out in the crowd. She also recognized me right away. The fact that we were somewhat look-alikes helped. My mother told me that her present husband wasn't aware that she had a son, and she wondered if it was okay if she introduced me as her cousin? "Sure," I said. "What should I call you?" "Just call me 'Patsy'," she smiled. "You know my middle name is Patricia?" I laughed, hiding some of the pain, "Okay Patsy, I'm your cousin Jim from Iowa."

I spent a few days with Patsy and her husband Bob, and then re-boarded the train for Iowa. It was good to be back in Iowa but, after a couple of weeks, California began "calling." I figured it might be more fun waiting for induction there and so I flagged a "Super Chief" and railed back to Hollywood.

I had been told that if an air candidate had passed his written, he could "voluntarily enlist" into the Air Corps. That option would speed up the induction process, and it would also look good on one's service record. I figured anything that might help get me to the stick and rudder was worth a shot so I signed up. The Air Corps ordered me to March Field at Riverside, California to take my physical. I was sweating out whether or not the doctor would thumb me down again for the short leg problem, but not a word was mentioned. I passed with flying colors and then tripped back to Hollywood to fun it up until my magic induction day.

FROM MUSCLE BEACH TO SHEPPARD FIELD BASIC TRAINING

I found some California hilarity at muscle beach in Santa Monica and kept half way in shape, running and pumping iron between beers. One of the regulars was Gene Berg who was destined to become a famous acrobatic dancer and film star. Armand and Vic Tanny of Vic Tanny's Gyms were also part of our muscle beach crowd.

I finally received my long awaited orders. I was sworn into the Army in Los Angeles, and ordered to report to Sheppard Field, Witchita, Texas, for basic training. On 14 September 1943, I was clicking along in a troop train bound for the infamous dust bowl called Sheppard Field. Bob Moeller had written to me that he had been ordered to Sheppard, also, and we planned to hook up.

I was shown to quarters and then marched directly to the quartermaster where I received my government issue. After spending most of the day reporting to indoctrination lectures and films, we were ordered to stand barracks inspection. Having just left the muscle beach set where trips between haircuts were a little longer than most, I caught the attention of the inspecting officer. He pushed his face into mine, and then eased around to the back of me, quite obviously examining my long locks. His voice exploded into my right ear, "How long have you been in the

Army soldier?" "Sir, since this morning sir," was my scared knee jerk reply. I could hear snickering throughout the barracks, including one from the inspecting officer. "You're dismissed to go to the barber shop and report back to your barracks sergeant at 1600 hours. Do you know why I'm sending you to the barber shop soldier?" "Yes sir, to get a haircut". "That's right soldier, you're catching on. Tell the barber that you have been ordered to get a one and a half inch regulation cut. Dismissed!"

I reported to the base barber and gave him my orders. The barber smiled, "How do you really want it cut young fellow?" I thought, what a nice guy. I smiled at the barber and gave him a friendly pat on the shoulder, "Leave it as long as possible please. Just so it gets me by inspection." The barber winked knowingly and I settled confidently into the chair. He kept me turned away from the mirror while he worked and it seemed to me that he was doing a lot of cutting and buzzing. Then he spun me face to face with the mirror. "How do you like it," the beaming barber asked?" I was missing. All I could see was this weird looking skin headed stranger looking back at me with a piteous, bewildered look. I wheeled around to 'Mr. Scissors,' "But I thought you were going to cut it just short enough for me to get by inspection." "Yeah," laughed the barber. "They all do. Welcome to the Army." I was too shaken to reply. I just pulled my G.I. cap out of my belt, threw it on my bald head and split.

That night I fell into the sack exhausted, and some one had not only short-sheeted my cot (rigging the sheet so that you couldn't stretch out), but they had dumped a bucket of water on it. I wasn't being singled out because there were a half a dozen other beds that were tricked up just

like mine. It was a bad first day and a bad first night. If the guys that short sheeted me are reading this book, please call me. I would like very much to discuss this thing with you.

The next day the barracks sergeant ask for volunteers to attend a "great" G.I. party that was to be held that night starting around 8:00 o'clock. A lot of us volunteered for the "party", and by the time we found out that a G.I. party meant cleaning the latrine, it was too late. We were even ordered to use toothbrushes to clean out the hard to get at places and, after that enlightening and disgusting experience, we never volunteered again. All of us inductees were ever vigilant for ways to get even with the military. For example, we were ordered to mop our floors every day, but we found a great way to save time and energy. We just slopped water around the area when the Sergeant wasn't around, and when he checked us for inspection, the half dried floors had that fresh mopped look. "The inspection Sarge would smile proudly, "That's the way to mop floors men." Our secret was never discovered as long as I was there, thank God. If it had been, I have a feeling that we'd never been released from the Army. We'd still be pulling K.P.

I FIND MY OLD GROUNDED DOW CITY BUDDY, BOB MOELLER

As soon as I got a break, I searched the field for Bob Moeller. I finally located him at the base hospital. He had been admitted there for appendicitis. I found him lounging in an overstuffed chair reading an aviation book. Bob looked good despite his missing appendix and we were glad to see one another. His first words were, "I see you've had an introduction to one of our base barbers." "Yeah, I snorted. "I wish they had issued my G.I. cap after I got the haircut." With that, I put my now oversized cap on and spun it around on my head. Bob laughed until he felt his stitches pull. We knew that we probably wouldn't have a chance to see one another again. Bob put his hand on my shoulder and said sadly, "You'll have to do all my flying for me Jim; looks like I'll be busting my knuckles on the ground for the duration." "Don't lose your hope", I counseled, "you'll fly yet." Bob took a deep breath and looked down as I tried to speak a word of encouragement, "You have to fly, you're the best. It'll take more than flat feet to keep you on the ground." He didn't believe me, but he smiled gamely and gave me a thumbs up. We put our arms around one another and, almost in harmony, said, "See you later."

It was hot and dusty at Sheppard Field and a couple of guys literally didn't make it through the physical fitness tests alive. Fortunately my cavorting with the muscle set in Santa Monica had given me a semblance of conditioning and I survived the ordeal. I soon learned that there was almost more chicken in the Army than I could swallow, and also more horse meat. That's right, the Army tried horse meat out on us motley inductees, and tried to disguise it as hash. The stuff was red and stringy, salty, and had a sweet sickening taste to it. There was no way to camouflage horse meat. Of course we weren't served the delicacy every day and that was our saving grace. Where were Doris Day and the other animal activists when we needed them?

THE DAY I DROPPED MY RIFLE

I accidentally dropped my rifle during one orientation, and I thought I was going to face the firing squad. We were attending an outside lecture; we set our rifle butts on the ground and leaned the barrel against our leg. I needed to get something out of my right pocket, and in that process I let the rifle fall. The Sergeant screamed, "Who dropped that rifle", and I had no where to hide. So, just like a little man I yelled, "Sir, I did, Sir". The sergeant inflated his chest and dog trotted over to me. He called me to attention. I stood there for five minutes while he chewed me out, and then in the middle of the chewing he barked, "And you'll be assigned to Kitchen Police beginning at "0" three thirty tomorrow morning." The only good thing about K.P. is that you could eat without waiting in the chow line, but that wasn't quite enough to make it worth while. I never dropped the rifle again but I did manage to pull K.P. a few more times.

Once I was pulling all-night guard duty, and I didn't challenge an officer properly. I figured that I might be court marshalled if I cocked my bolt action gun as we had been instructed. That wasn't good thinking. I received another lecture and another tour at K.P. I began to wonder why I had voluntarily enlisted. I knew that procedure speeded up the induction process. Why was I so all fired patriotic? After all, I might have been able to postpone all of this Bovine Scatology until the war was over.

THE GESTAPO

There were two Sergeants who used to patrol the base trying to find someone who had broken regulations. If they couldn't find anyone, they'd grab the nearest G.I. and cite some made-up base regulation that the inductee had broken.

20

There wasn't any grievance committee available at Sheppard to listen to our complaints, and we didn't have much of a choice but to go along with this farce. The two guys were generally known around the base as the "Gestapo", the name coming from and inspired by Hitler's hated and infamous German secret police.

The Gestapo stopped me on one occasion and claimed that my trousers were a half inch longer than regulation. Another K.P. tour. Hair measuring was another big deal with the Gestapo. A quarter inch over the limit and more K.P.

Along the way we were given an I.Q. test to see if we were still qualified for the air cadet program. It's a wonder to me that any of us passed, considering our fatigue and state of mind. I always wondered what the Gestapo guys would have scored? Very high on the chicken section for sure. The one thing that kept me going was the thought that the next time I saw this chicken farm I would be flying over it as a commissioned officer.

HAROLD SHARP FLYING B-17'S OUT OF ENGLAND

I received a letter from my old pal, Harold Sharp, and he was now a First Lieutenant flying B-17's out of England. The letter had been pretty well censored, but I could guess that he was in the thick of the air battle over Germany. I was proud of him, and I remembered our good times growing up in Dow City. I thought of Harold's skunk gag, and his incredible Dow City buzz job. Bob Moeller, Harold, and I were like the three musketeers and, whatever happened now, it was good to know that at least one of us had made it into the wild blue.

It seemed as if we had been in Sheppard a year, but it had only been a little over six weeks. Next stop would be the cadet college training detachment at Creighton University in Omaha, Nebraska. The program called for six months of intense training after which we would be shipped off to Santa Ana, California for classification.

I knew that we'd begin flying at Creighton, and I was happily anticipating the challenge. Then, too, Omaha was only 70 miles from Dow City, and a little over 200 miles from Des Moines where the folks lived; that gave me a feeling of home. Also I had cousins in Omaha, including Major Lee Huff, commander of Offutt Air Force Base. I hadn't seen some of those relatives for years, but the prospect of meeting up with them again was a measure of comfort and pleasant anticipation. The rumors held that Omaha was a great liberty town and we were all looking forward to week-end passes. Actually, after Sheppard we looked forward to anything.

Jim B. Smith and his father

Smith and his step-mother

Smith at Creighton College

Smith (r) during training at Puerto Rico

Smith at Fairmont

Smith (front row left) with his first crew at Puerto Rico

Chapter Three

THE MARCH OF TEARS

The date was October 16, 1943. Our troop train braked to a steam-blowing stop in the Omaha station and one hundred eager cadets disembarked to take in the new surroundings. Omaha looked like Shangri-la compared to Sheppard, and we hadn't even left the train station. A Sergeant was barking out orders so nothing was new in that department. We threw our duffle bags into personnel trucks and then jumped up beside them for our trip to Creighton University. The trucks swept past traditional two-story houses, all guarded by proud spreading trees aflame with red and gold autumn leaves. Some were being blown free from their moorings and wafting lazily to the street below. I watched in fascination as they swirled in a multicolored wake behind our troop truck. There was a chill in the air that fanned fresh excitement into our new adventure. At Creighton we were to study subjects that would prepare us for military flying, but the most exciting part would be taking actual flying instruction at the Omaha airport.

We arrived at quarters which turned out to be regular Creighton University dormitories. The sergeant called us to attention and then placed us at ease, lecturing us briefly on the do's and don'ts of an air cadet: "I can put my hand in my pocket and relax, but you better not be caught in a relaxed mode at any time or you'll spend your weekends walking tours with a parachute strapped to your achin'

backs."

The Sergeant called our assigned quarters and dismissed us to set up. Compared to Sheppard Field, these were strictly first class accommodations; four men to a room. I was getting that officer feeling already.

THE FLYING CURRICULUM

The teaching staff was composed of civilian instructors and Jesuit Fathers. The curriculum was tough, and included Physics, Mathematics (Trigonometry, Navigational Calculus), Geography, History, English (Rhetoric and Composition), Civil Air Regulations, and Speech. The Jesuit Fathers were strict and demanding; the civilian teachers were top echelon and dished out heavy assignments. There was also a strenuous physical fitness program which kept everyone lean and mean. Flight training was conducted at the Omaha Municipal Airport where we cadets were instructed in high wing, tail dragger aircraft: Taylorcraft, Piper, and Aeroncas.

My first take off was a memorable one, and shook my confidence a little. We flew a Taylorcraft trainer "D" which featured tandem cockpits and dual controls. The instructor sat in the front seat and the student in the back. My seat was too far back, but that check list item escaped the attention of my instructor. I could barely reach the rudder pedals. When I did reach one, my big old G.I. shoe had a tendency to hang up in the rudder space just long enough to put me behind on the controls. The instructor never mentioned that shifting ones body from left to right to reach the pedals was not standard procedure. We started a takeoff roll. I got behind on the rudders and we began to zig zag back and forth across the center line. I tried to correct by angling my body to one side and the other to work the rudders, but that awkward procedure contributed to making things worse. We finally wound up out of control and spun into a clockwise ground loop. The instructor pulled power and stopped the loop. I sat there looking down at my oversized shoes, while my legs did a nerve dance. I was afraid to look at my teacher. I could see a big thumbs down coming up and maybe my career as a pilot. The instructor began to laugh, and that broke the tension enough for me to face him once more. "Let's taxi back to the runway numbers and try again. This time I want you to bring your seat up so that you can catch those rudder pedals." We tried it again. This time we birded off in good shape, and I recouped some of my lost self confidence.

OMAHA LIBERTY

The Creighton curriculum was tough, but those wonderful Omaha weekend liberties and the vision of becoming a flying officer, gave us all the motivation we needed to keep our noses to the grindstone.

Squadron Four took over the Fontenelle Hotel from Friday night through Sunday and, if you called any room, you would likely hear a cadet answer, "Squadron Four!" The King Cole Room in the Fontenelle Hotel was considered liberty headquarters. We tipped a few beers, met a few girls, and wore out the Nickelodeon with repeated plays of "Don't Fence Me In", by Bing Crosby and the Andrew Sisters, and "There, I've Said It Again," by Vaughn Monroe. On one occasion a couple of cadets heard me singing along with the Nickelodeon, and asked me if I'd become a member of the musical quintet they were organizing. Even though I had learned never to volunteer for anything in the Army, I believed this situation was safe enough and I agreed. I sang the lead, which was the easiest part, of course, and we performed at every gala cadet event. We sang old songs such as "Shanty Town", "Sweet Adeline", "So High", and "Lazy River" with a musical accent on the old "Barber Shop" sound. It was great public relations and we had a ball entertaining the various groups. By the same token, we escaped some of the lowly detail work by always complaining that it interfered with our singing or rehearsal schedule. I was beginning to see that there were some advantages in being a cadet, especially a performing cadet.

PLENTY AT "STEAK" IN THE STOCK YARDS

Omaha featured some of the best steak houses in the world. They were generally located in south Omaha next to the stock yards. Years before, I had ridden shotgun with my Dow City truckin' buddies on cattle runs to Omaha. I was just twelve years old at the time, but I remembered the fabulous hamburgers that were served up in the fast food places. We dreamed of having enough money one day to buy a big steak, but we never seemed to pull that one off. Boy, how things changed now that

I had become a big-time cadet with gold wings on my sleeve and some jingling change in my pocket. My buddies and I were frequent weekend visitors to the stockyard steak houses (no one was talking about cholesterol in those days), and I never even looked at the right side of the menu. There was no question in my mind that I had "arrived."

GUARD DUTY AT 20 BELOW AND WHITE GLOVE INSPECTIONS

Omaha became a little frosty in the winter time, and it wasn't a lot of laughs pulling 12 hour night guard duty in a blizzard with two hours on and three hours off until the end of the shift. In my mind we earned our keep with the guard duty assignment alone. The cadets were always studying for examinations and, in the middle of it all, we'd get those infamous white glove inspections. That's when the inspecting officers put on clean white gloves and examined your room for dust or dirt and organization. Their search for dust later reminded me of the guys who were scrounging for gold in the classic film, "Treasure of Sierra Madre." The inspecting officers turned furniture upside down, stood on chairs to check light bulbs and shades, and examined every nook and cranny with their white gloves. If a glove showed any soil, the room was "gigged" and, after a certain number of these demerits, cadets were ordered to strap on the old parachute and walk weekend tours in the courtyard. We went to any length to avoid weekend tours since missing liberty in Omaha was considered the worst punishment in the world. Our room made the courtyard one time, and we were all convinced that the King Cole Room would come tumbling down; happily, the beer and ladies were waiting for us when we returned the following Friday night.

I learned another interesting lesson about human nature while I was enrolled in the cadets' program at Creighton. Some of the student cadets were picked at random to be acting officers in the squadron. They were known as "Bottle Cap Captains." Most of these fellows were first rate nice guys, but with the addition of authority many of them turned into real monsters. It seems to be one of the sad facts of life. A little rank and some folks lose their balance.

YOU HAVE THE MUMPS

One snowy morning I noticed one of my intrepid roommates peering into the mirror. He looked worried. "What's the matter?" I asked. "I don't know, Jim, but I have a weird swelling in front of my ear. It's real tender too." Both my grandmother Smith and my dad loved to play doctor. I guess it left a visible mark on me because ever since I can remember, my friends have sought my counsel when they've had a medical problem. My roommates in Creighton were no exception. I took a closer look at my buddy's swollen cheek and then gave my diagnosis: "My friend, I believe that you have the mumps." My roomie laughingly challenged me, "The mumps! That's a kid's disease." "Not necessarily so," I said, "and if you catch them at your age, the virus can settle in one or both testicles and cause sterility. You also might have to use a wheelbarrow to carry em' around for a while. And I've been told that the pain—well, it's like slipping off your bike pedals and landing on the cross bar. Better head for the dispensary now!" I began thinking that I might have been a little heavy handed so I back pedaled a bit, "Hey, remember I'm no doctor. I'm probably wrong." My worried roommate, however, bought my original diagnosis and comments; he took off post haste with no further questions. The dispensary confirmed my guess, and then I began to wonder if I'd ever had the mumps? A prior infection meant a life time immunity. Actually I was worrying more about missing the festivities in the King Cole Room than contracting the disease. I wrote to my mother and asked her if I had ever contracted mumps. She wrote back confirming that I definitely had, so I knew I was home free. Hot damn!

One by one the Cadets began to fall prey to the big "M" and, as they were diagnosed, they were taken to the Offutt Air Base hospital for treatment. The treatment meant staying in bed so that the mumps wouldn't settle in the testicles or cause other problems. I informed all hands that I was immune to the disease due to prior exposure so I would be free to messenger any communiqués to their girl friends or, indeed, provide a personal escort service. I also suggested to each of the victims that I would be happy to babysit their charges at the King Cole Room but my "kindly overtures", received a frigid reception. It was all in good fun but there weren't many laughing—until they saw me checking into the mumps ward at Offutt. Yes, me—the immune one!

THE IMMUNE ONE CHECKS IN THE MUMPS WARD

I couldn't believe it but I, too, woke up one morning with a swollen parotid and salivary gland. I called my Mother and she remained unmoved in her declaration that I had fallen victim to the mumps at a very young age. I told that story to the Doc and

he smiled, "You obviously contracted the viral infection on just one side when you were a child and now you have the virus on the other side—simple." I was a sad looking individual when I arrived at Offutt with my barracks bag slung over my shoulder and sporting a swollen right cheek. My comrades invited me into their ward with open arms and a variety of horse laughs. I definitely had it coming.

The lying in bed became a drag, and yet any strenuous movement could send the virus to the testicles. We had no choice but to cool it for at least three weeks. We kept ourselves busy with projects such as trying to make alcohol from yeast and fruit juice. We bartered with the orderlies for the ingredients and then we placed the large can of juice with yeast and sugar on the radiator and hoped our expected three to six week stay would be a proper fermentation period so that we could sprinkle a little frivolity into the ward. One of the guys had a better idea. He had one of his friends bring him oranges that had been injected with Vodka. He ate one too many oranges one day and we suspected from his demeanor that he was getting some abuse substance from somewhere. He finally admitted that his oranges had been spiked. After considerable pressure from the group, he offered to sell his remaining oranges and that set the customers scrambling over one another trying to get their money down. The old fruit can-sugar-yeast trick didn't pan out to be too palatable but, if nothing else, it kept us high with anticipation.

My cousin, Major Lee Huff, commander of Omaha's Offutt Army Air Base, made a surprise visit to our ward. He was an older distinguished fellow with charismatic charm. He spoke to each of the patients, and then asked where Jim Smith's bed was? The Major made a fuss over me and we talked about our mutual relatives at some length. The word of the Major's and my relationship spread throughout the ward and, for some reason, I seemed to be more popular after the Major left than before he entered. That convinced me that politics works everywhere, even in the Army Air Corps.

THE SUNSHINE NURSE

I fell in love with one particular nurse. She was blonde, beautiful, and always upbeat. I called her Sunshine because she brightened my every day. I still remember her taking my blood pressure and temperature as a recording of Vaugh Monroe played, "Oh What a Beautiful Morning" wafted over the ward's speaker system. Let me tell you, Sunshine made all of my mornings beautiful.

The medical staff sprung me after three and a half weeks, and I really had mixed emotions. I didn't want to leave Sunshine because I knew that I might not ever see her again, but I wanted to get back to school and weekend liberty.

It was extra hard trying to catch up with the Physics and Mathematics courses that we missed during our hospitalization, and I was wondering how many of us would pass our subjects satisfactorily.

One of my buddies, Louis Webb, a big, prematurely bald practical joker type, bet me five bucks that I wouldn't be able to run the five miles that was currently required by the gym instructor. He didn't think anyone could be confined to bed for three weeks and have enough physical conditioning left to run five miles. I took on Louie's challenge, and finished the

course. When he asked me how I did it, I said simply, "Every time I felt like quitting, I'd figure how many beers that "fiver" would buy in the King Cole Room. It kept me going for the win." Louie didn't think the remark was that cute. He growled a little, but he paid off.

THE DIRTY RAG AND BROKEN RIBS

There was never a dull moment with good old Louie. One day we were ordered to a G.I. party (cleaning up headquarters) and I became the brunt of Louie's horseplay. I have to believe that he was still thinking about the bet he lost. Louie was cleaning the banisters leading to the second floor and I was cleaning up the first floor. He yelled at me and when I looked up, he caught me full in the face with his dirty cleaning rag. I gave him a tight little smile—like, one for you Louie. Then he tagged me again with the same filthy rag and I warned him, "Next time the rag hits me, I hit you! Fair enough?" Louie flashed a devilish, challenging grin. Fifteen minutes later, and before I could duck, I was eating another dust rag. My adrenaline shot me up the steps and I drove a tackle into the big guy. Louie must have outweighed me by sixty pounds but I caught him by surprise and down the stairs we thundered. Luckily I landed on top of him. I heard a cracking sound and later it turned out to be a couple of Louie's ribs. He could have killed me if I hadn't surprised him, but interestingly enough, I was the subject of some adulation after the incident. That was pretty funny, I thought.

Occasionally we used to sneak down to the commanding officer's desk after bed check and use his telephone to call girl friends. We took the chance even though we knew getting caught would mean serious disciplinary action or, at the very least, a series of parachute-on-the-back tours. One night I thought I needed to call one of my girl friends and I quietly sneaked down the stairs wearing only my skivvies. I slipped into the commanding officer's office and turned on the light. It was like a scene from a horror movie. There, sitting in the commanding officer's chair, was the commanding officer himself, Lieutenant Campbell. He apparently had suspected that cadets were using his phone and he was going to put a stop to the practice. I was so shocked that I couldn't say a word; I just came to attention, saluted and then ran back up the stairs. The reality sank in a few minutes later and I stayed awake most of the night, embarrassed and worried over the punishment that would certainly be coming my way.

MAJOR LEE HUFF'S SUNDAY PARTY, AND MISSING THE BULLET

The following Sunday Major Lee Huff and his wife, my cousin "Babe", and their daughter, Sally, invited Squadron Four to their home for an afternoon party. I spotted Lt. Campbell there and I tried my best to avoid any confrontation with him. The guy had the looks of a big time movie star, somewhat belying the fact that he could be just plain hard nosed. Major Huff came over to greet me and, out of the corner of my eye, I could see Lt. Campbell looking on. Before I had a chance to slip away, Campbell moved in to shake hands with our host. Major Huff put his arm on my shoulder and addressed the Lieutenant, "Lt. Campbell, do you know my cousin, Cadet Smith?" Lt. Campbell was surprised, "Your cousin, Sir, is that right? A small world, as they say. Yes Sir I've

met Cadet Smith on several occasions. As a matter of fact just the other night..." Some well wishers pushed in at that point, and Major Huff turned his attention to them. I gave the Lieutenant a pathetic smile and just waited for the blade to fall. To my surprise, he was chuckling. "You know, Smith, I've had guys salute me out of uniform, but you're the first one that ever saluted me wearing nothing but G.I. shorts." I stammered, "I'm sorry, Sir." "Hey, not at all Smith, you get me through the day. Every time things get serious I just think of you standing there in your shorts saluting and I start to laugh." Campbell was laughing again as he recalled the incident and I went along with him, forcing a weak courtesy smile. Several cadets came over to greet Lt. Campbell and I segued out of there while I was ahead. Another bullet missed. Perhaps I owed my reprieve to my high ranking officer cousin, Major Huff. However, I always wanted to believe that Lt. Campbell let me off the hook simply because he was a nice guy. I'll stay with that thought.

It was getting close to graduation which meant that Squadron Four would be moving on to Santa Ana for classification. We were beginning to hear ominous rumors that the Army Air Corps was over booked, and that classification might be closing. Hospitalization for those of us who had been stricken with the mumps lowered our grade averages as we were obliged to take finals without the benefit of much needed study. Still, I graduated with an eighty seven percent average in my courses. I also received an eighty seven percent in my flying which was considered an "A". My last check ride was a major contributor to my flying grade and I'll never forget it.

THE TENTH HOUR CHECK RIDE

My tenth hour check was a memorable one and gave me a lifetime lesson in human psychology. There was one instructor on staff that was known for his tough, unforgiving treatment of cadets, and I was unlucky enough to draw him. All of my buddies began holding a wake for me the minute they learned I was the one who was going to be fed to the bad guy. I couldn't sleep much the night before the ride. My brain was working overtime trying to figure the best fame plan to counter my unfortunate luck of the draw. I decided on a psychological approach. I'd keep this tough instructor busy, bombarding him with so many questions that he wouldn't have time to chew me out for every little detail. That might keep enough pressure off me so that I could give my best effort.

We were flying another Taylorcraft for this check ride. I climbed into the back cockpit after the instructor pilot had settled into his forward position. First thing, he began lecturing me on the art of buckling and adjusting my seat belt. I hadn't buckled it in the most efficient way or something. I took a deep breath and figured that this was going to be a very long day. I leaped into my game plan as quickly as I could and began asking questions like: "The other instructors never explained this or that to me and I never understood exactly how to perform this maneuver etc... "

We made some short field takeoffs and landings and then climbed to altitude for a series of left and right 360 degree steep turns. The next maneuvers were power-on and power-off stalls, after which we descended for low level work: figure eight turns and turns around pylons. It was back to altitude again for engine failure procedures and a power-off landing in a short grass field. Takeoff from this short field would be a challenge. I let down twenty degrees of flaps, stood on the brakes, and pushed the throttle full forward. In seconds we were at full r.p.m. I released the brakes, and we were into our take off roll. I eased forward on the stick just enough to lift the tail and then when I felt that we were reaching flying speed I came back on the stick; the little plane was airborne a good hundred and fifty yards before we reached the end of the strip. I climbed to altitude and pointed the Taylorcraft toward the Omaha Municipal Airport. I kept my "diversionary" questions going throughout the check ride.

We taxied to base operations and shut down. The fearsome check-out instructor couldn't have been nicer. He told me that I had done an excellent job and that I would have no trouble making it as a pilot. A handful of buddies were waiting for me to help pick up the pieces. They were shocked to see me climb out of the airplane smiling and shaking hands with my also smiling check-out instructor. All I can tell you is that this "Mr. Bad" was a delight. He taught me more in that check-out ride than I had learned from all the other instructors combines. I was eager and relaxed. The instructor gave me an overall score of 87 which proved to be one of the highest grades given to any cadet on this 10 hour check. My buddies couldn't wait to corner me and get the gory details. It was a kick. I just made a "meal" out of how great the guy was while my fellow cadets kept shaking their heads in disbelief. There was a valuable lesson learned here: When someone is putting pressure on you, start asking questions. Well, at least it worked that day.

HAROLD SCOTT SHARP MISSING IN ACTION

I felt proud of my accomplishments at Creighton and I was feeling confident and eager to take the next giant step toward that left seat. I had often thought of Harold Sharp's last letter to me. He wrote, "Hang in there, Jim, you'll be a pilot just like me. We'll beat up on these bad guys, and then celebrate our win at the Chicken Shack" (one of our favorite growing up places in Harlan, Iowa). I answered Harold's letter and, at the end, I penned these lines, "Here's to the Chicken Shack--Give em' hell!" I had been thinking of Harold when the letter I wrote to him was returned. It had a stamped imprint in the upper left hand corner which was the likeness of a hand pointing to these shocking words: "Harold Scott Sharp missing in action." I don't remember how long I stared at the letter in disbelief. I went outside and walked somewhere. I didn't want any cadets to see me cry. I opened my returned letter and all I could see was the ending that I had written: "Here's to the Chicken Shack--Give em hell." The reality of war had reached out and touched me for the first time. It hurt a lot.

Note: Warren G. McFadden, tail gunner on Harold Sharp's crew has now been located. He reports that their B-17, "Flak Happy", was shot down over Bremen, Germany October 8th, 1943. According to McFadden, an ME 109 came out of the sun and raked the fuselage before anyone knew what was happening. Three of them were able to bail out, and the last thing McFadden saw was the wingless fuselage of "Flak Happy" falling end over end. The three men were captured by Germans and were finally taken to another areas by a truck with seven wooden caskets in it, so McFadden said he knew that the bodies were buried.

SQUADRON FOUR LEAVES CREIGHTON UNIVERSITY

On March 18, 1944 we loaded our bags onto the back of troop trucks and stood by for our ride to the train station. At long last we were headed for classification where we'd be classified flying officers. Most everyone wanted to a pilot but classification would determine whether the cadet would be a pilot, bombardier, or navigator. The University of Creighton had given us a great start and, even though we would miss our friends, we were eager to move on.

At the last minute one of the young Catholic Fathers, Callihan, came out to say good-bye. He had been a wonderful teacher and a great motivator. He spoke to us in emotional, loving terms, hugged each one of us, and pledged his prayers for our safety. We were all touched by Father Callihan's concern for us, and by his caring. None of us would ever forget him.

A large number of civilians had gathered at the Omaha train station to see us off: buddies, girl friends, and some of the families that had taken us in as their own. Even the tough Squadron Sergeant Pruitt had a tear in his eye as he said good-bye. Lieutenant Campbell, and his adjutant, Lieutenant Green, gave their best wishes to all of us, and we in turn thanked them for their considerations and excellent training. There was no question that leaving Omaha was a deeply emotional experience for everyone.

THE SCAM IN CHEYENNE

The Santa Ana bound troop train had a one hour stop in Cheyenne, Wyoming. The cadets had time to play some "no-win", one-way slot machines, and buy some frolic juice in a nearby liquor store. I had been given some pool money for that detail, and I brought back a full pint of whiskey which we agreed to savor until the right moment. The troop train was just an hour out of Cheyenne when I poured the first drink for one of the contributors. We anxiously anticipated his smiling approval, but instead, the cadet took a modest swig, held it in his mouth for a moment of taste testing, then spewed it out all over the floor. The strangest look came over his face. He locked his eyes and stiffened as if he'd been poisoned. Then he let it all out, "We've been had", he bellowed— "it's brown sugar and water—or worse." I could feel the hair standing up on my neck. One by one we cautiously smelled the contents, wet a finger and tasted the stuff. Brown sugar and water—at least that's what it tasted like. The bottle had been sealed perfectly and displayed a government stamp, but when you looked closely, you could see that the bottom of the bottle had been tampered with. The guy in the store knew that he would never see us again. I have wondered to this day how many other troop trains had stopped there, and how many other soldiers had been victimized?

All the talk on the train eventually got around to that ugly rumor which held that classification was closing at Santa Ana. It was being said that the fellows who couldn't qualify for flying would be sent to the infantry. Not a good alternative. If there was any truth at all to the classification scuttle, I just hoped that we'd all make it through before the flight

selection system actually closed. All of us tried to face the possibility that we might be eliminated from the cadet program, but no one was fully prepared to be washed out after all the rigorous training we had endured.

SANTA ANA, CALIFORNIA AND THE BIG WASH OUT

The train ride from Omaha to Los Angeles had been a long one, and we couldn't wait to hit the exits. Our trusty quintet quickly organized and we serenaded the crowd with "California Here We Come" (we had practiced that one on the train), and then we gave them our best rendition of our favorite "Shanty Town" for a closer. As it played out that was the last song we ever sang together. The group was soon scattered to the four winds and we never saw one another again.

As soon as the troop buses arrived we were informed by a Transportation Sergeant that classification had been closed temporarily so all those bad rumors, unfortunately, turned out to have substance. We tried to shake off our disappointment by telling one another that classification might reopen and everything might turn around for us. Hope springs eternal, especially in the young, but the reality of a wash-out could not be denied. We settled into quarters and awaited further instructions. There was a large pool of cadets that had preceded us, and they were also standing by for orders.

The next morning we were told that classification had re-opened but only for a few days. That was enough to get us all charged up again. Some were then ordered to classification and others, like myself, waited to be called. I finally saw my name on the list of those who would begin classification. There was a psychological interview that followed all of the testing, and the officer cautioned me not to get my hopes up. "There is a heavy overload of pilots," he said. "You had high marks in the navigation section so perhaps you'll be classified as a navigator. However there's not much chance at this stage since the selection process is about to be shut down permanently." I related this message to one of my buddies who tried to encourage me: "Don't worry, Smith. If you don't make it, none of us will. You've got one of the best grade averages in the squadron."

WASH-OUT WAITING ROOMS

Declassified information now shows that the cadet college training program was instituted because there was a growing surplus of flying officers and the military didn't know what to do with the newly inducted cadets. The college training detachment facilities became, in effect, wash-out waiting rooms regardless of grades or accomplishments. A handful of cadets that were first scheduled for classification slipped through the cracks and became flying officers. The rest of us were ordered to tote our barracks bags from cadet quarters to the enlisted men quarters across the field. It was literally a march of tears. I can speak for all of us when I say that the trip from a "gentleman" cadet to an enlisted man is a long one. My mother leaving my dad and me was emotionally shattering, but this wash-out was crippling.

The attitudes of those in charge changed at once. We were the same, but now we were treated like non-persons. A washed

out cadet was viewed as a loser and, unfortunately, some of us were beginning to think of ourselves in the same light. The fact that it wasn't our fault didn't seem to make any difference.

In Craven and Cate's, The Army Air Forces in W.W. II., the editors cite the closing of classification as creating one of the biggest morale problems of the war. I can personally vouch for the accuracy of this statement.

THE SADDEST TRAIN RIDE

It was the agony of defeat for all of us. I was especially bitter about being eliminated from the flying program considering the fact I had finished Creighton University and the student flying course with very high marks. Since I was qualified as a flying crew member, I was given the choice of radio school or gunnery. A couselor advised me: "The top ten percent of radio school graduates will be transferred to officers' candidate school where they will become communication officers. There is no such opportunity in gunnery." I thought gunnery school sounded like more fun than the "dit and dah" deal, but the chance to get those bars made my decision easy. I was ordered to Sioux Falls, South Dakota for radio operator/mechanics school.

The train was crammed with fellow cadets who, like me, had just been axed out of the cadet program. No one was saying much. We were mourning the passing of our dreams. I was emotionally sick, and to make a bad situation worse, I was suffering chest pains from a bad cold. I remember that someone passed around a bottle of whiskey and a large bottle of orange crush soda for a chaser. Orange

Crush and whiskey wasn't really such a terrible combination, especially when you were a hurting washed-out cadet. Anything that would take away pain for awhile. The morale of these troops was scraping bottom.

Although it was late March, old man winter was still on display in the midwest showing plenty of banked up snow at the crossings and main streets. The train whistled mournfully through the hamlets and towns, appropriately reflecting the mood of its occupants. We could see occasional remnants of Christmas lights and decorations that were waiting to be dismantled and, in view of the depression we were all feeling, those scenes pulled us even lower. I think we resented anything that reminded us of joy and happiness. All of us had been polished and buffed by the military and then suddenly tossed away like old bones. The cadets had run on wings of hope and high expectations and, just when everything was in the "green", the brass chopped our power and we spun out.

"Off We Go Into The Wild Blue Yonder"... The Army Air Corps had taken that song away from us.

Chapter Four

(S) DIT DIT DIT (F) DIT DIT DAH DIT

The ex-cadets arrived at Sioux Falls in the early evening. We might have landed at the North Pole for all I knew; it couldn't have been much colder there. The Army bus wheeled us down snow- patched, icy roads on our way to the Sioux Falls Army Air Field. We were driven into Section "R" where we unloaded our gear in sub-zero temperatures and received our barracks assignments.

No sooner had we arranged our footlockers and climbed into our double bunks than one of the pot bellied stoves backed up and began belching out huge clouds of black coal smoke. I joined a couple of other G.I.'s, who were coughing and choking like myself, and we managed to clear the flue enough to redirect the smoke up the chimney. The damage had been done, however, and there was still enough smoke lingering in the barracks to make breathing a challenge, but no one was eager to open doors to clear things with Arctic-cold air. We figured that was a bad trade-off at the moment. One guy figured the best way to get to sleep in the remaining cloud of irritating coal dust was to strap on his issued gas mask. It worked for him so the rest of us tried it, and, eventually, we were all able to grab a few "Z's". Any way you look at it, it was a very memorable first nighter.

The next morning was as bright and clear as it was cold. We had a typical S.O.S. (sh-t on a shingle) Army breakfast, and then marched to orientation. We were then shown the different class rooms and facilities used for teaching International Morse Code and radio mechanics. I was impressed with all that I saw at Sioux Falls, and I was determined to get the best grades on the field. They weren't going to skunk me twice. I wanted those officer bars, and I was willing to do whatever it took to get them. The sting of the wash-out I had been feeling turned into just enough resentment and anger to motivate me to fight like hell for the goal line.

INTERNATIONAL MORSE CODE

School began and I pushed the throttle all the way forward. I loved it. I soon found out that a natural musical ability was tremendously helpful in learning code and, fortunately, I had received musical genes from both sides of the family. Our code rooms were huge and there was row after row of long shiny tables, each accommodating about a dozen students. We used earphones for receiving code, and the old J-4 and J-37 Morse keys for sending. The instructors taught us code by demonstration. They described each character with dits and dahs and then sent them to us. We copied and then sent the code back, one student sending at a time.

As our code proficiency increased, we were moved to higher code speed tables.

At first we began to count the dits and dahs that made up letters or numbers. It was possible to memorize the dots and dashed and count them for each character up to a speed of about six words a minute, and that was "max" for that concept. After six words per minute you had to hear the dits and dahs of each character (or number) as an overall sound. If you didn't grab hold of that theory, you were headed for a wash-out. The folks that didn't have any music in their bones could get to a code speed of about fourteen words per minute, and that was tops. That speed would get you into the Air Transport Command but then you'd miss the excitement of flying bombing missions. We had to pass sixteen words per minute to qualify for bombers. There were no short cuts here, no gifts or politics to bail anyone out. It was like the yes or no binary principle. You could either send and receive, or you couldn't, and there was no way to fake it. The guys that couldn't or wouldn't hack it, were looking at the infantry. You had to work hard and practice every day, and even then it took months to gain speed and proficiency.

Everytime I saw a sign or lettering of any kind I'd translate it into Morse code in my head. It didn't make any difference what I was doing or where I was. I'm convinced that my brain was practicing the dit and dah language even while I was sleeping.

In International Morse Code, the dit sounds are the dots (.) and the dah sounds are the dashes (-). We used phrases, and rhythms to help us. For example you would think of "L" as the phrase: "To hell with it". The letter "L" in Morse code is: dit dah dit dit which sounds like "To hell with it." There was a popular song at the time entitled "Deep in The Heart of Texas". It started out, "The stars at night".

Well, that was perfect for the letter "P", which in Morse code is: dit dah dah dit (The Stars at Night). We used a plaintive Army phrase that we couldn't forget for the letter "C": "Balls and all dit", which in code is: dah dit dah dit. It was the phrase: "Balls and all dah," for the letter "Y". In code, "Y" is: dah dit dah dah. For "F" we used the phrase: "Get a haircut." In code, "F" is: dit dit dah dit. "X" was "Slide Kelly slide." In code, "X" is dah dit dit dah. "Q" was everyone's favorite: "Pay day today," and in code "Q" is: dah dah dit dah.

If you make a mistake when you're receiving code you can't think about it even for a split second or you'll miss the next character coming up. A lot of people flunked tests because of the tendency to think back on their mistakes. It's an unwritten law of life: think back on your errors and you'll invariably blow the next opportunity. Also, if you are the least bit tense, that will diminish your code speed proficiency. Many of the students at Sioux Falls made sure that they drank a few beers the night before a code test. A slight hangover seemed to keep one loose and concentrated. However I learned that the very best way to pass the tests was to be prepared by constantly practicing.

HUT ONE, HUT TWO

Having been assigned to section "R" at the Sioux Falls Army Air Base meant that I drew Lieutenant Gerber for a physical education instructor. He was a hard-nosed guy who stood about six feet two inches, built like he was going to last forever, and had an extremely raspy, comical sounding voice. Gerber was an ex-sparring partner of Max Bear (one time heavy weight champion of the world), and I suspected that he might have taken one too many punches. The man was in such powerful good shape, however, that he didn't know his own strength. He almost killed every G.I. in the section with his work out routines. (He exercised right along with us as he called cadence.) Gerber assembled us at the exercise field and started us out with stretching and calisthenics. When we were about ready to drop, he'd order us to run six miles around the air station. After we returned to the field, Gerber always had a surprise for us—like running wind sprints. There were no fat boys in Section R.

One day when we were well into our calisthenics routine, I had an urge to imitate the Lieutenant's raspy count. I didn't think he'd hear me, but I underestimated his audio receptors. He stopped in the middle of a jumping jack, and screamed in his fog horn voice, "Who did that, who tried to imitate me?" I prayed that no one would rat on me, and of course I had learned by now not to volunteer anything. "You might as well tell me," he fogged, "because if I have to find out on my own, you'll be doing K.P. for the rest of your Army career." After what seemed like an hour Gerber said, "All right, back to the jumping jack—one two, one two..." I sweated being found out for the rest of my stay in Sioux Falls, but nothing more was said about the incident. If you read this book, Lt. Gerber, I'll finally confess that I'm the one who did your impression. No offense, and thanks for getting me down to 164 pounds of solid muscle. I still think it was great impersonation though.

JOE MAY'S HORSE TRICK

Week-end passes in Sioux Falls were always relaxing, and in the summer a few of us would chip in on a fifty-five gallon barrel of Grainbelt Beer and head for the park with a cache of picnic goodies. It was a blast. Joe May, another cadet wash-out, was always aboard for the picnic bit. He was a good guy and easy company. Joe's quiet demeanor understated the real man. He was slight of build and tipped the Toledos at about a hundred and forty five pounds. The hundred and forty five, however, was metamorphic rock.

On one happy park occasion an over-dressed rider pranced through our area on a Palomino stud. The horse was high-spirited and it caught Joe's attention immediately. He yelled to the over-dressed rider, "Can you stop for a minute? That's a fine looking horse you got there." The fellow smiled and pulled up his fractious, prancing steed. As the horse wheeled around in a 360 the rider called, "He's got a lot of fire, pretty hard to handle." Joe grabbed the halter and the horse steadied, "How much would you take to let me ride him for a minute or two?" The rider smiled, "You couldn't keep your mount on this one." J. M. scratched his head, "Well two things to consider here: if I don't keep my mount, I won't blame you for any damage I suffer; secondly, we have a 55 gallon barrel of Grainbelt beer that we've just tapped. You let me ride your horse and you can drink all the beer you can hold." The guy laughed, "Okay you asked for it, but don't say I didn't warn you." The fellow dismounted cautiously and handed Joe the reins. With that my friend stepped quickly into the stirrup and swung up into the saddle and the next minute and a half was a happening that will be etched in my memory forever.

Joe raked the horse and the horse jumped off the ground with all fours. When the quadruped hit terra firma again, May pulled him into tight circles, first to the right, and then to the left. The snorting horse was pounding the ground and kicking turf all over the place. The owner was spilling his beer as he moved tightly in concert with the action. Joe pulled back on the reins and the horse reared; then he kicked his steed into a run. The big animal kicked up huge clouds of dust, partially hiding himself and his rider. The frightened owner, obviously anticipating the worst, ran after them until the horse and rider were lost in dust and distance. The fellow, who had tenaciously hung on to his Grainbelt, gave up his chase and just stood there in the middle of the bridle path alternately shaking his head and emptying what was left of his large cup of suds. We all watched in stunned silence as Joe brought a contented walking horse back. The fellow horseman ran over to his Palomino and looked up wide-eyed at the rider, "My God man, who are you? I've never seen anyone handle a horse like that, especially this one. I don't believe it. Look at him, he's as calm as anything." May dismounted with an athletic hop. "He'll be fine now. He just needed a little work. Nice horse!" He tied the horse to a small tree and invited the owner to have another beer. We all rushed over to shake our new hero's hand and tell him how he had blown us away with his one-man horse show. The other rider was gushing all over him, "Where did you ever learn to handle a horse like that." We all wanted to know, "Yeah, where Joe?". Ol' Joe May took a long sip of Grainbelt and then threw a leg up on the picnic table bench. "Heck, I grew up on these animals. I'm from Wyoming you know; I rodeo'd for three years before I ever got caught up in this man's Army."

PLANNED ELECTROCUTION

I went to sleep with the dits and dahs, and woke up with them. They obsessed me. Obsession with code was crucial if one was to do well with that new language.

The radio mechanics course fascinated me. We studied the Superheterodyne receiver and were required to build both receivers and transmitters before we graduated. We learned all about the inner and outer workings of the hardware, including the capacitor. Unfortunately we learned about the workings of the capacitor by way of some real life experiences. There was always a character (among others, I suspected the instructor) who would charge one up and leave it loose on a work bench. We all had our turn at being the unsuspecting person to pick up one of these charged condensers. When we did, zzzaaaaap! The electrical discharge had enough kick to drive the yowling victim across the room. This tom foolery finally stopped as everyone became wiser, and learned to carefully discharge every loose condenser with a screwdriver before handling it.

My soldering wasn't first class, but I did manage to put a Superheterodyne receiver together and it worked like a charm. I was elated. Then I put a transmitter together and it transmitted. Exciting stuff! It still amazes me that one can electronically transmit or receive without wires. Amazing, even with wires.

It was late fall of forty four and we were getting ready to graduate from radio school. There were many who had failed the course, and some of those people were sent to the infantry. Others who qualified at lower speeds only were sent to the A.T.C. (Air Transport Command). My musical genes and my determination served me well. I passed a code speed of twenty one words per minute, both sending and receiving. I could understand up to thirty words per minute, but I couldn't physically print that fast. As for sending, the standard code key was not designed for sending above 25 words a minute.

At regular speeds 'S' was: dit dit dit--'H', dit dit dit dit--'I', dit dit--'T',dah!) In international code at thirty words a minute S.H.I.T. sounded like: Thrrrrip Dah. A "bug" sender was used for code speeds in excess of twenty words a minute. You operated it with a thumb and first finger technique which required a separate learning process. A typewriter was necessary to copy high speed code, and the typing and receiving of code had to be learned together. The best typists and fastest code receivers could not just simply put those two skills together. It was an evolving process and had to be learned simultaneously.

LIGHT SIGNAL CODE

Understanding Morse code from signal lamps was required and we had to pass six words per minute. That was tricky. You were using the sense of sight and not of sound. Then too, once you achieved a high code speed, it was tough to slow down to 6 words per minute because of the change in rhythm. Even so, I found that repeating the dits and dahs as I watched the light source was a big help.

The last requirement was for radio operators to send and receive code while actually air borne. They used the old Lockheed twin engine Hudson Bomber for that chore and the reception was so poor that it took terrific concentration to pick up any words at all. That was a real sweat but, fortunately for us all, there were no

thumbs up or thumbs down on that ride. The ride was merely a requirement and there was no grade given.

COMMUNICATION CADETS SCRUBBED

I finished my classes well within the top ten percent and I know that I was going to make communications cadets. I and the other ten per centers were notified and ordered to a lecture theater where a Major congratulated us for our high grades, and then unceremoniously announced that the communication cadet officer program had been terminated. That brought the troops out of their chairs momentarily as we experienced another Air Corps "whiplash". I swore under my breath: "Here we go again." The Major then advised us that we 10 per centers were the chosen few and the luckiest guys in the Air Corps because we were being assigned to the new Super Bomber, the B-29 Superfort. The Major went on to advise us that we would soon become "Flight Officers," (special rank), and we would make the same amount of pay as a group captain. At this point in time my buddies and I viewed all military promises with total skepticism. As we used to say in Iowa, "I guess we'd been shucked just one too many times to get excited." As far as the B-29's were concerned, they were reportedly plagued by engine fires and explosions. Those reports had a decided dampening effect on our enthusiasm. The Air Corps had a unique way of pointing out unsafe aircraft. We were beginning to hear the B-29 described as the B dash, two crash, nine.

GENERAL HENRY HARLEY "HAP" ARNOLD'S B DASH 2 CRASH 9

The military had been looking for a

strategic long range bomber since the 1930's. As early as 1939 Commander of the Army Air Forces, General Henry H. (Hap) Arnold was insisting that the Air Force develop a long-range, very heavy bomber to fulfill future tactical requirements. The idea gained support when it looked like England might be defeated. In that eventuality there would be no place for the United States to base its planes for future operations against the Axis powers. General Arnold challenged the engineering staff at Wright Field, Dayton, Ohio to design a super bomber that would be the biggest, most heavily armed, and have the longest operating range of any airplane in the world. It would have to be specifically designed to control all strategic bombardment operations on a world wide basis. Several aircraft companies submitted proposals based on the Wright Field engineer's specification, and Boeing's model 345 was the one that rang the bell. The Army Air Corps gave it a designation of XB-29, and Boeing was awarded three million, six hundred thousand dollars to start developing the prototype.

The experimental B-29's encountered big time trouble in the beginning which seriously jeopardized the program; jammed gears, dead power plants, and fires in the engine nacelles prompted an outcry from the critics to scrap all B-29 development. General Arnold stubbornly stood his ground and won back some major support in June 27, 1943 when Colonel Leonard "Jake" Harmon successfully flew the XB-29 at Boeing's plant in Wichita, Kansas. What had been characterized as a shaky three billion dollar gamble, was beginning to look like a winner. Interesting to note that General Arnold, in a bold move of anticipation, had ordered mass production of 1664

B-29's before the first test flight.

By February 1943 it appeared that the B-29 program was finally on course when a second flight test being flown by chief test pilot Eddie Allen at Boeing aircraft in Seattle, ended in tragedy. Allen and his crew were all killed and the multimillion dollar B-29 development program was once again in big trouble. General Arnold again remained steadfast and fought back to re-establish support for the big plane. His perseverance paid off and, by 1944, Superfortresses were being produced at four factories: Boeing's Witchita Kansas plant; Boeing, Renton, Washington; Martin Aircraft at Omaha, Nebraska; and Bell at Marietta in Georgia. Five years after the Boeing Company submitted its design, the B-29's were bombing Japan.

GOOD BYE TO SIOUX FALLS

The Major wished us luck and dismissed us from the Sioux Falls lecture hall. All of the guys had mixed feelings. I wasn't charmed by the scuttle describing B-29 engine fires and explosions on takeoff, but the airplane was new, and I figured that safety modifications would be occurring at a fast rate. However, I did have my fingers crossed that the problems would be solved before I climbed aboard. There was some comfort, though, in knowing that B-29 crew positions were being filled by the best people in the Air Corps. We'd also be flying in the biggest and greatest bomber the world had ever seen, and that, in itself, was pretty heady stuff. The B-29 was being characterized as the "Queen Mary" of the skies. One ex-cadet turned to me as we made our way out of the lecture theatre and put it all into perspective, "Well, Smith, whatever the 29 turns out to be, it sure as hell beats the infantry." I put a thumbs up, "Amen, brother."

LINCOLN, NEBRASKA

The next stop was the Army Air Field in Lincoln, Nebraska where we were to be given orientation lectures and high altitude decompression chamber tests. Once qualified, we'd be assigned to appropriate B-29 training bases. Our group arrived at the Lincoln Army Air Field station in November 1944.

Orientation lectures with films came first, and they offered a wide assortment of boring subjects. The one exception was the sex orientation film. It started out by showing a great looking female then cut to an old worn out "B" movie actor, portraying a doctor sitting at his office desk. The old Doc, surrounded by framed diplomas, turned dramatically into the camera and warned: "She may look good but do you know how many girls have venereal disease?" Then the pretend doctor pointed out different parts of the country, and gave percentages of the populace that were afflicted with venereal disease. The film depicted every kind of sexually transmitted contagion, and every type of venereal sore one could imagine. It was the only orientation I remember where the audience didn't drift off. At the end of the lecture, a live in-person medical officer made the remarkable statement that one's alimentary canal was actually cleaner than one's mouth. I never knew exactly what the message was there, but the entire experience was definitely an anti-aphrodisiac.

Everyone drew K. P. in Lincoln sooner or later. Infractions of rules and regulations had nothing to do with it this trip. It was a logistic necessity and everyone took turns whipping the potatoes. We began at 3:30 a. m. which seemed even earlier after a night of liberty. The bars featured a drink called Glick's Stite Ale. It was inexpensive and several bottles would set you free--for about three days. Rumors had it that the stuff was laced with ether. I don't know about that one, but I learned quickly to leave it alone. For me, a dozen nickelodeon plays of "Don't Fence Me In" with Bing Crosby and the Andrew sisters was enough to make my night.

There was a beautiful old Staff Sergeant at Lincoln who used to wake us up at reveille by singing a song instead of blowing the customary ear shattering whistle. This, the S.O.P. wake-up call would generally bring you out of your bunk cussing, and ready for a fight. We couldn't believe this Sergeant, but he'd come in every morning singing, "Wake up sleepy heads wake up, wake up sleepy heads wake up". It was straight from a nursery portfolio but I promise you that none of us "macho" guys ever complained. Guess the old Sarge thought we were all his kids and, although we laughed about it, we privately thought it was pretty neat. God Bless him.

EXPLOSIVE DECOMPRESSION

The Lincoln Army Air Field was known for its sophisticated high altitude decompression chambers. These were large sealed chambers in which any pressure altitude could be achieved, and then explosively discharged to lower pressures. The purpose of the chambers were to simulate conditions that might occur in a high flying B-29 that was penetrated by anti-aircraft fire or lost pressure from some other reason. (A B-29 was pressurized to a density altitude of eight thousand feet, and could operate at 35,000 feet and more.) If a test subject had an ear equalization problem, the chamber would reveal it to him in a most painful way.

We were given instructions and then explosively depressurized from an 8000 foot pressure altitude to the very low altitude pressure of 35,000 feet. We held on to an oxygen mask, but we didn't use it until we felt ourselves passing out. The command wanted us to get acquainted with the symptoms and effects of hypoxia, and how to relieve that condition with the correct use of an oxygen mask. A few guys passed out before they opted to put on their mask and medical personnel had to move in. The exercise was enlightening if not a little scary.

After several short weeks I was qualified for duty in B-29 air crews, and on December 1, 1944, I was transferred to the Fairmont Army Air Field, Geneva, Nebraska. My new assignment: B-29B aircraft, 2nd Air Force, 17th Bomb Training Wing, 16th Bomb Group, Very Heavy, 17th Bomb Squadron, Very Heavy.

We were really a part of the 315th Bombardment Wing VH (very heavy) which had been established on 17 July 1944 and headquartered at Peterson Field, Colorado Springs, Colorado. We were placed under the control of the Second Air Force for combat training because of its status as the principal pioneer in heavy bombardment training, and also because the Second Air Force had available training facilities. When our Wing reached combat we would be directly under the command of the 20th Air Force.

FAIRMONT, NEBRASKA ARMY AIR FIELD

The Chicago & North Western Railway delivered our little band of sky warriors to Geneva in good fettle, and deposited us at the train station. The population of this small community was 1,888; I could identify with small towns since I grew up in Dow City, Iowa, which was almost half as big. We bussed out to the Fairmont Field located just four and one half miles to the Northeast, and it was a great looking facility covering some 1,844 acres. A very large water tower claimed my attention. I nudged a fellow G.I. and pointed to the tower, "Well, I'm thrilled that they have some water here. I was getting a little tired of Glick's Stite."

The facilities were outstanding and I figured this was a class set up. The concrete runways were N/S, NE/SW, each 6,965 feet long and 150 feet wide. I reckoned that the big B-29 birds could use every bit of that cement. I was still a Private at this point, and by now I knew that the latest information about my becoming a flight officer was so much Bovine Scatology! I had no choice, though, but to make the best of it, and I was heartened by the thought that the war couldn't last forever.

My heart beat fast when I first saw the huge tail of a B-29 rising almost thirty feet above the hardstand. Buildings blocked out any view of the rest of the airplane, but it was enough of a teaser for me and the other guys to get us racing back to the flight line after we set up our quarters.

THE BIG BIRD
The B-29 was the world's first pressurized bomber, the world's heaviest production airplane, had the most powerful reciprocating engines, and the highest wing loading of the time. The first glimpse

took my breath away and the dimensions were unbelievable. This airplane dwarfed the B-17 Flying Fortress. The B-29 Superfortress was the most complex aircraft ever conceived—60 tons of fighting fury. It was 99 feet long with a wing span of 141' 2.76"compared to the B-17 which was 73 feet long and had a wing span of 104 feet. The wing area of a B-17 was 1,420 Square Feet while the B-29 was 1,738 Square Feet. The basic weight of a B-17 was 37,000 pounds, compared to a B-29 which was 72,000 pounds. The B-17's gross weight was 60,000 pounds; the B-29, 140,000 pounds with bombs and gasoline. The B-17's takeoff power was 4800 H. P., and the B-29's four R-3350 Wright Cyclones engines generated 8800 H. P. on takeoff.

The B-29 had two main gears with two wheels each, and a nose gear with two wheels. The nose was bullet shaped, rounding off on top at approximately 14 feet above the ground with gear down, and the tail stood 27 feet 9 inches above the hardstand. The diameter of the four bladed Hamilton propellers was 16 feet 7 inches. As some said, it was a bomber of superlatives.

NO GUNS

There was one spine tingling mystery to the whole scenario: there were no turrets on these Fairmont B-29's except the tail turret which showed two 50 caliber machine guns, and a 20 millimeter cannon. The standard B-29's had five turrets: two forward; top and bottom; two aft; top and bottom, plus the tail turret. The immediate speculation was that the airplanes we were seeing would soon be flown to Boeing's Witchita factory for armament installation.

They weren't kidding around at Fairmont. Within four days after I arrived there, I had been assigned to crew 1712, and was climbing up the nose wheel ladder of what the Air Corps was calling the greatest bomber ever devised by man. The crew consisted of AC (aircraft commander), Earl W. Bentley Jr.; Pilot, Rodger B. Jensen (replaced by an instructor for that trip); Navigator James E. McClellan Jr.; Bombardier, Paul O'Brien; Flight Engineer, E, George R. Martinonis; (myself) ROM, Jimmie Smith; Central Fire Gunner Robert K. Emmons (was not aboard); waist gunners, Russell J. Willette, and John E. Schutz; Radar Operator, August St. George; Tail Gunner, Ronald E. Vanderhoof.

Note: My first B-29B pilot, Lieutenant Rodger B. Jensen (crew #1712), was among those of us who were ordered to stand by in a replacement pool. Lt. Jensen was subsequently assigned to a crew who became part of the 315th Bomb Wing stationed at Northwest Field, Guam. By reason of a unique twist of fate, Jensen's crew figured prominently in the historic last mission. The details will be described by Jensen's former radio operator mechanic in a later chapter dealing with the last mission.

I stepped onto the flight deck, took a deep breath and filled up on the "essence of new airplane." I had first experienced that olfactory sensation while working at Consolidated Aircraft in San Diego. I've always thought that this fetching fragrance comes from a combination of anodized aluminum and new materials that make up a freshly manufactured aircraft. Whatever the source, the smell of a new airplane is pleasantly addictive, and a flier never forgets it.

The command pilot took his left seat position, while the check ride instructor took the pilot's seat on the right. The bombardier settled into his position which was a step down from the pilots station and forward in the Plexi-glas nose. That was the best seat in the house and it provided a remarkably clear view for the bombardier. I turned to my right, took two steps and was in the middle of the B-29 control center, the engineer's station. I surveyed the maze of gauges, instruments, switches, throttles and mixture controls, and suddenly felt a growing respect for the engineer. He was loud and clear the heart beat of things. The radio man's station was located just aft of the engineer's bulkhead. The absence of the upper forward turret gave us enough room to dance. I planned to enjoy this luxury as long as possible because I knew those new central fire control turrets would be installed soon, and the dance would be over.

I sat down in my swivel seat and studied the equipment. It was all familiar to me except the new Collins' transmitter. Instead of having to change coils for certain frequencies as we did in radio school (the radio operators had to change frequency coils on B-17's and some early B-29's), these B-29's featured the new Collins' transmitter which gave the radio operator the capability of presetting 10 frequencies. Thankfully, the Collins made the changing of coils a thing of the past. This new sophisticated transmitter was made in Cedar Rapids, Iowa and the radio guys were calling it the "Maytag". (I liked the idea that it was made in my home state where quality had always been the hallmark.) As you punched in one frequency after another, all the dials spun one way, and then the other until the selected frequency was set up and the

antenna loading was completed. That was the "Maytag" part. It was a wonderful, time-saving, innovative piece of equipment and featured 75 watts of power. It transmitted carrier wave (CW), and of course, modulated carrier wave for voice transmissions. There was a trailing antenna that could be let out when low frequency, long distance communication was required.

The navigator's position was opposite and slightly forward of the radio position. The station included some flight instruments: long range navigation indicator (Loran), radio compass control box, outside air thermometer, and altitude-airspeed handset unit. The radar operator's station (the operator facing aft), featuring the AN/APQ-7 radar synchronous bombing system, was located behind the navigator and directly across from the radio position. I swiveled my chair to my right and unlatched the round, port hole shaped forward bomb bay entry door, which in flight served also as an air pressure door. There was a second bomb bay aft, and that pressure/entry door was accessed from the waist gunners position. Each bomb bay could carry more than five tons of bombs. There was a tunnel running above the forward bay back through the length of the second bay, which allowed crews access to the forward and aft positions of the aircraft. There was just enough room for one person to crawl through the tunnel, and you could get more than a little claustrophobic before reaching the other end. If you happened to be in the tunnel at altitude and the airplane experienced sudden depressurization, forget it. You were a bean in a bean shooter.

THE HANDBOOK OF FLIGHT OPERATING INSTRUCTIONS,

SECTION 16., MOVEMENT OF FLIGHT PERSONNEL, PUTS IT THIS WAY:

"a. GENERAL: The forward and rear pressurized compartments afford ample room for crew members to move around as necessary, and the tunnel may be used whether or not the compartments are pressurized. Attention is called to the potential danger that exists in the use of the tunnel under pressurized conditions. If pressure were lost rapidly in either the forward or rear compartment while maintaining a high pressure differential, anyone in the tunnel could be ejected with sufficient velocity to sustain serious injury."

I crawled to the waist gunners positions; another ballroom with no turret congestion. The tail gunners position was a different story. The space was adequate but since the gunner shared his quarters with two fifties and a 20 millimeter cannon, it was cozy close.

I climbed back through the tunnel and re-checked my radio gear for a few minutes. We all sensed the majesty and importance of this great Superfortress. It was a pressurized bomber with 50,000 separate parts, a million rivets, thousands of miles of complex wiring, and capable of flying over sixteen hours with full fuel and bomb load. I knew that I was a top radio operator, and I was now entrusted to demonstrate my skills in the world's greatest bomber. My despair at being eliminated from pilot training was now being overshadowed by the pride I felt in my new assignment. I knew that I could contribute, and that made everything better.

A radio instructor who was checked out on the Collins' equipment, climbed aboard and showed me how to pre-set the new transmitter. He told me that he would hang in for this orientation flight and suggested that I could get a bird's eye view of takeoff from the tunnel astrodome. (The astrodome was at the top of the tunnel and a step way from my position.) I climbed up and saw ground crew personnel with fire extinguishers waiting on the right side. Number three inboard engine began to turn slowly; it shuddered, belched smoke, and then finally kicked the Hamilton four-bladed propeller into a smooth circle of enormous power. The propellers had to be slowed down with 35/100 reduction gears to keep the tip speed under the speed of sound. These massive 18 cylinder R-3350 Wright Cyclone engines with dual sets of turbo-superchargers, were the most powerful reciprocating engines in the world with each engine representing 2200 horses of raw power. Number four outboard kicked into action, then on the port side, number two inboard, and finally number one outboard. Carl pushed his throat mike button and ordered, "Crew interphone check". Beginning with Dick Marshall, the bombardier, we all checked in by stating our position followed by the quality of the transmission. For example if the transmission were loud and clear the crew would respond: bombardier, five by five (readability best, and signal strength best), copilot five by five, engineer five by five, radio operator five by five, and ending with the tail position. Carl would respond to each call with a "roger". If any position had a problem with reception, I was the one to correct the problem.

FIRST TAKEOFF AND LANDING IN THE BIG BIRD

We taxied to the active runway and took our position. As we held for takeoff, I was wondering if the 6,965 foot runway was enough for this great bird to accelerate to flying speed. The pilot released the brakes just before full throttle and we were on our way. We rolled more slowly at the beginning than I had expected, but then accelerated faster than I could have anticipated. The engines roared and the world swept by faster than I had ever seen it before. At 90 miles per hour, the nose rotated and at 120 miles per hour the plane flew itself off the runway. For a split second I thought about those B-29's that had exploded on takeoff. If it happened to us at this moment, and with this momentum, there wouldn't be enough pieces left for anyone to worry about.

Only the pilots and the engineer had control of the aircraft, and everyone else, except the bombardier, was literally a back seat driver. You always had to keep faith in God, and your commander, hoping that one or the other would bring you back in the same condition as when you started. I didn't like that back seat, no control deal, but it was one of the prices that I had to pay for the classification SNAFU in Santa Ana.

The check out pilot put the commander through his paces. The giant bird handled the stalls and steep turns gracefully. The engineer worked with fuel transfer systems, airflow systems, air and temperature gauges, monitored engine settings, and adjusted cowl settings. The cowls had to be adjusted at regular intervals in order to keep the R-3350's engines from over heating. There was no question that the engineer's most formidable challenge was to keep those 2200 horsepower Wright-Cyclone engines cool. With all its problems, this B-29 Superfort was still a great airplane, and with the addition of the much heralded

central fire control system, we would be ready for the Japanese.

The pilot extended the gear on the downwind leg and just before base he added 25 degree flaps. We went to full flaps as we turned onto final. Everyone was "up" for this first B-29 landing. The bombardier called out the air speed as we approached touch down. One hundred thirty; one hundred twenty; one hundred fifteen, and the tires kissed. I took in a deep breath, blew up my cheeks, and slowly let the air out in measured relief. For most of us this was our first flight in the B-29 Superfortress.

Many of our questions regarding the flying characteristics of the new B-29 were answered on that first flight, but the lack of armament on the bird still remained a large mystery. That speculation was the prime topic of conversation bantered around over coffee and doughnuts and in the barracks. Most everyone still believed that the airplanes would be armed at Boeing's plant in Wichita, but when? Combat training was intensifying, and we knew that the crews had to be checked out with central fire control armament before being deployed overseas. The addition of the appropriate armament would effect every crew position in one way or another. Training with all the equipment was essential.

THE CASE OF THE STRIPPED SHIPS

The question of armament was finally cleared up. All crews were ordered to assemble in the large lecture hall. We stood to attention as a General from Washington, D.C. was introduced by a Captain who was adjutant to the base commander.

THE GENERAL'S SPEECH:

"At ease gentlemen. The information that I am about to reveal is highly sensitive--top secret. You are hereby advised that any discussion of this information with anyone not present in this meeting will be considered a serious Court Martial offense. Is that understood by all?" There was an affirmative murmur from the crews. "The Air Corps has known from the beginning that the United States could gain a major tactical advantage over the enemy if we could design an airplane that would fly higher, faster, farther, and carry a heavier payload than any of the world's existing aircraft. We knew that objective was attainable when the first flight of the XB-29 took place on September 21, 1942.

"Everyone here has been hand picked for his excellence. You are expected to make a difference and you will. You have no doubt noticed that the B-29's here at Fairmont do not show any turrets except for the tail turret. I have been sent from Washington to explain some of these curiosities."

The crews shuffled and straightened to catch every word.

The General continued:

"The Shinto, Buddhist-worshiping Japanese, are dedicated to winning this war down to the last man, woman and child. Every tactical effort has been initiated by the United States to end this conflict as quickly as possible without having to invade the mainland. However, if we are compelled by circumstances to invade Japan, we are prepared. The Joint Chiefs of Staff have been planning this action for months. Intelligence estimates that an invasion will cost us at least one million men, and ten million Japanese lives. The daytime bombing of Japanese Industry has been extremely effective, but we have to apply more around the clock bombing pressure. You have been selected to fly the graveyard shift, and please don't take the last phrase literally." There was no laughter in response to the attempted pun.

The General had more to say:

"The Japanese have always been 90% dependent on foreign oil. Intelligence has come to the opinion that the petroleum industry in Japan is in such a critical state that the destruction of facilities and stores will react promptly upon the tactical situation. Major General Curtis LeMay, Commanding General of the XXI Bomber Command, and Lt. General Barney Giles, commanding the Army Air Forces in the Pacific Ocean Areas, have decided that you will devote your bombing efforts exclusively to oil targets. you will use the radar bombsight, synchronous bombing technique. The H2X AN/APQ-13 equipment that you are familiar with will be replaced by the more efficient Eagle system that has been developed by Professor Luis W. Alvarez of the Massachusetts Institute of Technology. This system is called the AN/APQ-7 system. It will only search 6 degrees, plus or minus 30 degrees, instead of the 360 degrees as the AN/APQ 13, but it will operated in the X-band and produce a four degree beam that will give a greatly improved picture on the indicator screen. It also has added pre-set ballistics in its computer such as the time of fall and trail values of bombs, and data concerning wind, direction of flight, ground speed, and altitude. The radar operator will sit aft of the navigator's compartment and his radar will be synchronized electronically with the Norden bombsight. The parabolic 30 inch antenna that's mounted on the lower part of the fuselage, giving your AN/APQ-13 a rotational scan, will be replaced by the AN/APQ 7 antenna. The antenna, a linear array about 16 feet long, is housed in an 18 foot airfoil having a 40 inch chord and a leading edge 8 inches thick. The airfoil will be mounted perpendicularly to the fuselage, almost giving you a biplane look. The AN/APQ 7 Eagle system gives a more accurate measurement of angle position than the AN/APQ 13 being used in other B-29s. The effective probability factor of your missions will be greatly enhanced with this Eagle Radar System." Our radar operator caught the navigator's attention and gave him a thumbs up.

The General continued:
"Now I'll reveal some of the most sensitive intelligence data of the Pacific air war:

"The B-29B models that you see at Fairmont do not carry guns except in the tail. We didn't forget to install armament on these airplanes. This is the B-29 that you will be flying in combat." There was an audible gasp heard throughout the lecture theatre. "We have stripped your B-29 of all armament with the exception of the tail turret which has two fifty caliber machine guns and a twenty millimeter cannon. The cannon has had some problems in operation and may be removed later on." (The cannon was removed from some of the early B29's and replaced with a broom stick).

The crews were being pummeled with one shocking revelation after another, and we were squirming in our seats.

The General anticipated our concerns:

"You are thinking that stripping your aircraft and ordering you to fly at night, which will take away your fighter cover, is going to compromise your safety. Actually the opposite is true. The absence of heavy armament weight will enable you to fly higher, faster, and give you a greater range capability. You will also enjoy more maneuverability in any evasive action that you have to take. The bomb load will remain the same—ten tons. Your cruising speed will be increased by twenty knots with this weight modification. You will be bombing your targets from an altitude of thirty to forty thousand feet. The Japanese night fighters are not effective at those altitudes, nor is the enemy's anti-aircraft fire. Your odds of survival will be dramatically increased. You will be the new, all-weather, high altitude, precision bombing wing, and you will make a dramatic impact on the course of the Pacific War." Our engineer, George Martinonis, was shaking his head.

The General concluded:

"You will begin your training immediately. You will fly some three thousand mile simulated bombing missions in the States, but most of these simulated missions will be conducted from the Antilles Command Caribbean bases, under a program the Second Air Force has designated as 'Gypsy Task Force'. And you'll be flying from Vernam, Jamaica; Batista, Cuba, or Borinquin Field, Puerto Rico. These bases are advanced training bases for very heavy bomb units preparing to deploy overseas. Good luck and Godspeed."

NO GUNS, NO WAY

The crews filed out of the meeting sober and concerned. George Martinonis, from

APG-15 Tail Turret

New Jersey, exploded, "No way can we keep cruise control with the altitudes given, and if we fly lower we get belted with anti-aircraft fire. If the Japs catch on that we don't have any guns, we're ducks in a barrel. Stripped ships will be our epitaph." I added my sentiments, "Going to war without guns—that's incredible. Welcome to the Kamikaze corps!"

On 17 December, a few days after our top secret meeting, official orders came down from the 315th Wing to remove any remaining armament from the B-29s except the AN/APG-15 tail turret. The Plexi-glas blisters protruding from the sides of the B29B's were to be replaced with smooth enclosures. The AN/APQ-13 radar system was to be replaced by the AN/APQ-7 Eagle Radar system, and the 17th Bomb Training Wing crews were reduced from 11 to 10 men by replacing the 3 original gunners with 2 visual scanner positions.

Modifications to the 315th Wing B-29s came as a result of Alamogordo, New Mexico studies testing the vulnerability of B-29s to fighter attacks. Lt. Colonel Paul Tibbets, while assigned to Grand Island AAF, had been ordered to test the B-29 in simulated combat with fighters at Alamogordo AAF. The fully armed B-29 proved difficult to control at 30,000 feet. Tibbets reported that a steep bank or sudden movement of the controls could cause the plane to stall. Then one day, his test B-29 was down for repairs at Grand Island and he borrowed another B-29 equipped only with tail guns and took off for Alamogordo. The lighter weight B-29 had remarkably improved climb characteristics and, at 30,000 feet, Colonel Tibbets found that he could turn in a shorter radius than an attacking P-47. Further tests showed that the lightweight

B-29 could also fly well above 30,000 feet and at speeds greater than some fighters were capable.

CATALINA

Our first simulated combat mission took us to Catalina Island, California and back to Fairmont. I had phoned my mother in Hollywood and told her that I would try to get the commander to fly over the Griffith Park Observatory area since her apartment was just a few blocks south of that location. My commander, Earl Bentley, Jr. pulled it off, my mother saw us, and it was a thrill that she and I often re-lived.

THE OLD KING COLE ROOM RE-VISITED

Fairmont liberty was about the same as liberty at Creighton inasmuch as we retreated to the Fontenelle Hotel and the King Cole Room for rest and recuperation. It was still the favorite place for all military fliers in the area. The logistics from Fairmont (less than 140 miles) were a little more complicated, but that didn't slow us down. We either took a bus or hitchhiked, whichever way we thought would be the fastest transport to the Fontenelle. Sometimes, however, survival dictated the mode of travel. The Nebraska winters were painfully cold and if sputum froze before it hit the ground, we took the bus.

Nothing had changed in the King Cole except there were no more guys with propellers on their sleeves. The Creighton Cadets were history. Vaughn Monroe and Bing Crosby and the Andrew sisters were still getting the big plays in the juke box along with "Don't Fence Me In," and "There, I've Said It Again." Officers and enlisted men all fraternized together here, and we were now thinking team instead of rank. We were growing up a little.

I met a voluptuous girl by the name of Alberta on one of my three day liberties, and we dated as often as I could get passes. You should have seen Alberta. She looked like she had just stepped out of one of those enticing B-17 nose art paintings. Alberta stirred the coals of passion in all of my comrades but, in reality, she was rigidly mid-west traditional, and there was no chance for intimacy before the ring. My relationship with Alberta was frustratingly platonic, but still she had all the parts to hold my undivided interest.

THE B-17

A few B-17's were flown into Fairmont as gap fillers until new B-29Bs could be acquired from the Bell-Marietta aircraft factory in Georgia. On February 7, 1945, I was ordered to fly as the radio operator on a B-17 with operations commander Major William Schmock. The B-17 was clearly a celebrity airplane posting a brilliant war record; it was an awesome experience for me to fly in it. The 17 didn't have the heating problems, the engine fires, and the runaway props that plagued the 29 and, for the first time, I flew without any anxiety at all. What a great feeling.

The radio operators' swivel chair in the B-17 was a large comfortable bucket seat. What class, I thought. However, the radio equipment was the old standard kind in which you had to change coils for different frequency ranges. We flew to Wichita, Kansas, and Major Schmock, bless his heart, searched with magnifying glass scrutiny until he found a legitimate mechanical reason to ground the B-17 so that our skeleton crew could R. O. N. (rest over night). Wichita was known as one of the best liberty cities in the United States and Major Schmock knew that we all wanted to spend some time there. We chose a popular hotel for our temporary quarters. The crew had dinner, met some girls in the bar and partied most of the night. Major Schmock proved to me that not all officers were hard nosed. The Major was a tall, affable, handsome guy, and the salt of the earth. In addition, he was a smart and capable officer. The Major was one of us, and we loved him for it. The B-17 was more airworthy next day than we were, but we "hung tough" and crewed the machine back to Fairmont.

SIMULATED 3000 MILERS FROM BORINQUEN FIELD, PUERTO RICO, AND TEDDY BEARS

The Second Air Force inaugurated the Caribbean mission simulation program, Gypsy Task Force, in December, 1944. In February we began those simulated mission training flights from Borinquen Field, Puerto Rico, which was located on the northeast part of the Island. Having shivered through most of the Nebraska winter, the crews viewed Borinquen as a tropical paradise. The weather was beautiful, and so were the girls. There were first class swimming pools for the sun ray "baggers" like myself, and beautiful golf courses for the "Spaulding spankers." Back at quarters we were spoiled by civilians that made up our net covered bunks and cleaned our barracks for just a few coins. It was the first time I had my

Army cot made up for me since civilian life, and I viewed it as a wonderful luxury.

There was a first class shopping complex on the base which, besides good shopping, presented great looking sales girls. Along with a variety of music and public service announcements, the public address system featured the Andrew sisters new recording, "Drinking Rum and Coca Cola"; that song added even more magic to our island adventure. I met Alicia (one of the most beautiful girls I had ever seen) on this first trip. Alicia sold Teddy bears and other stuffed "cuddlies" for one of the department stores. I made excuses to check out the Teddy bears almost every day and, each time I showed, Alicia made a big fuss over me. She would clap her hands and say, "Jeeeeeemie, I'm so glad to see you." Alicia was scintillatingly gorgeous and I vibrated every time she laid those beautiful brown "Bambi" orbs on me. I yearned to date this young lady in the worst way, but there was just one small problem. We had been told in an orientation lecture that if we dated a native Puerto Rican we had better be prepared to marry her. Otherwise, the family would be looking to do great harm to our young G. I. bodies. We decided in favor of longevity and opted to concentrate on other pleasures.

THE RAT OF AQUADILLA

We chose the closest-to-base town, Aguadilla, for our hunger and thirst needs, and I'll never forget our first visit to the little town's most popular restaurant/night club. Two of my buddies and I were working on our first drink when a most unusual scene took place on the long back bar. Two rats half the size of Polo Ponies were threading their way along the bar between bottles of booze. I caught the bar tenders' eye and pointed to the monsters with dramatic concern. He merely smiled and said, "Don't worry, Señor, they won't hurt you." He didn't elaborate beyond that, which was just as amazing to me as the phenomenon we were watching. The pair of skinny tails finally disappeared at the far end of the bar and we carried our skinny tails up the stairs to the restaurant part, trying to forget what we had seen while we chowed down.

WE BEGIN THE OVER-WATER 3000 MILE SIMULATED MISSIONS

On the flip side of fun and merriment, there was the serious business of flying three thousand mile over-water missions at night in relatively untested B-29's. Once the B-29 had climbed to altitude and was trimmed for cruise configuration, it was quite reliable. Until you reached cruise, however, it was anybody's guess whether or not the engines would hold up. By now we knew that the cylinder baffles on the massive R-3350 engine were simply inadequate to cool the engines properly. The design couldn't dissipate enough heat under power conditions to keep the engine within normal operating limits. In addition, Boeing's design of the landing-gear door and bomb door systems led to engine over-heating. The landing-gear doors were operated by an electric jackscrew and didn't come up until the gear was up. The bomb-bay doors were also operated by jackscrews. The systems took too long to complete their cycles. On takeoff the engines would overheat just waiting for the gear doors to get closed. The twin turbo-superchargers were made out of magnesium and once they caught fire in the air, they were nearly impossible to extinguish. The maximum cylinder head temperature limitations in the R-3350 was 260 degrees centigrade for five minutes, and it was not unusual for us to exceed those limitations on our takeoff. Prop runaways were not infrequent and then you hoped that you were able to feather the engine. Leaky carburetors caused frequent engine fires until it was discovered that the mounting bolts were bottoming out before they were snug enough to seal the carburetor. "Too hot" was the bottom line. Over heating accounted for most of the B-29's mechanical problems.

THE NEW B-29 FROM GENERAL LEMAY'S POINT OF VIEW

General LeMay, a pioneer of strategic bombing who commanded the Third Bombardment Division against Germany, and who took over the B-29 command in China and the Marianas, made this observation early on:

"Fuel economy is difficult to regulate or even measure because present fuel quantity gauges are practically useless." After flying a long mission, pilots could only guess whether they were running short of gas. The indicators were inaccurate. LeMay observed, "The B-29 feathering mechanism was dismally unreliable. (Propellers on dead or dying engines had to be 'feathered' or turned with the thin sides of their blades facing the air flow to reduce drag on the plane.) Inability to feather almost always results in the loss of the aircraft. The B-29 airplane is capable of a considerably higher performance than the R-3350 engine now installed will permit, as the maximum gross operating weight is limited by the power available for takeoff and climb. Until more power is available, we cannot

fully capitalize on the capabilities of the airplane. Most of our difficulties center around the engine."

The crews didn't talk much about operational problems but, believe me when I say that we who crewed B-29's paid a heavy price in anxiety. Our over-water training flights from Puerto Rico and our combat missions over Japan, were flown at night and averaged between 13 and 17 hours. We were all well acquainted with the R-3350 engine limitations and the dangers that were lurking in the waters beneath us in the event of a night bail-out. In the Carribean Area chances were that barracudas would dine on you, and in the Pacific it would be the sharks. Flying B-29s was a little like waiting for the other shoe to drop.

The number of Gypsy Task Force training accidents that occurred the month before we arrived at Borinquen Field did not lessen our concerns. On 31 December a B-29 crashed during a training flight at Borinquen Field. Captain Frank H. Beales, pilot, and First Lieutenant Barclay H. Beeby, instructor pilot, had tried to immediately return to the airfield to land following the failure of their number one engine on takeoff. The aircraft rolled over and crashed just 500 yards from the end of the runway. Five of the six men on board were killed.

In the first incident of 1945, a B-29 ditched off the coast of Haiti due to an uncontrollable fire in the number two engine. The plane broke in half and only five men were rescued. The other five were never found. Later, on 26 January, a crew crashed near Fort Riley, Kansas while en route from the Caribbean. Another B-29 crashed near Lexington, Missouri while flying to home base.

The final accident of the month occurred on 27 January. Crew 203 from the 402nd Squadron took off from Borinquen on a practice bombing mission when their number one and two engines and electrical system malfunctioned. The crew had to shut down the number two engine and operate number one with drastically reduced power. After checking the electrical problem, the crew found that they could not extend the landing gear or wing flaps. The young aircraft commander, Captain Arthur W. Dippel, and his crew headed for Borinquen Field, losing altitude all of the way. Once over land and at an altitude of four thousand feet, Capt. Dippel rang the alarm bell for his crew to bail out. Four men in the front of the plane bailed out, but those in the rear did not hear the bell. By the time Dippel discovered this, he knew the aircraft was too low for the remaining crew to bail out. An instructor was in the pilot's seat and he began flying the airplane to the runway at Borinquen. On the final approach, Captain Dippel took over the controls and made a perfect no-gear, no-flaps landing. The aircraft skidded along the runway on its belly and caught on fire. In this rare instance everyone escaped without serious injury.

THE SPARK GAP THAT KILLED

My crew and I were at the Borinquen airfield pre-flighting our airplane in preparation for a simulated bombing mission that would take us from Borinquen to Venezuela and then back to base. The antenna insulation from my Collins' transmitter consisted of segmented lengths of ceramic material. I noticed that as the antenna took sharp bends to conform with the fuselage, it caused gaps in the ceramic insulation which exposed the antenna. At some points the exposed antenna appeared to be close enough to the skin of the airplane to cause radio frequency shorting. We always send a message back to base on takeoff and a thought hit me: a radio frequency spark shorting out to the skin of the airplane could certainly ignite any gasoline fumes that were in the bomb bays and cause an explosion. There had been reports of explosions and fires immediately after takeoff and this could be one of the reasons. I asked the Ground Crew Chief to check the antenna when I keyed the transmitter, and, sure enough, he found an R.F. spark. That confirmed my theory on the subject. The Ground Chief told me that he would write up a technical order on the problem, and I assured him that I would do the same just as soon as we returned from our over-water training flight.

We took off for our mission at approximately 1640 and you can believe that I checked the bomb bay for fumes before I sent my takeoff message back to base. About seven hours into the flight my navigator, Jim McClelland, turned to me with an "I don't know where I am" look and asked me if I had any procedure that would help double check his figures. I smiled at the opportunity and gave him a thumbs up. The radio operators were given a number of emergency procedures that were designated as "Q" signals, and the Q signal for location fix was called a "QDM". I sent a Morse code message to the appropriate station on the East coast requesting a QDM procedure and then transmitted three twenty second dashes holding my key down each time. Within seconds they contacted two other stations and gave me a fix. I passed it over to McClelland. He studied his figures for a minute, apparently discovered a mistake he had made, and then gave me the biggest most relieved grin you've ever seen. "You just pinpointed our position and saved my navigational neck. You are right on the money," McClelland said gratefully. "You know what you're doing, Smitty, that's for sure." I shrugged that it was nothing, but I could feel myself blushing with pride. We made it back next morning after a thirteen plus hour flight, and I wrote up the tech order on the radio antenna.

A month later all the ceramic type of insulation had been changed to a running plastic insulation and I felt that I had a part in making the B-29 a safer operating airplane. My self worth had taken a bad beating in Santa Ana, but graduating with high marks at Sioux Falls had given me an emotional boost. Now, having established a successful over-water navigational fix while on the job, and discovering a potentially serious antenna problem, my self-confidence had begun its return trip.

The crew completed training at Borinquen and flew back to Fairmont for more ground classes. Instruction was given in the new navigational Loran radar system. The navigator used the Loran to determine his position; the radar and radio operator were back-up operators.

PINNING THE TONGUE TO THE CHEEK

The radio man was also chosen to be the medic on board. We had to attend classes where we practiced drawing blood from one another's arm. The instruction was conducted by the group's medical doctor. I can still hear him caution, "Don't look for the biggest vein you can see, look for the best anchored vein". I learned that it was much easier to give blood than to take someone else's. There were a lot of pale faces in that class and, for some reason, it seemed that it was always the big tough types that had problems holding up. A couple of these guys asked to be excused when the doctor instructed us on how to use a safety pin for pinning a victim's tongue to his cheek. This procedure was to be used in the event a wounded crew member was unconscious and had begun to swallow his tongue.

B-29'S FALL

In the meantime, more B-29's were falling. Two more fatal aircraft accidents occurred in March within the Gypsy Task Force. One B-29B crashed into the golf course near the Borinquen Field runway. The aircraft had been flying at 10,000 feet when number one and three propellers malfunctioned. By the time the pilot, Second Lieutenant Harold C. Anderson, and his crew returned to Borinquen, the number three engine had been feathered and the number one engine was on fire. The aircraft stalled while trying to land and crashed short of the runway. Six of the nine crew members were killed. Then on 12 March, a B-29 piloted by First Lieutenant V. Tulla crashed while trying to land at Alexandra AAF, Louisiana. The ten-man crew was killed.

THE NEW AIRCRAFT COMMANDER CANDIDATE

The B-29, 501st Bomb Group was stationed at Harvard AAF, Nebraska, and the 502nd at Grand Island, Nebraska. These crews were getting ready for deployment overseas. Occasionally, one of the groups would lose a crew member for one reason or another, and that position would be filled with personnel from crews of lesser priority. We of the 17th Bomb Training Wing supplied a good share of those replacements and, just as we were getting acquainted with our crew commander, First Lieutenant Earl Bentley Jr., he was ordered to replace a priority crew pilot at a staging base. Losing our aircraft commander was a morale shaker for sure, and we felt a little orphaned.

A First Lieutenant was assigned to replace Bentley, pending the Lt. logging additional B-29 hours. The Lieutenant was an experienced B-17 pilot, but he lacked the necessary B-29 hours required for an aircraft commander. By April we were planning another simulated mission training tour at Borinquen Field. A commander, Lt. Shea, was ordered to fly us to Puerto Rico while our replacement candidate for aircraft commander was scheduled to rejoin us after we arrived there. He would be training alongside an instructor pilot until he logged enough hours to qualify for aircraft commander. The candidate was a great guy, an unusually caring fellow. He took time to write letters to our families telling them not to worry about us. As aircraft commander he promised to do everything in his power to take care of his crew. Needless to say, our families were very impressed and moved by the Lieutenant's unprecedented gesture. We, the crew, appreciated his extraordinary considerations, but we viewed him as a bit too protective.

THE BERMUDA TRIANGLE NIGHTMARE

The flight back to Puerto Rico with aircraft commander Lt. Shea, began the afternoon of April 11, 1945, and it would be one that none of us aboard could ever forget. It was my job to clear our flight for weather through the Galveston, Texas station "APQ 4." I received clearance and advised that there were no weather systems between our present position and Borinquen Field.

As soon as we had cleared the mainland, my orders were to contact Batista, Cuba by Morse code. It was nighttime and, in light of the clear weather advisory, transmission and reception should have been excellent. Instead there was so much weather static and interference that I couldn't make contact. I called Lt. Shea, who had, early on, established himself as a blustery, tough talking Irishman. I advised Shea that we were flying into a weather front. Shea waved me off, "Hell, there's no weather out here. You just cleared us through Galveston. I heard the contact. It's clear all the... " Shea didn't have a chance to finish his sentence. It was like we had hit a wall, and then a horrendous thermal lifted us skyward at a terrific speed. Shea slammed the yoke down but it had absolutely no effect on the climb. Suddenly, the airplane shuddered, stalled out, and headed down at an alarming rate of descent. I knew that this was it. We were going to plunge into the ocean. We bottomed out with a tremendous "G" force that drove us back hard into our positions, and then the process repeated itself. Shea alternately jammed the yoke forward and then back into his lap trying to counter the violent up and down lurching track of the airplane. It was futile; the controls had absolutely no effect on the airplane. We were terrified captives of some awesome force that was trying to kill us.

We were thrust upward again at an

incredible rate of climb; again the airplane shuddered and we stalled into a death defying plunge toward the ocean. Hail and rain began pounding on the Plexiglas nose and aluminum parts. It sounded like we had been thrown under the roaring wheels of a fast moving freight train. Somehow, through all the noise, I heard the pilot yell, "There's no airspeed indication; the compass is spinning like a top!" Shea yelled back that the pitot tubes must be froze up; then he screamed for me and the engineer to open the nose wheel hatch and prepare for bail out. That was a hysterical order; we would have been eaten up by the elements before we even hit the water. It was just that we were desperate to get out of whatever was destroying us. The guy in the tail screamed that the wings were coming off. The engineer and I tried to lift the nose wheel hatch but we were repeatedly knocked down by the thermals. We scrambled back to our positions and figured that we would be better off to die with our seat belts on.

Then, as suddenly as the violence had begun, it stopped and we were flying straight and level in total calm. Thinking that we must be in the eye of the storm, we braced for more violence but, for some strange reason, it never came. We were to later discover that this area was considered to be within the parameters of the infamous Bermuda Triangle, and perhaps that had something to do with it. We'll never know the truth of what took us over and shook us beyond the limits of our imagination.

There was no discussion of the horrifying event that had just taken place. Every crew member was in shock. The first words were finally uttered by Shea as he tried to line up for final approach into Borinquen, "C'mon you big son-of-a-bitch,

let's stay on the center line." He kept his eyes straight ahead, but leaned his head toward the pilot, "It won't track right. Something's wrong." Shea was bringing the bird in as hot as he dared so he could get maximum effect from the control surfaces. He fought the airplane all the way down. We touched and bounced, and then hit back down hard. It sounded as if the gear were being driven up through the fuselage. The bird finally, if not begrudginly, settled and rolled out.

I'll never forget the scene that followed. The crew disembarked and gathered around Lt. Shea at the nose wheel. He waited as we slowly formed a group in front of him. No one but Shea had spoken at this point. We were all white-faced and shaken from the experience. Big, tough, profane Lieutenant Shea was deadly serious and kitten calm now. His demeanor was almost spiritual. He spoke in tones barely above a whisper: "I want you all to know something. I don't know who brought us through this thing, but I know I didn't." That's all he said. He gathered up his gear and headed toward operations. Sometimes, when the going gets tough, I think back to that event and count my blessings. I've considered every sunrise since a bonus.

Next day word came back from maintenance that rivets had popped out all over our B-29, both wings had been sprung, and the tail section had been ripped open by those unknown forces we had encountered. It was a miracle that we had landed with any tail section at all. No wonder Shea had more than a little trouble keeping the airplane centered on final approach. To this day I can still hear his words, "I don't know who brought us through this thing, but I know I didn't."

PRESIDENT ROOSEVELT DIES

Two days later, April 12, 1945 this shocking news was blared from the base public address system: "President Franklin Delano Roosevelt has died from a massive cerebral hemorrhage." The crews were stunned and openly worried that Vice President Truman might not possess the strength of leadership to guide the country to victory. A sad day.

THE LIEUTENANT COULDN'T LAND

The crew met at operations at 1600 hours, and we were assigned a new aircraft. The damage to our aircraft was going to take days or weeks to repair. Our new aircraft commander candidate and his instructor pilot were present. We were briefed to fly the local area and the Lieutenant would be asked to execute basic B-29 training maneuvers. In addition to logging the required time in the left seat, the candidate was to be proficiency rated. He would be required to perform a number of day and night takeoffs and landings.

It was pretty much all straight-ahead stuff but the Lieutenant was having a terrible time handling the airplane. He seemed to be consistently behind on the controls. Takeoffs were fine but every landing was just short of a crash. The night landings were the worst. The Lieutenant was soaked with perspiration and trying with everything he had, but he couldn't find the touch. He'd invariably stall the bird high and hit the runway with enough force to test the integrity of the aircraft. We all worried about the airplane breaking in two. Finally, the instructor called it a night and we taxied back to the operations area. We were heading toward operations for the debrief when the Lieutenant stopped

suddenly and broke down. He couldn't talk. He just sobbed. It was awful to see this, just awful. My heart ached for the fellow. I thought about the wash-out in Santa Ana and I knew that our aircraft commander candidate had been overcome with some of those same feelings this night. It was a sad fact, but the Lieutenant was just not emotionally equipped to command a B-29 combat crew.

We flew a simulated mission the next day with a different commander, and two days later the crew was headed back to Fairmont. Soon after our return we were told that our A/C candidate had been relieved of his flying duties.

Without an aircraft commander, crew 1712 was in big trouble. The problem with our replacement candidate occurred just when we crew members were becoming highly proficient at our individual positions and coming together as a team. Having lost Bentley and the new A/C candidate, the commanding officer had no choice but to order the rest of us to stand by as replacements for priority crews. The broken crew's morale dipped to an all time low, and we converted our depression to thoughts of liberty passes. I reasoned with the others that the passes were kind of like consolation prizes for the series of bad breaks we had suffered.

THE ENGAGEMENT RING OR THE MONKEY

We were given one more four-day pass and every one knew that it would probably be our last one at Fairmont. The crews were ready for deployment and I figured that I would be going somewhere as a replacement. I called my friend, Alberta, and we met in the Fontenelle's King Cole

Room. I poured out my tale of woe over some bubbly and told her that this would be my last trip until after the war. There were a number of B-29 crews present and we began building a four-day bon voyage party.

A Lieutenant from my same group suggested that we all adjourn to a suite that he was sharing with a couple other buddies. About thirty of us, including Alberta and some other local girl friend types poured into the two large rooms which had been set up with champagne, snacks and sandwiches. We had all met at one time or another in the King Cole, so there were no strangers here.

Just as the party began to roll, the Lieutenant gave me a funny little grin, then called the group to quiet. Oh, oh, what does the Lieutenant have in mind, I wondered? He singled out Alberta and me and without further adieu he asked, "Alberta do you love Jim?" She laughed good naturedly as did the rest of the us, and said, "Yes, of course!" The Lt. then asked me if I loved Alberta? Under normal circumstances the unexpected question would have been quite embarrassing, but this was party fun and no one was taking things all that seriously. Notwithstanding the fun however, if I answered with anything but a yes, I'd be in serious trouble with my playmate Alberta, so I gave a large Air Corps style, "Affirmative!"

Our host continued with his ceremonial rhetoric, "Alberta if you love Jim and Jim if you love Alberta, why aren't you engaged?" "Well for one thing," I grinned, "This Air Corps corporal doesn't have enough green left to buy a cigar band, much less an engagement ring." That line played well with the Lieutenant who then gleefully revealed his "benevolent" motive for this little true confession drama. "Hey boys," he said, "these poor kids don't have enough money to buy an engagement ring. There's a jewelry store in the next block, and we're going to take up a collection. I'll pass my hat around and let's fill it up with some ring money." Alberta and I laughingly objected to the idea, but by now party madness was taking over, and around went the hat. By the time it returned to our perpetrator, it had been hit with about seventy dollars (that would have bought a nice engagement band in 1945).

"Okay," said the fun loving Lieutenant, "I'm going to take these two lovers to the jewelry store". The three of us laughingly swept out of the room, and headed for the jewelry store. In the frivolity of the moment, we had forgotten that it was Sunday afternoon; the jewelry store was closed. There was a pet store open next door and we ventured in to ask if they had the jewelers' home number. As the sales person looked for the number, our Lieutenant friend became especially fascinated with a monkey that was on sale. It was about the size of one of those monkeys you see standing on an accordion player's shoulder and holding a tin cup. The sales person found the jeweler's number and handed it to the Lieutenant. Our mentor thanked the fellow and then asked him the price of the monkey. "Sixty bucks", replied the clerk. The Lieutenant liked the price and advised the fellow, "We're going back to the Fontenelle and try to get in touch with the jeweler; if he won't come down and open up, I'll be back here to buy this primate." The unbelieving clerk laughed at the fun. Alberta and I grinned at one another. "From a ring to a monkey," I pondered. "Well, what the heck, at this point we're still top billing."

We sashayed back to Fontenelle, and to my extreme relief, the jeweler could not be reached. The Lieutenant hung up the phone and shrugged, "Oh, what the hell, that's the way it goes." He headed for the door explaining, "I'll be back shortly." Fifteen minutes later a slightly inebriated Lieutenant with his leash-tethered, perky little monkey friend, returned for admittance to party headquarters. The little fellow stared wide eyed at the crazy two-leggers around him, and then scampered up the drapes to get a wipe view of the group from a loge seat on the valance. We coaxed him down after a while and decided to introduce him to the King Cole Room. Everyone thought the monkey was cute stuff until he upset some drinks, and emptied himself on a bar stool. As the party wore down, the Lieutenant realized that he was in over his head with the monkey gag; he wisely decided to get rid of the animal by making a gift of it to our favorite waitress. She asked for an accordion and a tip cup, too, but that one didn't come off. I had a private talk with Alberta and promised her that I'd come back to see her. We said our good-byes, and I headed back to Fairmont.

THE LIEUTENANT PARKING ATTENDANT MAKES AN OFFER

A few days later a First Lieutenant aircraft commander whom I knew, stopped me on base. (This fellow had a reputation for being pompous and overly impressed with his rank.) As expected, he addressed me with stilted formality and his best Orson Wells' voice, "Corporal Smith, our radio operator has some problems and I'm looking around for someone to fill his position. I've been told that you are one of the best R.O.M.'s (radio operator mechanic) in the Wing and I know that

you are on a replacement status. Would you like to fly with us, permanently?" I squared with a touch of military for the Lieutenant's benefit, "Well, thank you, sir, I..." The Lieutenant jumped my line, "I hear that your old crew was pretty informal." He straightened a little and tried to flatten his over weight gut. "I'm proud to say that I demand strict military protocol at all times." That's all I had to hear but his statement fired me to respond, "Our crew all respected one another Lieutenant, however no worshipping was allowed—except on Sunday." The Lieutenant didn't appreciate my smart reply. "I don't think that attitude would find a place on my crew." I couldn't restrain my enthusiasm, "No, sir, it wouldn't!" I saluted and the Lieutenant gave me a half hearted return along with a slight growl. I took off while I was still ahead. He was just another "Bottle Cap" type.

GERMANY SURRENDERS, AND I'M ORDERED TO KEARNEY, NEBRASKA AS A REPLACEMENT ON LIEUTENANT SCHAHRER'S CREW

May 7th, 1945. It was announced that Germany had surrendered and the camp went crazy with jubilation. We all began chanting: "One down and one to go", one down and one to go." I could visualize the war ending soon, but I wanted my chance to help beat up on the Japs before they surrendered. On May 18th it looked as if I might get my wish. I was ordered to the overseas staging area at Kearney, Nebraska to replace radio operator, Donald Groen, crew #346-3, 315th Bomb Wing, 501 Bomb Group.

I called Alberta and told her that I was being transferred to another group and that I would keep in touch. I wanted to lighten our subject matter at one point and I asked about the monkey that the Lieutenant had given to the waitress. Alberta laughingly told me that the monkey had been given a return trip back to the pet store, but not before the frisky little guy had dismantled the waitress's apartment.

I met my new airplane commander, First Lieutenant Carl Schahrer in Kearney's Commanding Officer's quarters. The Commanding Officer, a Major, was sitting behind a desk and a First Lieutenant was sitting in a chair to the major's right. I approached the desk of the Major, "Sir, I'm Corporal Smith, Jimmie B. 396-99-665, from Fairmont Army Air Field reporting as ordered." The Major placed me at ease and I handed him my transmittal papers. The Major studied me for a moment; "Corporal Smith," he nodded toward First Lieutenant Carl Schahrer, "this is your new aircraft commander, Lt. Schahrer."

I was expecting a big, good looking, intimidating type of fellow who would fit the aircraft commander stereotype. Schahrer blew that profile all to pieces. He qualified for the good looking part, but he was small in stature, soft spoken and gentle. Still he emanated a confidence that you could feel. I liked him. Carl stood up and we shook hands. He got right into the subject matter, "We have an excellent radio operator, Donald Groen, but unfortunately, he was taken to the hospital three days ago for an emergency appendectomy. My crew is scheduled for final overseas staging at Mather Field, Sacramento in two days. We have to replace him." Before I could respond Carl suggested, "All of the fellows, except Groen, are over at the airplane right now checking out equipment. Let's go over

there and I'll introduce you around." "Yes, Sir, that would be fine. I'm anxious to meet your crew and see your airplane." I looked back at the Major and he handed me my billeting papers, "One of the enlisted crew will show you to your quarters." I squared up, "Thank you, Sir", and the Major went back to his paper work.

Carl put on his cap and opened the door for us to exit. Usually the enlisted man stayed one pace to the rear on the officer's left so that the officer had room to salute oncoming personnel. I hesitated for a moment as Carl exited the commanding officer's quarters, but he motioned for me to walk with him. I felt a warmth that worked up to a grin, and Carl grinned back; I knew this was my man. As we walked, Carl told me a bit about his training at Alamorgordo, New Mexico. He had begun his Army career as a non-commissioned officer. Now I knew why I liked him so much. He knew the system and he had perspective. "I've looked over your papers, Smith, and they show me that you have a good background and that you are well qualified." I wanted to fill Carl in a little bit more: "I went through Air Cadet College Training Detachment in Omaha, and came out with a high grade average. My Squadron arrived at classification at the wrong time and I was eliminated when the program closed. I picked radio because they told me I would go to communication cadets if I made the top ten percent and come out with a commission. Well, I made the top ten, but for some reason I'm still one of these..." I pointed to my corporal stripes. Carl smiled with an understanding that I hadn't seen for a while, "It's called operation SNAFU; standard operating procedure, Smitty. Too bad, but we all go through it in the Army--one time or another."

THE TALE OF "THE BOOMERANG"

Carl and I approached the bird and it was a brand new beauty. Carl told me that the navigator, Tony Cosola, had been given an authentic Australian boomerang which he carried with him on every flight. "A friend of Tony's gave it to him and Tony likes to think of it as a good luck charm. The crew agreed that "The Boomerang" would be a good name for our airplane and so that's what we call it." I smiled, "Always comes back to the place where it was launched". Carl smiled, "That's the idea." "The Boomerang", I mused, Hey, that's a great name."

TONY'S OWN TAPED, TRANSCRIBED WORDS (1983):

"Jimmie, you remember the story of how we named the aircraft "The Boomerang"? Somehow or other I got home in California for a short time just before we went overseas. The father of one of my buddies was an old Australian--he was working for the Oakland Tribune news paper over here in Oakland, California. He was a typesetter, Linotype operator or something in those days. He said, "What are you going to call your airplane?" I said, "We haven't settled for a name or insignia on it." He said, "Well I'll tell ya, if you'll call it "The Boomerang", I've got an original old Australian boomerang that was given to me in the early part of World War I by an aborigine, and an aborigine chief of Australia." That sucker was old when he gave it to me. Carl and you guys agreed that would be a good thing to do if I picked up the boomerang. Got a little newspaper publicity out here; there was an article in the Oakland Tribune-I've got the article around here somewhere. Well, we named

the plane "The Boomerang" and we lettered it up as we flew each mission: We have Northwest Field, Guam. I've got it here in front of me right now while I talk to you. The crew of "The Boomerang" and all the names of the people are on there: Technical Sergeant Floyd Jennings, and all of our missions ending with the surrender ceremonies in Tokyo Bay on September 2, 1945 and the P.O.W. supply drop on Tokyo August 30th, 1945. In May 1947 I gave the boomerang back to Mr. Fraser, John Fraser was the guy's name-the father of my buddy. See, the theory was that if the boomerang is handled properly it will always come back, and that's the symbolism of the whole shot. So I told him that the boomerang came back, and I gave it to him. Well, we had our picture taken and a little something in the paper about that. He kept it and several years later he died, and his family indicated that when he died he wanted the boomerang to come back to me. So I've got it. I'm not sure what to do with this thing when I die, as I must some day. You know, I've been hearing about this thing where a bunch of buddies have a pledge and there's a certain thing of some value; when the second to the last one dies it winds up in the hands of the last one to live. I thought maybe I'd set it up that way and have the addresses of all you guys; if I die and Carl is still alive we'll pass the boomerang over to him, and when Carl goes it'll move to Johnny Waltershausen, Dick Marshall or Dick Ginster or whomever till it finally ends up with the last surviving member of "The Boomerang". Maybe we should write something up about it anyway, and maybe the Smithsonian would take it for the National Aviation and Space museum there in Washington. God knows they've got everything else. Maybe a picture of our airplane which we all have, "The Boomerang", a couple of newspaper

"The Boomerang"

The front office of "The Boomerang"

View from the pilot's seat, "The Boomerang"

Looking through "The Boomerang's" nose

articles concerning it. Might as well pass it around from hand to hand until it's handed off somewhere and it won't actually die. We weren't great heros and I don't know whether we did such great things, but we did the best we could. We didn't do too badly. I know that my kids would love to have it but I feel that it kind of belongs to all of us. I'd like to see it passed along in some kind of a format."

"THE BOOMERANG" CREW

We arrived at the airplane and the crew gathered around us. I felt like a visiting V.I.P. Carl gave me a nice introduction, "This is Jim Smith, guys, he is our new radio replacement and he's a highly qualified man. We're lucky to have him." As Carl introduced me, the fellows came over and we shook hands. My initial impressions of the fellows was one that never changed. What you saw was what you got. The crew:

Carl Schahrer the 26 year old aircraft commander, from Oildale, California. My once-over impression of Carl: a neat guy-a diminutive giant.

John Waltershausen, the pilot, 23 years old, a movie star look, an impish face and a ready smile. John was from Colorado. I thought, women have to love this guy-and they did.

Dick Marshall, the bombardier, was 27 years old and mature for his years. He exuded confidence along with an air of aristocracy, but he was personable and friendly. I figured that Dick must be financially well-heeled. He was a neat and fastidious, all-together kind of a guy. Dick had a furniture business and lived in Tustin, California.

The engineer was Hank Gorder. Hank was from the small town of Grafton, North Dakota. He was a tall, raw-boned Swede with an easy-going friendly manner, and showed a serious, quiet, confidence. My thought: Here's a case where still waters run deep. A ton of character in this man.

The Radar Operator, Rich Ginster, was from Georgia. Twenty-three years old, quiet and, as I guessed, extremely efficient. An unobtrusively nice guy.

Tony Cosola, Navigator, was from San Francisco, a good looking Italian-American with a great outgoing personality. Tony had a flair about him; I figured him to be a highly sensitive, emotional type, but a top man at any job.

Hank Lefler was left scanner, a 21-year-old from Colorado. Hank was a stocky, tough-looking guy with a mischievous grin. You had a feeling that he could deal with any emergency.

Henry Carlson, the right scanner, was another 21-year-old, and he hailed from New Jersey. Henry was a good looking, happy, good-natured type. It was my impression that Carlson was an honest caring type and that he would be a strong asset to the crew.

Sid Siegel, tail gunner, was also 21 years old, and came from Connecticut. He was upbeat, wore a permanent smile, and I had the feeling that Sid might have a tendency to exaggerate just a bit. One thing for sure, there wouldn't be any dull moments around this imaginative guy.

Carl invited me up the nose wheel ladder to check out my radio gear. Everything seemed to be in fine order and,

Carl Schahrer, AC, "The Boomerang"

Jim B. Smith

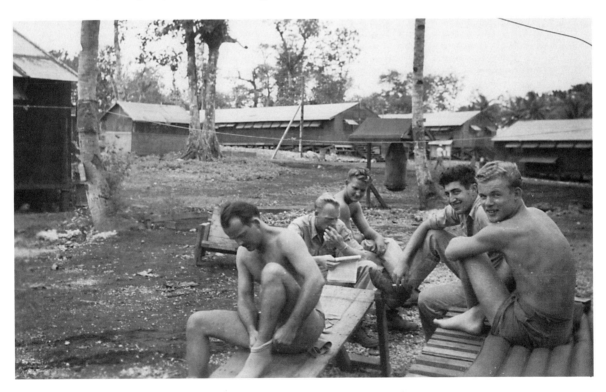

"The Boomerang" crew between missions

Sid Siegel

Hank Leffler

Henry Carlson

Hank Gorder

68

surprisingly enough, I felt right at home. Carl sat in the navigator's seat, studied me for a minute, and then asked me if I had any questions? I looked at Carl squarely, "Is there relaxed protocol on your crew or do I have to address the officers by their rank and last name? That's important to me as a team member. I respect rank but..." Carl didn't let me finish. Carl grinned. "I'm Carl and you're Smitty--except when there's an inspection." We looked at one another with a nod and a knowing smile. I thought, thank God for this man.

MATHER FIELD--LAST STOP

The date was May 20th. There was barely time to have my equipment checked out by the quartermaster before we were off and winging toward our final staging area at Mather Field, Sacramento. Every position worked with excellence and I was smooth in all of my radio procedures. We were on final approach for Mather, and since I had experienced so many nearly disastrous landings by various aircraft commanders, I found myself slightly apprehensive. This would be my very first landing with Commander Carl Schahrer. I swiveled my seat around and strained to watch him handle the controls. He was working especially hard in the cockpit or perhaps his lack of height made it appear that way. (There were no hydraulic assists built into the controls and real strength and effort were required to handle this bird.) I was going through all the motions with him and the "two" of us "greased" the B-29B in without breaking an "egg." None of the crew looked surprised and so I figured these smooth landings were par for Carl. I felt much better about everything.

All positions were required to take tests at

Mather Field, and that didn't make much sense to me. If someone failed, what were they going to do, wash him out? Barring an emergency, it was much too late for anyone to be replaced now that we were en route to combat. Nevertheless I sweated the code tests; I guess it was just because I wanted to do a great job. After all, I was supposed to be a professional at this stage and I wanted everyone to know it--most importantly, myself. Moreover, I didn't want to lose a position on this crew. These guys were unusually talented; I had jostled around with enough of the others so that I would know. I figured that Carl and his gang would give me the very best chance of survival.

The enlisted crew and I became much better acquainted during our nine day stop at Mather. There was liberty every night and we checked out a number of night spots and restaurants in the Sacramento/Oakland area. Hank Gorder, the engineer, was the fellow that I took to immediately. Tall, rangy Hank was only four years older than I but he showed middle-aged maturity. The engineer was the center of the B-29's operation, no question, and his job required concentration, application and knowledge. Hank had that shy, cool, quiet self-confidence that gave me and the others a feeling that everything was always under control.

I think that Hank viewed me kind of like a kid brother, because that's the way he treated me. Hank was the only other enlisted man in my section of the airplane and I had the opportunity of seeing him work close up. He was smooth and masterful at his position and he was most respected by all of the crew. I had found a solid friend in Hank Gorder. Henry

Carlson and Hank Leffler, the scanners, were fun guys, and Sid Siegel, the tail gunner, was always upbeat and good for a laugh. We all had a great liberty time together at Mather. It was quite a family, and we looked forward to getting to the Pacific and giving the Japs hell. Our game plan was still the same. Get the war over and get back home. Some guys wouldn't make it back. We were well aware of the realities of combat.

The enlisted guys and I met a young Lieutenant on the last night of liberty and we all fell into tight camaraderie. The guy was from Bay City, Michigan and a totally genuine person. We drank and sang and speculated where we were going to be based. We knew that the first stop would be Honolulu but that's all we knew.

The discussion came around to the rumored price of booze in the Pacific and all of us had heard that modestly priced stateside whiskey such as "Three Feathers," was going for as much as two hundred bucks a fifth in the islands. The command gave us a quota of three bottles per man, but we were all so tapped out by the end of the 9 day liberty that we couldn't even buy our allotment. The Lieutenant friend from Bay City asked us to go with him to a liquor store that was up the street as he wanted to buy a couple of cases of Canadian Club whiskey. We caught a pair of waiting taxi cabs and followed one another back to Mather Field. As we all were shaking hands and saying good night, the Lieutenant presented us with a case of whiskey, "Here's a small memento of our last night in the States--good luck to you guys." We were thrilled, shocked, and completely taken off guard by the Lieutenant's benevolent gesture. We sputtered some sort of thank you and vowed to pay him back when we caught up with him. The Lieutenant just laughed, "Nope, it's a gift, my friends, it's a gift." He gave us a thumbs up and we returned the gesture with a grateful smile of appreciation. What a special fellow. I'll never forget this super gent from Bay City. It would be great to see him once again before silver taps. If he reads this book I want him to know that the next time we meet, the fermented laugh water's on me!

Chapter Five

13° 26′ NORTH/144° 39′ EAST

29 May, 1600 hours. My new crew and I had just finished pushing props through in preparation for our first leg flight to Honolulu. I could feel an elevator in the pit of my stomach. This was the last time I would see the United States until after the war. Maybe I'd never see it again. That was the reality. I took a deep breath and a long last look at things then climbed up the nose wheel ladder.

All positions were busy pre-flighting. Commander Carl Schahrer was checking out all flight controls and he found a problem. Carl called over the interphone, "The rudder controls are hanging up. Everyone check the cables in the front and back bomb bay and see if they're clear." Pilot John Waltershausen came back and opened the forward bomb bay pressure door just behind me. He checked the control cables and every thing appeared to be normal. Now he had to check the aft bomb bay. Instead of climbing through the tunnel which began just above the pressure door, he exited through the nose wheel hatch and walked back to the scanner's entrance door on the right side of the airplane. Carlson met John as he arrived and sheepishly informed him that he and Leffler had found the problem. It was the case of booze. The boys had tried to tuck it out of sight in the bomb bay, and, in so doing, they had jammed some control cables. They had since moved the booty to another area and camouflaged it with personal gear.

Leffler and Carlson begged John not to tell Carl fearing that he might order the precious contraband off the ship. Good guy John never breathed a word that the mechanical dysfunction was caused by a case of 80 proof whiskey. He just told Carl that some gear had accidently been stashed too close to the control cables but that it had been cleared. Carl tried the controls again and, sure enough, they were free. He didn't know who the responsible culprits were, of course, so he called the crew on the interphone and gave us all a five minute lecture on safety procedures to be taken when loading the airplane. So the fun juice remained; thanks be to John for not blowing our cover. He saved the fun nectar and our enlisted posteriors.

Takeoff and climb were smooth but, as usual, cylinder head temperatures peaked above the 260 degrees Centigrade maximum. With Hank and Carl working together on the power systems, all the horses cooled off nicely after we reached cruising altitude. Hank adjusted cowls, RPM., fuel flow, synchronized props, and we were on our way to war. Tony and I were quietly apprehensive since this over-water leg had to be on the money and we were both being tested.

IN TONY'S OWN WORDS

"I remember that fly-out 'cause we had to

observe radio silence. and we couldn't show any lights so the Japanese subs or whatever couldn't get any idea of what kind of movement was going out from the States towards Honolulu. But they had two picket ships out there; one a third of the way to Honolulu, and another one 2/3rds of the way out. They'd given us their coordinates and charts, and it was going to be dark when we hit that first picket ship. You were to send out a radio signal on a certain frequency to make contact. They weren't going to answer us. You sent out some kind of a (Morse) coded signal and, when they received that signal, they were going to shoot a shielded light straight up above the ship. From where we were in the air we could see that light, know how close we were to our proper track, and I could adjust accordingly in case I screwed up. I was never all that certain that I was that good of a navigator anyway, and I was pretty concerned about this flight with all you guys while I'm trying to find Honolulu out there without any navigational aids. There wasn't any Loran and all I had to rely on was dead reckoning, my Sextant and those stars. I don't know whether you guys knew it but I almost flunked Celestial in Navigation school. But I would up as an instructor in Navigational school and I taught Celestial so I learned it pretty good then. I recall really sweatin' out that first third: shooting stars and computing and plotting like mad, and making my new course direction. Finally I had my estimated time and the last correction into that ship. Just about thirty seconds before the E.T.A. ran out we asked you to send out that signal, and I was standing up there lookin' out between the aircraft commander and pilot. You sent out the signal, and after what seemed like and eternity, a light flashed directly under our nose. We hit that thing right on the head and, as I recall, all you guy let out a

cheer on the airplane and a huge sigh of relief that this big Italian klutz that had managed to get us one third of the way with reasonable accuracy."

If Tony felt better, well, so did I. If I had been unable to set up and handle the transmission just right we would never have received the light, and the heat would have been on both Tony and me. Ten hours and fifty minutes later we touched down at John Rogers Field, Honolulu. (Hickam Field, which had been attacked by the Japanese at Pearl Harbor, was still undergoing repair and reconstruction from time to time.) Another perfect touch down by my new commander, Lt. Carl Schahrer. I was beginning to enjoy landings instead of bracing for them.

HONOLULU AND THE PEARL REMINDERS

We were comfortably quartered and enjoyed a good night's sleep. Next day we took a small tour of the Island, beginning with Pearl Harbor. It had been more than four years since the Japanese launched their sneak attack on Pearl. On December 7th, 1941, 360 planes from six Japanese aircraft carriers sank the Arizona, West Virginia, and California; the Oklahoma capsized; the Nevada ran aground; the Maryland, Utah, and Tennessee were damaged and put out of action. 65 U.S. Army Planes were destroyed. Of the Navy and Marine aircraft, only 54 out of 225 were flyable. 2,335 sailors and soldiers were killed; 68 civilians died and 1,178 persons (military and civilian) were wounded. Five times as many sailors were killed as had died in World War I. The military result of the Japanese sneak attack on Pearl Harbor resulted in the command of the Pacific being passed to the Imperial Japanese Navy. The mementos of Pearl re-fired our determination to kick the hell out of the Japs.

We checked out a couple of night clubs in Oahu but for some reason there seemed to be a general feeling of animosity by management toward the G.I.'s. The bouncers' blew police whistles every time we got a little chatty and threatened to give us the old heave-ho. I don't know what sociological or political problems lay behind their attitudes then, but it was sure different than what we had expected. One good thing about it, the unfriendly ambience in the clubs didn't encourage us to miss curfew.

SECOND LEG KWAJALEIN

We were rolling down the John Rogers runway on 1 June, destination unknown. Carl had been given orders that he was instructed to open after we reached cruise. I sent my takeoff message to ground and then I hung out watching instruments until we throttled back at 15,000 feet. Tony and I sidled up behind Carl to watch him open the sealed papers. Carl looked at the orders for a moment, turned to John and us and announced, "We're going to Kwajalein." Tony looked at the map he was holding. "Kwajalein, let's see, that's about 2400 miles south west; a little over ten hours from here." John thumbed through his charts until he found Kwajalein, "I'm glad that you're landing boss, we've got less than 5000 feet to set it down; there's water waiting at both ends. If we make a mistake, we get wet." Carl thought about it a moment, "I'd like our standard 7000 but you take what they give you. One thing for sure, we'll be burning

fuel for ten hours, and that'll leave us nice and light for a short field landing. John nodded, as I added, "I'm surprised that there's enough of that Island left to land on, after all the military action. One thing, I'll bet there aren't enough Japs left to worry about." Carl clucked, "I hope not, Smitty." Tony reminded us that there were still Japs in the Marshall Islands south of the Kwajalein Atoll, and briefing had cautioned him to stay exactly on course. Carl turned to Tony and smiled, "Well, let's get to work, Tony, and give me some good headings."

Kwajalein was one of the last of the Marshall Islands taken by the American forces as a result of Admiral Nimitz' and MacArthur's joint military effort that was called "Operation Cartwheel." Kwajalein was populated by Japanese forces before Pearl Harbor. It is the largest coral atoll in the world, 66 miles long and 20 miles wide.

Prior to the assault on Kwajalein, Admiral Spruance and Marine General Holland Smith presented the argument to Admiral Nimitz that a direct attack on Kwajalein would expose them to air attack from nearby Japanese bases. Nimitz persisted, however, and Spruance and Smith were over-ruled. On February 1, 1944, the main island of Kyajalein was subjected to the most concentrated bombardment of the Pacific war. Thirty-six thousand shells from naval vessels and field artillery, emplaced on an outlying islet, ravaged Kwajalein. Above the trajectory of shells droned formations of Liberators which released bombs into the exploding inferno. One observer reported; "The entire island looked as if it had been picked up to 20,000 feet and then dropped." There was nothing standing after the shelling. Tanks led the invasion for the U.S. forces; there were 8,122 Japanese soldiers killed, and 264 taken prisoner. The Americans lost 356 men.

This was another long mechanical test for "The Boomerang", as it took us exactly ten hours and forty minutes to reach Kwajalein. We weren't challenged with any major hardware problems on this leg, but the short 4000 plus runway presented a formidable test for Carl and John. Any mistakes and, like John said, we'd all get dunked. Carl put on another show for us and set the bird down at the numbers stopping just short of the salt water on run out. There had been a small number of 29's that ran off the runway on landing and several ran out of cement on takeoff. The pilots and crews always sweated the Kwajalein runway, and for good reason.

The ground crews had seen a good number of B-29's by the time we had arrived, but the Superfort still held its celebrity status. Ground personnel viewed the bird with wonder as they checked the airplane out on their post flight walk around. As always, there were questions concerning our lack of firepower. We had been advised to say only that turrets would be added before we flew missions, and we stuck to our story.

THE SPRUANCE HAIRCUT

The crew regrouped early next morning to take a fast look at the Island before the command briefed us on our final leg. It was weird not seeing any trees on what we understood was once a lush island. The now barren landscape was characterized as the "Spruance haircut." Surprisingly, there were still remnants of destroyed American assault vessels and other military litter sticking out of the water; touchable

evidence of the violent fighting that had taken place there. You could almost hear the wounded and dying screaming from the beaches.

We had breakfast at the Navy mess hall and it was pleasantly unlike anything we had ever experienced in the Air Corps. These guys even made their own bread and served up a meal that made us wonder if we were civilians again. I was looking forward to the return trip and more of this great homemade bread.

The crew briefed and by mid-morning we were in position and holding for takeoff on the short Kwajalein runway. We had landed on this war torn coral island less than 24 hours before. The date now was 2 June. We were heading for somewhere in the South Pacific, but no one knew exactly where that somewhere was. Carl had been given new sealed orders and commanded to open them after reaching cruising altitude. There were enough logical possibilities to confuse the issue, which pushed our intrigue even higher. Carl angled "The Boomerang" slightly to the right with the nose wheel straight to compensate for the airplane's tendency to turn to the left. John let out 25 degree flaps, and Carl and John both stood on the brakes advancing the throttles smoothly. Everybody could feel their heart pump on this one. When the manifold pressure had been stabilized in all engines at 56.5 inches, Carl and John took the brakes off and we were rolling. Carl kept back pressure on the yoke to hold the tail down. At 125 miles an hour we could see water coming up fast and everyone held their breath (my thoughts turned back to those newsreel shots of Charles Lindberg bouncing along in the "Spirit of St. Louis" trying to get the plane airborne). In the next second or two the bird lifted itself off; we saw runway and then water flash by and we were on our way.

FINAL DESTINATION...

We reached ten thousand feet leveled off and throttled back. Hank, Tony, Dick Ginster (radar) and I met on the flight deck to watch Carl open the sealed orders. Tony had grabbed a map and held it ready. It was the academy award this time, and everybody was breathless with excitement. Carl slowly opened the envelope, using all the drama the moment would hold, and then announced: "The winner is: 13 degrees 27 minutes north, 144 degrees 45 minutes east..." Carl held his dramatic pause long enough for Tony to check the coordinates and yell, "Guam! Carl grinned, "You know, Tony, you're a heck of a navigator."

None of us knew much about Guam except that in July 1944 U.S. troops had fought and recaptured this Mariana Island from the Japanese who had held it since December 1941.

Note: After 17 days of air and naval bombardment, American landing forces on July 20, 1944, went ashore on Guam, which the Japanese had seized the day after Pearl Harbor. "This campaign," wrote Rear Admiral W. L. Ainsworth in his action report, "was brilliantly conceived, splendidly planned, and precisely executed." It took three weeks of fighting, but the island came back into American hands. Ledger: "Killed, 10,693 Japanese; 1,290 Americans."

Having grown up in land-locked Iowa, it was hard to believe that 70 percent of the planet earth was water, but after flying over ocean for 10 hours and 40 minutes

between Honolulu and Kwajalein, and then seven more hours between Kwajalein and Guam, the 70 percent figure seemed a bit too conservative. We were almost to the 7 hour mark when Dick Marshall, bombardier, called out, "land ahead." We were all elated to see a chunk of ground again. I now had a small idea of how the ancient explorers must have felt when, after seeing nothing but water for days, they finally sighted pay dirt.

From the air Guam looked like solid jungle with a clearing sprinkled here and there. We could make out the capitol, Agana, the largest town on Guam, and various Naval installations. You could see the outline of huge coral reefs showing beneath the surface of the coastal shores, especially on the southern side. We swept past the runways on a "fly-by" to look everything over. There were two 8500 foot runways and we learned later that the south one had only been operational for one day at the time of our arrival. There were dangerous four to five hundred foot cliffs that dropped off cleanly from either end. Carl offered some positive rationale on that subject: "The cliffs will be a challenge on landing, but on takeoff we can nose the bird down, cool the power plants off a little and pick up more flying speed."

THE BRASS HAD ARRIVED IN JANUARY AND THE SEABEES WERE IN FULL SWING BUILDING RUNWAYS BY MID-APRIL:

In January of 1945 Brigadier General Tommy Power arrived at Northwest Field Guam, with the 314th Bomb Wing. In April of 1945 Brigadier General Frank Armstrong arrived at Northwest Field to take command of the 315th Wing. (He

Chapter 5 - 13° 26′ North/144° 39′ East

Northwest Field

Control Tower

Ground Controlled Approach Radar

Base Operations

had just returned to the states from combat in England, when he was ordered to Guam.) Colonel Boyd Hubbard had been ordered to command our 501st Bomb Group attached to the 315th Wing.

By mid-April 1945, ten Army Engineer and Navy Seabee construction battalions were struggling to complete the airstrip at Northwest Field. The engineers worked night and day to transform the jungle into heavy bomber runways that would meet Air Force specifications. Three feet of compacted rock bases and a paved surface were required to accommodate the B-29's 140,000 gross weight. The Northwest runways were required to have a minimum width of 200 feet and a minimum length of 8,500 feet. There had to be hundreds of paved hardstands and miles of taxi ways. The approaches had to be free from mountains and other obstructions for 15 miles at either end of the runway. The European airfields represented approximately 30,000 cubic yards of ground while Northwest Field represented over a million cubic yards. The hard coral rock lying beneath the jungle offered a tough challenge to jack hammers and bulldozers. Sometimes dynamite was the only solution to breaking up the coral.

FLUFFY FUZ III

There had been a formal dedication ceremony for Northwest Field held on the south runway the day before we touched down. General Armstrong circled the field in his "Fluffy Fuz III" to begin the ceremony, then landed on the newly completed south runway. He taxied the aircraft and parked facing the distinguished visitor ceremonial platform. Hundreds of men from various military services cheered and rendered a rousing

applause. On the speakers' platform with the Naval executive Admiral of the Fleet Chester W. Nimitz were: Lt Gen Barney M. Giles, commanding the Army Air Forces in the Pacific Ocean Areas; Maj Gen Curtis E. LeMay, Commanding General of the XXI Bomber Command; Maj Gen Henry L. Larson of the Marine Corps, the Island Commander; Brig Gen Frank A. Armstrong Jr., Commanding General of the 315th Wing; and Col Lee B. Washburn, Commanding Officer of the 933red Engineer Aviation Regiment, the construction director.

The speakers highlighted the significance of the event in a brief ceremony. Admiral Nimitz, the honored guest for the occasion, commended the Army Aviation Engineers and Naval Construction Battalions (Seabees) for their superhuman efforts to build Northwest Field. He also stressed the connection between the mission of the troops on Guam to the total war effort in the Pacific. Col Washburn spoke and declared Northwest Field operational. Gen Armstrong promised excellent results from the 315th. Gen Larson called Northwest a milestone in the march to Tokyo. Finally, Gen Giles commended the engineers and revealed that Japanese engineers had told the Japanese Imperial Command that insurmountable terrain problems would never permit American B-29 forces to operate out of the Marianas. Giles wondered what these Japanese engineers would say after the upcoming B-29 Superfort raids.

CLEARING THE CLIFFS

Carl took a long final and added full flaps. We came in with indicated air speed of 130. The ominous looking 400 foot cliff

General Armstrong

"Fluffy Fuzz IV"

was waiting to greet us if the bird landed short. Carl came in a little high for an extra measure of safety, leveled out, used the ground effect and sat down gently. We used up a lot of pavement, but then we had a lot to work with. A jeep with a checkered flag met us and showed us back to our hardstand. The crew deplaned forward and aft and then retrieved our gear which was stored in the scanners' area. One runway and most of the hardstands were all completed but one runway was still being laid down. The remnants of construction could be seen all around the field, especially on the south and east sides, and you knew that this field represented a monumental effort on the part of the Seabees and Aviation Engineers. They truly performed miracles for the Air Force, and we all had enormous respect for these talented and dedicated troops. History has tried to give the engineers the salute they deserve, but from the perspective of the 315th Wing, their accomplishments can never be overstated.

IN THE WORDS OF DICK MARSHALL, BOMBARDIER

"Upon reaching Guam we could then understand why we had so many delays since leaving Kearney, Nebraska. There were two runways but the south runway had barely been completed at the time of our arrival. All the delays we were encountering were giving the Seabees time to complete the landing strips. I couldn't help but marvel at these troops. I had always heard how capable and resourceful they were and how proficiently they performed. Gun in holster, strapped to their waist, going about their work in a very methodical manner. They reminded me of an ant colony swarming all over the

place with their bulldozers and heavy earth-hauling equipment, working feverishly around the clock to complete the other landing strip which ran parallel to the one we landed on a few days earlier. In less than two weeks after we arrived, they had completed the entire air field including taxing areas. In a little over one month, they had carved out of what was a jungle on the northwest tip of Guam, a complete air field ready for operation—a remarkable task and accomplishment. The Seabees were truly unsung heroes, but then that's what they were noted for. The success of the war effort in the Pacific had to be due in great measure to the Seabees. Without them, there could not have been air bases cut out of jungles on Tinian and Saipan Islands in the Marianas or on Guam from which hundreds of B-29s struck the Japanese Empire. June 16, two weeks after we had arrived, the field was completely finished including all taxi ways and hardstands; we made our first combat shake down mission to the Island of Truk."

GUAM

The 90 degree air felt caressingly soft and relaxing; it reminded me of Puerto Rico. Hundreds of massive Superforts sitting poised on their hardstands gave the only visible hint that there was a war going on. Crew trucks for officers and men drove up and the G.I. drivers welcomed us aboard. I threw my gear into the truck and then hopped in beside it. We were all eyes on they way to quarters. The jungle was thicker than I could have imagined. Our tail gunner, Sid Siegel, made this observation as we bounced along a graveled road: "The jungle looks about the same as it does in National Geographic, but the nude girls are missing." I turned to

Sid, "Maybe they're hiding behind the palm trees." Sid grinned, "You can bet that I'll check that one out." "Better check it out before dark Sid, otherwise one of those left over Japs might check you out." We had heard "scuttle" that there were still a number of Japanese dug in around the island.

Our housing was a mere one half mile south of the field. We unloaded from our crew truck, and took a good look around. Our barracks was frame construction, well built and elevated off the ground about a foot to prevent flooding during the monsoon season. We all settled into individual areas. Each man had a foot locker, a cot, small clothes space, and a shelf. Leffler had a cot to my left and Henry Carlson was next to me on my right. Sid was four cots east of me, and Hank was five cots away on the other side of the barracks.

BARRACKS RATS

An old regular Army Staff Sergeant called us to attention and then ordered us: "At ease! Welcome to Guam. It's not bad duty for those of you who love hot, humid weather, lots of rain, and, uh--rats. Oh yeah, there's no mosquitos, snakes, or bugs, but there are a billion rats that nest mainly in the palm trees, and so far the military hasn't been able to find an effective way to eliminate these charmers. In fact they haven't even slowed em' down. The other day a G.I. in the 314th Wing was sittin' on a three holer and one of the varmints took a chunk out of his left testicle." That line brought some grunts from the group. The Sarge added, "What the hell, it didn't kill him. He'd had his Bubonic Plague shot, and I take it you've all had yours. You'll need that

protection, for sure."

A few hours later we were all sacked out. The flying, plus excitement, anxiety, and strange new quarters had done us in. I roused a couple of times, and then fell back into a deep sleep. I was lying on my back when I realized that something was exploring my hair, or was I dreaming? No, I was awake and I could feel a small, slick furred animal standing on my forehead. I knew it was a rat. I froze for a second, and then I instinctively jerked my head and body towards my right side. The thing departed so fast that his toe nails raked a track across my forehead, just above the eyebrows. It was dark and I couldn't see anything, but I didn't need any confirmation; I knew it was a skinny tail. "Rat, rat," I yelled, as I jumped out of my sack and looked for the chain on the overhead light. I pulled on the light, and the other barracks lights clicked on one by one. The rat had apparently entered by a vent screen and then he couldn't find the exit. The rat scurried up one side and then down the other as guys jumped on top their cots and flipped their G.I. issued knives at the creatures. Sid, groggy from sleep, grabbed his 45, and yelled, "Japs, Japs, Japs!" I hollered back, "It's a rat Sid, a rat—not a Jap. Put that damned thing away before you kill somebody." Hank Leffler stood his ground, and all of a sudden I heard a high pitched squeal. Leffler had run him through. It was gory, but Leff just smiled and said, "Leave 'em to me men, leave 'em to me." Leff carried his victim out of the barracks on the point of his knife and threw it into the jungle. I took out some iodine from my emergency first aid kit and daubed my skinned forehead. Once again it was lights out.

The eager Sergeant blew the old reveille whistle a step ahead of dawn. We slowly

315th Officers - Carl Schahrer 2nd from left

20th Air Force Headquarters

315th Wing Headquarters

20th Air Force Chapel

Rain and mud flowed freely

Chuck Martin (Crew 63) dealing with mud and laundry

373 General Hospital

shook off the effects of exhausted sleep, and as morning chased away the lingering shadows of night, we assessed our new jungle surroundings. It was intriguing and exciting. It was also warm and humid, and the day had barely begun. Now I knew why Tarzan and Jane favored loin cloths for their uniform of the day. We walked a couple blocks distance to the mess hall, dunked our mess kits into luke-warm water, and swallowed one of the worst breakfasts in our young experience. All the chow was imported from Australia, and it tasted like it had been buried for a year. The Australian butter looked like swiss cheese and had a distinctively weird taste. Our only hope of survival, I thought, was that our mission food would be more palatable.

Note: Portable ovens with trays were placed in the aircraft before missions, and the food was prepared by specially trained cooks. That chow was a vast improvement over the mess hall fare, and provided an element of pleasant anticipation.

THE ORIENTATION

After breakfast the crews rendezvoused at an orientation tent which was located a short way from our enlisted barracks. For me tents had always meant church reunions, boy scout retreats, a circus, and the Iowa State Fair. The realities were different here, but the tent mixed in some of yesterday's enchantment with the serious business of war. The crews gathered at assigned tables with a G-2 (intelligence) officer.

The officer assigned to our crew pulled a small booklet from his briefcase: "I'm going to give you a short history lesson on your new jungle home: Guam is 30 miles long and 4 to 8 and one half miles wide; an area of 225 square miles. The northern half of the island is covered with a high wooded plateau and is bounded on the coast by sheer cliffs and steep bluffs 200 to 600 feet high. There are no harbors along this part of island and so called bays are shallow. Broken mountain country rising from central lowland 1300 feet characterizes the south half of the island. The southern valleys, in which numerous mountain streams flow, are very fertile and largely under cultivation. Apra harbor is in the south half, as are the small harbors, Umato, Merizo, Inarajan, and Tulofafa. Guam was discovered in 1521 by Magellan's crew during his historic voyage around the world. Spain formally took possession of the Marianas in 1564. During the Spanish American war the United States took possession of Guam and later, by the Treaty of Paris, Guam was formally ceded to the United States. President McKinley placed the Island under control of the Navy Department in 1898. The Governor of the Island was a naval officer appointed by the President. The Island was designated as a Naval Station for the purposes of Government and protection. Isolated as it was in the midst of Japanese controlled islands, the small garrison at Guam was overcome quickly by the Japanese on 10 December 1941. On 21 July 1944, American Forces launched their assault and regained Guam.

"The Chamorros, who make up most of the civilian population, are descendants of the original island inhabitants: Spanish, Mexican, and Philippine soldiers, who were brought to Guam for conquest, as well as Americans, British, Japanese, and Chinese who came later. The native language is Chamorro but Spanish and English are spoken also. The official language is English.

"The average temperature range is 68 degrees to 90 degrees, and the average rainfall is 90 inches per year. The rainy season is from May to November so you will see plenty of rain. Most of it will come in the form of island squalls. If you are on final approach and a squall line closes in on you, abort and fly around for 15 minutes. The weather will generally clear in that length of time. There are occasional typhoons, and, believe it or not, some earthquakes." The intelligence officer took a deep breath and paused to look at his notes.

"There are virtually no mosquitos left on the Island since defoliation, so malaria is not a concern here. There are awful looking lizards that grow big enough to saddle, but they are no threat to the human population. Rats are a problem and we have not been able to eliminate them. They even get into airplanes and start chewing up insulation on the wiring. We don't know all the ways they get in, but they will go up an entry ladder if a crew chief leaves it down long enough. Henry and Leffler pointed to the scratch on my head and Leff broke in, "One autographed Jim Smith's head last night, and I autographed him with my knife." The Intelligence officer took a close look at Jim's head, "Sorry about that. The damned things get into the barracks some way, and then can't find their way out. Among other things, I guess your barracks would qualify for a rat trap." No one smiled. "Caution is the word. Try to avoid being bitten."

"Japanese propaganda has been so effective we suspect that even the propagandists' themselves believe they're winning the war. Actually they are losing badly, and taking a terrible beating. The Japanese are Shintoists and Buddhists;

their Emperor Hirohito represents a God. They feel that they have just one choice; to fight on, even if they have to chew grass, eat earth and live in the fields. They believe that in their death is the country's chance for survival. For the Japanese, dying for their country is the highest honor attainable, and the assurance of a peaceful spiritual life after death."

THE OFFICE OF STRATEGIC SERVICES ASSESSED THE WARTIME SITUATION IN JAPAN THAT COVERED THE WINTER OF 1944--1945 IN THE HOME ISLANDS:

"For the average Japanese the winter just past was one of constant strain. The weather was said to be the coldest in 25 years; severe earthquakes occurred in Hokkaido and in central Japan; and Allied air raids steadily mounted in scale. War plant dispersal, evacuation and the destruction of housing facilities in air raids has caused severe dislocation not only in the cities but also in the rural areas receiving the flow of refugees.

"Every phase of Japanese life has been constricted by the war. The Government has demanded increased sacrifices of all kinds from the citizenry including a 7-day work week. The first tendency toward dangerous currency inflation since the start of the war followed a recent steep rise in war expenditure. The people, caught between inflated costs, high taxes, and compulsory savings, are finding it hard to make ends meet in spite of increased salaries.

"Despite claims that Japan's existing labor supply is sufficient, the Government has continued to take measures to enlarge it. On 10 March 1945 males between 12 and

40 were made subject to call for home defense as well as for war production. Previously these groups could only be called up for work in certain essential industries. Much emphasis has been placed on monthly production quotas in war plants, and in November Tokyo promoted the "special-attack spirit" as a propaganda device designed to inspire civilians as well as the military to make greater sacrifices for the war...

"Evacuation has reduced Tokyo City's 1994 population of over 7 million to less than 4 million. Compulsory mass evacuation measures, with special emphasis on children and nonessential adults, were intensified after the heavy March air raids demonstrated the inadequacy of shelters and defense precautions. Measures taken to restrain essential workers from fleeing the city indicate a high degree of confusion and terror. Many people have been forced to live in cellars or shacks constructed from debris. Family life has been severely disrupted...

"With a reduced number of movies and nightclubs as a result of air raids and Government edicts, the Japanese are turning more and more to the radio for entertainment, but even here they complain about the excessive 'sermons and preaching.' The populace is constantly told that the war may last ten or twenty years and that 100,000,000 Japanese must be killed before Japan can be defeated."

ACCORDING TO AN O.S.S. REPORT ISSUED THE THIRD WEEK IN JULY, JAPAN'S 'SECRET' WEAPON: SUICIDE

"Specifically, the Japanese High Command began to stress in 1944 that the death of an individual in combat should serve a military purpose. That is, any suicide attack should inflict damage on the enemy. If a Japanese soldier is to die in combat, especially in a suicide effort, the least he must do is kill an Allied soldier at the time he gives up his own life. Too often, the Japanese soldier, rather than surrender, committed suicide to no end, without killing his mortal enemy. Soldiers' diaries and letters repeatedly referred to the necessity and desirability of death in a hopeless battle situation. On Saipan, a division commander ordered his remaining troops to follow him into the hills where all physically capable officers and enlisted men committed suicide in the ancient tradition of bushido, in which hara-kiri was the only honorable course in peace or war for the responsible warrior or samurai who has met with failure, whether or not as a result of his own personal actions. Banzai suicide charges, another manifestation of the suicide indoctrination, had become commonplace in battle in the Pacific. Officers, and the soldiers whom they commanded, were inculcated with the spirit of accepting suffering and pain in pursuit of their military careers, and to bear physical hardship and torture without flinching. Soldiers were taught from youth that 'the way of the warrior is to die, and to die in battle with a fortress for a pillow.'"

The O.S.S. issued a SECRET report warning the Joint Chiefs of Staff that the Japanese High Command had consciously expanded the traditional bushido concept to encompass the employment of suicide tactics as a standard military device. The Japanese pushed this theme one step further by insisting that a suicidal defense to the last man would meet Allied forces daring to invade the home islands. The O.S.S. report warned the Joint Chiefs of

Staff what this one problem might mean for the United State's planned invasion of Japan, November 1945.

The report further advised the JCS that the Japanese High Command had gone on record stating all air and naval activity would be based mainly on suicide tactics (kamikaze attacks) which the nation already had accepted as a legitimate basic part of ground defense: "Secret weapons' such as suicide planes, suicide flying bombs, and human-bomb gliders have emerged... They are planned to exact the maximum toll of Allied Forces at the most advantageous times."

On Okinawa, the Japanese demonstrated their defense philosophy by ordering massive kamikaze attacks on the Americans. They exacted an enormous naval toll: 36 ships sunk, nearly 400 damaged, more than 700 fleet aircraft lost, 4,900 sailors killed or missing and 4,800 wounded.

O.S.S. reported: "Human-Suicide swimmers, have been used in recent campaigns to destroy landing craft, transports and cargo ships. These men, generally organized in platoon strength, swim under water in the direction of an approaching landing craft and then surface throwing a grenade. Or they swim toward the landing craft, pushing antiboat mines until they explode in contact with the oncoming craft...

"Many small depth-charge suicide boats intended for large-scale use in smashing Allied landing and supply operations in the Pacific were discovered in the Philippines and in the Ryukyu Islands. More than 300 of the boats and tons of explosives were captured in caves near the beaches in the Kerama Islands before the Japanese could use them. The boats, intended for attacking Allied convoys approaching a beach landing area, were to be manned by units composed of 100-150 young men with special physical, educational, and character qualifications.

"Most recently the Japanese, in an effort to stimulate home front morale and also to frighten the Allies into a revision of the unconditional surrender formula, have been threatening a last-ditch civilian resistance in the home islands. Addressing the 87th Extraordinary Session of the Imperial Diet in June 1945, Premier Suzuki declared: 'Judging from the trends within enemy countries and considering the developments in the international situation, I cannot help feel strongly that the only way for us to do is to fight to the last.' Other Japanese spokesmen have described 'the natural aptitude of the Japanese is to die to the last man,' and have pictured 'an entire nation armed physically and spiritually to stamp out any attempt to defile Japan's sacred soil...' The national song of the Civilian Volunteer Corps promised, 'Our orders have come, O land of Japan: To death we fight, to our last man.' If carried out, these threats would exploit to the final limit the Japanese capacity for suicide.

"The Japanese soldier's willingness to sacrifice his individual life in his country's interest is based in part on his strong feeling on the continuity of Japan's national life. Regardless of the current propaganda, should the continued existence of Japan as a nation be threatened by the possibility of anything approaching the total extinction of its population, many Japanese soldiers and civilians might well come to prefer surrender to death."

THE G-2 ORIENTATION OFFICER CONTINUES

"There has been a buildup of U.S. heavy bomber forces operating primarily from Chinese bases, but they have not been effective in destroying Japan's desire to continue the war. There is a variety of reasons for this including technical, political, and geographical."

HISTORIANS CRAVEN AND CATE

Craven and Cate, the official historians for the Army Air Forces in World War II, have stated that the bombing was neither early or sustained, and achieved no significant results of a tangible sort, and the intangible effects were obtained at a dear price.

ORIENTATION OFFICER CONTINUES:

"Consequently," the G-2 orientation officer went on to say, "the whole weight of the B-29 Superfortresses has shifted to the Pacific Islands which have been captured so that airfields could be constructed within range of the Japanese home islands. The cost to the U.S. and its troops has been great.

"The B-29 bombing raids on Tokyo began in November 1944 from the recently captured Saipan, but the distance was so great that it forced a reduction of bomb loads, and because of lack of fighter protection the B-29's had to bomb from a high altitude with a resulting loss of accuracy.

"The U.S. decided that it was essential to capture Iwo Jima, and Okinawa to provide airfields for fighters to accompany B-29's

to their Japanese targets. You will be flying airplanes that have been stripped of all armament excepting a tail turret, and so maximum bomb loads can now be reinstated."

ORIENTATION OFFICER EXPLAINS THE SPECIAL OPERATION OF THE 315TH WING

"As you know you will be the all-weather, precision, synchronized radar bombing Wing, and you will bomb oil refineries exclusively. The 315th Wing is made up of four Bomb Groups, each Group had three Squadrons, and each Squadron has 10 aircraft. There are in excess of thirty back-up aircraft so that we can put up approximately 145 aircraft in a maximum effort. Generally a mission will send 80 to 100 aircraft. The Joint Chiefs of Staff believe the Japanese are starved for oil, and that attacks on their refineries will bring them to the peace table with great dispatch."

THE 315TH SHOULD ATTACK THE JAPANESE OIL INDUSTRY

In April, General LeMay had decided that the 315th would attack the Japanese oil industry. It had not been a high priority objective on the Joint Target Group assigned target list. Nonetheless, General Lemay believed that Japan's oil industry was in a critical state and should be knocked out. He further reasoned that the 315th should strike the refineries because they were located on or near the coastline, and would provide an excellent ground/water contrast; the Eagle radar system could easily define those targets. Lieutenant General Barney Giles, the new Deputy Commander of the Twentieth Air

Force, supported LeMay's decision along with General Carl A. Spaatz, Commander of the U.S. Army Strategic Air Forces Pacific Ocean Area (USASAFPOA). Spaatz had seen the German war machine crippled following the strategic bombing campaign against the German oil industry. Moreover the Strategic Intelligence Section of the Air Staff in Washington concluded that the destruction of the Japanese oil targets would have an immediate effect upon the tactical situation. LeMay had all the support he needed, and the 315th's first objective, then, was the decimation of Japan's oil industry.

LeMay was under extreme pressure to perform. His previous attempts to test selective target bombing using the AN/APQ-13 radar was inadequate. Now it was time for the AN/APQ-7 to show what it could do. Japanese oil targets had been left intact, and so the 315th's effectiveness could be easily evaluated.

JAPANESE OIL

The Japanese produced only 2,470,000 barrels of oil in the peak year of 1937, and only 1,941,000 (less than .1 per cent of the world's total) in 1941. During the 1930's the military built up a backlog of 55,000,000 barrels by extensive importation and severe restrictions on civilian use, but by Pearl Harbor heavy consumption and the U.S. embargo had reduced the stock to 43,000,000 barrels. It was the need for oil that fired Japan's drive southward, and her quick success in the Netherlands East Indies had given her access to petroleum and its refined products, but Japan had to depend on shipping and had begun the war without adequate tonnage in tankers. The

demands of the war consumed much of her newly gained production, and the Allies took an ever increasing toll with attacks on her shipping with submarines and carrier-and land-based planes. By August of 1943 oil shipments from the south had begun to decline, and as the Allied forces moved northwestward into the Marianas and Philippines, the flow of oil decreased sharply. There had been no chance to build up capacity or technological skill to build a synthetic oil industry equal to that which had served Germany after the loss of her stolen Balkan wells. By 1 April, the Allied blockade had effectively shut off all of Japan's foreign oil. B-29 mine drops by the 313th Bomb Wing resulted in shutting down the shipping of oil in and out of Japan and between islands. The Japanese made desperate efforts early in 1945 to improvise a synthetic industry, including a pine-root project, but it was too late.

OIL CRISIS PROMOTES KAMIKAZE TACTICS

It was thought that the fuel crisis in Japan promoted kamikaze tactics which were considered the only way possible to launch effective attacks with untrained pilots lacking fuel. The Japanese had calculated that eight bombers and sixteen fighters were required to sink an American battleship or carrier in a normal attack, but that the same job could be done with three suicide planes.

Lieutenant Colonel Jin, who was operations staff officer for the Sixth Air Army, recalled that there was no prospect of victory in the air by the employment of orthodox methods. Kamikaze attacks were more effective because the power of the impact of the plane was added to that of the bomb, and the exploded gasoline caused fires. Suicide attack was the only reliable means of compensating for the lack of fuel.

THE INTELLIGENCE OFFICER CONTINUES:

"The J. C. S. has made plans for an invasion of Japan. If that invasion occurs it will cost an enormous number of lives on either side. We estimate that one million Americans could die and ten million Japanese. Your efforts, if they are successful, may make an invasion unnecessary."

JOINT CHIEFS OF STAFF PLAN INVASION OF JAPAN

A month before the test explosion of the atomic bomb, the service Secretaries and Joint Chiefs of Staff had laid their detailed plans for the defeat of Japan before President Truman for approval. When General George C. Marshall, Army Chief of Staff, presented his two-phase invasion of Japan, Admiral King, and General Arnold supported the proposal whole heartedly. Three days after receipt of the J.C.S. directive, and after consultation with Admiral Nimitz' representatives, General MacArthur issued a strategic outline for the November 1, ("OLYMPIC") invasion of southern Kyushu Island. This would be accomplished by the Sixth Army, under the command of General Walter Krueger. The second March 1 invasion ("CORONET") armies would go ashore in the Kanto plains area near Tokyo. This invasion would be carried out by our Eighth and Tenth Armies followed by the First Army which would be transferred from Europe.

MacArthur planned to undertake OLYMPIC mainly with the Sixth Army; on D-day, Marine V Amphibious Corps were to land near Kushikino on the southwestern peninsula, Army XI Corps in Ariake Bay, and Army I Corps near Miyazaki on the east coast of Kyushu.

LASSO A SUBMARINE

The intelligence officer advised us that the Japanese had shown no mercy to captured fliers, and he gave us some unique instructions for avoiding capture: "You will be flying combat over Japan at night, and if you are forced to bail out, chances are that you will be within walking distance of a rice paddy. Dig in for the night. If you are discovered, don't analyze the situation. Shoot first. If you don't, the four score and ten that's been promised to you in the 'Big Book' could very easily be amended. Find your way to the coast, and steal a boat. If the boat is chained and locked, use the steel saw that's in your survival vest and cut the chain. Row a mile out to sea, and by that time a U.S. rescue submarine will find you. If the sub can't surface for safety reasons, then use a line and throw it around the periscope. The submarine will tow you until it's safe to surface. Stay in the boat and you will be top side the submarine when it surfaces." The crew looked at one another with mock disbelief whereas the officer advised, "This is no Buck Rogers make-believe scenario. The action has been tested, it works, and if you want to survive you had better use it. You will have coordinates of our air sea rescue submarines and if you are forced to ditch, it is to your survival advantage to ditch as close to one of the submarine areas as possible.

"If you are captured and are interrogated, answer any questions that you can. It may save your life and you can be assured that their intelligence knows almost as much about your operation as you do. However, we're gambling that they will not discover you are flying stripped ships. (It looked to me that the crews were the real gamblers here; it was our flesh against this untried military tactic.) Avoid that subject at all costs. One more thing - never smile when you are being interrogated. To the Japanese that means you are making fun of them."

CRUEL BEASTS IN WARFARE

Our concerns of being captured were framed in reality. Everyone was acquainted with the Bataan death march in 1942 after the Americans lost the battle of Corregidor. The Japanese inflicted murder, starvation, and atrocities on American prisoners, even compelling them to bury one another alive. President Truman characterized the Japanese as "beasts and a terribly cruel and uncivilized nation in warfare." It was reported later by a surviving prisoner: "A Japanese officer rushed to one American and they embraced. The two had been students at the University of California at Los Angeles."

We know now that as late as May and June of 1945, captured B-29 airmen were used for vivisection experiments at Kyushu Imperial University under orders of the Western Japan Military Command. The experiments involved removing the prisoner's lung or stomach and were fatal. The Japanese knew that surrender to the U.S. would mean punishment for these kinds of crimes. (One more reason for the Japanese to fight unto their death.)

ROTA

The officer looked at his briefing papers and continued, " In four days you will fly a bombing training mission to the island of Rota. Rota is a small Island located 32 miles Northeast of Guam. It was attacked by the U.S. June 14/15, 1944 after which the U.S. military bypassed the island. It has a rag tag army that has been cut off and is probably starving right now. They have one runway on the island, and we use it for target practice. We bomb the runway, the Japs repair it, and then we bomb it again." Some chuckles come from the crew. "It's really sort of funny, but the runway offers excellent training and there is negligible resistance. Ineffectual rifle fire has been reported, and that's about it. The mission to Rota will be a daytime training mission and you will be notified about briefing."

Note: We now know that Rota was a valuable listening post for B-29 operations, so it was of a higher military priority than initial intelligence had known or revealed.

"THE BOOMERANG"

The officer shuffled through some more papers, "I see that you are calling your airplane "The Boomerang", and that you have requested nose art. Also, the bottom of your aircraft will be spray painted black to make you harder to find at night. That's all that I have-- so sign your names on this orientation briefing form, and you are dismissed."

DICK MARSHALL RECALLS "THE BOOMERANG" ART WORK

"While we were waiting for the field to be

completed, I drew up an insignia design of a right angle curve shaped boomerang with the words "The Boomerang". Everyone approved the design and I made a stencil of it so we could paint it on each side of the nose of the plane just under the aircraft commander and pilot's windows. We then all had a hand in painting it black and it really stood out against the aluminum skin of the plane. "The Boomerang" was our mascot and Tony was responsible that it was on board for every flight we made. It served us very well."

TRAINING MISSION TO ROTA AND THE "BLACK LIGHT" BRIEFING

7 July, 0800 hours we reported to the briefing building for our daylight mission to Rota. The briefing room was located just walking distance away, and it was something to behold. Phosphorescent and luminescent paints were used with ultraviolet light for briefing presentations. With this concept, personnel could project pictures, maps, and radarscope photographs with great clarity. Specific points of interest could be emphasized in more prominent relief through the use of different colors, and the ultraviolet light brought out vivid colors that were unseen with ordinary electric light. There were also relief maps and topographical maps to illustrate the target areas. The briefing was like a visit to a science and technology display, and it was hard to realize in this setting that the purpose was the ultimate destruction of Japan.

Bombing Rota was not a worrisome operation. The mission would be flown in the daylight, the distance to Rota was only thirty two miles northeast, and the resistance would be nill. However, as we discovered, dress rehearsal was just as tough as the actual show. Not as dangerous, but it required just as much concentrated effort.

We lined up two by two and pushed 12 blades through to circulate oil. Early discovery of a liquid lock would permit the removal of spark plugs, and still allow for takeoff at the scheduled time. (Our engines were equipped with Hamilton Standard 4 bladed hydromatic, constant speed, full feathering propellers.) If engines had been stopped more than thirty minutes, the ground crew or air crew pushed the prop through 12 blades; if less than thirty minutes, we pushed through four blades.

We were carrying less than a full load of 500 pound bombs and we got off the runway at about 125 miles an hour. Carl eased the nose down over the cliff at the end of the runway, and picked up a little more protection speed. We rendezvoused with some other B-29's on the southeast side of Guam and flew formation according to our briefing orders. Thank God the Wing would bomb targets only at night, thereby eliminating any formation flying. We learned that formation flying under the best of conditions was hard, challenging work, and could be dangerous.

Dick Ginster, our radar operator found the initial point at Rota Island and gave Carl the target heading. Hank depressurized and Dick Marshall opened the bomb bay doors. We were holding our bombing altitude at 10,000 feet. Ginster was tracking the target on the radar scope cross hairs. He called out to Dick Marshal, bombardier, "Clutch in point is approaching". At 70 degrees sighting angle Ginster called, "Ready...Mark--coming up on 68 degrees...Ready, Mark." I climbed up into my target position in the tunnel astrodome to watch the action.

THE SYNCHRONIZED AN/APQ-7 EAGLE RADAR BOMBING METHOD

The radar operator sat aft of the navigator and also faced aft. The AN/APQ-7, being electrically synchronized with the optical Norden bomb sight in the nose, passed along its sighting information. This tracking information, including drift, was then fed from the bombardier's bomb sight into the pilots' direction indicator, (PDI). The pilot set the plane on automatic pilot, turned to the track displayed on the PDI and held that course to target. He also stabilized the airplane speed and altitude so that the pilot was controlling all three parameters on the bomb run. In the usual approach to optical bombing, the pilot only controlled speed and altitude; the bombardier held the course. (The radar operator could also steer the airplane on the bomb run with the autopilot turn control located on his radar rack.)

WE BOMBED THE PRIMARY TARGETS: BY RADAR AND VISUAL, BY RADAR ALONE, OR BY OPTICAL ALONE

If the bombardier and radar operator were using the radar and visual bombing technique, the bombardier used the AN/APQ-7 radar information and visual sighting to spot the target while the autopilot's gyroscopes kept the aircraft straight and level. In this scenario, the bombardier held the course on the bomb run. If the primary target was obscured by weather, then we would use the radar method and the pilot would hold course

on the bomb run using his pilot's direction indicator. If we used optical alone, then the bombardier again held course during the bombing run. The bombing procedures required great precision, and the crews logged many practice hours in maintaining their proficiency.

Even though the Rota mission was flown in daylight, we were using the standard APQ-7 radar synchronous bombing method for purposes of training. At the target the bombsight indicators came together, a red light flashed in the cockpit to signal the bomb bay doors had snapped open, and the bombs were released.

The bombardier, Dick Marshall called, "bombs away", and I watched the five hundred pounders eat up the runway. It looked as if we were in the target ten ring on our first training mission. I sent in my strike report by Morse code and reported no fighters and no anti-aircraft fire. During debriefing the scanners, Hank Leffler and Henry Carlson, reported that they saw small arms fire, and Sid Siegel, our tail gunner, agreed.

Shakedown training resumed the next night with landings on Northwest using localizer procedures (transmitter that, when used with glide path receivers on the airplane, guides the pilot to the runway). This procedure would come in handy when runway visibility was compromised by one of the frequent island rain squalls.

AIR SEA RESCUE

A new air sea rescue system was being implemented on Guam. Under this system an LCI (landing craft, infantry) would patrol the shoreline just off the runways and monitor the Superforts as they took

APQ-7 Radar Unit

APQ-7 Antenna

off for their Empire missions. In addition, a Dumbo (rescue aircraft, usually a Consolidated PBY 5, a PB2Y3 or a B-24) would cruise over the shoreline area and direct the LCI to any aircraft and crew in distress. B-29s were also used for air sea rescue and they were referred to as "Super Dumbos." The individual crews were required to train for this eventuality, and training exercises were conducted from an LCI a few miles off shore. We were required to jump into the water with just our Mae West life vests and one man-dinghy (attached to our bottom side), then follow various procedures for water rescue. The one-man dinghy could get you more than a little sea sick if you were in choppy water. It was definitely a hard way to go, and just the visualization of bobbing around in the ocean at night in this little unstable dinghy could upset your equilibrium. You wondered who would discover you first: the Japanese, a shark, a U.S. submarine, or an air sea rescue plane? We strongly favored the latter two possibilities.

The Dumbo dropped flares to mark our positions and then dropped two five-man dinghys for us to board. The prevailing winds blew the sulphur marking flares into our faces, and we were all instantly sick. By the time we climbed into the five-man boats, we were heaving up as we "heaved to."

The LCI rescued us after a few minutes. I stumbled to the bow, grabbed hold of a cable railing and lay down. Everytime we hit a good sized wave I was buried in spray. A concerned seaman warned me that I could be washed overboard. I assured him, in between retchings, that's exactly what I had in mind. I decided that I'd take the risk of flying any day over this nautical torture.

14 June we continued training exercises that included landings at Agana, and Harmon Fields located due south of Northwest.

FLEET ADMIRAL NIMITZ

On 15 June we attended a special dedication ceremony at the Field's south taxi strip. General Armstrong wanted the 315th to give special recognition and tribute to Admiral Nimitz who's troops had given so much logistic support to the building of Northwest Field. General Hap Arnold was in the area on an inspection tour and he was the keynote speaker. A B-29B named the "Fleet Admiral Nimitz" was dedicated to the Admiral and our 501st commander, Colonel Boyd Hubbard, was designated as Aircraft Commander.

Flak helmets and vests were issued to us and sometime later we were given a small allotment of flak curtains to reinforce our positions. Since the curtains were in short supply, crew members bought, bartered, and conducted "moonlight requisitions" to get as many of the protective curtains as possible. (Tells you something about self-preservation.) I set up a curtain back of my radio gear and I cut another one to sit on. It hadn't been necessary to wear flak vests and helmets during the Rota exercise, but now we would be flying a combat mission to Moen in the Truk Island Group about 600 miles southeast of Guam. This was a different story than Rota. We expected some resistance at Truk, and one good hit from a fighter or anti-aircraft fire could mess things up pretty good. We had to be prepared as much as possible.

TRUK ISLAND

Truk was the former Japanese Gibraltar in

Fleet Admiral Chester W. Nimitz looks out from Col. Boyd Hubbard's aircraft during dedication ceremonies 15 June 1945

Fleet Admiral Nimitz addresses the Wing

(l-r) Adm. Nimitz, Col. Hubbard, Gen. "Hap" Arnold

the midst of the Carolina Islands, 7 degrees 25 minutes North latitude and 151 degrees 47 minutes East longitude. It is made up of a cluster of 57 volcanos and surrounded by an atoll reef consisting of 40 large coral Islands. Truk had been a great naval and air base from which Japanese sent reinforcements to New Britain, New Guinea, and the Solomons. On February 16, 1944 Admiral Raymond A. Spruance led a powerful task force to the Carolinas and the Japanese fleet was caught off guard. A huge air force roared off the American flattops and, a few days later, 201 Japanese aircraft, 2 light cruisers, 2 destroyers, 1 ammunition ship, 1 seaplane tender, 20 oilers, 2 gunboats and 8 cargo ships were destroyed. The United States lost 17 aircraft. No attempt was made to storm the Japanese garrison of 50,000. The island was rendered useless.

It wasn't long after our 1930 hours takeoff that we encountered some cumulonimbus build ups and began a bucking bronco ride that was to continue until we returned to Guam. I had been a little gun-shy of storms since the weird and frightening encounter with the elements on that trip to Puerto Rico, and I felt the pressure. There, again, it was tougher to be a back seat driver where you didn't know exactly what was going on. The weather added a further challenge to the Wing on this mission.

We were flying single file at 30 second intervals with an altitude separation of 200 feet, and mid-airs would be a concern, especially in heavy weather, with each pilot correcting a little differently than the other. Our briefing altitude for target was 15,000 feet which was a far cry from the 30 to 40 thousand feet promised us at the Fairmont, Nebraska top secret meeting.

We weren't terribly surprised because scuttle had it that General LeMay had not been able to get enough accuracy with high altitude bombing, and if that was the case, then altitudes obviously would be lowered. Whatever the altitude, flying single file with stripped ships and no fighter escort was not encouraging. We offered up a huge unprotected target.

ST. ELMO'S FIRE

The electrically charged clouds present in the weather system set the stage for a phenomenon that got our adrenalin pumping: an eerie blue glow suddenly appeared around the propellers, the cowl flaps, the wings and tail. The scanners yelled that the airplane was on fire. I scrambled up into the astrodome and it looked to me like the whole ship was burning. I could see blue flame licking at the propellers, the engine nacelles and the leading edges of the wings. Tony took a quick look out Hank's window and then hurried back to his navigators table. He had his hands full. Tony hadn't been able to perform any celestial navigation because of the weather, and our mission success depended on accurate ETA's and headings. Carl got on the interphone, "All right, relax everybody. This phenomenon is called St. Elmo's fire. It's caused by these electrically charged clouds that we're flying in. Nothing to worry about." (St. Elmo's fire is not dangerous, but it will definitely get everyone's full attention.) Carl later admitted that he wasn't as cool as he let on. The prop tips were making rings of fire, and as Hank Gorder recalled, "Dick Marshall could lead the St. Elmo's fire around with his finger." But the most heart stopping part: The phenomenon caused a strobe effect that made the propellors look like they had stopped

98

turning!

We were depressurized and about fifteen minutes from the target. I hauled on my heavy flak vest and helmet, put on my oxygen mask, then climbed up into the lip of the tunnel to assume my target position. I had a tight time squeezing into the tunnel with all my flak gear. (As I look back I must have appeared pretty clumsy and funny with all that gear.) I was taking the self-preservation idea all the way. I never dressed up like that again, but I did like the idea of wearing a flak helmet. I sat in the tunnel looking forward through the astrodome bubble while my feet extended down in front of the forward bomb bay pressure door. The astrodome was designed for celestial navigational star fixes, and it was the second best seat in the house for a view--the first being the Bombardier's nose seat. This was our first real combat mission and all of us were wired with anxiety. The free roller coaster ride, compliments of severe weather, made our every move more difficult.

It wasn't long until I heard our radar operator, Dick Ginster, say, "I.P."(initial point) and minutes later, "Ready--Mark, coming up on 68 degrees. I knew that the radar operator and bombardier were synchronized. Suddenly the airplane lit up. There was so much electrical activity from the weather system that it was hard to tell whether we were being illuminated by search lights or lightning, but we soon learned to differentiate between the two. If a search light caught you, it would stay with you for a while, and then flak bursts were sure to follow.

I didn't see any fighters but there were plenty of B-29's on divergent courses just missing one another. Some of the 29s really got screwed up on their bomb run,

and they were coming back through us on a reciprocal. What a mess! We took several short evasive actions to avoid mid-airs, and then lined up on course again. Carl was having a tough time holding his PDI heading. Search lights found "The Boomerang", and Carl yelled for the scanners to dispense "rope". (Radar chaff was aluminum tinsel designed to confuse the ground anti-aircraft radar systems.)

BACKGROUND OF THE WUERTZBURG RADAR AND "WINDOW"

British and American bombers had begun to suffer heavy losses because of the "Wuerzburg radars" that the Germans were using. German flak, in particular, directed accurately by the Wuerzburg, was taking an ever-heavier toll until the British developed "Window", which was nothing more than aluminum foil strips that, when dropped from an airplane, sent back multitudinous radar echoes and blinded the enemy oscilloscopes so that the aircraft's own echo became indistinguishable in the display.

Henry and Leff shoved the rope through the flare chute and the ground lights wiggled off us. The bomb bay doors had been opened minutes before. Down in the nose the bomb-sight indicators came together in the Norden bomb sight; a red light flashed in the cockpit. The airplane lurched upward as the 500 pounders dropped away and we immediately broke right. Our bomb load was well on its way to target.

A few minutes later we had separated from the action. Nervous chatter spilled out as we set up for our return leg. I was glad to get out of my flak gear; I sent a strike report back to base by Morse code: Time 1032 hours. Bombed target. Target altitude 15,000 feet. Cumulonimbus seven tenths. Search lights and light flak. Heavy turbulence. One enemy fighter pacing us from just out of firing range. Returning to base.

We sat back down on Northwest at 1:30 a.m. local time. It had been an extremely rough ride and we were glad to feel the stability of earth once again. We were trucked to debriefing, given the standard 2 ounces of whiskey, and directed to a table with a debriefing officer. Carl, who was normally quiet and reserved, complained to the officer in charge: "The initial points have to be chosen more carefully and better defined. B-29's were coming in from all directions, and it's a damned wonder that a lot of us weren't victims of mid-airs." (Damn was a strong word for Carl.)

IN BETWEEN MISSIONS

The crews would have a week off before getting back into the air, and we used the time to orient ourselves to our new island home. There were a couple more rats carved up in the barracks, and each one was memorialized with a painting of its likeness on the front of the barracks. (Just like painting bombs on the airplane to indicate the number of missions.) You could hear the varmints scurrying around high up in the palm trees, and you could hear them squealing under the barracks at night. They were everywhere, even in the three holers. We learned to check around the three holer reinforcement beams to make sure one wasn't waiting to bite an appendage when we sat down. The medics threw lye into the out-houses every few

days to keep things neat; that discouraged the rats some, but not altogether.

Water supply was the most critical problem at Northwest Field. One 800 gallon per minute deep well was located within 2 miles but the Navy held first priority and wouldn't release a pump to the 315th. As a result water had to be hauled 47 miles round trip by truck from Agana and chlorinated again before use. We used Lister bags for our drinking water and 5 gallon cans for bathing and washing. (Everyone preferred the available green three-two beer to the ill tasting drinking water although it was certain that both would contribute to the diarrhea problem.) Our steel flak helmets (piss pots) became a very important piece of equipment and we used it for shaving, bathing, and washing clothes. We had a canvas covered structure close to the barracks that we used for general utility and laundry purposes. Everytime it rained, the water would collect in the sags and that became our shower. One guy would stand underneath the collection area and another guy would use a pole to push the water out. It worked. Amazing the innovations that spring from basic needs. Later on we were treated to real salt water showers, and that was a luxury beyond words.

The chow was atrocious. The menus always included Australian goat, Australian butter, Australian eggs, and Australian cheese. All of it was as ripe as catfish bait and almost impossible to stomach. The food might have started out in fair condition, but it was in lousy shape by the time it reached our chow hall. We never had to ask what was being served at the mess hall; you could smell it for two miles. There was never enough boiling water to sterilize mess kits, and so many of us suffered from diarrhea the entire time we were in Guam. I came over weighing 185 and went back at 145 pounds. My normal weight was 164 pounds.

The mission food placed on-board in the portable warmers was 100% better than the chow hall groceries and probably saved us from malnutrition. We plugged the oven in after takeoff and by Iwo Jima the food was ready to be served. The meat entrees included ham, and steak which were strictly a feast for a king compared to all that mess hall garbage. The food on board was a much needed morale builder.

We learned early on to eat coconuts and drink the juice, but we soon learned to drink only juice from the green coconut and eat only the meat of a ripe coconut. Switch that one around and you logged extra time in the three holer. Those of us who were smitten by the G.I. problem took toilet paper and boxes with us on the missions. We dropped the used boxes with the bombs. That posed an additional threat to the Japanese, I'm sure.

The crews were continually searching for recreation: there was poker; kicking and throwing the football around; exploring the jungle, and at night the big deal was attending the "Coconut Grove" open air movie which had been built about two hundred yards west of quarters. Good films were in short supply, and the Eddie Bracken/Peggy Ryan "B" films were run until the sprocket holes failed (we enjoyed them anyway). It was necessary to bring steel helmets and rain gear to the movie since there was a great chance that an island squall would dump rain on us before the film was over. It was amazing. Sometimes the show began under a moon-lit, star-studded sky, and before it was over we were watching the picture in a monsoon.

THE SHARK SHOOT AND THE DEAD JAPANESE

Some of us developed a rather unique recreational idea--shooting at sharks. We kept our G.I. shoes on to protect us from the coral, waded out a quarter of a mile on the reef, and looked for triangles (dorsal shark fins). We often found them and then took target practice with our very inaccurate 45's. I don't remember anyone ever hitting a shark and if we had, we might have been caught up in the middle of a feeding frenzy. It was a pretty "lame" practice but, fortunate for us, we lost interest in that festive sport before anyone was hurt.

I well remember the day "The Boomerang" enlisted men emptied their 45's at the sharks. Leff was patrolling the beach while the rest of us were taking pot shots at the "triangles". Suddenly we heard Leff yell, "Hey come on in here, I've found a Jap." I yelled back, "If he's alive, I'll take my chances with the sharks." Leff responded, "He's definitely not alive." With that we all waded back to shore to see what the fuss was all about. Leff pointed to the remains of a partially decomposed Japanese soldier. The helmet was still on the skull, and a blue denim jacket remained as a covering for the upper part of the body. There were no pants or other garments or gear to be found. I was amazed that there was still some skin and sinew holding some of the bones together. We figured that salt from the high tides had helped preserve the cadaver's bones and body tissue. Leff turned to me, "Hey, Jim, you're the doctor on the crew; let's do an autopsy."

101

We examined the remains and found two large metal fragments in the middle of the chest cavity. One was the size of my fist and the other one was half that size. I remarked that the shrapnel must have come from large caliber Navy guns. One thing seemed certain: he couldn't have suffered much after taking that kind of hit. Then Leff and I examined the jacket and my eyes riveted on the label. It read, "made in San Francisco." (I never have figured that one out.) I reached into the inside pocket and there was a thin leather holder with pictures inside it. The pictures were still discernible. They were family pictures: A man, a woman, and three children (two girls and a boy). None of us said anything for a long time, and then I voiced my thoughts, "Those kids and their mother won't be seeing their Dad again--ever. Damned war! Damn their leaders for starting it." It kind of put everything into perspective.

We buried the remains and fashioned a cross out of driftwood. Leff hung the helmet on the cross; the guys and I headed back to the base. That evening we were all sitting at a mess hall table contemplating what we had experienced a few hours before and attempting to eat the over-ripe goat entree. Our blood drained faces suggested that no one was really in the mood to partake of any food. Finally Hank Gorder spoke, "I think I'll grab a beer and go back to the barracks." We got up one by one and left the mess hall. It had been a heavy day!

While we were shooting at sharks, and burying dead Japs on the beach, Dick Marshall and his fellows were involved in other adventures.

DICK MARSHALL BOMBARDIER--

JOHNNY WALKER BUYS THE ISLAND

"I had accumulated a foot locker full of liquor which we were able to purchase from the Navy when the ration supply ship would arrive at the Naval Base at Agana. After the bell bottom kids got their rations, then the fly boys got what was left. I always managed to get a bottle and tucked it away in my footlocker. A Navigator, his name escapes me, from another crew who had his tent across from mine, was a naval architect in Massachusetts. We had decided to build a small boat on our off days to give us something to do, so he drew up a set of plans. I had plenty of liquor, which on Guam was worth it's weight in gold. I delegated myself as a committee of one to do some barter shopping. I checked out a Jeep and headed for the Naval Supply Depot in search of marine plywood. The Shore Patrol Guard, at first, was not going to allow me to enter the supply yard until I prevailed upon him, while stroking a bottle of Johnny Walker Red Label Scotch, that it would be in his best interest if he would direct me to the person in charge of lumber. With very little hesitation, he cautiously stooped down to pick up the bottle I was offering him without being obvious. He not only gave me the party's name, he even drew me a map how to get there. The sailor in charge, after learning what I wanted and what I wanted it for, succumbed to the same technique. He even assured me there would be no problem with the marine plywood or anything else I might want. I came away confident we could proceed with our plans to build the boat, but more important, I had the leverage in my footlocker that would get me anything I wanted. At this point I felt I could buy the island."

LAST TUNE-UP

We flew our last tune-up training assignment 23 June to Farallon De Parajaros Island; the next time out would be for real. Farallon De Parajaros, which was approximately 500 miles to the North, was a volcanic island 1 mile in diameter and located at the far northern end of the Saipan District. It featured an active volcano which rose 1,047 feet above sea level. There were no Japanese military or civilians on the island so there would be no resistance. That was good news to all of us. I could watch the action this time without the encumbering flak equipment. What a joy. The briefing order was to bomb Parajaros, continue to Iwo Jima. make one landing and then return to base. The mission was a full dress rehearsal for the first mission. Tony had an awesome responsibility of navigating those long 3000 milers without making any mistakes. Loran, Dick Ginster, and I backed him up but I couldn't ask for a fix unless it were an extreme emergency for security reasons. As for Dick Ginster and his navigational equipment, Loran was as accurate as the navigator's skill in using it and the AN/APQ 7 was dependent upon a water/land contrast in order to be effective. We found Parajaros without any problem, dropped out bombs, and headed for Iwo Jima which was almost another four hundred miles north. We'd be flying over Iwo in the next few days en route to Japan, and the command wanted us to get acquainted with our navigational routes and the landing strip facility at Iwo. The island was a life saver for many B-29's which had been shot up, were low of fuel, or encountering mechanical problems. Carl gave the controls to the right seat pilot, John Waltershausen, for the Iwo landing. I looked over things from my watch in the tunnel astrodome. I could see Mt. Suribachi in the distance and I thought about the Marines who raised the American flag there. Correspondent Robert Sherrod, who had covered the action, wired: "to watch the Jap mortars crash into the men as they climbed. They died with the greatest possible violence. Nowhere in the Pacific War have I seen such badly mangled bodies."

IWO JIMA

Iwo was a volcanic island 8 square miles in area, 660 miles south of Tokyo, and the site of one of the most costly U.S. military campaigns in history. The Japanese had a garrison of 23,000 men under Lt. General Tadamichi Kuribayashi. The Japanese had transformed the island into a miniature Maginot line. Among their other defensive measures, they combined volcanic ash, cement, and steel into fortified caves with 8 foot thick walls. Iwo was honeycombed with caves, tunnels and pillboxes, which was a familiar pattern to the U.S. island hoppers. The enemy had also heavily mined all of the beaches.

THE BATTLE FOR IWO

For six weeks Iwo Jima had been bombed daily by B-24's and occasionally by B-29's. By February 15, warships had bombarded the island with thousands of ammo rounds. On February 19,1945 the Marines stormed ashore commanded by Lt. General "Howlin' Mad" Smith. Three days later on February 22, General Harry Schmidt came ashore, ready to direct the Landing Force, the largest body of Marines to fight under a single command, three full divisions. On March 14 General Kuribayashi radioed Tokyo what he thought would be his farewell message: "The battle is approaching its end. Since the enemy's landing, even the Gods would weep at the bravery of the officers and men under my command. In particular, I am pleased that our troops with empty hands carried out a series of desperate fights against an enemy possessing overwhelming material superiority on land, sea and air. However, my men died one by one and I regret very much that I have allowed the enemy to occupy a piece of Japanese territory. Now there is no more ammunition, no more water. All the survivors will engage in a general attack. As I think of my debt of gratitude to my country I have no regrets. Unless this island is retaken, I believe Japan can never be safe. I sincerely hope my soul will spearhead a future attack. Praying to God for the final victory and safety of our Motherland, let me say "Sayonara" everlastingly..."

He ended with three of his poems:

> Without ammunition
> It is sad for me to leave this world,
> Having failed to achieve my important mission
> For the Motherland
> I could never rot in the fields
> Unless my soul took vengeance
> May I take up arms,
> Even unto the seventh life.

> I worry over what Japan's future will be
> When weeds cover this Island.

His final orders:

1. The battle is approaching its ultimate phase.
2. Our garrison will make a general attack against the enemy tonight. Starting time will be 0001 hours, 18 March, 1945.
3. Everyone will fight to the death. No man will be concerned about his life.
4. I will always be at the head of our troops.

Only one other U.S. offensive action, Pickett's Civil War charge at Gettysburg, had so great a percentage of casualties. For one hellish month it was the most populated area in the world, with 10,000 battling men per square mile. Before it was over on 27 March 6,800 Marines were killed and more than 18,200 wounded. The Japanese left more than 20,000 dead. Nimitz said "Uncommon valor was a common virtue."

FINAL APPROACH FOR IWO JIMA

"The Boomerang" was on final approach for the Iwo runway. John set us down hard, but he did a great job considering he was in the right seat and didn't have the opportunity to practice proficiency like Carl. Besides, the runway was a little rougher than Northwest. We taxied back to the numbers again, and took off for Northwest. We touched down back on Guam without incident. The next takeoff would be the one we were all waiting for; the one that would launch us on our first bombing mission to the Japanese Empire. Pre-season was over; it was time for the play offs. We were as proficient as we'd ever be, and we were confident and ready. Still the anxieties and real fears of combat pulled at our insides.

Chapter Six

"THE BOOMERANG" STRIKES OIL

By the 20th of June, the United States was rushing plans to concentrate the preponderance of its military might toward ending the war in the Pacific. President Harry S. Truman in his memoirs: "We were doing this at a time when our military and political experts in Europe were tackling the enormously complicated task of rebuilding Europe and peace in the West. The war in the Pacific had been hard and costly in the years since December 7, 1941. We had come a long way back from Pearl Harbor and Bataan, from Australia and New Caledonia in the south, and island bases, the Philippines, and to the last island chain before the Japanese home islands. Okinawa and Iwo Jima had been defended fiercely by the enemy, and our loss of lives had been very heavy. But we now had bases from which direct attacks could be launched on Japan. We also knew that the closer we came to the home islands the more determined and fanatical would be the resistance. There were still more than four million men in the Japanese armed forces to defend the main Japanese islands, Korea, Manchuria, and North China. The Japanese were also building up a 'National Volunteer Army' at home for a last-ditch stand. The Chiefs of Staff were grim in their estimates of the cost in casualties we would have to pay to invade the Japanese mainland. As our forces in the Pacific were pushing ahead, paying a heavy toll in lives, the urgency of getting Russia into the war became more compelling. Russia's

entry into the war would mean the saving of hundreds of thousands of American casualties."

JUNE 1945 THE U.S. NAVY'S CRYPTANALYTICAL BRANCH INTERCEPTED A TELEGRAM FROM THE FORMER JAPANESE PRIME MINISTER, FUMIMARO KONOYE, TO THE JAPANESE AMBASSADOR IN MOSCOW, NAOTAKE SATO:

"His Majesty is extremely anxious to terminate the war as soon as possible, being deeply concerned that any further hostilities will not only aggravate the untold miseries of the millions and millions of innocent men and women in the countries at war. Should, however, the United States and Great Britain insist on unconditional surrender, Japan would be forced to fight to the bitter end."

MISSION #1

It was the 26th of June. The jungle dawn splashed brightly across the rows of G.I. bunks and one by one the crew's members began shaking off the numbing effects of humid sleep. This day would be like no other for us. We were scheduled to fly our first mission to the Japanese Empire. Reality is hard to come by sometimes, but here it was. The drills and exercises were all over, this was it--the real thing. I lay in my bunk feigning sleep. I didn't want a conversation with anyone just yet. I wanted to think about things for a few minutes.

The real world was often too painful for me to accept, and I had a tendency to skitter away from the basic truth of things now and then. Perhaps that problem began when my mother walked away from my dad and me. I was seven and I didn't handle that experience very well at all. Then, too, I sometimes leaned more to the dramatic side of things rather than view situations in the unemotional light of objectivity. Well, there was no opportunity to escape the truth of today. We were putting our flesh and blood on the line beginning at 1730 hours.

The trick was to fly 1500 miles to the enemy's Empire, decimate an oil refinery, and return safety to Northwest Field. Oil is the life support system to any war, and Japan had been cut off from foreign oil since April 1 (Japan was and is 90% dependent on imported oil). The Japanese would try to blow us up before we reached their oil fields; we would try to thread our way through their defenses and destroy the designated target. There was no childish make-believe here. Those were the facts, and there was no brushing them aside.

I thought about the morality of war. An oil refinery had no soul, but the refineries were operated by humans just like the Jap we'd found on the beach. Some innocent people would die when we dropped our bombs. I felt a shudder ripple through my insides. Of course, if they got to us first, it would be a different story. If the Japs knew about our stripped B-29's, chances were excellent that we'd never reach the target. Then I bristled as I remembered the Japs' sneak attack on Pearl Harbor which killed over 2000 Americans, and I thought of the tens of thousands of Americans who had been killed since, fighting the Japanese aggression in the Pacific. I thought about the newsreels I had seen of Japanese soldiers walking up behind kneeling and bound American captured fliers and firing bullets into their heads. Then there were the Japanese atrocities: On Guam the remains of American Marines were found staked down in a spread eagle fashion, having been eaten alive by ants. There was the infamous Bataan Death March that occurred after the Japanese rounded up American GI prisoners at Corregidor and marched them to camps 60 miles away. Unthinkable atrocities were meted out by the Japanese captors such as forcing Americans to bury one another alive. Any compassion that I was feeling for the Japanese turned to a strong feeling of retribution.

JAPAN'S GIRDLE OF DEFENSE

By December 7th, 1941 the Japanese had seized Manchuria, invaded China, and committed atrocities among the Chinese people which placed them on a collision course with the U.S. Special Envoy Saburo Kurusu and Japanese Ambassador Kichisaburo Nomura had gone to Washington to meet with President Roosevelt and Secretary of State Cordell Hull to ease tensions between the two countries. While the two Japanese representatives were talking peace, Japan unleashed a devastating sneak attack upon our Naval fleet at Pearl Harbor, Hawaii from the decks of six carriers. The attack left all the U.S. Pacific Fleet's Battleships sunk in the mud, and Japan owned the Pacific. Guam, Wake, Hong Kong and Singapore fell. Thailand was overrun. Burma was lost and, with it, land access to

Bomb storage area

Incendiary bombs

China. The Netherlands East Indies were taken. Australia was attacked, and then the Philippines fell. With these island conquests, Japan planned to set up a girdle of defense that would enable them to exploit the oil and raw-material riches of Malaya and The East Indies, Japan's "Greater East Asia Co-Prosperity Sphere."

ENGINEER HANK GORDER'S THOUGHTS ABOUT BOMBING

Years later Hank Gorder gave me his thought and concern for the Japanese despite their cruelties in war: "Jim, do you remember the time Tony Cosola couldn't find the I.P. for our target. The procedure then was to bomb at random the nearest large coastal city. Guess I'm a softie-my blood ran cold. All I could think of was what if this was my home town being bombed. Thank God the problem was corrected and we got on target."

We all felt compassion for the Japanese civilians, but no one had to remind us of our patriotism in those days, and what we had to do. We didn't have to talk about it. Our love and total dedication to America was as much a part of us as breathing. The troops and the country were of one mind. The Japanese would have to pay for their attack on America. We were willing to pay any cost and bear any burden in defeating the Japanese and preserving our American freedom. Yet we weren't a rubber stamp bunch. We were young, tough, and single minded enough to question everything. All of us bitched and griped about each inequity, but never about our country or our common purpose. We knew that we were on the right side of things, and we were proud to be serving.

Hank Gorder yelled at me, "C'mon, Jim, we've got a lot of ground to cover today--and even more water to cover tonight." I smiled at the pun, and waved a hand in agreement, "I'm up."

There was excitement in the briefing room that hadn't been there before. It was a room full of butterflies. This was the big game; we were eager to play, but we were also concerned about the dangers of the mission. Self preservation is an instinct that's always there. It was common scuttle that General LeMay had scrubbed the 30,000 feet bombing program, but we were hoping that he'd compromise and perhaps adjust the target altitude down, say to 25,000 feet. At that height we'd at least have a fighting chance.

The field order specified a maximum wing effort against the Utsube River Oil Refinery at Yokkaichi approximately 200 miles south of Tokyo. This refinery was situated where the Mitsube River emptied into Ise Bay, about the middle of the main Japanese Island of Honshu. General Armstrong, our commanding officer, took center stage and addressed us squarely, "The 315th Bomb Wing is making history today. If this mission is successful, this raid will revolutionize aerial bombardment." We were ready.

The pre-takeoff information was given and illustrated using the 315th special illuminated briefing technique. This mission, and all of our future missions, would take place at night for two special reasons:

1. To permit daylight takeoff and landings.
2. To compensate for our lack of firepower and fighter

protection by using the cover of darkness.

A 28 mile synchronous radar bombing run was planned (a 70 mile bomb run was desired). The briefing officer paused briefly, took a deep breath in anticipation of a negative reaction from the crews, and announced our bombing altitude: "Your bombing altitude for this mission will be 10,000 feet in compliance with General LeMay's XXI Bomber Command policy. I looked at Hank, "Ducks in a barrel". Hank grinned, "Ducks in a barrel but at least we'll have enough gas to make it back." Henry Carlson, the right scanner chimed in, "Dead ducks don't make it back." The line gave us all pause.

The intelligence officer described the enemy's defenses and the weather officer gave the mission forecast. We of "The Boomerang" crew and the others then conducted our special briefing and reviewed the mission profile, route check points, and radarscope photographs of the target.

We were trucked to "The Boomerang"'s hard stand on Northwest. The combination of the fresh nose art with the last addition of the black underside gave the plane a whole new exciting character. We all admired the art work to which we had collectively contributed in one way or another.

The black camouflage extended from the bottom of the aircraft to well over half way up the fuselage. On the starboard side of the nose, just underneath the flight deck and centered high over the nose wheel hatch doors, was the word "The", and just beneath it was the word "Boomerang" printed within the outlined configuration of a boomerang. Both words had been painted on the aluminum fuselage against the black camouflage background. The painted symbol was about twenty times larger than the real boomerang that Tony carried on board. As we stood there checking out the new look, Tony grinned and made believe that he was throwing the authentic Australian boomerang toward the Empire. "Hey boys, if we fly it just right, it will always come back to this spot." Floyd Jennings, our ground crew chief, put a thumbs up on that thought.

Just under Hank's position and toward the nose was the word "Anne" (Hank's wife), and under John's pilot window was the name Jinx which stood for Jinx Falkenburg (at that time a well known Hollywood film star rage). Jinx would have claimed the personable, and good looking John for sure. On the port side of the nose under Tony's position was the word "Naomi" who was Tony's fiancé (later his wife), and just back of Carl's position was the word "Geneva" which was his wife's name. The area directly under Carl's position was being saved for bomb symbols which would represent missions flown. There on the port side nose wheel hatch door was the name of our crew chief: "T/S L. Jennings". T .S. standing for Technical Sergeant. The L. stood for Lloyd but we all called him Floyd for some reason. I figured that the Crew Chief's name on that nose wheel hatch door had to be good luck. Jennings and his crew were proud of their old "Boom", and God knows where we would have been without their dedication to have the best running airplane in the Wing.

In addition to Geneva's name on the airplane, Carl carried her picture above and to the left corner of the instrument panel. The boys were taking their loved

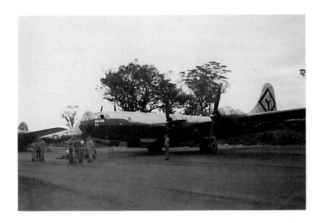

"The Boomerang"

"The Boomerang's" engines received
TLC from TSgt. Lloyd Benson

"The Boomerang"

ones with them, if only in spirit. Dick's wife, Fern, had stayed with him through training in Nebraska, and she had been there at Mather Field to see us off. The family touches gave us all a feeling of togetherness.

At precisely 1700 hours, Wing Commander General Armstrong started his takeoff roll in the "Fluffy Fuz III" to lead the mission. Thirty four B-29Bs from the 16th and 501st Bomb Group followed at 30 second intervals. "The Boomerang" ran a temperature on takeoff as always, and this time she was huffing and puffing a little more from the ten ton bomb load, and sucking in hotter-than-usual tropical air. We used most of the runway to lift off and then Carl dropped the bird down just above the water. He wanted "The Boomerang" to drink in some cool air which would reduce engine temperatures so we could make the long climb to altitude. One B-29 turned back with engine trouble.

It was a strange new feeling flying to war. I began thinking over my 21 years, and it didn't seem like I had done very much. I had taken some lumps, but with it all, life was wonderful, incredible, and I was just getting started. It would be a shame, I thought, if I had to give it all up after such a small taste. Still that's what happened to my Dow City buddy, Harold Sharp. Here was this handsome, cock sure guy, shot down and lost over Germany. Harold always seemed invincible to me; I couldn't believe the Germans had got him--I still looked for him to show up one day with that cocky grin, and saying something like, "Hey, you didn't think those Huns could whip my butt did you? I was shot down and then I worked my way back through the French underground. With all those beautiful French girls, it took me a long

time. Let me tell you something, Smith-- I took a few Krauts with me for good luck." That's the scenario that I had imagined and hoped for, but, sadly, it never happened. Harold was never coming back.

I thought back to the Dow City Consolidated High School and smiled as I pictured Harold pulling the "skunk" to class on a leash. God Bless old Harold and his humor. I could visualize my Dad and step-mother receiving a "Jimmie B. Smith Missing in Action" notice; I could see the tears well up in my Dad's eyes. Well, I had to make it through somehow; I simply had too much to accomplish to get knocked off now. I wanted to graduate from college, get married, have a family. I needed to contribute. I shook off the dark thoughts; I knew that I had to keep focused on my job if I were to function with top proficiency. I silently asked my Maker to protect me and the crew. I went to work.

"The Boomerang" was purring now. Once those over-heated engines cooled down, and the props were synchronized, she was a smooth bird. In the meantime, we had to fly over three thousand miles of water and these marginally powered Wright Cyclone engines were always being stretched to the limits of their operating envelopes. The odds weren't good if we were forced to bail out at night, and ditching didn't improve ones chances of survival very much, if any. Our best alternative was to stay airborne and in one piece.

If anyone could keep "The Boomerang" in the air, it was Hank Gorder. Every time I felt a little shaky about things I would slip up to Hank's station and check with him. If he said all was well, then you could bet your life on it.

IN HANK'S OWN WORDS

"I was the flight engineer (Technical Sergeant). My duties were mainly mechanical pre-flight inspection and fueling (6725 gallons minimum) for our max range missions. About 80 B-29s taking off at 30 second intervals alternately on parallel runways. Takeoff: 2 minutes at full power, gear up at 160 m.p.h., and just barely airborne over the edge of the 550 foot cliff at the end of the nearly two mile runway. We'd lose altitude almost to the water to gain flying speed of 195 m.p.h. (necessary to prevent over heating). My engineer panel had about 75 instruments and 75 controls. Duties: monitor instruments very closely; maintain minimum cowl flaps, carburetor air and oil cooler settings to minimize drag; make power settings each hour or when necessary to maintain maximum range. The exact airspeed (determined by gross weight, altitude, temperature etc.); to maintain most efficient flying attitude; transfer fuel; pressurize cabin; keep cruise control charts, etc."

I wondered what would happen after we hit the Japanese mainland? There would be fighters and searchlights for sure, and since we didn't have any protection from escorts, we were hoping Sid could at least take care of our rear end in case of an emergency.

TAIL GUNNER SID SIEGEL ABOUT THE CANNON

"The twin fifties worked okay but the 20 millimeter cannon didn't make it. The gun had a slower rate of fire and a lower trajectory than the 50 calibers. The bullets were heavier and that caused the lower trajectory. It jammed occasionally and

really was an inept piece of equipment. Far as I was concerned the only effective firepower we owned was the fifties."

Sid's instructions were not to shoot until fired upon since the tracers would pin point our position. Carl was the only one who could give Sid permission to unload. Then I had a chilling thought: if the Japs find out we've been stripped of guns, the party's over. Flying a long bomb run to the target in trail at 10,000 feet was made to order for the Jap defenses. We were presenting them with a beautiful target. How in hell can they miss, I wondered. This was all General LeMay's big idea, and none of us was thinking very kindly of him at this point.

I remembered the instructions intelligence had given us during orientation: "If you have to bail out, find a rice paddy, and stay there all night. If some Japs find you, blow em up." And then the officer's line, "If you don't, your 'four score' promised to you in the Book, could be very easily amended. At dawn, make your way to the sea shore, steal a boat and row out until an American 'sub spots you. If the sub can't surface, throw a line around the periscope and he'll tow you until he can surface." I thought, well, that's just fine, if I survive the bail out; if I can find a rice paddy; if I have enough rounds to take care of any Japanese that might discover me; if I can find the shore line and a boat; if I can saw through the chain, and if I can find an American submarine... Way too many if's for my money. Like trying to win a horse race, but the stakes were a little higher here.

I checked my 45 in my holster to make sure it was secure and that I had slipped in a live ammo clip. I began to wonder if I could really kill another human being?

Well, I guessed I could if it were life or death-- him or me kind of thing.

None of us had been able to sleep much before the mission with all the excitement and anxiety pounding in our veins. Then there was a longer than average briefing for the mission that took away from our preflight relaxation. Tony predicted that we'd be in the air over 14 hours, so we were in for a very long night with not much shut eye in the bank. I hoped the lack of sleep wouldn't dull our proficiency too much.

I was the medical man on the crew so if we got shot up, and someone was wounded, it was my job to patch them up. I thought about what the Doc had told us at Fairmont: "If a crew member is wounded, and then tries to swallow his tongue, take a safety pin and pin it to his cheek." I took a deep breath and pondered that one as I slowly exhaled. There were no options here. If I have to, I have to, that's all!

I wondered how long it would be before the Japs discovered that our ships had been stripped of armament? They were bound to find out sooner or later, and when they did, we'd be taken out of the ball game fast. Our only hope was that the war would come to an end before our secret was revealed.

I slipped my head phones down around my neck, where I could still catch any transmitted message, and walked up to Hank in his engineer's position. Hank was concentrating so hard on the airplanes systems that he didn't even notice me. He finally sensed my presence and smiled. I scanned the instruments briefly. "Looks like they're in the green," I said. (My comment was a subtle approach to a more

serious subject.) Hank nodded, "Yep, everything is looking good Jim." I studied Hank for a minute. At the ripe old age of 30, I think he represented a father image to me. He was married, and lived in the small town of Grafton, North Dakota. I could best identify with small towns, and I think that brought me even closer to Hank. I felt there wasn't a better, more honest guy anywhere than Hank Gorder. I respected and trusted him as much as anyone I had ever known. It was like everything would be all right as long as Hank was there.

I shuffled a bit, as I was about to expose my 21 year old macho image with an honest confession: "Hank, are you scared?" Hank looked up at me, and grinned that big slow grin of his, "Yeah"! I never took my eyes off his, "So am I Hank." It was a good measure of comfort to me that Hank felt the same fear that I did. I guessed I was not much different than anyone else.

We opened our food warmer which had been stocked with ham, and potatoes (no stringed beans or other gas forming foods). We passed trays around, and I poured black coffee which the crew had voted for in lieu of water or fruit juice. (Facing those all-night runs tipped the voting in favor of caffeine). Ham and potatoes! What a beautiful reprieve from the green Australian goat. It almost balanced out the odds.

I went back to the radio and put the head phones back over my ears. There was an attempt being made to jam my monitoring frequency. The jam signal was a carrier wave transmission: the letters "C" & "B", dah dit dah dit, dah dit dit dit, and then it repeated over and over: (C) dah dit dah dit, (B) dah dit dit dit; (C) dah dit dah dit, (B) dah dit dit dit! The jammer varied the frequency slightly so the signal would go from low to high and high to low, like a siren. I could read through the jam with no problem, but the oscillating frequency was somewhat of an irritant. Especially when you consider that I had to listen to this stuff 10 to 16 hours per mission. Radio silence was always the rule and there was no communication going on between me and base unless it was the strike report or an emergency communiqué. But if the ground wanted to contact us for any reason, I had to be there to receive the Morse Code carrier wave message. That meant guarding my assigned frequencies at all times.

A modulated signal broke through on my monitoring frequency. It was a propaganda broadcaster speaking without any trace of an accent, and articulating perfect English. I called Carl and hooked the crew into the broadcast. None of us was really shocked that a propagandist had found our frequency, since everyone was acquainted with the notorious Tokyo Rose who had been dishing out propaganda to the U.S. Pacific troops since the early 1940's.

TOKYO ROSE

Tokyo rose was as American girl of Japanese descent who had graduated from the University of California at Los Angeles and became one of the first propaganda broadcasters for Japan. She was visiting her sick aunt in Japan when the war broke out, and was enlisted by the Japanese government to broadcast lies to the American troops. The propagandist was nicknamed "Tokyo Rose" by the Americans, although she first went on the air as "Ann", short for "announcer." Tokyo Rose then began calling herself "Orphan

Annie", your favorite enemy, and speaking from our standpoint, the Americans were more amused than swayed.

The propagandist who had intercepted my watch frequency had little tid bits of accurate information, but 99% of his act was pure bull. Some of it was so ludicrous that it was funny. However everyone had their serious fingers crossed, hoping the fellow didn't have any information concerning our stripped ships. That would have been a big morale buster.

The propaganda broadcaster said that the Japanese were aware that the 315th Wing had arrived on Guam, and he named General Armstrong as the wing commander, and several other commanding officers: "You will all be destroyed in your attempt to bomb our homeland. Your leaders will tell you that the U.S. is winning the war. This is a blatant American lie. The truth is that Japan has borne America's feeble military attempts to destroy her and is now prepared to deliver an overwhelming counter attack. We will shoot you out of the sky and when your ground troops attempt to invade our homeland, we will massacre them as they step onto our beaches. Be smart and live. Drop your bombs in the ocean and turn back before it's too late..." Carl piped, "I've heard enough;" I switched the crew off the broadcast.

THE U.S. WAS ALSO BROADCASTING PROPAGANDA

By 1945 the Allies were listening to Japan through a myriad of communication networks, and, in addition, the U.S. was broadcasting its own propaganda to Japan. For example, in April 1945, an OSS

(Office of Strategic Services) "black propaganda" radio station on Saipan was established. It was staffed by American Nisei under the direction of 27-year-old Stanford graduate John Zuckerman, and began beaming long range broadcasts to the Japanese islands in an attempt to "soften" the enemy's morale prior to the planned U.S. invasion.

SIGNAL CORPS ARMY COMMUNICATIONS SERVICE

The commodity dispatch overseas in greatest quantity during World War II, and at the greatest speed, was neither munitions, nor rations, clothing or supply items. It was billions and billions of words, messages of strategy and command, plans of campaigns and reports of action, requests for troops and schedules of their movements, list of supplies requisitioned and of supplies in shipment, administrative messages, and casualty lists. Then there were services for the press and services for the soldiers (expeditionary force messages), poured over far-flung wire, cable, and radio circuits and channels-routine and urgent, plain text and enciphered. All this was work of the Signal Corps Army Communications Service, ACAN. Major General Frank E. Stoner, Chief of Army Communications Service throughout the war, estimated that eight words were sent overseas for every bullet fired by allied troops.

The bulk of information during World War II was communicated long distance by radio, and anyone with a short wave receiver and a knowledge of Morse code could eaves-drop on radio messages. Virtually every nation had listening posts established throughout the world. The U.S. had several on Pacific Islands even before the beginning of hostilities.

There were a number of communication facilities on Guam by 1945: Switchboard, telephone, teletype, telegraph, radio transmitters, radio stations, foreign broadcast intelligence service transmitters, recorders, receivers, test sets, and radio antenna equipment. Navigational aids included: radio range, radar beacons, homing device, and instrument approach equipment. There were 101 teletypewriter stations, and cable connections to Honolulu, Saipan, Midway and San Francisco.

Telephone exchanges on Guam in 1945: Boston, Atlanta, Denver, Chicago, Barrigada, Georgetown, Erie, and Fresno. There were 8,050 telephones.

ARMY AIR FORCES COMMUNICATION SYSTEM

The first Army Air Forces Communication System (AACS) went into operation on 5 December 1942 at Amberley Field, some 30 miles from Brisbane, Australia, thereby completing a network of airway communications extending from San Francisco through Hawaii and the South Pacific to Brisbane. Pacific Airway Communications Systems (PACS) was activated at Hickam Field, Honolulu 11 January 1943, and then spread westward. The Pacific Airways Communications Area became, on 15 May 1944, the 7th AACS Wing. Biak, Saipan, Guam, Leyte, Luzon, Iwo Jima, Okinawa--all found their way into the history of the 7th Wings, as finally did Tokyo. On the morning of 28 August 1945, two weeks after the official surrender, some two dozen C-47's (one of them a fully equipped mobile radio station) flew from Okinawa to Atsugi carrying technical equipment and technicians for the establishment of an emergency air base in Japan's homeland.

SECRET WAR--CRYPTOGRAPHERS AND CRYPTANALYSTS

Most governments employed hundreds of cryptographers who devised secret ways of passing information. Hundreds of cryptanalysts were also employed who tried to unravel the secret codes and ciphers. This activity became a major preoccupation of the "secret war."

ENIGMA, ULTRA, MAGIC

The British (preceded by the Poles)-from 1940 on-broke German signals enciphered on the "ENIGMA" machine. The intelligence information obtained was known as "ULTRA".

Japanese signals beginning shortly before Pearl Harbor were protected by encipherment on a machine that came to be called "PURPLE". The information gathered from this source was known as "MAGIC".

ULTRA was combined with MAGIC and, until the last day of war, there was a constant flow of rich sources of intelligence for the Allies about the thoughts, the plans, the resources, and the actions of the men in Tokyo and Berlin--on a world wide scale.

CIPHERS AND CODES

Captain Joseph Rochefort, one of the most distinguished code breakers of the U.S. Navy explains: "Code has a group of letters or numbers-sometimes the letters are pronounceable and sometimes not-which designates a letter or a number, a phrase, perhaps a whole sentence or complete thought. The original people would require a book to interpret.

"A pure cipher would interchange each letter of the original text so that rather than having a group of letters meaning a whole thought, sentence, or phrase, each letter would be changed, or each numeral. i.e. where you interchange your letter by another letter, or a numeral by another numeral is a pure cipher".

U.S. COULD NOT DECIPHER WORD OF JAPANESE CARRIER ATTACK ON PEARL HARBOR

On Sunday, December 7, 1941 (the date of the Japanese attack of Pearl Harbor) the 14th installment of a Japanese encoded message reached the Japanese Embassy in Washington D.C. by the way of the Radio Corporation of America circuits-the same system used by the public for everyday international communication. The Japanese Navy alone employed more than 25 different systems at a time. At the time of Pearl Harbor, the U.S. could decipher messages exchanged between Japanese diplomats, but not those between officers of the Japanese Navy. U.S. government Officials therefore had no inkling that Japanese aircraft carriers were already preparing for an air strike at Pearl Harbor.

EXCERPTS FROM KEY DECLASSIFIED DOCUMENTS ON THE ROLE OF COMMUNICATIONS INTELLIGENCE IN THE WAR WITH JAPAN. JAPAN

MONITORS OUR B-29 OPERATION FROM GUAM

The exploitation of communications intelligence was not a monopoly of the Allies in World War II. The short memo, "Enemy Analysis of Allied Communications," contains an intriguing reference to the Japanese ability to read encoded American messages, while the longer "Ultra Supplement to Report of Study of Communications of Twenty First Bomber Command" (our command) illustrates a specific case in which the Japanese were able to employ radio analysis to obtain intelligence on B-29 operations from the Marianas. Further specific information on Japanese communications intelligence efforts and their effectiveness no doubt will be forthcoming as the declassification of ULTRA documents continues.

ULTRA SUPPLEMENT TO REPORT OF STUDY OF COMMUNICATIONS OF TWENTY-FIRST BOMBER COMMAND

I. STATEMENT OF PROBLEM

To determine whether Japanese radio intelligence activities relating to B-29 activities, as revealed by Ultra intelligence, are producing accurate information about the activities of the XXI Bomber Command.

II. FACTS

Ultra intelligence shows that the Japanese have been studying the radio communications of the XXI Bomber Command and from such study have made estimates of the number of B-29s in the Marianas and predictions of B-29 raids. Many of the Japanese reports are available and information and conclusions contained in them have been checked so far as possible against the actual facts to determine the extent to which the Japanese have obtained accurate information.

    A.   Japanese Study of B-29 Air-Ground Call Signs and Frequencies.

        1.   The Japanese have obtained a good deal of accurate information and have reached a number of accurate conclusions about the frequencies and call signs used by B-29s on air-ground circuits.

    B.   Japanese Estimates of Number of B-29s.

        1.   As noted in the Secret part of this report, use of individual call signs for each group and plane permits the enemy by monitoring traffic to individual planes to count the total number of planes airborne. He can thus ascertain or estimate the total number with considerable accuracy.

CONCLUSIONS

A.) The Japanese have identified the

frequencies and most of the call signs used in air-ground communications and control tower contacts of B-29s. They are constantly monitoring these frequencies and studying the communications intercepted.

B.) Through monitoring of air-ground communications, the Japanese have been able to make substantially accurate estimates of the number of B-29s in the Marianas at various times.

j.) Constant study of Ultra intelligence about enemy analysis of
B-29 communications is essential.

(I.P.) INITIAL POINT

Fifty miles before land fall we cut off all the lights except instrument lights, and we wouldn't turn them back on until we were 50 miles from lands end on our return. Dick Ginster, our radar operator, called out "Initial Point", and Carl ordered all crew members into battle position. His voice cracked a little, revealing the tension that all of us were feeling. Dick Marshall actuated an electrical switch and the bomb bay doors opened. Hank depressurized, and since our target altitude was only 10,000 feet we didn't really need oxygen masks. I donned my flak gear and squeezed into my tunnel position. I cradled my throat mike hand switch in my right hand, and surveyed the world around me from my astrodome position. The sky was totally undercast which was bad for the Japanese defenses but perfect for our synchronized bombing technique. The undercover of clouds helped camouflage us, and yet our AN/APQ-7 radar could easily read the target.

Later on cloud cover didn't give us much

advantage. Some targets threw up extremely accurate antiaircraft fire that intelligence believed was launched from imported German radar systems. Intelligence officers told us that Japan had received this German weaponry by submarines that had found a hole in our perimeter blockade. On a clear night these units could be identified by their different colored lights.

Dick Marshall yelled, "Fighters at 12 o'clock high," and two Japanese fighters spitting tracers dived at our nose. They missed, but they came so close that we wondered if they were Kamikazes. Carl told Sid to keep his guns ready but not to fire until the fighters made a run at us. Leff and Henry, the scanners, got on the interphone and said the fighters were flying along side us just out of range. Carl responded, "They think we have guns, and so they're staying away from us and pacing us into target. They're giving the ground units our altitude, speed and bearing." I wondered how the hell the fighters could find us between cloud layers. But they pulled if off, and now they were setting us up for their antiaircraft guns. We were sitting ducks anyway, and now—well the pacers weren't good news anyway you looked at it.

I heard Dick call, "Clutch in", and I knew that we were getting close to target. I saw searchlights sweeping through the undercover ahead of us, and Carl called for Leff and Henry to dispense chaff. The pacing fighters turned away and that meant flak would be coming soon. There it was! Flak at two hundred yards port side and flak meager but reaching up menacingly close on my starboard side.

A replay of my life passed through my consciousness with the speed of light. I remembered all the good things, and all the stupid things I had done in my life, and lastly my mind turned to the hopes and dreams of the future. I found myself mouthing a prayer, and I remembered the statement some general had made: "There are no atheists in foxholes." I could relate.

BOMB SIGHT INDICATORS COME TOGETHER

I heard Dick call, "Ready Mark", and then call it out once again. Carl was crabbing to his starboard to hold course. The wind was fierce. Dick Marshall's Norden bomb-sight indicators came together, Carl's red light came on, and the bomb bay doors snapped open. Dick had pulled all the safety pins and counted them to make sure every bomb was armed. "The Boomerang" lurched upward assuring me that she had just released her nearly ten ton load of 500 pound bombs. We broke away and headed back to the promised land. Carl made several sharp turns to avoid the airspace of other B-29's. We had discovered at Truk that mid airs during and after the bomb run were a real possibility.

Carl turned his interphone to "Call", pushed the switch on his control yoke and said, "Good job everybody." We began to unwind; Tony turned to me with a big smile; I gave him and Dick Ginster a double thumbs up. Radio silence had to be broken now and I sent my strike message 1500 miles back to base: Bombing altitude 10,000 feet, 10/10th cloud undercover, flak meager, searchlights, four out-of-range fighters, bombs away at 1241, no damage to aircraft. Returning to Northwest. Out.

Hank was busy with his slide rule, figuring the cruise control for our return. We had a long 1500 plus miles to go over water and most of it would be at night. We'd been nervously awake with anxiety, excitement, fear and "iodine strong" G.I. coffee. Now we experienced that post-bombing let down. We were running low of adrenaline and being pulled down by bone aching fatigue. I clamped my ear phones tight to my head. All was clear on my assigned frequency except the incessant jamming attempts: (C) Dah dit dah dit, (B) Dah dit dit dit. The jammer was still oscillating the frequency from high to low and low to high. Even though it was disconcerting, I learned that it broke the boredom of a long flight and kept me on my toes. You might say that the Japs were actually aiding and abetting my job. If they only knew...

I woke up with a start about 4:00 a.m. My head had been face down on my radio table. My forehead was sore and I felt a bump on the upper right side just a fingers width below the hairline. I quickly surmised that I had collapsed onto my radio table from fatigue and had fallen into an unconscious sleep. I looked around and saw others sacked out and I hoped that someone was flying the airplane other than the automatic pilot. I peered into the flight deck; Carl was awake and doing his job. John Waltershausen, the pilot was fully "sacked", as was bombardier Dick Marshall in his nose position. If Carl got too zonked he'd change shifts with John, so nothing to worry about there. I didn't even have to look at Hank. I knew that he'd be scanning gauges, transferring gasoline, adjusting cowl settings, synchronizing props, and performing other magic to keep the engines from overheating. I was in good hands. How lucky I was to have been transferred to this crew. I guessed that maybe everything in life worked out for the best.

Dawn gave "The Boomerang" crew our wake-up call. I slipped up into the tunnel and checked the world out again. No artist could have captured the beauty of this South Pacific morning. All was calm now, making sharp contrast to the fiery hell that we had witnessed a few hours before. An occasional white cap caught the eye as we slanted down from altitude. Were we really at war? It was hard to believe in this peaceful sky-blue setting. The world was gentle and loving again. Wouldn't it be wonderful, I mused, if the combat part had just been a bad dream? I climbed back down from the tunnel and discovered reality once again.

This was a big day for "The Boomerang" crew. We had bombed our first Empire target and survived. It had also been a big day for the world with the signing of the United Nations charter in San Francisco. President Harry S. Truman was present at the Veteran's War Memorial Building to witness the signing of the charter (Secretary of State Edward R. Stettinius Jr. signed for the United States). The President then proceeded to the Opera House where he addressed the final session of the plenary conference.

PRESIDENT TRUMAN COMMENTS ON THE SIGNING OF THE UNITED NATIONS CHARTER JUNE 26, 1945

"The charter of the United Nations, which you have just signed is a solid structure upon which we can build a better world. History will honor you for it. Between the victory in Europe and the final victory in Japan, in this most destructive of all wars, you have won a victory against war itself."

NORTHWEST AND HOME

We made a long down-wind for the Northeast/Southwest (N 65 degrees, 47 minutes E) runway and turned onto final. Carl pressed his yoke mike button and told us to prepare for landing. John let down the flaps from twenty-five degrees to full and we kissed the coral at 100 miles per hour (the time was 0700 hours). I figured we weighed about 100,000 pounds at this point since we didn't have any bombs and there was very little gasoline left in the tanks after our 14 hour trip.

We taxied to our hard stand and Technical Sergeant Lloyd Jennings was there with his crew to meet us. The ground guys were as excited as little kids, asking us all about the mission and how all "The Boomerang" systems worked? What a man this ground chief Jennings! He and his team were every bit as dedicated as the flying crew. We had a solid respect for those guys. Funny thing, though, we could never get Jennings to fly with us. He had a penchant for terra firma that we couldn't move. He took great pride in his work and in his crew, but he didn't care to check-out the airplane at altitude. The fact that these guys kept "The Boomerang" in the air despite a myriad of engine problems and a lack of replacement parts (Wright Cyclone engine strikes in Cincinatti, Ohio added to the problems) attested to their excellence.

"The Boomerang" group was uncharacteristically quiet as we trucked back to the debriefing building. (The debriefing facility was located near the mess hall and I gagged quietly as I detected the essence of green goat.) We were exhausted from our ordeal and lack of sleep. We found our assigned table. There was an officer standing by to pour out our mandatory 2 ounce shot of debriefing whiskey, and a G2 (intelligence) officer seated at the head of the table. The effects of the whiskey was immediate, and everybody felt like talking. Guess that was the idea.

We discussed the short bomb run, the high winds, and the problems of establishing a track for the AN/APQ 7. We were told that the winds aloft over Japan were some of the most erratic and strongest in the world. They generally were clocked at 100 to 175 miles an hour. G2 thought the head-on fighter attacks that we encountered could have been Kamikaze, and the fact that the other fighters were pacing us in to target instead of attacking meant that they believed we were equipped with the fearsome Central Fire Control turrets. "They obviously haven't discovered that you are flying without guns," smiled G2. Carl added his thoughts, "Let's hope it remains that way. We all know that the Japs will discover our secret as soon as they find a downed B-29B, and then there'll be trouble." G2 nodded in agreement, but added: "Let's hope the war will be over by then."

Each crew member was asked questions and we all delivered similar answers, but Sid Siegel our tail gunner always "improved" on all the stories a little. I suspected that Sid had an extra keen sense of drama, but then too, he had an unobstructed view from his tail spot. He could see more than most of us, especially at "six" (six o'clock position.) One thing for sure, there was never a dull moment with Sid around. He kept things interesting, and that was important.

We learned from our debriefing officer that First Lieutenant Davis had an engine fail and, undeterred, he completed a

three-engine bombing of a secondary target at Kuata. One Superfort commanded by First Lieutenant Whitted, ran low on fuel and landed at Iwo Jima. The first mission was a success in some ways but it fell short in others. There were no major injuries to personnel and only one B-29 sustained damage.

Sid Siegel told me recently that Lt. Davis was set down pretty good by the command for "endangering" his crew with that 3 engine bombing attack. Personally, I salute Davis for his dedication to duty.

We were all too tired to eat so we had a cigarette, and split for the barracks. Not a recommended health regimen for any kind of longevity. Nonstop diarrhea, coupled with our reduced desire to devour green Australian mutton, kept our weight down to starvation standards, and that didn't contribute to our well being either.

The air mattress that we used on our cots felt like heaven and the next ten hours was comatose time.

Reconnaissance photos of our first mission showed that 539,330 square feet or 30 percent of the Mitsubi refinery's roof area was damaged, but the refinery had not been knocked out, and another mission would be needed to complete the job. The erratic high velocity wind had been more of a problem since we had a short bomb run and it was difficult for Ginster to compute the corrections. The wind had also adversely effected the flight path of the bombs as they dropped.

Our Wing Commander General Armstrong decided that, in future bombings, he would send a B-29 to the target a few minutes before the main strike and broadcast wind drift,

Chapter Seven

NIGHT BIRDS OF PREY

MISSION #2

On 29/30 June, we flew our second mission to Japan's home islands. "The Boomerang" and 35 other 315 Wing B-29s attacked the Nippon Oil Company's plant at Kudamatsu. The Kudamatsu plant was one of the largest petroleum producers in Japan and located about 50 miles south of Hiroshima. Superforts from the 16th and 501st Groups flew in separate waves starting at 1811 hours using 45 second takeoff intervals. Our assigned bombing altitude once again was 10,000 feet. Four B-29s had engine problems and did not reach the target. For the second time the weather was overcast and ideal for radar bombing. One fighter dived at our nose, and a number of other fighters paced "The Boomerang" just out of range. Searchlights and flak were light. We used 500 pound General Purpose (GP) bombs. The Wing returned to Guam with a logged total mission flight time of 14 hours 45 minutes.

The bombing results for Empire Mission number 2 were similar to the first mission.

Photo-reconnaissance showed the Kudamatsu plant sustained only 5 percent damage with a 45,000 square foot refining unit and several small storage tanks and buildings totally destroyed. We missed on this one and Dick Ginster admitted that the I.P. was confusing. We had mistakenly dropped our bombs on the Haitachi Manufacturing Company, a locomotive factory located adjacent to the Kudamatsu plant. Other B-29s had followed suit and, and as it ended up, 40 percent of the locomotive plant was destroyed. Wrong target but not a bad damage percentage.

General Armstrong was not happy with our bombing results, and neither were we. The bomb runs were still too short, and Armstrong vowed to correct that situation once and for all. A longer single stream bomb run would allow the APQ-7 radar to align itself with the target, but it would also mean that each single file B-29 would be exposed to more enemy fire. Captain William C. Leasure, General Armstrong's staff navigator and Wing Tactical Plans Officer, developed a "compressibility" procedure to solve the problem. The key to his procedure was a method of aircraft cruise control the crews would use en route to Japan.

COMPRESSIBILITY

Captain William C. Leasure: "We planned that each aircraft would fly at 100' elevation intervals--using the same indicated airspeed for all, i.e., the first aircraft would fly at 2,000' from Guam to the point where the climb was started to achieve the bombing altitude prior to the IP; the second at 2,100' etc. The True Air Speed factor of 2 percent increase over indicated per 1,000 feet gave me the closure over a great distance that was necessary to compress the aircraft bombing times to perhaps 20 percent of the elapsed takeoff time outlined to match the needs."

The compressed stream of aircraft would cross the initial point at the planned altitude and maintain their compressed spacing to the target. Captain Leasure's procedure increased aircraft compressibility during the longer bombing run and minimized the flight crew exposure to enemy fire. Interestingly enough, commanders opposed the longer bombing run and compressibility plan because of factors unknown that might compromise the safety of their men. Gen. Armstrong listened to all of the objections, but supported the plan by stating, "That's the way it will be." Consequently we prepared to use Capt Leasure's procedure on the next Empire mission.

AIRCRAFT COMMANDER 1ST LIEUTENANT CARL SCHAHRER ON COMPRESSIBILITY

It all looked good on paper but this was Carl Schahrer's assessment of the Captain Leasure strategy: "Theoretically we were in a long string of aircraft about 30 seconds apart, but I recall many times going over the target, particularly if we were in clouds, there would be 6 aircraft within a quarter of a mile from me. In front of me, behind me, and on either side. So flying that distance trying to maintain an exact air speed just doesn't work. We'd always get a little shuffled up. However, as far as I know, no one ran into anybody. I still wonder how it happened that we didn't."

LIVE ENTERTAINMENT

The Army Air Corps engineers built two outside theaters, El Gecko, and The Target which provided live entertainment for the crews. "This Is The Army Show" was playing at the El Gecko and "The Boomerang" crew was aboard. The performing military troupe was from Stateside, and they were terrific. I was dumbfounded to discover that Gene Berg, a stateside friend, was the featured acrobatic dancer in the troupe. Gene and I first met at Santa Monica California's famous Muscle Beach. We and a number of other draftees hung out there while waiting for Uncle Sam's orders. Famous "Mr. America" weight lifters Vic and Armand Tanny held court at "Muscle", and film stars such as Peter Lawford, were among the regulars. I loved to run the beach and body surf while Gene generally practiced acrobatic floor exercises and adagio dancing on the Muscle Beach outdoor stage.

I hurried back stage after the show and found Gene. He looked at me in total disbelief for a moment, and then we put our arms around one another. "Jim, what the heck are you doing here?" "Well", I said, "the Air Corps assigned me to Guam, and asked me to tour Japanese targets in a B-29. What about yourself?" Gene grinned, "Special Services thought I should tour the islands as an acrobatic dancer." Gene added, "I think I might have the best deal." We reminisced about Muscle Beach and agreed that our meeting in Guam was against all odds of probability. Gene was attached to the Army Specialist Corps Special Services. He had wanted to join the Air Corps in the worst way, but he had injured an eye during his teen years and he couldn't qualify. I told Gene where I had been sitting during the show. Curiously enough, he told me that his attention had been drawn to that spot. He

didn't recognize me from the stage, but he said that an overhead light made my eyes reflect like a cat's. That added even more intrigue to our unlikely meeting. I jokingly invited Gene to join us on our next mission over the Empire; he smiled and excused himself, explaining that he and his troupe had to catch a Military Air Transport Aircraft for Iwo Jima early next morning. We said good bye and wished one another the best. The performers in "This Is The Army Show" had definitely lifted our morale, which was living proof that Gene and the cast were making a positive difference in the war. The show illustrated the importance of Special Services in the theatre of combat.

Gene Berg later became a big star in Hollywood and he underwent a small name change: "Gene Nelson!" I had one more no-odds encounter with him after the war. I was auditioning for a singing role in a Hollywood Show, Lend an Ear. (Gene was a member of the cast.)

MISSION #3

"The Boomerang" crew was scheduled to fly mission #3 on 2/3 July. The target was the Maruzen Oil Refinery at Shimotsu/Wakayama located 266 miles south of Tokyo and 40 miles from Kobe Osaka. The plant was a major producer of aviation gasoline, lube oil, ordinary gasoline, and fuel oil. It also provided extensive oil storage facilities for the Japanese Navy.

General Curtis LeMay made an appearance at this briefing, and his appearance left a lasting impression on me. He took center stage while mashing his ever present cigar in his bulldog-like jaws. He took the cigar out of his mouth

just long enough to catch us with a "trap block". The General complimented us for a good job, and when we relaxed a little, he slammed us: "But it's not good enough. We'll either get better results or we'll take you down to a altitude where you can see your target close up. You'll go over with flaps and gear down if need be." Then he had guts enough to wish us good luck. LeMay jammed the cigar back in his face and strode off. He was respected as a great military man, but he certainly did not project a lovable charisma. All of us fully believed that the 315th was a championship team, and we knew that we'd soon achieve the bombing success that the General demanded.

I had taken my tunnel battle position before the Shimotsu I. P. and was snugly sardined in place by the time we began the bomb run. The weather was ideal with undercast and overcast skies hampering the enemy's heavy searchlight and flak defenses. I was back in my ringside seat on the bomb run. At the beginning I was feeling pretty secure as we were flying in thick clouds. I couldn't see any pacing fighters and so everything was going well. Then it happened! A pattern of bursts exploded on the starboard side next to my astrodome position. The bursts were so close that I ducked in a reflex action, I could feel the concussion of the exploding bursts of flak and I could hear the fall-out raining down on the Plexi-glas astrodome that enclosed my head. I knew that we were being coned by German automatic radar weapons. I called to Carl and told him that flak was exploding close to my station. Carl ordered Henry and Leff to dispense more radar chaff. Carl pushed his throttles forward and I saw the bursts moving back and biting at our tail. We dropped our ten ton bomb load and "The Boomerang" ballooned upward as she gave up the weight. Soon we were out of the action--thank God.

CARL SCHAHRER YEARS LATER

"I do recall the night we bombed the oil refinery at Shimotsu/Wakayama which is close to Kobe. We drove in about 15,000 feet from the I.P. into the target. We were in the clouds. I could feel a chunk, chunk, chunk, chunk. They had a German antiaircraft gun that was radar directed. "One thing for sure, no one wanted to challenge the German antiaircraft radar systems again. It takes just one well placed flak burst to take you off the active roster, and the Japs had the range that night.

Col Hubbard's crew had called back wind data this time and we were much better prepared to attack our target. There was a lot of smoke and turbulence from the thermals and we figured that we'd laid in the 500 pounders pretty good.

Aircraft compressibility was good over the target, but reconnaissance showed that we had mixed results on Maruzen. Although we were somewhat disappointed, we knew that we were getting closer to the bull's eye.

Col Hubbard, the 501st Group commanding officer, took care of the clean up on Maruzen three days later, July 6/7. On that mission Hubbard led a force of 60 Superforts. Col Gurney led the 16th Bomb Group's element of 31 B-29s. As the B-29s approached Japan at 10,000/11,000 feet, 34 enemy fighters jumped them and made several attempts to ram the Superforts. Col Hubbard led and sent back wind and other pertinent data to the other 29s. Photo analysis demonstrated that Maruzen was completely destroyed. Gen LeMay sent a congratulatory message to the 315th., "I have just reviewed the post-strike photography of your strike on target 1764, The Maruzen Oil Refinery at Shimotsu, the night of 6/7 July. With a half-wing effort you achieved ninety-five percent destruction, definitely establishing the ability of your crews to hit and destroy precision targets at night using the AN/APQ-7 synchronous radar bombing system. This performance is the most successful radar bombing of the Command to date. Congratulations to you and your men."

MISSION #4

"The Boomerang" missed the Maruzen mission but we got back into some big action on 9/10 July. This would be our 4th trip over the Empire. We were ordered to re-bomb the Utsube River Oil Refinery at Yokkaichi 200 miles south of Tokyo. Yokkaichi had been our first bombing mission and reconnaissance had sighted meager results so we were ordered back to complete the job. 64 Birds were launched from Northwest at 30 second intervals.

I was surveying things through the astrodome when I felt something move on my right forearm. I looked down cautiously and my eyes riveted on a huge rat that was looking up at me with cocked head curiosity. The rodent was parked between my elbow and wrist and completely took up all that space. It looked to be about the size of an alley cat. I could feel sweat explode out of my pores. I didn't want to antagonize the creature in those close quarters and lose part of my face. I ever so gently pressed my hand mike switch, and in a measured guttural sound I called to Tony, "Tony there is a rat on my arm." Tony's immediate response was uncharacteristic and charged with disbelief: "Bullshit." Whatever I said to Tony in the next transmission moved him. Tony was a long, lanky type. He grabbed a K-2 Signal Light, took one long step and illuminated me and the rat. Tony, being an emotional fellow, jumped back and yelled out the information I had just given him, "Oh my God there's a rat on your arm." Tony gave ground and collapsed back into his navigator's station. The light and Tony's wild movement was enough to scare the skinny tail. He jumped through the space between my cramped shoulder and neck and high tailed it down the tunnel. Tony, in his shock, had not turned the light off, and three guys yelled at the same time, "Kill the light Tony!" I just looked for fighters and took deep breaths until my heart rate came back down. Carl yelled fighters at 12 O'clock. I saw one of them dive for the nose spitting tracers, and I froze until I knew he was clear. There were more fighters pacing us just out of range, and so once again it appeared that the Japs had not yet discovered that our B-29s had been stripped of armament.

Another long ride back to Northwest Field. We shut our engines down and exited by way of the nose wheel ladder. I related the rat caper story to Staff Sergeant Jennings. Floyd scratched his head, "How the hell do you find a rat in this bird? Too many places for em' to hide. Just hope to hell that he doesn't start chewin' up insulation and screwin' up systems." Jennings' response wasn't much consolation.

We'd encountered more fighters in the target area than usual, and one crew, commanded by First Lieutenant Maurer,

exchanged fire with one. Flak was moderate and four aircraft suffered minor battle damage. Sixty-one Superforts reached the primary target and dropped 469 tons of GP bombs on Utsube. Aircraft compressibility was excellent with 50 aircraft crossing the target in 33 minutes. One aircraft crashed and burned on the runway after its landing gear collapsed on landing. Photo reconnaissance showed the raid successfully knocked the plant out of operation and perhaps crippled it beyond repair. Now "The Boomerang" crew was beginning to smile a little.

We learned that another operational loss occurred the night of our Yokkaichi raid. A B-29 had headed for Truk, and crashed shortly after takeoff from Northwest. The LCI (landing craft infantry) patrolling the coastline saw the aircraft explode. Personnel at Northwest heard a secondary explosion and saw a huge fireball light up the night sky. Air-sea rescue units searched the area thoroughly, but no survivors were found. A piece of material containing the plane number was recovered which identified the crashed plane. 1 Mae West, 1 glove, and 4 green oxygen bottles were identified as accessories of the plane. It was thought that an engine malfunction caused the crash.

THE 3350 WRIGHT CYCLONE AND LABOR STRIKES

The 3350 engine was known for swallowing valves. It was a tough engine to trouble-shoot because the problems and the indications were not consistent. The Wright Cyclone 3350 engines that powered our B-29 were far better than those on the aircraft used in training, but they still had a lot of valve problems. According to one

Undergoing repairs

The Wright R-3350

Dale Stoner, Asst. Crew Chief for "Late Date", is dwarfed by the B-29B tail

Even something as serious as engine work could generate a few laughs

maintenance man, "We pulled one 29 out of the taxi line because we could hear the familiar loud tapping noise as it went by. The engineer had no indication of a problem, and the pilot was furious because he wanted to make the mission. We soon found the problem--zero compression on one cylinder, which meant a cylinder change."

When the maintenance crews first arrived on Guam, they were authorized to change a maximum of three cylinders on an engine. However, in the summer of 1945 they received a TWX authorizing them to change all 18 cylinders, if necessary, because labor strikes in the U.S. had pinched off the flow of replacement engines to the Pacific Theatre. This TWX dramatically increased the work load of the 315th's already over worked maintenance crews. (It has always been my view that some crashes and loss of life occurred because of the Ohio Wright/Cyclone engine strikes ordered by labor unions.)

MISSION ABORTED

On 12 July the field briefing order directed us to strike the Kawasaki Petroleum Center near Tokyo. This would be mission number 5. There were four separate, but adjacent companies: Standard Oil, Rising Sun Oil, Nippon Oil, and Mitsui Products. The target was protected by heavy antiaircraft defenses, and we were eager to get in on the action. Everyone had pre-flighted and pulled four prop blades through. We were in place at our individual stations waiting for engine start. Hank started number 3 and reported, "Engine running normally." The procedure continued until all four engines were running. Then Hank advanced the

number 1 engine to 2200 RPM for a magneto check. Hank called out, "Right-- Both, Left-- Both". Readings were normal until he got to number 3. Carl got on the 'horn', "Hold everything, we've got a 65 RPM mag drop on 3." I walked up to the engineers station to look at things myself. Sure enough number three was dropping over 65 RPM. Hank added power and leaned it out in an attempt to clear any fouled plugs. It didn't work. Carl turned around and yelled back to Hank, "If you want to ground the airplane, give me the word." Hank tried to clear the engine by adding power and leaning it out, but with negative results. He called back to Carl, "Something's wrong, and I can't fix it. We'll have to scrub." That was it. Hank reluctantly shut down and a disappointed crew began gathering up gear. Although we had heard that Kawasaki was a dangerous target, we were "bummed" out because we wouldn't be there to help our teammates.

I turned on Hank and exploded, "I think scrubbing for a mag drop is pure chicken." Hank looked at me cooly like a Grizzly might look at a cub who had just nipped him. He wasn't going to fight me over the incident, but he wanted me to know that I was out of line. "We're allowed an RPM drop of 50 Max. If it had been 55, that would've been okay, but a 65 RPM drop can mean trouble out there." I was still unhappy, and I just stormed away. I had as many fears as the next guy, but I was frustrated because we wouldn't be there to do our part. All of us in the 315th were team players. We all felt the same way about being grounded; it was like sitting on the bench during a big grudge game--worse--we couldn't even watch the game. Hank had shown the maturity to separate emotion from the safety of the crew, and that said a lot about his character. I cooled down after a bit and apologized to him. We both grinned knowingly and buried the hatchet.

HANK GORDER ON THE SCRUBBED MISSION

Yeasr later Hank reminded me why he had scrubbed the mission: "Jim do you remember the time I called a mission off? The whole crew pitched in pulling cowling, changing plugs etc. After that our mag drop was still borderline and we were late. We would have been tail end Charlie. Carl told me I was the boss and I called the mission because we had an on going problem with fuel consumption and back firing. When on high power, I hardly dared take my four fingers off the 4 throttles."

After reading Hank's explanation I felt even worse about jumping on him that afternoon. I really believe that the scrub was meant to be, and that it saved our back sides. I remember the guys from the other crews coming back into the barracks after the mission. They were somber and pale as zombis. No jokes this time. Several of the crew members agreed that the mission was a full-fledged nightmare. One of them got to the bottom line, "The Japs threw up everything they had. We didn't think we'd make it back."

There were two B-29s that failed to return. First Lieutenant Milford Berry's B-29 developed three runaway propellers, and they were forced to ditch at sea approximately 125 miles north of Guam in daylight. At least five men of Crew 28 were known to have bailed out before the crash. Of these, three were picked up alive by surface rescue vessels, one was found dead, and the fifth man was never located.

The other five men went down with their Superfort. That unfortunate accident re-enforced my position that ditching in the ocean or bailing out over water was equally hazardous to one's health--especially at night. In the second incident, First Lieutenant James C. Crim's crew completed their bombing run but failed to return to Northwest Field. Lt. Crim's and his crew were listed as missing, and no word was ever received from them. It was speculated that they were shot down shortly after they had released their bombs.

The Kawasaki strike was successful; the target was virtually destroyed. All the refinery units were damaged or destroyed, and there was also extensive damage done to the adjacent warehouse buildings and a crude oil tank farm. 341,000 barrels, or 85 percent of the original crude oil tank capacity (400,000 barrels) destroyed or damaged; 49,300 barrels or approximately 70 percent of the original intermediate oil tank capacity and 71,300 barrels or approximately 15 percent of the original refined oil tank capacity (115,700 barrels) destroyed or damaged; 2 oil bunkering piers on the south side of the refinery destroyed.

THE AN/APQ-7 MAINTENANCE TRAINER

A radar operator training program was initiated to correct deficiencies that had become evident in the first Empire missions. The major problem areas noted included wind drift corrections for the bomb run, coordination between radar operators and bombardiers, and radar identification of landfall points. Training classes that taught radar film analysis were started to correct these problems, and to improve mission planning. A mock-up of the AN/APQ-7 was built so that radar operators could practice in flight maintenance procedures. Early radar operators were poorly trained, but those in the 315th had the best training of all. Our radar operators had to spend hours going over pre-briefing material, including scope-reconnaissance photos of the target, and they had to prove they could draw the details of the target from memory. The radar training program was designed to increase the radar bombing accuracy of the crews already in combat, and as a means to share their experiences with the newly arrived crews.

THE AN/APG-15 TAIL TURRET SYSTEM PROBLEM

As previously established, our total fire power was integrated in a tail turret which was equipped with two 50 caliber machine guns, and a 20 millimeter cannon. It was reported in early July that the AN/APG-15 radar directed tail turret system was hampered with serious malfunctions. The gunners were reporting that they were forced to recalibrate the APG-15 in flight even though maintenance personnel had calibrated the system perfectly prior to takeoff. In addition the AN/APG-15 frequently locked on to a target without searching or would search but refuse to lock on to a target. Our only fragile line of defense was in jeopardy. In the interim our constant hope was that the Japs would continue to believe we carried the deadly Central Fire Control armament. On Friday 13 July 1945, the Wing initiated Special Project EPR No. 1 to solve the AN/APG-15 problem. Major William G. Pierce was assigned as director to accomplish the project's purpose.

UNITED STATES ARMY STRATEGIC AIR FORCE, PACIFIC OCEAN AREA (USASAFPOA), ESTABLISHED ON GUAM TO COORDINATE PRE-INVASION OPERATIONS WITH THE EIGHTH AIR FORCE

Also in July there were major changes to the organizational and command structure for strategic forces operating in the Pacific. With the end of the war in Europe, the Eighth Air Force was being converted to very heavy bombardment operations and scheduled to deploy to Okinawa. As a result, the United States Army Strategic Air Force (USASTAF) of the Pacific was established at Guam on 5 July to control and coordinate the pre-invasion combat operations of the Twentieth Air force and the redeploying Eighth Air Force. On 16 July, the XXI Bomber Command officially became known as the Twentieth Air Force and headquartered at Guam with five B-29 wings, the 509th Composite Group (part of the 313th Wing), the Seventh Fighter Command, and the Guam Air Depot under its command. So the USASTAF became the guiding force for the final assault on Japan with the Twentieth Air force carrying the load until the Eighth Air Force became operational.

JAPANESE DISCOVERED IN CHOW LINE

Japanese soldiers had been reported in the Northwest Field area, and one showed up in G. I. clothes in our chow line with his cap pulled low over his face. Guess he thought he wouldn't be recognized but as you might guess, he stood out like a "skunk at a lawn party" and was taken into custody. The 315th's military police sent out a patrol to search for Japanese soldiers on 16 July. Six days earlier, security guards patrolling the jungle area east of Northwest Field had found evidence of recent Japanese habitation. A patrol was organized and sent into the designated sector. On the first day they killed four Japanese soldiers and wounded another who later died. Two more Japanese were killed during the following 48 hours. Intelligence figured that there were more Japanese on the island, and two weapons carriers equipped with 50 caliber machine guns were used to guard against reprisal action.

MISSION #5

19 July "The Boomerang" was ordered to bomb the Nippon Oil Refinery at Amagasaki, in the Kobe Osaka area. This would be only mission number #5 for us since we were forced to scrub our previous mission.

We were part of a force of 83 B-29s that crossed the target in 34 minutes. Once again there were fighter passes, pacing fighters and searchlights. I had my loge seat in the balcony and I saw a B-29 coned in searchlights. He was executing every maneuver thinkable, but he couldn't shake the lights. The bird looked like a fish trying to run and shake free. I could see flak exploding closer and closer to the trapped 29, and I felt sick. Our bomb doors had been open since the I.P. and we dropped our pay load. The B-29 trapped in the search lights suddenly disappeared. I figured the airplane took a hit and blew up.

We climbed out of the target area and turned to a heading that would take us back to Northwest Field. The stress of 14-hour missions was beginning to show; this B-29 combat life style was taking a toll on our young bodies. I had lost a lot of weight and so had many others. Diarrhea was the big problem. We were supposed to dip our mess kits into a barrel of boiling water to sterilize them after we ate, but the barrels of water were often not hot enough to sterilize the remnants of over-aged goat. That situation surely contributed to the gastrointestinal difficulties. Even though we were suffering mentally and physically, our morale was intact. We were still tightly bound together by our commitment to defeat the Japs and end the war.

MISSION #6

On 22/23 July "The Boomerang" and 81 other 315th aircraft were ordered to the Ube Coal Liquefaction Company. This mission was to be "The Boomerang"'s 6th mission. Ube was a leading producer of synthetic oil and a high priority target in a Japanese petroleum industry that had been crippled by the U. S. naval blockade. Seventy four B-29Bs bombed the primary from 12,000 feet to 13,000 feet. Four other aircraft struck targets of opportunity due to radar malfunction. All aircraft returned safely with only four receiving minor flak damage. 19 crews landed in Iwo on the way back. We damaged 31 structures at the plant, but most of the refinery was still operating. We were destined to fly one more mission to Ube, and this time the mission would be recorded as one of the most unique in all of history.

Nerves were getting raw from the accumulated stress of the all night missions. Tony and I lost it shortly after our return from the Ube mission. We were hauling equipment to the crew trucks and Tony began chewing me out for

B-29Bs, Northwest Field

137

something I did or did not do. He became so exercised at one point that he called me Sergeant instead of Jimmie or Smitty. The formality in this case was to remind me that I was outranked, and I ended my rather spirited rebuttal by addressing Tony, in turn, by his rank. The way it came off was funny enough to crack us both up.

Tony was a super navigator, a very talented and exceptional person. He was a class act all the way, and I respected him. Tony and I both were emotional types, and the small disagreement had to be chalked up to exhaustion and stress. We never exchanged another unkind word, and it has to be said that Tony's dedication to his job as navigator contributed greatly to the crew's survival.

I had trouble getting to sleep that morning. Even though my encounter with Tony was quite benign, it brought back those unpleasant memories of the Santa Ana debacle, and the Communication Cadet snafu at Sioux Falls. I thought about the high grade average that I had maintained in Creighton, only to get squeezed out at Santa Ana when they closed down classification. I could never forget the heartbreak of getting washed out, and then there was the Communication Cadet snafu at Sioux Falls following my all out effort to graduate in the top ten percent. I remembered the Air Corps promise that the top 10 "percenters" would be sent to Communication Cadets and wind up with a commission, but of course they changed that regulation just as I completed my courses and, instead of being sent to Communication Cadets, I was ordered to B-29s. Then there was that bull about we B-29 guys being promoted to the special rank of "Flight Officer" and receiving the same pay as a ground

Captain. Despite all of the promises, I flew my first missions over Japan as a Corporal and eventually ended up a buck Sergeant. I was pretty much disillusioned with the military but, on the other side, they had put me with top people in the world's greatest bomber; that took some of the sting off. Still the frustration was there.

Many times I secretly slipped down to the hardstand, climbed up into Carl's left seat and pretended that I was the aircraft commander. After the war I obtained a flying license and that made up for a whole bunch of disappointment that I had experienced in the service.

"The Boomerang" crew needed some rest and recuperation and by the grace of a mechanical problem, we drew a "by" on the next scheduled trip to Japan.

While "The Boomerang" crew sacked out, the 315th flew their 10th Empire mission on 25/26 July. Of the 85 aircraft launched on the mission, 7 aborted prior to the target. The Japanese took advantage of the clear night and maximized their anti-aircraft fire and fighter defenses. One B-29, commanded by a Capt. Dillingham, was hit and exploded in midair. 34 percent target damage was the figure given by reconnaissance.

I speculated that the remains of Captain Dillingham's airplane would provide one more opportunity for the Japanese to discover that we had been stripped of our major firepower. We couldn't stretch our luck forever, and just as soon as the Japs found out... I really didn't want to think about it.

I knew that the ground crews would have "The Boomerang" airworthy for the next scheduled mission. The 315th's ground support system did a remarkable job in restoring ailing birds quickly and putting them back into the fight.

B-29B MAINTENANCE

The Electronics Section achieved a 96 percent effectiveness rate for the AN/APQ-7 radar equipment (the AN/APQ-13 reached 92 per cent) while the aerial photo section personnel kept the 0-5 radarscope cameras operational. Maintenance work stands and towing tugs were in short supply so the engineering sections built their own stands and used jeeps to tow equipment. The Armament and Ordnance Sections completed all bomb loading requirements on schedule despite shortages in B-7 bomb shackles and C-6 bomb hoists. The flight-line maintenance crews kept the aircraft fueled and completed the 50, 100, and 200 hour inspections. All the 315th ground support personnel deserved a share of the credit for the wing's outstanding record during the first 10 Empire missions with 618 aircraft launched out of 636 scheduled.

MISSION #7

On 28/29 July, we of "The Boomerang" were back in the saddle to fly our seventh mission against the Nippon Oil Refinery at Shimotsu. This was a return trip. The first time, we bombed the Shimotsu area was 2/3 July, and our designated target then was the Maruzen Refinery.

The target was an important refiner of crude oil with large and modern facilities and good shipping and rail connections.

DICK MARSHALL BOMBARDIER

Dick Marshall's account: "We were in real heavy weather on the way up to the Empire that night. There was a lot of cloud cover and the turbulence within those clouds was frightening. We were about two hours from the coast line, flying at 10,000 feet when all of a sudden the turbulence dropped us 2000 feet just that quick. I looked out to see if we had any wings left on the plane. The winds were bouncing us around like a feather in front of a fan. The wings were flapping up and down like a sea gull taking off. All the time I was wondering low long they could take this punishment, when everything started settling down except our stomachs. Carl started to regain his altitude and we were glad that was over. As we were on our bomb run, we were getting some flak bursting below us and I looked up just momentarily from the bombsight to see this Jap Fighter pass directly across our path. I could have reached out and touched his wing tip. I don't believe he saw us any more than we saw him, other wise he would have fired upon us. It was bombs away and I said to Carl, 'Let's get the hell out of here." According to Murphy's Law, if anything can go wrong, it will. This was our mission for getting shook up and putting Murphy's Law into practice..."

CARL SCHAHRER AIRCRAFT COMMANDER

Carl described the front this way: "We went through a violent front. It was so rough: a 50 pound can of emergency ration was lashed down with 1/2 inch rope and the lurching broke the rope leaving the can pounding around in the section with the two scanners. The air was so rough that it took us about 20 minutes to penetrate and go through. The only thing

Walt and I could do was hold the airplane level and let it go with the up and down drafts. We'd fall in a down draft for 2000 feet, and it took about 30 seconds to do it. Then an up draft would take us back 2000 feet. It was as rough as it could be."

We climbed out of the target area, and turned to a heading that would take us back to Northwest Field. Thirty minutes later we were cruising at 11,000 feet and being thrown around by the rough air when a tremendous jolt caused a rippling shudder from nose to tail. Carl checked his controls and yelled into the interphone, "Anyone see a Kamikazi or anything hit the airplane?" Carl rechecked his controls and everything seemed to be normal. No one relaxed; we figured that an impact like this one must have damaged the airplane somewhere. I flipped on the light switch in the forward bomb bay to give that a look, and what I saw momentarily suspended my mental processes. There was a 500 pound bomb rolling back and forth in the bottom of the bay. The bomb had apparently hung up when the others were released, and then finally dropped from its mooring into the closed bomb bay. The bomb had pulled away from the safety wires that ran through the nose and tail fuse so the arming props were free to spin. The bomb bay doors had been damaged when the bomb fell, and they wouldn't close properly. The gap created by the damaged doors allowed a stream of air to course over the bomb, spinning the arming propellers. The bomb was bumping around and as soon as an arming propeller came off, we'd be blown higher than Mars. I called Carl on the interphone and grimly spelled out the situation in measured speech. I didn't figure there would be time to repeat it; I knew that I had to explain the emergency in such a way that there could be no misinterpretation.

Dick monitored my call and flicked his bomb bay door release switch. The doors wouldn't budge. (One emergency handle for opening the bomb bay doors was located at Carl's A/C control stand, and another emergency release valve was located on the starboard side of the forward bomb bay.) Carl pulled his emergency handle--nothing. Hank had depressurized so that we could access the bomb bay pressure door. Tony was waving his arm like a windmill and yelling at Dick Marshall, "There's a bomb in the bomb bay. It's going to explode." I unlatched the bomb bay pressure door, and climbed into the bomb bay. I stood on the cat walk, grabbed a hand hold with my left hand and turned the red knurled emergency valve wheel with my right. Nothing happened. The damaged doors were hanging up on one another. I began to climb back into the radio station, and Dick was there waiting to get into the bomb bay. He quickly stepped through the bomb bay access onto the cat walk and tried the emergency valve control himself--with the same results that I had experienced. The bent, damaged doors wouldn't budge. The props on the bomb were spinning faster and starting to wobble. I knew that one would come off any second and arm the bomb. The 500 pounder was still being jostled back and forth by the turbulence, and once armed, it would have to explode.

The strangest thing: A very peaceful feeling came over me. I knew I was going to die. I also knew that I'd never hear the bomb explode. There would be no pain--I had accepted the inevitable and I was at peace. Dick could just reach the upper part of the starboard bay door with his right foot. He turned the emergency valve to the release position once again, grabbed a hand hold with his left hand and began kicking the bomb bay door with all his might. All of a sudden the doors banged open and the bomb dropped. Dick reached to the right of the emergency release knob and pulled the emergency handle that closed the doors again. I steadied him as he spilled back inside my radio position. There was a moment of shivering silence, and then we all began applauding our deliverance. Between the hellish storm that tried to devour me and my Fairmont crew en route to Puerto Rico, and this hung-up 500 pound bomb, I had used up a lot of luck—a lot of luck.

The trip back to Northwest Field was without incident. We related the story to the briefing G2 officer. He smiled, scratched his head and said, "There was a U.S. sub positioned along your course that reported a depth charge at 0100 hours. It shook up the sub but fortunately no one was hurt. I just wonder..." We all agreed— it could have been our 500 pounder.

JOHN WALTERSHAUSEN PILOT

Many years after the incident I received a letter from John Waltershausen, our pilot: "I am handling the estate of a fellow who was a navigator on a B-29 flying out of India and China before they moved them all to the Pacific. His widow told me that on one of their flights all the bombs were dropped except one which hung up and dropped on the bomb bay doors. Her husband went out in the bay and opened the doors and dropped the bomb. He received a medal for his bravery. Dick Marshall did the same thing but no medal."

We scored heavily on the Shimotsu target. Reconnaissance photos showed that we would not be required to return to this place. The target was almost completely destroyed. 927,000 barrels of the 1,246,000 barrel capacity were damaged while the 1,274,100 cubic foot gasometer capacity was nearly destroyed. Sixty nine percent of the 21,254 square foot area was destroyed. The target was beyond repair. Target photo-reconnaissance also showed 60 percent of the Wings crews placed their bomb salvo centers within 1,000 feet of the aiming point. Now we were achieving the results of which we knew we were capable.

THE RUNAWAY PROP ON MISSION #8

On 1/2 August it was a multi-strike mission against three of the previously bombed targets and "The Boomerang" was ordered to participate. The mission plan split the wing's B-29s into two forces to strike three adjacent targets in the heavily defended Kawasaki area south of Tokyo. One force was to attack the Kawasaki Petroleum center previously raided on 12 July. The other force would concentrate on the Hayama and Mitsubishi Oil Refineries partially destroyed on the 25 July Empire mission. Since these facilities had already claimed 315th aircraft and lives, the flight crews were apprehensive but eager to knock them out.

This mission would be #8 for "The Boomerang". We were well into our takeoff run, and lifting off when number three engine began running away. I heard Carl and Hank confirm the runaway on the interphone. We were potentially in big trouble. Carl initiated the procedures he had long ago memorized from the Handbook of Flight Operating Instructions:

(1) If a runaway propeller occurs during takeoff, throttle back the engine of the propeller affected to below 2800 RPM. This provides as much thrust as possible from the runaway propeller during takeoff. The propeller will be dragging at 150 MPH, IAS (indicated air speed). If the propeller is wind milling, keep down the RPM by intermittently pushing in and pulling out the feathering button. (The button has to be pulled out, otherwise it will not pop out until the propeller is completely feathered.) Sometimes the governor will control the propeller after the feathering button is used to bring down RPM. It is possible that the propeller will govern at 2400 RPM and not a high RPM as the governor setting is reduced and RPM lowered as above. Avoid applying sudden power to the engine if the above procedure is successful. Check engine oil pressures and temperatures and correct if necessary or possible.

(2) If the propeller cannot be made to govern, it should be feathered as soon as practical. This is very important when the hydraulic oil feathering system is installed, since feathering is impossible once all the oil is gone. Do not use the feathering button over three (3) times to control the propeller intermittently.

(3) If the propeller cannot be governed or feathered it will be necessary to throttle back and reduce airspeed to a point where the wind milling RPM will not exceed allowable limits. Handle the throttles carefully and land as soon as possible.

We were carrying a full bomb load on takeoff and to make things worse, Carl had to reduce RPM's on the runaway, number three. We lifted without any safety net of extra air speed. Carl pushed the nose over the cliff and down to the water to get our normal speed back and to cool off the engines. We inched back to altitude with Carl working with Hank on procedures. Number three would not govern or feather so Carl was obliged to pull back power even further. Runaway props were known to centrifugally explode and slice through a nose section so we were full into a serious emergency. Carl and John finally got the engine feathered and used VHF radio frequency to contact ground. We were told to jettison our bombs on the runway of our old training target Rota, 32 miles northeast of Guam. I figured the Japs had probably just finished repairing the runway damage from our first training mission, and now we would bomb them back to square one again.

TONY COSOLA RECALLS THE RUNAWAY PROP

"Just about the time we got off and got our gear and flaps up we lost an engine. The prop ran away on us. Carl and Johnny Waltershausen finally brought it under control and got it feathered up. They told us to go over to that little Island of Rota, dump our load of bombs on the runway to lighten up our fuel load, and then we'd come on in and land when the other airplanes had taken off. We went over there and did that. We got over Rota, and Dick Marshall salvoed our bombs on the runway. Something fouled up because only ten bombs went away in each bomb bay out of the twenty in each bomb bay; all the bombs on the left side of the airplane, the port side both front and rear bomb bays, stayed there. One of the scanners, Hank Carlson or Hank Leffler, and I went out in that bomb bay and wedged in behind those bomb racks, and each with a big screw driver; we pried loose the release and kicked those bombs out of the bomb bay and dropped them. For me around that age of almost 22, that was high adventure."

We all sweated out our approach and landing since the tendency would be to turn-in towards the feathered engine, and the bird was hard enough to hold on track during normal operation (no hydraulic assist). Mr. Reliable made a perfect landing and we made the most out of what proved to be a short vacation.

In the meantime Colonel William A. Miller, wing Deputy Chief of Staff, flew with First Lieutenant Larson's crew, 502nd Bomb Group, and led the entire wing on the Kawasaki multi-strike mission. The weather in the target area ranged from clear to 9/10 thin overcast. Two enemy fighters attached First Lieutenant Ethier's aircraft. An estimated 130 blue and green searchlights blanketed the skies, and antiaircraft fire was medium to heavy. Two aircraft sustained heavy flak damage while 13 others received minor damage. One plane, H-5, commanded by Captain Woida, received major damage. The number one engine was shot out, fuel cells and gas lines were damaged, and other damage was done to the bomb bay doors, wing, and other surfaces of the plane. It landed on Iwo Jima. Captain Woida's aircraft was one of five forced to land at Iwo with heavy battle damage or engine trouble. The crews reported that the Kawasaki Petroleum Center and Hayam-Mitsubishi refineries were burning fiercely.

The 315th's raid on the Kawasaki area was part of the largest single bombing efforts by the 20th Air Force dropping 1,025 tons of bombs on their targets. Three Kawasaki plants were rendered useless to the enemy.

"The Boomerang" was back to fly a mission to Ube August 5/6. It would become one of the most unique and significant missions of all time.

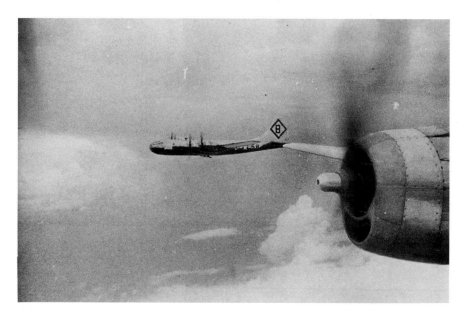

Chapter Eight

UBE AND THE ATOMIC CONNECTION

On July 17, 1945, President Harry S. Truman, British Prime Minister Winston Churchill, Russian Premier Joseph Stalin, and their staffs began a historic conference at Potsdam, Germany. The goal of the conference was to settle the European post-war issues and to share plans for Japan's defeat. Truman had come to the conference with a draft of an ultimatum calling upon the Japanese to surrender. Stalin could not sign the document since Russia was still at peace with Japan. Churchill and President Truman agreed that Chiang Kai-shek should be asked to join in the issuance of the document and that China should be listed as one of the sponsoring governments.

At nine-twenty on the night of July 26 Truman issued the joint proclamation from Berlin. This was the ultimatum that became known as the Potsdam Declaration. President Truman directed the Office of War Information in Washington to begin immediately to get the message to the Japanese people in every possible way.

POTSDAM DECLARATION BY HEADS OF GOVERNMENTS, UNITED STATES, UNITED KINGDOM, AND CHINA

"(1) We—the President of the United States, the president of the National Government of the Republic of China, and the Prime Minister of Great Britain, representing the hundreds of millions of our countrymen, have conferred and agree that Japan shall be given an opportunity to end this war.

"(2) The prodigious land, sea and air forces of the United States, the British Empire and of China, many times reinforced by their armies and air fleets from the west, are poised to strike the final blows upon Japan. This military power is sustained and inspired by the determination of all the Allied Nations to prosecute the war against Japan until she ceases to resist.

"(3) The result of the futile and senseless German resistance to the might of the aroused free peoples of the world stands forth in awful clarity as an example to the people of Japan. The might that now converges on Japan is immeasurably greater than that which, when applied to the resisting Nazis, necessarily laid waste to the lands, the industry and method of life of the whole German people. The full application of our military power backed by our resolve will mean the inevitable and complete destruction of the Japanese armed forces and just as inevitably the utter devastation of the Japanese homeland.

"(4) The time has come for Japan to decide whether she will continue to be controlled by those self-willed militaristic advisers whose unintelligent calculations have brought the Empire of Japan to the threshold of annihilation or whether she will follow the path of reason.

"(5) Following are our terms. We shall not deviate from them. There are no alternatives. We shall brook no delay.

"(6) There must be eliminated for all time the authority and influence of those who have deceived and misled the people of Japan into embarking on world conquest, for we insist that a new order of peace, security and justice will be impossible until irresponsible militarism is driven from the world.

"(7) Until such a new order is established and until there is convincing proof that Japan's war-making power is destroyed, points in Japanese territory to be designated by the Allies shall be occupied to secure the achievement of the basic objectives we are here setting forth.

"(8) The terms of the Cairo Declaration shall be carried out and Japanese sovereignty shall be limited to the islands of Honshu, Hokkaido, Kyushu, Shikoku and such minor islands as we determine.

"(9) The Japanese military forces, after being completely disarmed, shall be permitted to return to their homes with the opportunity to lead peaceful and productive lives.

"(10) We do not intend that the Japanese shall be enslaved as a race or destroyed as a nation, but stern justice shall be meted out to all war criminals, including those who have visited cruelties upon our prisoners. The Japanese Government shall remove all obstacles to the revival and strengthening of democratic tendencies among the Japanese people. Freedom of speech, of religion, and of thought, as well as respect for the fundamental human rights shall be established.

"(11) Japan shall be permitted to maintain such industries as will sustain her economy and permit the exaction of just reparations in kind, but not those which would enable her to re-arm for war. To this end, access to, as distinguished from control of, raw materials, shall be permitted. Eventual Japanese participation in world trade relations shall be permitted.

"(12) The occupying forces of the Allies shall be withdrawn from Japan as soon as these objectives have been accomplished and there has been established in accordance with the freely expressed will of the Japanese people a peacefully inclined and responsible government.

"(13) We call upon the government of Japan to proclaim now the unconditional surrender of all Japanese armed forces, and to provide proper and adequate assurances of their good faith in such action. The alternative for Japan is prompt and utter destruction."

The Proclamation was signed by President Truman, the President of the Chinese Republic, and the Prime Minister of Great Britain.

TOKYO MONITORS THE POTSDAM PROCLAMATION

At six o'clock in the morning on 27 July, the overseas radio bureau in Tokyo had monitored a broadcast from San Francisco announcing the Potsdam Declaration. The Foreign Office gathered to study the terms of the Proclamation and, at the same time, a translation was being made ready.

Shunichi Matsumoto, Vice-Minister of Foreign Affairs, was the first man in the government to take a position of agreement that Japan should accept the Declaration. He counseled the Minister of Foreign Affairs, Shigenori Togo, that it would be foolhardy if Japan rejected the terms for surrender. Matsumoto began immediately to shape the draft of Japanese acceptance that would be cabled to Japan's ministers in Switzerland and Sweden; from there the acceptance would be transmitted to the Allies.

Togo said that the Army would never accept the Declaration as it stood. He wanted to use the good offices of the Soviets to negotiate for more favorable and face saving terms. (Little did he know that the United States and Britain had already agreed to major concessions in the Far East if Stalin, within two or three months after the end of the war in Europe, entered the war against Japan.) Togo further argued that if the Potsdam Proclamation was the sole basis for peace negotiations, he believed that no announcement should be made until the government was able to make a decision to continue the fight or the tortuous decision to surrender.

The one living Japanese model of a Samurai warrior, tough War Minister General Korechika Anami, was the most powerful man in the country. Anami advised that if the terms of the Proclamation were to be released, then the government must object and dictate the manner of response by the Japanese people. Anami was seconded by the Army and Navy Chiefs of Staff.

Finally a compromise was reached. The government's own position was not to be announced; the newspapers were to attach little significance to the story. They were allowed to publish part of the text of the Proclamation, but without any editorializing.

MOKUSATSU

The Japanese government wanted to totally ignore the Proclamation while Anami appealed for a powerful protest and rejection. Prime Minister Baron Kantaro Suzuki agreed with Togo that the government should "mokusatsu" the Proclamation. Moku meaning to be silent and satsu to kill; take no notice of; treat with silent contempt; ignore by keeping silent. It also means "remain in a wise and masterly inactivity".

At four o'clock the following day, Saturday, July 28th, Premier Suzuki held a press conference. He told the press that the Proclamation was just similar to the Cairo Declaration and that the government considered it worthless. He added, "We will simply mokusatsu it," after which he insisted that Japan would continue to fight the enemy until she had won. Suzuki's statement was picked up by the world press agencies, and they in turn communicated statements that Japan had not even bothered to reject the Allied Potsdam Proclamation.

MISSION #8, WE BOMB UBE ONCE AGAIN

On August 5 "The Boomerang" was ordered to bomb the Ube Coal Liquefaction Company in south Honshu. It was to be one of the most unique missions of World War II, and one that would have far reaching historical significance.

147

Ube had been attacked first on July 1, by 530 plus B-29s, who carried out incendiary raids on Ube, Kure, Shimononseki, and Kumamoto. On July22/23 "The Boomerang" and 71 other B-29s bombed the Coal Liquefaction Company at Ube. Now on 5 August we were ordered to strike that target once again. "The Boomerang" was to be part of an attacking force which numbered 106 B-29s. We figured that Ube had to be a very high priority objective for the JCS to order a third bombing.

The briefing officer described the target: "Ube Coal Liquefaction Company is located on the waterfront at Ube to the east of the mouth of the Kota Gawa. Ube is located on the Inland Sea about 20 miles east of Shimonoseki Straits (approximately 70 miles south of Hiroshima and about 100 miles north of Nagasaki). This is the largest synthetic plant in Japan proper. It measures 3000 by 3500 feet overall and has a rated capacity of 475,000 barrels."

We were briefed to carry 500 pound general-purpose bombs since the Ube Company contained buildings of reinforced concrete. (We had begun to mix 100 pound bombs with the 500 pounders since the lighter bomb would not only penetrate an oil storage tank, but the 5 to 1 ratio permitted us to achieve a "shotgun" pattern.) But for this mission, the use of the larger size bomb would prove more effective against the concrete structures. On the other side of the "ledger", the 500 pounders would not permit maximum tonnage to be carried, and we couldn't expect to have as many direct hits. However, it was concluded that, in selecting the 500 bomb, we would be capable of destroying the wood frame structures and seriously damaging the

reinforced installations. The ordnance: 18,500 pound bomb load, 600 pounds of ammunition. Each aircraft would carry approximately 6500 gallons of fuel.

On the question of bomb fuses for the Ube mission: Fusing of .01-second delay were selected as it would allow detonation beneath the roof level of the wood structures as well as allow penetration of the concrete installations.

The selected navigational route would take us from Northwest Field direct to Iwo Jima; direct to Inamino Misaki Point on the southwest coast of Shikoku Island (this point was expected to be easily identified). The route would then take us to the initial point of Hime Jima (a large island which would be easily identified by radar) and then direct to target. It was believed that the use of the islands and peninsular coast line of the Inland Sea would facilitate radar navigation. The initial point of Hime Jima was expected to provide a good run to the target. It was believed that the course from landfall to the target, which approximates a straight line, would allow the radar operator ample time for computing all important data. The target, located on a coastal projection just north of the city of Ube, would be resolved as a separate return. It was planned to employ a direct radar synchronous release on this target.

Our axis of attack would be 298 degrees from an altitude of 10,000/11,000 feet. Intelligence estimated that 15 to 20 enemy fighters would be sent against us, most of which we would intercept in the Shimonoseki straits area. Fifty bundles of rope (radar jamming tinsel) were carried on each aircraft and dispensed at the rate of three bundles per second when protection against search lights was

Take-off over the cliffs, Northwest Field

needed.

The final weather summary gave this information:
(1) Base at take-off: Scattered to broken middle clouds.
(2) Route: Scattered to broken clouds with a few towering cumulus, broken middle clouds, with light showers to 20 degrees north.
(3) Target: Ube: 2/10 stratus, tops 4000 ft. Winds at 10,000 feet were 125 degrees at 12 knots.
(4) Base on Return: Scattered low and high clouds.

Pretty good weather for a change. In the event we had problems on takeoff there would be 11 submarines, 11 Dumbos, and 4 surface vessels in the area.

We were "graced" this trip with a "Full Bird" Colonel who joined us at the line just before take-off. He was sent from headquarters to serve as a mission check-out officer. Carl introduced the colonel to the crew and his responses were cold and uninviting. It appeared that the Colonel was heavily impressed with his rank. We expected a 15 hour plus trip so I knew that Carl was hoping that the "Rank" didn't crowd him too much.

BOMBARDIER DICK MARSHALL DESCRIBES TAKEOFF

"On August 5th we taxied out awaiting our turn to takeoff. On the other runway, parallel to ours, there was a long line of B-29s on the taxi approach waiting. With the two runways, each takeoff was timed every 30 seconds. First one runway, then the other allowed two planes airborne every minute. We were in position to take off, waiting for the plane ahead of us to get airborne. It was using every inch of

runway and it didn't appear they were going to make it. At the end of the runway was a steep cliff, dropping straight down 500 feet into the ocean below. They ran out of runway—they didn't make it. It was awful—something you can never forget. This turned out to be our next to longest mission. It took 15 hours and 30 minutes.

"As if nothing had happened, Carl was given his clearance from the tower for takeoff and began our acceleration. John was counting off the airspeed to Carl. He had it full throttle and numbers were coming faster and faster. I could see the end of the runway coming closer and closer and then there was that wonderful floating feeling of knowing we were airborne and the cliff was behind us."

The takeoff was long but smooth; we picked up some good speed by nosing down the cliff. Carl flew low over the water for fifteen minutes to let the engines cool down and then we climbed to our assigned en route altitude of 8000 feet. The Colonel sternly observed the flight deck crew without comment or notation.

My radio cracked with the familiar and incessant jamming signal that oscillated over my watch frequency. Intelligence noted the jamming code as BC, however it was a case of which came first, the chicken or the egg. I listened to the jamming fourteen to fifteen hours per mission and I heard it (C), Dah di dah dit, (B) Dah dit, dit, dit. BC or CB it was all the same, and it had only a nuisance value.

THE PROPAGANDA BROADCASTER

Our nightly propaganda broadcaster came on again predicting our imminent extinction, and he again reminded us that Japan was dug in and ready for us. This time the fellow gave a large count of B-29s that he claimed had been shot down and promised that many more would be blown out of the sky. The propagandist had become progressively more cocky and brazen. Still no mention of our stripped ships, thank God. Waiting for that shoe to drop was tortuous. Our concern over stripped ships had begun with the top secret meeting in Fairmont, and it intensified with each mission.

The Colonel had used Hank's bulkhead to relax and he had fallen asleep. We were approaching our island initial point, Hime Jima, and Carl suggested that Hank inform the sleeping Colonel that we had reached our Initial Point. The Colonel yawned and stretched back to life, then took a position back of Carl.

We picked up some searchlights; Henry and Leff began dispensing radar rope. We were now flying at our target altitude of 11,000 feet. Perfect altitude for antiaircraft I reasoned. We were barely crabbing so I knew that the wind was negligible (the briefing information was right on: wind 125 degrees at 12 knots). There was a little bit of everything this time: flak, two engine fighters, single engine fighters, and a formation. A couple of fighters dove past our nose and other fighters paced us just out of gun range; the old routine to which we had become so accustomed. I climbed into my ringside tunnel astrodome position for the bomb run. It was a remarkably clear night—CAVU (clear and visibility unlimited), and once again our weather briefing information was on the money: 2.10 status undercast at about 4000 feet.

I saw something that I hadn't seen before. It was like a sheet of flame coming from a Japanese fighter. Later G-2 told us that

intelligence gathering from technical sources and prisoners of war, reported that the Japanese were fitting some of their fighters with rocket units to provide an extra measure of power.

Carlson and Lefler reported three aircraft flying formation. The lead plane seemed to be bigger than the other two, and in the center of each plane appeared a white light. Debriefers said that it was possible that the V-formation consisted of a night fighter, to lead, and 2 day fighters to fly wing positions. Some of the enemy fighters showed red lights port and green lights starboard, and others displayed the reverse. A good trick as it would make them tougher to track for the gunner.

One twin engine fighter made a pass at us on the bomb run from the right beam and level. The fighter came within 100 yards but didn't give our tail gunner Sid a shot. A green rocket exploded into a green light 500 yards in front of us. The flak was meager but accurate on the run; Carl called for Leff and Henry to dispense more radar rope.

I heard Dick Marshall say, "I can see the target perfectly in this moon light. I'm going to bomb visually." Dick Ginster disconnected but stayed with his APQ-7 radarscope just in case the bombardier needed him. Carl punched his throat mike button, and told Dick, "It's all yours." Dick bent over his sight and took over the tracking control of the airplane. He fine tuned for a few seconds, the bomb-sight indicators came together, Carl's red light came on and it was bombs away (the time was 12:30 a.m.). I watched the tight pattern of exploding bombs as Dick yelled, "It's a bulls eye!" We had to stay below 11,000 on breakaway between target and the point of turn. Towards lands end we saw another twin engine fighter that did not attack us, but chose to attack a 29 in front of us. There had been 111 B-29s ordered to fly the mission; three had mechanicals and did not bomb, and two bombed other targets. 106 B-29s bombed Ube and compressibility for the Wing was 127 minutes. Out of the 106 B-29s that bombed Ube, "The Boomerang" and six other B-29s bombed visually.

DICK MARSHALL ON THE BOMBING OF UBE

"In retrospect, the interesting thing about this mission was the time frame. We had taken off about 4:45 p.m. August 5. We hit our target at 12:30 A.M. August 6th, a day that will live in the annals of history forever. This was the morning that the first Atomic Bomb was released on Hiroshima. We had just flow by Hiroshima and were on our way back, not realizing that within a few hours, this city that had been spared the ravages of war, would be completely destroyed by one super bomb. Had it been daylight, I could have looked down to my right and seen the Aioi Bridge, which was the aiming point for the "Enola Gay"'s bombardier, Major Thomas Ferebee."

Marshall Continues:

"At 2:45 A.M., on the morning of August 6, 1945, two hours and fifteen minutes after we had dropped our load on Ube, "Enola Gay", commanded by Colonel Paul Tibbets Jr., had just taken off from Tinian with the first Atomic Bomb. The "Enola Gay" was escorted by two B-29s, "The Great Artiste," and ""Number 91"." "The Great Artiste", the instrument plane, carried scientific data recording instruments; "Number 91" carried photographic equipment. Both airplanes carried military and civilian scientific personnel. The purposes of the two accompanying aircraft were to monitor the effects of the detonation and photograph it's display. We landed back on Guam at 8:15 a.m., the same time the Atomic Bomb was detonating 660 yards above the hypo-center, or ground zero over Hiroshima."

Since the Colonel had slept all the way to the initial point, Carl was obliged to give him a full replay of procedures prior to the bombing run. The Colonel, noticing that I had moved out of the tunnel, decided to take my place and go back to bed. Normally the tunnel was not used as a place to sleep since there was always a danger of explosive decompression at higher altitudes. However, at our flight plan altitude of 8000 feet, decompression was not a factor, and the Colonel could do his thing with no sweat.

It had been a long flight and I was beginning to feel every minute of it by the time we approached our Iwo Jima check point. The dawn had begun to chase away the long Pacific night, and we were surprised to see three B-29s on our reciprocal about 2000 feet higher. The crew didn't think much about it and agreed with Carl that the planes were "photo reconnaissance" heading for Ube. Later we learned that these airplanes were no doubt weather planes attached to the "Enola Gay" mission.

About 40 minutes south of Iwo we sighted two or three more 29s in trail heading North at approximately the same altitude. Tony quipped, "More photo reconnaissance! I guess we blew so much hell out of Ube they had to send a squadron of cameras to cover the

damage."

After the facts of the Hiroshima mission were known, we believed that these B-29s were the "Enola Gay", and her two supporting aircraft: "The Great Artiste", and "Number 91".

The Colonel woke up when Carl called, "Prepare for landing." We touched down at approximately 8:15 a.m. Our mission time was 15 hours and 30 minutes. "The Boomerang" had consumed more than 5,384 gallons of fuel. It had been a very long, tiring mission. Debriefing was routine except we were all chattering about our bulls eye hit on the target. The Colonel didn't add anything. He couldn't—he really wasn't involved in very much.

THE SACK RAT SHOW

The crew was exhausted and a little giddy from the two ounces of pre-debriefing whiskey. All we wanted to do was to take a shower and hit the old cot for a fast 8. We arrived at the enlisted barracks and someone had tuned in the local "Sack Rat" radio show. The creator of this one man G.I. program always announced the latest news to the returning crews, then step by step he'd pretend to undress us and get us ready to hit the sack: "Well, Sack Rats, you've had a busy mission and you're ready for some heavy "Z's". Now just sit down on your cot that you've fitted with that nice air mattress (we all had placed air mattresses on our cots for added comfort), and take off those old heavy G. I. shoes. Umph, doesn't that feel good? Now just stretch out and relax. That's a good G.I. etc." Then the guy would sprinkle in some funnies about "Sack WACs" (Woman's Army Corps). He

began the same routine: he undressed the imaginary WACs, and, as usual, cautioned us not to look. It was all pretty juvenile stuff, but most of us were only a couple of years out of our teens and we loved the show. The fellow combined cleverness with a great sense of humor. The radio personality was in the middle of his act when someone in the studio handed him a bulletin. There was a pause and then he announced in gathering somber tones: "A super bomb was dropped on Hiroshima by a lone B-29 this morning, and Hiroshima has been destroyed. The time of explosion was 8:16 a.m." Everyone looked at one another and then someone laughed, "This guy had really gone Asiatic!" I laughed back in response, "Oh, what the hell, let him have his fun." The information was repeated, and the fellow cautioned that this was no drill. We began to get curiously serious and several of us turned up the radio. The announcement was repeated again: "One B-29 dropped a super bomb on Hiroshima this morning at 0816 hundred hours and the city has been destroyed. The attacking B-29 was based on Tinian Island and took off at 2:45 a. m. this morning. Three weather ships and two technical support B-29s accompanied the lone bomber."

One crew member gave voice to what the rest of us were thinking: "Tinian—hell we would have heard some scuttle on this thing."

I turned to Hank and the others, "Those lone B-29s that we spotted this morning..." Everyone was up to speed with me, and then Henry Carlson posed a question: "There was only one B-29 that bombed, do you suppose those others were..." I jumped his line, "Yeah they must have been the weather planes and the other supporting aircraft."

We were still a little suspicious that the super bomb stuff might be a gag since the broadcast was always a little far out, but the same information was being announced over and over, and it didn't have any funny punch lines. We began to realize that this unbelievable event had actually occurred. I turned to Hank Gorder, "My God, one bomb, and one city gone?" I turned to the guys around me, "This has got to shorten our stay here friends. I'm going to start packing for the States." Our speculations welled up into excited exchanges and war whoops. The shocking and dramatic news had propelled us high above our fatigue.

At first no one had a clue that the bomb was Atomic and even if we'd known, we couldn't have grasped the enormity of the explosion and the long range significance of the event. However we all believed that this "Super Bomb" would help effect a Japanese surrender. We finally showered and fell into our sacks with a good feeling that the war would soon be over.

THE SUPER BOMB

Thomas T. Handy, General, G.S.C., acting Chief of Staff, had sent the following order to General Carl Spaatz, Commanding General United States Army Strategic Air forces, 25 July 1945:

"1. The 509 Composite Group, 20th Air force will deliver its first special bomb as soon as weather will permit visual bombing after about 3 August 1945 on one of the following targets: Hiroshima, Kokura, Niigata and Nagasaki. To carry military and civilian scientific personnel from the War Department to observe and record the effects of the explosion of the bomb, additional aircraft will accompany the airplane carrying the bomb. The observing planes will stay several miles distant from the point of impact of the bomb.

"2. Additional bombs will be delivered on the above targets as soon as made ready by the project staff. Further instructions will be issued concerning targets other than those listed above.

"3. Dissemination of any and all information concerning the use of the weapon against Japan is reserved to the Secretary of War and President of the United States. No communiqué on the subject or releases of information will be issued in the field without specific prior authority. Any news stories will be sent to the War Department for special clearance.

"4. The foregoing directive is issued to you by direction and with the approval of the Secretary of War and of the Chief of Staff, USA. It is desired that you personally deliver one copy of this directive to General MacArthur and one copy to Admiral Nimitz for their information."

PRESIDENT TRUMAN DAYS BEFORE THE ATOMIC BOMBING OF HIROSHIMA

"This weapon is to be used against Japan between now and August 10th. I have told the Secretary of War, Mr. Stimson, to use it so that military objectives and soldiers and sailors are the target and not women and children. Even if the Japs are savages, ruthless, merciless and fanatic, we as the leader of the world for the common welfare cannot drop this terrible bomb on the old capital [Kyoto] or the new [Tokyo], where the Imperial Palace has been spared so far.

"He and I are in accord. The target will be a purely military one and we will issue a warning statement asking the Japs to surrender and save lives. I'm sure they will not do that, but we will have given them a chance. It is certainly a good thing for the world that Hitler's crowd or Stalin's did not discover this atomic bomb. It seems to be the most terrible thing ever discovered, but it can be made useful."

UBE POST-MISSION REPORT: TARGET DESTROYED AND SUNK

Post-Ube mission reports arrived revealing that we had damaged that target beyond the limits of our imagination: The refining units of the plant were 100 percent destroyed or damaged. In addition, 50 percent of the adjacent Iron Works Co. had been damaged. Ube was built on reclaimed land and it was protected from the ocean by dikes. The target photo-interpreter who analyzed the damage sent a special post-strike to Admiral Nimitz with a note attached reporting: "Target destroyed and sunk! Nimitz remarked that it was the first time bombers had ever sunk a factory.

"The Boomerang" and the 315th Wing received a Presidential Distinguished Unit Citation for this mission. The "sleeping Colonel" received a Distinguished Flying Cross. (Once again I was reminded of the Air Corp's in-equities.)

THE DIVERSION

Our bombing mission not only destroyed Ube, the largest synthetic oil producer in Japan, but the mission had a diversionary effect which convinced the Japanese early warning radar operators that the "Enola Gay" and her supporting aircraft were photo reconnaissance B-29s en route to Ube. As a result no enemy action was initiated. We can only speculate what would have happened if the "Enola Gay", stripped of fuselage turrets, had been engaged by enemy aircraft and ground fire. Our mission to Ube, in effect, was the perfect diversion for the atomic bombing of Hiroshima.

QUOTE FROM PAGE 20 OF JAPAN'S LONGEST DAY WRITTEN BY 14 JAPANESE HISTORIANS WHO DEVOTED YEARS TO RESEARCHING THE LAST DAYS OF WAR:

"At eight o'clock Hiroshima radar operators detected two B-29s. A warning was sounded. The planes mounted to an extremely high altitude: the radio announced that they were on a reconnaissance flight. Most of the city's quarter of a million people didn't bother to seek shelter, anticipating no bombing. Many gazed up into the sky to watch the maneuver."

HIROSHIMA BOMBING REPORTED TO TRUMAN

Meanwhile President Harry S. Truman was aboard the U.S.S. Augusta sailing back to the U.S. from the Potsdam conference. Captain Frank Graham, White House Map Room watch officer handed the following note to the President:

"Following info regarding Manhattan received, "Hiroshima bombed visually with only one tenth cover at 052315. There were no fighter opposition and no flak (as stated above, the "Enola Gay" and her accompanying aircraft were thought to be reconnaissance planes en route to Ube and no Japanese military response was initiated). Parsons (Captain William Parsons, a Navy ordnance expert who was responsible for arming the bomb) reported 15 minutes after drop as follows: "Results clear cut successful in all respects. Visible effects greater than in any test. Conditions normal in airplane following delivery."

FROM THE MEMOIRS OF HARRY S. TRUMAN AFTER DROPPING OF THE "A" BOMB ON HIROSHIMA:

"We are now prepared to obliterate more rapidly and completely every productive enterprise the Japanese have above ground in any city. We shall destroy their docks, their factories, and their communications. Let there be no mistake; we shall completely destroy Japan's power to make war.

"It was to spare the Japanese people from utter destruction that the ultimatum of July 26 was issued at Potsdam. Their leaders promptly rejected that ultimatum. If they do not now accept our terms, they many expect a rain of ruin from the air, the like of which has never been seen on this earth. Behind this air attack will follow sea and land forces in such numbers and power as they have not yet seen and with the fighting skill of which they are already well aware.

"The fact that we can release atomic energy ushers in a new era in man's understanding of nature's forces. Atomic energy may in the future supplement the power that now comes from coal, oil, and falling water, but at present it cannot be produced on a basis to compete with them commercially. Before that comes there must a long period of intensive research."

EXCERPTS FROM TACTICAL MISSION REPORTS OF THE 509TH COMPOSITE GROUP DURING JULY AND AUGUST 1945 (this Document was declassified from Top Secret July 30, 1973):

"Tactical Application of the Atomic Bomb: Because of the almost inconceivable expense of each individual Atomic bomb, it is obvious that no live, i.e. "atomic-smashing", munitions could be used for practice or training. However, a very close simulation of the employment of the Atomic bomb could be had by using dummy munitions with ballistic qualities similar to those of the combat munitions, using the same techniques that would be necessary when dropping the combat munition. These dummy munitions originally had an inert filler for use in the Zone of the Interior. However, it was believed advisable, in giving the 393rd Squadron combat crews training in the theatre of operations, to use a practice bomb with a high explosive filler in order to cause destruction to practice (enemy) targets and to give the crews experience in dropping demolition bombs. During these training missions in the theatre of operations, as close a similarity as possible to the projected operation was established. In studying the operation of the 509th Group during these training missions, it is important to keep this fact in mind because many of the techniques were at variance with normal combat procedures.

"One of the initial problems of the tactical application of the Atomic bomb was the necessity for using an air burst to derive the most advantage from the terrific blast effect of the bomb. This necessity for an air burst meant that no delay fusing could be used, which would have enabled the dropping aircraft to fly to a safe distance from the target before the explosion regardless of altitude. It was necessary for the aircraft to fly at altitudes of approximately 30,000 feet and to use special breakaway procedures in order to avoid the explosion. This permitted the removal of fuselage turrets, which would have interfered with the special equipment and personnel necessary for the Atomic bomb Missions.

"In addition, it would be necessary for the aircraft, immediately after bombs away to make a turn of at least 150 degrees in order to increase its distance from the point of detonation of the bomb. This distance was to be further increased by making an upwind bombing run so that the turn after bombs away would be down wind. Although no Atomic Bomb had previously been dropped (one had been statically detonated in a steel tower), scientists had been able to compute that an aircraft at a distance of approximately ten miles from the point of explosion would be subject to a 2G acceleration. A B-29 releasing from 30,000 feet would have a slant range of six and one half miles from the target. By making an immediate turn, it was estimated that the B-29 would be at least ten miles from the explosion. Since the B-29 had been designed with a safety factor of 4Gs, it seemed that a sufficient margin of safety had been provided.

"To get the greatest possible accuracy (using visual instead of radar bombing) with such an expensive weapon, it would be necessary to accomplish daylight attacks.

"Because of the wide destructive area of the bomb it would be necessary for only a single bomb to be dropped during any one attack on any one target. This would eliminate the necessity for formation flying and all attacks would be by individual aircraft.

INTRODUCTION SECTION OF THE TACTICAL MISSION REPORT

"Early in June, 1945, this headquarters was informed that one Atomic Bomb would be available for use against the enemy by 6 August 1945. By 5 August the bomb was ready, weather was satisfactory, and the carefully selected crew was well trained to drop the first Atomic Bomb. Weather aircraft were dispatched to all targets to relay strike-time weather forecasts back to the strike force. However, since it was so desirable that the primary be hit if possible, rather than the other targets, instructions were given to the strike aircraft to pass close enough to the primary targets, regardless of the weather aircraft's broadcasts, to insure that a visual bombing opportunity on the primaries was not missed. However, after that check, the strike aircraft were to proceed to either the secondary or tertiary, depending on the weather aircraft. It was essential that visual bombing be accomplished to make the attacks effective. Radar was to be used as an aid, but if a visual check on the target-sighting operation could not be made with the Norden bombsight, the crews were to bring the bomb back to base.

"Munitions: One Atomic Bomb for each mission."

NAVIGATOR'S PLAN

Routes in all cases were to be planned to pass by Iwo Jima on the way to the target. Landfall and land's end were to be selected on basis of location, radar and visual check points, and flak. All aircraft were to be instructed to return to base via Iwo Jima. Altitudes to and from the target area were to be dependent upon engineering and weather factors. En route to the target the altitude was to be 10,000 feet or less. The return altitude to be specified was to be at 18,000 feet when passing Iwo Jima in order to prevent unnecessary alerting of defenses.

REASON FOR SELECTION OF TARGETS:

Mission Number 13 (Hiroshima)

Hiroshima is highly important as an industrial target. Prior to this attack, Hiroshima ranked as the largest city in the Japanese homeland (except Kyoto) which remained undamaged by the B-29 incendiary strikes. The city had a population of 344,000 in 1940. Hiroshima is an army city—headquarters of the 5th Division and a primary port of embarkation. The entire northeastern and eastern sides of the city are military zones. Prominent in the north central part of the city are Army Division Headquarters marked by the Hiroshima Castle, numerous barracks, administration buildings and ordnance storage houses. In addition, there are the following military targets: Army Reception Center, large Military Airport, Army Ordnance Depot, Army yards and ship building companies, the Japan Steel Company, railroad marshalling yards, and numerous aircraft component parts factories. The fact that Hiroshima was undamaged made it an ideal target. This was deemed necessary to assess correctly the damage which could be inflicted by the Atomic Bomb. The size of the city was another important factor in the selection. According to preliminary data, it was believed that the radius of damage which could be inflicted by the Atomic Bomb was 7500 feet. By placing the aiming point in the center of the city, the circle of prospective damage covered almost the entire area of Hiroshima with the exception of the dock area to the south.

Kokura and Nagasaki contained essentially the same characteristics for a good target as Hiroshima, with the exception that they both had prisoner of war camps nearby. Nagasaki was the poorest of the three targets as to situation and overall construction and for these reasons was made the tertiary target.

NARRATION OF MISSIONS AS FLOWN:

Note: Pilot Colonel Paul W. Tibbets Jr. named his B-29, The "Enola Gay", in honor of his mother. The bomb was named "Little Boy." Chuck Sweeney and Crew 15 flew "The Great Artiste" instrument ship. George Marquardt commanded the third plane, "Number 91", equipped with cameras.

"Cruise to the Mainland: Individual climbs were made immediately after take off to altitudes between 8,000 to 10,000 feet where the initial cruise was flown. No assemblies were made.

"Bomb Run: Bombing was conducted by individual aircraft at average altitudes of 30,000 feet.

"Return to Base: Return to the base was conducted by individual aircraft without difficulty. Return speeds consisted of cruising at 200 CAS (calibrated air speed) and descending at 210 CAS.

"Comments: All aircraft loaded a bomb bay tank. Because of the configuration of the A/C of the 509th Group, speeds higher than those recommended for a normal combat aircraft were used. Speeds on the route out averaged 15 mph higher, and on return, 30 mph higher. It was impossible to raise the bomb carrying capacity by better cruise control procedures because of the special type bomb carried. During the descent from high altitude, higher power than was necessary to maintain maximum range speeds was used to hold cabin pressurization.

MISSION NUMBER 13:

"a. Primary Target: Hiroshima Urban Industrial Area.
b. Secondary Target: Kokura Arsenal and City
c. Tertiary Target: Nagasaki Urban Area

"Primary Target (Hiroshima) The aircraft on Mission Number 13 dropped one Atomic Bomb on the primary target as follows:

"Time of Release: 052315Z (6 August 8:15 a.m. local time)
Altitude of Release: 31,600 feet.

"Mission Number 13 (Hiroshima August 6): It was estimated that 4.1 square miles or 60 percent of the build-up area of Hiroshima was destroyed."

Note: The "Little Boy" atomic bomb weighed 9000 pounds, and generated a heat of 300,000 degrees Centigrade as it exploded.

DOMEI NEWS AGENCY REPORTS ON

THE BOMB

In Tokyo The Domei News Agency dispatch indicated that a very few enemy planes had inflicted tremendous damage on Hiroshima with a bomb of an unknown type. The next morning General Torishiro Kawabe, vice-chief of the Army General Staff was informed that all of Hiroshima had been sacrificed with the explosion of one bomb. Later Kawabe speculated that the bomb was atomic.

On August 7 the Japanese Army issued a communiqué in which it said that a small number of B-29s attacked Hiroshima and caused a considerable amount of damage.

TRUMAN'S BROADCAST PICKED UP

Later, on the same day, Minister of Foreign Affairs Shigenori Togo informed the Cabinet of Truman's broadcasts from Washington, picked up by the government in Tokyo:

"We have spent two billion dollars on the greatest gamble in history, and won. If the Japanese do not now accept our terms they may expect a rain of ruin from the air, the like of which has never been seen on this earth..."

On August 8th, Togo counseled the Emperor that Japan must accept the terms of the Potsdam Proclamation immediately in light of this new horrible weapon. Emperor Hirohito told Marquis Kido, Lord Keeper of the Privy Seal, that his safety was secondary, and that the war had to be terminated at once. Prime Minister Baron Kantaro Suzuki called for an emergency meeting of the Supreme War Council for Direction of the War, also referred to as the Big Six. ("SCDW" was a coordinating, conferring body, which, with Imperial General Headquarters, decided war policy). The Big Six consisted of the Premier, Ministers of War, Navy, Foreign Affairs and Chiefs of Staff of Army and Navy.

RUSSIA BREAKS OFF NEGOTIATIONS WITH AMBASSADOR SATO

In Moscow that same afternoon Molotov cut off Japan's ambassador Sato's attempts to use the good offices of the Soviet Union to intercede and negotiate Japan's position in the peace process. He instead read a note that ended in these words: "...the Soviet Government declares that from tomorrow, that is from August 9, the Soviet Union will consider herself in a state of war against Japan." Two hours later the Red Army had entered Manchuria and begun its destruction of Japan's "invincible" Kwatung Army. The Japanese considered the Soviet action illegal since the Soviet-Japanese Neutrality Pact did not expire until April, 1946; but Stalin, with Truman's help, made a legal case for his act.

In Tokyo, Foreign Minister Togo demanded that Prime Minister Suzuki call emergency meetings of both the Supreme War Council and the Cabinet and also to counsel with the former Prime Ministers who composed a body called the Jushin, or Senior Statesmen, whose duty it was to advise the Throne.

THE BIG SIX DIVIDED

The "Big Six" of the Supreme War Council split in their positions. Suzuki, Togo, and Admiral Mitsumasa Yonai, Minister of the Navy, favored acceptance of the Potsdam Proclamation with the following stipulation:" that the Imperial polity would be preserved." The other three, War Minister Anami, and two Chiefs of Staff, Umezu of the Army and Toyoda for the Navy, wanted to write in other conditions: a minimal occupation force, trying of war criminals by Japan rather than the enemy, and demobilization of Japanese troops by Japanese officers. War Minister Anami was torn between his allegiance to the Emperor and his duty to fight to the end.

NAGASAKI BOMBED

While The Supreme Council was in session, the U.S. exploded its new horrendous Super Bomb on Nagasaki. The time was 10:58 a.m.

EXCERPTS FROM TACTICAL MISSION REPORTS OF THE 509TH COMPOSITE GROUP DURING JULY AND AUGUST 1945

Mission Number 16:

"a. Primary Target: Kokura Arsenal and City
b. Secondary Target: Nagasaki Urban Area

"Kokura:

"A city of 168,000 inhabitants according to the 1940 census, is situated on northern Kyushu near the industrial center of Yawata. This target is 3 miles by 2 miles in area and has many valuable industrial targets. The Kokura Arsenal, which is one of the largest Japanese arsenals and probably the most important in Japan for the manufacture of light automatic weapons and the smaller type antiaircraft

161

and anti-tank guns, also manufactures combat vehicles. Production rates are unknown at this arsenal because of such a diversity of activities, but probably is several thousand machine guns of all kinds per month. The arsenal is known to produce 6.5 mm and 7.7 mm light machine guns, 7.7 mm heavy machine guns, 20 mm antiaircraft, anti-tank guns and ammunition. It was reported to be equipped to mix poison gas, to load gas shells, and to store those shells underground. The most essential processes of this plant are the making and assembly of ordnance. Forging and pressing are also essential.

"Nagasaki:

"One of Japan's leading shipbuilding and repair centers, is also important for its production of naval ordnance and its function as a major military port. Outstanding among the shipbuilding and repair facilities, comprising a shipyard, dockyard, and marine engine works located on the western side of the harbor within an area measuring approximately 6500 feet by 2000 feet. The Mitshubishi Steel and Arm Works and its new rolling mill located along the Urakami River in northern Nagasaki is integrated with the shipyards that produce ship plate, castings, forgings, etc. Naval ordnance, timber and lumber storages, are located just to the south of the rolling mill and supplies lumber and wooden fittings to the shipyards. The Kawanami Industry Company Shipyard located on Koyagi Island to the south of the harbor entrance is believed to be an important producer of medium sized vessels in addition to its production of marine engines and boilers. The eastern side of Nagasaki Harbor contains all the important loading and storage facilities. Nagasaki's southwest

location made this city a primary embarkation and supply port for operations on the mainland, and the docks and freight yards are believed to be congested with military supplies. Numerous reports refer to large-scale expansion of dock and storage facilities, and the entire waterfront is lined with small shipyards, equipped with shops, foundries, slipways, and a patent slip. These yards build small wooden cargo vessels, shipping vessels, lifeboats, etc. Three unidentified factories are located along the railway to the north of the Mitsubishi Steel and Arms Works. Of these, the northernmost appears especially significant, comprising of some eight to ten shop-type buildings, the largest measuring approximately 9000 feet by 400 feet, a power plant and several storage buildings. The total area occupied by these buildings measures 2000 feet by 1500 feet. The plant's general arrangement and appearance suggests either a very large textile mill or a major assembly plant. Intelligence reports mention new munition plants in this area and an aircraft engine factory at Nagaskaki also has been reported. It is possible that this plant might be an engine works supplying the Omura Naval Aircraft Factory, located approximately 15 miles to the northeast. Nagasaki occupies a very limited, amphitheater like site, extending from reclaimed land along the waterfront to the lower slopes of the surrounding hills. Small strips of built-up districts extend along the valleys to the east and along both sides of the Urakami River to the north. In Nagasaki proper, commercial and public buildings are concentrated along the eastern and central parts of the city. Densely grouped houses crowd these buildings and extend in an almost solid mass to the hills. Four rivers and canals and a few wide streets constitute the only substantial firebreaks. It should be noted that all important industrial installations are located outside the city proper. Another factor which entered into the selection of Nagasaki as a target was the fact that it was virtually untouched by previous bombings, thus enabling an accurate damage assessment. The size of the city made it ideal for an Atomic Bomb attack. The city is the third largest on the island of Kyushu, with a population of 253,000 persons. The city measures approximately 5 miles from north to south and 5 miles from east to west and it was believed that an accurate drop would destroy the bulk of the city east of the harbor and possibly carry across to the western shore."

Note: Major Charles Sweeney, who had piloted the instrument plane Great Artiste over Hiroshima flew "Bock's Car," while her regular pilot, Captain Federick Bock Jr., flew the instrument plane. The bomb was named Fat Man.

Kokura was reported clear, but the city turned out to be partially obscured by smoke and haze, and Bombardier Kermit Beahan, who had been ordered to make a visual drop, could not find the aiming point. He called back to Sweeney, "We'll have to make another run." "Pilot to crew," Sweeney announced, "No drop. Repeat. No drop." They made a steep turn and came in for a second attempt. Beahan still could not pick up the target because of dense smoke; Sweeney and Commander Frederick Ashworth, the officer in charge of "Fat Man," decided to go on to the secondary target, Nagasaki.

Secondary Target (Nagasaki): the aircraft on Mission Number 16 dropped one Atomic Bomb on Nagasaki:

Time of Release: 090158Z (9 August 10:58 a.m. local)
Altitude of Release: 31,600 feet.

RESULTS OF MISSION:

Mission Number 16 (Nagasaki August 9): Photo coverage showed that 1.46 square miles or 42.4 per cent of the built-up area of Nagasaki was destroyed.

ONE OF THE MOST RESPECTED AND INFLUENTIAL SENATORS, RICHARD B. RUSSELL, JR., OF GEORGIA, SENT A TELEGRAM TO PRESIDENT TRUMAN AFTER THE NAGASAKI BOMBING:

"Let us carry the war to them until they beg us to accept unconditional surrender. The foul attack on Pearl Harbor brought us into the war, and I am unable to see any valid reason why we should be so much more considerate and lenient in dealing with Japan than Germany... If we do not have available a sufficient number of atomic bombs with which to finish the job immediately, let us carry on with TNT and fire bombs until we can produce them... This was total war as long as our enemies held all the cards. Why should we change the rule now, after the blood, treasure and enterprise of the American people have given us the upper hand?..."

TRUMAN SENT RUSSELL AN ANSWER THAT DAY AUGUST 9:

"I know that Japan is a terribly cruel and uncivilized nation in warfare but I can't bring myself to believe that, because they are beasts, we should ourselves act in that same manner.

"For myself I certainly regret the necessity of wiping out whole populations because of the "pigheadedness" of the leaders of a nation, and, for your information, I am not going to do it unless it is absolutely necessary. It is my opinion that after the Russians enter into the war the Japanese will very shortly fold up.

"My object is to save as many American lives as possible but I also have a human feeling for the women and children of Japan."

That night, in Truman's radio address on Potsdam, he made a point of urging all Japanese civilians to leave the industrial cities immediately and save themselves. To the American people he said: "I realize the tragic significance of the atomic bomb."

Back on Guam "The Boomerang" crew and others were being briefed on our scheduled mission to bomb the Nippon Oil Refinery at Amagasaki, 250 miles south of Tokyo. The briefing officer interrupted the briefing to read a one line statement that had been handed him: "Nagasaki has been decimated with one atomic bomb, with almost the same results that were witnessed at Hiroshima."

As the facts of the Super Bomb (that we now understood was an atomic bomb) came in, we of "The Boomerang" crew were convinced that the Japanese surrender was imminent. Certainly, no one questioned the fact that the bombing of Hiroshima and Nagasaki represented two giant steps to war's end. To make things worse for the Japanese, Manchuria was now practically in Soviet hands. We were hoping that the trip to the Nippon Oil

Refinery at Amagasaki would be cancelled in view of the events. But no such luck.

PRESIDENT TRUMAN SPEAKING OF THE BOMB IN A RADIO BROADCAST DECLARED:

"We shall continue to use it until we completely destroy Japan's power to make war. Only a Japanese surrender will stop us."

After all of this, the Supreme Council was still not able to reach a decision.

WAR MINISTER KORECHIKA ANAMI BELIEVES JAPAN CAN REVERSE THE SITUATION

In Japan, Admiral Yonai believed that the Japanese must surrender quickly to preserve their country, War Minister Anami summed up the view of the other side. He believed that it was possible for Japan to reverse the situation when the allies invaded, and bring Japan to victory. "Furthermore, he said, "our Army will not submit to demobilization. Our men simply will not lay down their arms. And since they know they are not permitted to surrender, since they know that a fighting man who surrenders is liable to extremely heavy punishment, there is really no alternative for us but to continue the war." Anami raised his voice in impatience, "We must fight the war through to the end no matter how great the odds against us."

EMPEROR HIROHITO AGREES TO MAKE A RECORDING TELLING THE NATION WHETHER THEY WOULD HAVE PEACE OR WAR

About the time that the Supreme Council

adjourned, Hiroshi Shimomura, Director of the Information Bureau was received in audience by the Emperor for an unprecedented two hours. During this audience the Emperor agreed to make a broadcast telling the nation whether they would have peace or war. The Emperor's voice had never been heard by the people of Japan. It would be unthinkable for the "Divine" Emperor to broadcast in person, so a plan was made for his highness to record the Rescript of surrender at the Imperial Household Ministry Building.

GENERAL HENRY H. (HAP) ARNOLD SENDS OUT THE ORDER FOR THE STRATEGIC AIR FORCES TO DROP LEAFLETS OVER CENTERS OF POPULATION IN JAPAN TO ADVISE THE PEOPLE THERE OF THE STATUS OF THE PEACE NEGOTIATIONS

"(1) Introduction:

"(a) On 7 August the Cincpac (Commander-in-Chief, Pacific) Advance Psychological Warfare Section was asked to institute a psychological warfare campaign with the Atomic Bomb as its focal point. Final arrangements for the program were made at the Saipan headquarters of the CINCPAC Psychological Warfare Section, when The Office of War Information agreed to make available its facilities to the project.

"(b) The text of the leaflet was drawn up by one of the CINCPAC Officers. The plan was drawn up to drop 3,600,000 leaflets daily for 9 days on Japanese cities having a population of more than 100,000 persons.

"(c) The Text was taken to headquarters of the Twentieth Air Force and United States Army Strategic Air Forces in Guam for approval. Additional approval was obtained from CINCPAC. As soon as this clearance was obtained, a Japanese language officer, with the help of Japanese officers assigned to Psychological Warfare, made the translation. After this was completed the text was made calligraphic and was taken to Saipan where it was made into plates and where the leaflets were printed.

"(d) A recording of the leaflet text in Japanese was made by a prisoner of war and broadcast on Office of War Information radio station to Japan starting at 1830K (local time) on 8 August. These broadcasts continued until the evening of 10 August.

"(e) The first delivery of leaflet bombs was to be made on 9 August to the 73rd Bomb Wing, which was to drop the leaflets. The plan called for the daily delivery for 9 days of 75 M-16 bomb cases, each containing 32,000 leaflets.

"(f) The plan was interrupted by the Russian declaration of war on 9 August and a change in the wording of the leaflet had to be made. However on 9 August 1,600,000 copies of the first leaflet [AB-11] were dropped on Osaka, Nagasaki and Fujuoka before the wording change. The revised text was translated into Japanese by a Japanese language officer working with a prisoner of war and a Nisei and was broadcast on the Office of War Information radio on the evening of August 9th. The text was then made a calligraphic by the Japanese prisoner. The new leaflets were designated AB-12. The transition from AB-11 to AB-12 was completed on the morning of 10 August, and on that morning 24 M-16 bombs, containing 768,000 AB-11 leaflets, were dropped on Tokyo. Also on 10 August 50 M-15 bombs containing over a million and a half copies of the new leaflet were dropped on Kumamoto, Yawata, Omuta and Yokohama."

The morning of 9 August, Thursday, had been eventful to say the least: Nagaskaki was nearly destroyed with one bomb as we were briefing for our mission to Amagasaki, Russia warned that she was declaring war on Japan, and 1,600,000 copies of AB-11 American leaflets were dropped on Osaka, Nagasaki, and Fujuoka.

The leaflets turned out to be a dangerous act relevant to the peace process since, upon reading, the Japanese would learn that they had been lied to regarding their progress in the war. The Army had kept the people in the dark for so many years; it was feared that the truth might send them into chaos and rebellion.

THE FIRST AB-11 LEAFLET

"TO THE JAPANESE PEOPLE:

"America asks that you take immediate heed of what we say on this leaflet.

"We are in possession of the most destructive explosive ever devised by man. A single one of our newly developed atomic bombs is actually the equivalent in explosive power to what 2000 of our giant B-29s can carry on a single mission. This awful fact is one for you to ponder and we solemnly assure you it is grimly accurate.

"We have just begun to use this weapon against your homeland. If you still have any doubt, make inquiry as to what happened to Hiroshima when just one atomic bomb fell on that city.

"Before using this bomb to destroy every resource of the military by which they are prolonging this useless war, we ask that you now petition the Emperor to end the war. Our President has outlined for you the thirteen consequences of an honorable surrender: We urge that you accept these consequences and begin the work of building a new, better, and peace loving Japan.

"You should take steps now to cease military resistance. Otherwise, we shall resolutely employ this bomb and all our other superior weapons to promptly and forcefully end the war.

"EVACUATE YOUR CITIES"

MISSION #9

The 9 August mission to Amagasaki seemed different. We all had the distinct feeling that the season for war was over. Then came the propaganda broadcaster to give us more reason to believe that the Japs were done. The fellow's tone had changed dramatically, as he leveled a scathing attack on America: "You filthy, in-human, American pigs have exploded a new super bomb on Hiroshima and Nagasaki." He lost all of his normally cool composure as he screamed, "You will pay, you will pay, you will pay..." It was a scream of defeat. I never heard the broadcaster again, although the old C B jamming signal continued through the last day of the war.

THE RAT

I couldn't believe it but my rat friend was still around. He popped his head out of the air duct just to the rear of my J 37

166

sending key. We were both startled as we eye balled one another, and before I recovered my composure the pointed face pulled back into the air duct and disappeared. (The rat looked thinner and I figured that living on an insulation diet might be doing him in.) These damned varmints must be mistaking me for the Pied Piper, I thought. I was beginning to develop a rodent paranoia.

It appeared that there were more pacing fighters this time out. Two made close passes at our nose in what might have been an attempt to ram us. Flak was moderate to heavy, and 11 Superforts were damaged. I yelled at Tony to turn off his navigator's light and he yelled back that it was off. A search light had zeroed in on us and you could literally read the fine print of a map. Some meager but accurate flak followed which told me that there was an increasing number of German built antiaircraft systems being used. The pacing fighters meant that the Japs still thought we carried central fire control armament. We kept our fingers crossed. This has to be the last mission, I was thinking. If we can make it back with these old engines we'll live to see the states again.

HIROHITO MEETS WITH THE SUPREME COUNCILORS, CHIEF CABINET SECRETARY SAKOMIZU, PRIVY COUNCIL PRESIDENT BARON HIRANUMA, AND TELLS THEM THAT JAPAN MUST SURRENDER. THE WAR COUNCIL WAS STILL SPLIT THREE AND THREE, AND THE WAR CABINET WAS SPLIT THREE WAYS. THEY WERE ALL CRYING

The Emperor Hirohito, accompanied by an aide, quietly entered his small underground bomb shelter at ten minutes to midnight just as our bombs were falling on the Amagasaki oil fields. The Supreme Councilors, with their aides and two invited guests, Chief Cabinet Secretary Sakomizu and Baron Hiranuma, President of the Privy Council, had been waiting since 11:37 p.m. as Kido's (Lord Keeper of the Privy Seal) diary indicates. The August night was stifling hot and humid; the room where the meeting took place was only eighteen feet by thirty, and poorly ventilated. Some of the Councilors and their guests were wearing formal morning clothes, and some were wearing uniforms with white handkerchiefs. The walls were paneled in dark wood; the tables were covered with cloth. Their were six men on one side and five on the other, facing one another. The Emperor seated himself at the head of the room in a large straight backed chair. There was a plain screen behind him; the Emperor's aide was in position near a door.

CHIEF CABINET SECRETARY SAKOMIZU READS THE POTSDAM PROCLAMATION

Premier Suzuki, standing at the Emperor's left, asked the Cabinet Secretary to read the Potsdam Proclamation aloud. Suzuki reviewed the situation indicating that the Supreme War Council was divided three to three, while the Cabinet, which alone had the constitutional authority to approve Japan's surrender, was split three ways--six members favored acceptance of the Proclamation provided that the Imperial House be guaranteed, three asked for the four conditions Anami had outlined, while five pushed for several conditions, but fewer than the War Minister's four.

Suzuki called upon Togo to give the

argument for surrender if the Imperial structure were guaranteed. The Minister of the Navy, Admiral Yonai agreed. General Anami slammed his fist on the table, jumped to his feet and proclaimed that Japan must fight on, insisting that the Battle for Japan would not be known until it was fought. Anami insisted that the Allies would have to agree to his four conditions or he would fight on. Anami's four conditions: Japan would retain the Imperial Polity, disarm her own soldiers, conduct her own war trials, and limit the forces of occupation. General Umezu (Chief of Army Staff) held that Japan was more than ready for the enemy; he joined Anami's position on the four conditions necessary before Japan could consider signing the Potsdam Proclamation of peace.

Admiral Toyoda (Chief of Navy Staff) gave further arguments in favor of Japan's continuing the war, and stated that he could not guarantee the Navy's response to surrender unless disarming was conducted by the Japanese themselves.

The national essence [Kotutai] of Japan, as a land of the gods, has existed because the Emperor reigns with undiminished power. His subjects thought him to be a god, and children were cautioned that if they looked at his face, they would go blind. Every child was taught that his conduct and moral sense was obligated to the emperor and one's parents. If a speaker mentioned the word, "Emperor" the entire body of listeners would come to attention.

Emperor Hirohito had named his reign "Showa" which meant enlightened peace. His grandfather, Mutshuhito, had chosen "Meiji" (Enlightened Rule); his era was known as the Meiji Restoration which was given credit for the greatest reforms and development in Japanese history. The Imperial Command was known as the Voice of the Crane. The Japanese believed that the Voice of the Crane could be heard in the sky long after the sight of it had disappeared. The Voice of the Crane was about to be heard from again. Japan was sounding its death rattle and as it gasped for breath, the Japanese people looked to their Emperor Hirohito for deliverance.

The emotionally charged deliberations and debates that preceded were all lost in the light of reverence for the Voice of The Crane, The Emperor Hirohito. Their god now held their spiritual essence:

"Continuing the war," the emperor said quietly, "can only result in the annihilation of the Japanese people and a prolongation of the suffering of all humanity. It seems obvious that the nation is no longer able to wage war, and its ability to defend its own shores is doubtful. It is unbearable for me to see my loyal troops disarmed, but it is time to bear the unbearable. I give my sanction to the proposal to accept the Allied Proclamation on the basis outlined by the Foreign Minister." The Emperor appeared tortured as he slowly made his way out of the room. Chief Cabinet Secretary Sakomizu later said that everyone in the room was crying, and that tears also fell from the Emperor's cheeks. The only body that had the constitutional authority to effect surrender was the Cabinet, and yet no one there would dishonor the Emperor's wishes.

AT FOUR IN THE MORNING CABLES WERE DISPATCHED TO SWITZERLAND AND SWEDEN FOR TRANSMISSION TO THE ALLIED

POWERS

"The Japanese Government [the note said in part] is ready to accept the terms enumerated in the joint declaration which was issued at Potsdam on July 26th, 1945, by the heads of the Governments of the United States, Great Britain, and China, and later subscribed to by the Soviet Government, with the understanding that the said declaration does not compromise any demand which prejudices the prerogatives of His Majesty as a Sovereign Ruler."

The part of the Japanese reply, "Which does not compromise any demand which prejudices the prerogatives of His Majesty", was destined to become a small fly in the Allied ointment.

Having dropped our bombs on Amagasaki, Hank calculated a high descending cruise back to Northwest. We pressurized and climbed to 27,000 feet for the ride home. I had just climbed back down from the tunnel position and prepared my strike report when ""The Boomerang"" explosively depressurized. We were all caught off guard and there was a violent scramble for oxygen masks which had been set aside with little thought that they would ever be needed. We weren't used to wearing the masks; they were considered an emergency item, like a walk around oxygen tank.

Carl called for positions to check in, and the Scanners sounded a little vague. Tony called Carl and told him he was going back aft and check the scanners, Leff and Hank Carlson.

TONY REMEMBERS THE DECOMPRESSION EMERGENCY

"I grabbed a walk around and crawled back through the tunnel. Both Leff and Carlson were obviously suffering from hypoxia. They were a little out of it--they hadn't hooked up to their oxygen just right. I re-connected their supply of oxygen and they came out of it. I crawled back through the tunnel and before I got back to my position my walk-around ran out, and I connected back up with some difficulty."

Henry later admitted that he had failed to close the aft bomb bay pressure door properly and the mounting pressure differential finally blew it into the aft bomb bay. We only suffered one casualty with the decompression--the rat. There was no way he could have survived without oxygen at 27,000 feet.

We landed on Northwest Field (10 August) dog tired, but in good spirits. I told our ground chief, Floyd Jennings that there was a dead rat waiting to be extricated from an air vent. Jennings exploded, "How the hell am I supposed to find a dead rat in a hundred miles of ventilation systems?" I smiled reassuringly and suggested, "Wait for three days and follow your nose." Jennings smiled back, "In three days I may be stateside, the war's about over."

Photo reports showed that our Nippon Oil Refinery target at Amagasaki was almost completely destroyed. Damage was evenly distributed. Only two tanks remained undamaged. Synthetic oil plants showed damage to a gasometer, four buildings, and a sulphur removal unit. In the refinery area, four refining units and 30 tanks were destroyed. In addition, nine other tanks and 25 buildings were damaged. Chalk up one more oil refinery for the 315th. The crews were getting sharp!

WE RECEIVED OUR THIRD DISTINGUISHED UNIT CITATION FOR THE AMAGASAKI MISSION.

We speculated that Japan would throw in the towel after the terrible destruction of Hiroshima and Nagasaki; each with one Super Bomb. Moreover, we learned at debriefing that Russia had officially entered the war against Japan (August 9,1945). The crew members were beginning to taste home.

However, like the Big Six, the Supreme Council, and the War Cabinet, Japan itself was divided into peace and war factions. The Japanese people had been told by the Army that they were winning. The Japanese military, which numbered more than four million men, would fanatically defend their main islands, then Korea, Manchuria, and North China unto their glorious death. The Japanese were also building up a "National Volunteer Army" at home for a last ditch stand.

On the morning of 10 August, 70 B-29s bombed Tokyo, and other B-29s mined Shimonoseki Strait, Nakaumi Lagoon, and waters at Sakai, Yonago, and Wonsan.

LEAFLETS DROPPED ON TOKYO, KUMAMOTO, YAWATA, OMUTA AND YOKOHAMA

On the morning of 10 August 24 M-16 bombs, containing 768,000 AB-11 leaflets, were dropped on Tokyo. Also on 10 August 50 M-15 bombs containing over a million and a half copies of the new AB-12 leaflet were dropped on Kumamoto, Yawata, Omuta and Yokohama. A recording of the leaflet text in Japanese was broadcast on Office of War Information radio station to Japan every half hour.

EXCERPTS FROM DECLASSIFIED MISSION REPORT: NEW AB-12 LEAFLETS TELL OF RUSSIA'S ENTRY INTO THE WAR

"ATTENTION JAPANESE PEOPLE"

"Because your military leaders have rejected the thirteen part surrender declaration, two momentous events have occurred in the last few days.

"The Soviet Union, because of this rejection on the part of the military has notified your Ambassador Sato that it has declared war on your nation. Thus, all powerful countries of the world are now at war against you.

"Also, because of you leaders' refusal to accept the surrender declaration that would enable Japan to honorably end this useless war, we have employed our atomic bomb.

"A single one of our newly developed atomic bombs is actually the equivalent in explosive power to what 2000 of our giant B-29s could have carried on a single mission. Radio Tokyo has told you that with the first use of this weapon of total destruction, Hiroshima was virtually destroyed.

"Before we use this bomb again and again to destroy every resource of the military by which they are prolonging this useless war, petition the Emperor now to end the war. Our President has outlined for you the thirteen consequences of an honorable surrender. We urge that you accept these consequences and begin the work of building a new, better, and peace loving Japan.

"Act at once or we shall resolutely employ this bomb and all our other superior weapons to promptly and forcefully end the war."

"EVACUATE YOUR CITIES."

The Japanese Army meanwhile attempted to counter the inflammatory effects of the U.S. leaflets by telling the people that the Allies desired to end the war without destroying Japan. The Japanese broadcast information from Manila and Okinawa telling the people that the United States could not manufacture and use an atomic weapon: it would be too variable and dangerous. Japan filed a formal protest through Switzerland against the government of the United States.

JAPANESE LEARN THE TRUTH ABOUT RUSSIA

The Japanese public learned from the leaflets and Friday morning's papers (August 10) that the Soviets had declared war on Japan. This was the first time that the Japanese knew that their government had been seeking the "good offices" of the Russians, and had failed to win them.

GENERAL ANAMI BRIEFS HIS PERSONNEL

Anami had ordered all personnel in the War Ministry above the chief-of-section rank to assemble in the Ministry's underground bomb shelter at 9:30 a.m. August 10. The General was close to his staff. He and they often attended a study group led by Tokyo University's Professor

Hiraizumi. The Professor was an ultra nationalist and condoned blood and even rebellion against the Emperor's will if the end results were in the best interests of Japan.

Anami told his men what had happened at the Imperial conference and said the decision to fight on would depend on the enemy's reply to the note that had been dispatched to them. The officers were stunned with shock and disbelief. They were convinced that the Emperor was being coerced by his traitorous advisors, and if Japan were to surrender, it would cease to exist in any recognizable form. Indeed, the Japanese would be enslaved by the enemy. The officers thought that every undying principle they stood for, and had fought for, was being stripped away from them.

THE DANGEROUS YOUNG TIGERS WANT TO FIGHT ON

Lt. Colonel Masahiko Takeshita, Anami's brother-in-law, the closest staff officer to Anami, silently vowed to resist any peace effort with blood. He would protect the Emperor from the forces who wished to destroy Japan. General Anami was torn in half between his undying loyalty to the Emperor and his life and death dedication to the Army which he served as War Minister. Anticipating the actions of his staff of "Young Tigers," as they were called, he warned that one man could bring about the ruin of the entire country. The one man could be any member of his staff, particularly Major Kenji Hatanaka, Military Affairs Section, Ministry of War, and a protégé of General Anami's. The young "patriot" was flushed and shaking with rage at the possibility of surrender. In a very few days he would join Takeshita,

に するんく す樹 るれないすつあ らで人人ちは全か部品 米つ ん助命
書様 都がてこかて戰んばたふア張りて 遊す達道る眠部せがをこ空か數でけをあ
いめ 市少もの て爭でも方のメリま 難かを主かが破るこ製の軍五日下た助な
て注 のく爆裏に 平をすつをはり込せ ら傷義分あ壞爲の造都はのさけけた 本
あ意 内と撃に 和止 と解たカん そつのりりしに勝す市爆都 いれよは
るし もこれて をる あゐ下にり でて声使日ろに撃 す。
～て 必さ書い 恢る様 敵ご書た ませすふの工はしに 面 思親告
かき 四のるてあ 復しな はいいく んけ兵な場軍まあ のビ兄ぐ
らま つ裏にもる た新ら たあ て は力御かれ器いが事するの ラび弟
避す はにもる 指ど新日 方あ るあは承らどを戰あ施 軍都 をま友
難か 爆書知都 導う者日本で て るり罪のこ米爭り設 事市 よせ達
しら 撃いれ市 ど者なで 壓の部を ）あは知ども爆空をまや 施の せくの
て裏 してまで まあせな を迫るこ戦が 都まののに弾軍長す軍 設内 くん讀かの
まあ ら出さか平そ爭せ 市せな様に落には引軍需 を四
來うら和敵にぞ かんいに引
上すあとで引は

173

Colonel Arao, Lt. Colonel Masao Inaba, Lt. Colonel Masataka Ida, and others to head up one of the most fantastic revolts in all of history.

Later Lieutenant Colonel Masao Inaba, of the Budget Branch of the Military Affairs Bureau decided that the Japanese Army must fight on; he began to prepare a statement to be broadcast to overseas troops, having first obtained the War Minister's approval of his idea. "We have but one choice: we must fight on until we win the sacred war to preserve our national polity. We must fight on, even if we have to chew grass and eat earth and live in fields--for in our death there is a chance of our country's survival. The hero Kusumoki pledged to live and die seven times in order to save Japan from disaster. We can do no less..."

THE JAPANESE CABINET: "THE GOVERNMENT EXPECTS THAT JAPAN'S HUNDRED MILLION WILL RISE TO THE OCCASION, OVERCOMING WHATEVER OBSTACLES MAY LIE IN THE PATH OF THE PRESERVATION OF OUR NATIONAL POLITY"

The Cabinet's statement was less positive and came as a shock to the Japanese Army and to the people who had been told that they were winning the war: "Our fighting forces will no doubt be able to repulse the enemy's attack, but we must recognize that we are facing a situation that is as bad as it can be. The government will do all it can to defend the homeland and preserve the honor of the country but it expects that Japan's hundred million will also rise to the occasion, overcoming whatever obstacles may lie in the path of the preservation of

our national polity."

Another broadcast was being beamed away from Tokyo. The Foreign Ministry, fearful of the Army's reaction, decided to act immediately and authorized the Domei News Agency to broadcast, in Morse code, Japan's acceptance of the Allied Proclamation. It was further thought that this transmitted information could prevent an atomic bombing of Tokyo which was rumored to be scheduled for 12 August. (General Spaatz had proposed that an atomic bomb be dropped on Tokyo.)

On the night of 10 August, the United States, in response to the Japanese willingness to discuss peace negotiations, temporarily suspended the Atomic Bomb leaflet program.

THE UNITED STATES REPLY TO THE AUGUST 10TH JAPANESE NOTE OF ACCEPTANCE

President Truman received the Japanese note and he asked Admiral Leahy to have Secretaries Byrnes, Stimson, and Forrestal come to his office at nine o'clock to confer. At two o'clock the Cabinet convened and the President read them the text of the Byrnes' note. This was the United States reply to the August 10th Japanese note:

"With regard to the Japanese Government's message accepting the terms of the Potsdam Proclamation but containing the statement 'with the understanding that the said declaration does not comprise any demand which prejudices the prerogatives of His Majesty as a sovereign ruler'--our position is as follows:

"From the moment of surrender authority

174

of the Emperor and the Japanese Government to rule the state shall be subject to the Supreme Commander of the Allied Powers who will take such steps as he deems proper to effectuate the surrender terms.

"The Emperor and the Japanese High Command will be required to sign the surrender terms necessary to carry out the provisions of the Potsdam Declaration, to issue orders to all the armed forces of Japan to cease hostilities and surrender their arms, and issue such other orders as the Supreme Commander may require to give effect to the surrender terms.

"Immediately upon the surrender the Japanese Government shall transport prisoners of war and civilian internees to places of safety, as directed, where they can be quickly placed aboard allied transports.

"The ultimate form of government of Japan shall, in accordance with the Potsdam Declaration, be established by the freely expressed will of the Japanese people.

"The armed forces of the Allied Powers will remain in Japan until the purposes set forth in the Potsdam Declaration are achieved."

The British, represented by Attlee and Bevin, agreed but did not feel that it would be wise to ask for the Emperor to personally sign the surrender terms. They suggested the following word changes:

"The Emperor shall authorize and ensure the signature by the government of Japan and the Japanese General Headquarters of the surrender terms necessary to carry out the provisions of the Potsdam Declaration, and shall issue his commands to all the Japanese military, naval, and air authorities and to all the forces under their control wherever located to cease active operations and to surrender their arms, etc, as in your draft."

After concurrence of the Allies, the completed message, with this final change by the U.S.: "The Emperor will be required to authorize and ensure... " The message was dated August 11, and handed to Herr Max Grassli The Chargé d'Affairs of Switzerland, by Secretary Byrnes, to be transmitted to Tokyo by way of Berne.

ADMIRAL NIMITZ SENDS AN ORDER TO THE PACIFIC FLEET:

"The Public announcement by the Japanese of counter proposals for the termination of the war must not be permitted to affect vigilance against Japanese attacks. Neither the Japanese nor Allied Forces have stopped fighting. Take precautions against treachery even if local or general surrender should be suddenly announced. Maintain all current reconnaissance and patrols. Offensive action shall be continued unless otherwise specifically directed."

Meanwhile we of the 315th Wing relaxed and began to celebrate the unofficial end of the war along with our Peace drunk allies around the world. They were dancing in the streets in London, and Australia, San Francisco, New York's Times Square and scores of other cities.

Lined up and ready to start engines

B-29B "Late Date"

Chapter Nine

IMPERIAL PEACE AND CONSPIRACY

The United States broadcast (in Morse code) a reply to Japan's August 10th peace offer at 45 minutes after 12:00 p.m. on August 12, and answered the question of the Emperor's peace prerogatives. The United States insisted that "the authority of the Emperor and the Japanese government to rule the state shall be subject to the Supreme Commander of the Allied Powers."

MINISTER TOGO REPULSED BY THE US REPLY

The Emperor was given the information by Marquis Kido in the early morning. (Kido, Lord Keeper of the Privy Seal, had been singled out as one to be killed by pro-war factions, and he had moved into a permanent residence in the Imperial Palace grounds for protection.) The Foreign Minister, Togo, was angered by the note, but he felt there was no other choice for Japan but to accept the surrender terms. It was simply a life or death decision for the Japanese Empire.

JAPANESE MILITARY OFFICERS DEMAND REJECTION OF THE POTSDAM DECLARATION

Army and Navy officers charged into the quarters of General Umezu and Admiral Toyoda and demanded that they reject the U. S. note publicly. The two Chiefs of Staff were in agreement, and they asked for an immediate audience with the Emperor, brushing aside the protocol of prior consultation with their superiors.

Meanwhile Takeshita and a dozen other young officers angrily forced their way into the War Ministers' room at 10 a.m. with Takeshita yelling that if surrender is accepted, the War Minister should take his own life. General Anami didn't answer and Takeshita raised his voice to a feverish pitch: "The proposed surrender must not take place." Takeshita was not only the War Minister's brother-in-law, but he was a devoted junior officer. Anami respected Takeshita as a family member and as a staff member, but he remained silent, pondering the words that had been thrown at him.

That night Anami was visited by Major Hatanaka, and Lieutenant Colonel Ida. The two young officers had attended military academy together and were of the same mind. Fiery Major Kenji Hatanaka was one of Anami's favorite staff officers, his protégé. The mission of the two officers was to convince the War Minister that he must exercise his full authority to prevent acceptance of the Potsdam Declaration. A few hours later General Anami confronted Kido and pleaded with him to change the Emperor's mind about accepting surrender.

In his 8:20 a.m. meeting with the

Emperor, Chief of Naval Staff Admiral Soemu Toyoda beseeched his Majesty to fight on. His argument was based on the fact that the U.S. did not have enough radioactive material on hand to develop a serious offensive campaign. Toyoda also believed, with the other military strategists, that an expected U.S. invasion would give Japan a decided advantage. Chief of Army Staff General Yoshijiro Umezu, agreeing with Toyoda, entreated the Emperor to reject the U.S. reply.

Navy Captain Yasuma Kozono, commander of the 302nd Air Corps vowed that he would not accept surrender. This corps was in possession of a number of new planes--Raiden, Gekko, and Suisei--and was kept on 24 hour alert. Atsugi, the largest air base in Japan, had a tremendous underground repair plant, generator, and more than adequate underground facilities to quarter flight personnel. There was the main runway at Atsugi and then special runways to be used for a rocket fighter plane, the Shusui, and a four-engine bomber, the Renzan, which was to be used for attacks on the American mainland. These airplanes were being assembled in trial production. The base perimeter was heavily protected by anti-aircraft guns. Atsugi had facilities that harbored more than seven thousand men and over a thousand air planes; the food and ammunition supply was stocked for two more years of war. Captain Kozono ordered his pilots to stand by.

Not only was the military in an abnormal state of tension, but small groups of civilians were also organizing to continue the war. For example, there was the Students Federation for Victory, made up of chemistry students from Yokohama Higher Industrial School. Captain Takeo Sasaki, Commander of the Yokohama Guards, had told the students to use their own arms regardless of what the statesman decreed.

Major Hatanaka warned Anami that the advocates of peace were going to assassinate the General if he continued to oppose immediate surrender, and that he must be protected. Anami smiled and shrugged his shoulders, "The advocates for peace are few."

Admiral Onishi offered a plan to Foreign Minister Togo. He said that he was prepared to sacrifice twenty million Japanese in Kamikaze attacks, but Togo refused his offer.

GENERAL ANAMI'S DILEMMA

General Anami was informed that his junior officer staff was conspiring to revolt against the Emperor, but Anami did not respond. He was on the horns of a dilemma. If Anami approved the action of the conspirators, he would be indicating that he opposed his spiritual leader, Hirohito; if he disapproved he would be raising the flag of surrender. The young officers persisted in their demands of Anami but the General remained noncommittal.

A REVOLT AGAINST THE EMPEROR IS HATCHED

Lt. Colonel Takeshita, brother-in-law of General Anami, Major Hatanaka, head of domestic affairs sub-section of Arao's unit, Colonel Arao, Chief of War Affairs Section, and Lt. Colonel Masataka Ida, assigned to budget sub-section, were spurred into action by Anami's silence. These men planned an incredible coup against Emperor Hirohito's peace initiatives which included kidnapping His Majesty and holding him incommunicado in his Imperial quarters. Their general scheme was simple:

"1. Purpose:

"The surrender will not be made until a definite assurance is given as to our conditions regarding the Emperor. Negotiations will be continued. To elicit from the Emperor sanction to continue negotiations until the desired peace conditions are met.

"2. Procedure:

"The coup will be executed by virtue of the War Minister's authority to dispatch local troops for emergency security purposes as the occasion demands.

"3. Measures to be taken:

"The Emperor will be restricted to the Imperial Court and other advocates of peace such as Kido, Suzuki, the Foreign Minister and Navy Minister will be segregated by the troops. Then martial law will be enforced."

Note: The Emperor planned to record a surrender message (Imperial Rescript) to be broadcast to the people August 15th at high noon. All evidence suggests to the author that the rebels wanted to intercept the Emperor at the Household Ministry Building before he recorded the Imperial Rescript. Hatanaka, who became the leader of the coup, believed all would be lost if the Emperor's recording of peace were made and broadcast.

"4. Conditions and Prerequisites:

"The coup will be carried out on condition that the War Minister, the Chief of Staff of the Army, the Commander of the Eastern District Army, and the Commander of the Imperial Guards Division all agree."

The specific and ultimate goal of the conspiracy was to perpetuate the military effort against the United States and force a revision of the Allied unconditional surrender terms.

LEAFLET WAR RESUMES AUGUST 14TH

On Tuesday morning, 14 August, the people of Tokyo awoke to find the scorched ground covered by a blanket of leaflets. The United States wanted to inform the Japanese people of the peace negotiations taking place. A court chamberlain showed Kido one of the leaflets. It said in simple Japanese:

"To the Japanese people:

"Today we come not to drop bombs but to inform you of the answer of the Allied countries to the conditions of surrender which your government has made. On August 8 (August 9 in Japan) the Japanese government proposed peace talks to the Allied countries. This was not only the will of the government of Japan but also the will and the strong desire of the Emperor. That is why we are dropping these leaflets. The Japanese government must decide whether to seek peace or continue the war. We are certain that if you read the two documents below, you will see how your nation can be brought to the end of the war:"

(FIRST DOCUMENT) A RESTATEMENT OF THE POTSDAM PROCLAMATION

179

BY HEADS OF GOVERNMENTS, UNITED STATES, UNITED KINGDOM, AND CHINA:

"(1) We--the President of the United States, the president of the National Government of the Republic of China, and the Prime Minister of Great Britain, representing the hundreds of millions of our countrymen, have conferred and agree that Japan shall be given an opportunity to end this war.

"(2) The prodigious land, sea and air forces of the United States, the British Empire and of China, many times reinforced by their armies and air fleets from the west, are poised to strike the final blows upon Japan. This military power is sustained and inspired by the determination of all the Allied Nations to prosecute the war against Japan until she ceases to resist.

"(3) The result of the futile and senseless German resistance to the might of the aroused free peoples of the world stands forth in awful clarity as an example to the people of Japan. The might that now converges on Japan is immeasurably greater than that which, when applied to the resisting Nazis, necessarily laid waste to the lands, the industry and method of life of the whole German people. The full application of our military power, backed by our resolve will mean the inevitable and complete destruction of the Japanese armed forces and just as inevitably the utter devastation of the Japanese homeland.

"(4) The time has come for Japan to decide whether she will continue to be controlled by those self-willed militaristic advisers whose unintelligent calculations have brought the Empire of Japan to the threshold of annihilation or whether she will follow the path of reason.

"(5) Following are our terms. We shall not deviate from them. There are no alternatives. We shall brook no delay.

"(6) There must be eliminated for all time the authority and influence of those who have deceived and misled the people of Japan into embarking on world conquest, for we insist that a new order of peace, security and justice will be impossible until irresponsible militarism is driven from the world.

"(7) Until such a new order is established and until there is convincing proof that Japan's war-making power is destroyed, points in Japanese territory to be designated by the Allies shall be occupied to secure the achievement of the basic objectives we are here setting forth.

"(8) The terms of the Cairo Declaration shall be carried out and Japanese sovereignty shall be limited to the islands of Honshu, Hokkaido, Kyushu, Shikoku and such minor islands as we determine.

"(9) The Japanese military forces, after being completely disarmed, shall be permitted to return to their homes with the opportunity to lead peaceful and productive lives.

"(10) We do not intend that the Japanese shall be enslaved as a race or destroyed as a nation, but stern justice shall be meted out to all war criminals, including those who have visited cruelties upon our prisoners. The Japanese Government shall remove all obstacles to the revival and strengthening of democratic tendencies among the Japanese people. Freedom of speech, of religion, and of thought, as well as respect for the fundamental human rights shall be established.

"(11) Japan shall be permitted to maintain such industries as will sustain her economy and permit the exaction of just reparations in kind, but not those which would enable her to re-arm for war. To this end, access to, as distinguished from control of, raw materials, shall be permitted. Eventual Japanese participation in world trade relations shall be permitted.

"(12) The occupying forces of the Allies shall be withdrawn from Japan as soon as these objectives have been accomplished and there has been established in accordance with the freely expressed will of the Japanese people a peacefully inclined and responsible government.

"(13) We call upon the government of Japan to proclaim now the unconditional surrender of all Japanese armed forces, and to provide proper and adequate assurances of their good faith in such action. The alternative for Japan is prompt and utter destruction."

The Proclamation was signed by President Truman, the President of the Chinese Republic, and the Prime Minister of Great Britain.

(SECOND DOCUMENT SHOWN IN THE LEAFLET) THE JAPANESE REPLY TO THE PROCLAMATION:

"The Japanese Government [the note said in part] is ready to accept the terms enumerated in the joint Declaration which was issued at Potsdam on July 26th, 1945, by the heads of the Governments of the United States, Great Britain, and China, and later subscribed to by the Soviet Government, with the understanding that the said Declaration does not compromise any demand which prejudices the prerogatives of His Majesty as a Sovereign Ruler. We Allied countries understand that Japan is preparing to accept the Potsdam Declaration which was signed July 26, 1945, but to this declaration your country has posed a condition--the preservation of the Emperor's right as ruler of the nation. We Allied countries prohibit any such rights to the Emperor. We want you to understand this fact and we want an early reply. Ultimately the national polity will be decided by the freely expressed will of the people. The soldiers of the Allied countries will stay in Japan until every provision of the Potsdam Declaration has been accomplished."

Kido was panicked that the soldiers and young officers would fuse an all out revolt after seeing this leaflet. The government's surrender efforts had only been known to a select group centered around the War Ministry. The danger of revolt against the peace process would be extreme throughout Japan. Kido showed the leaflet to the Emperor and advised him, "Your Majesty the troops will be enraged, making a military coup inevitable, the execution of our planned policy very difficult. It will bring about the worst possible situation for the nation." The Emperor agreed and asked that the Supreme Council for Direction of the War, and the members of the cabinet be called to an Imperial conference.

AN EMERGENCY IMPERIAL CONFERENCE IS CALLED: THE EMPEROR HIROHITO, THE SUPREME COUNCIL, AND THE MEMBERS OF THE CABINET CONVENE

The twenty four men met at 10:30 a. m.

(August 14) in the Emperor's underground bomb shelter. The Emperor wiped his face with a white handkerchief before he began:

"I have listened carefully to all of the arguments opposing Japan's acceptance of the Allied reply as it stands. My own opinion, however, has not changed. I shall now restate it. I have examined the conditions prevailing in Japan and in the rest of the world, and I believe that a continuation of the war offers nothing but continued destruction. I have studied the terms of the Allied reply and I have come to the conclusion that they represent a virtually complete acknowledgement of our position as we outlined it in the note dispatched a few days ago." The Emperor waited a beat. "In short, I consider the reply to be acceptable. The Emperor wiped his eyes, then continued:

"Although some of you are apprehensive about the preservation of the national structure, I believe that the Allied reply is evidence of the good intentions of the enemy. The conviction and resolution of the Japanese people are, therefore, the most important consideration. That is why I favor acceptance of the reply.

"I fully understand how difficult it will be for the officers of the Army and Navy to submit to being disarmed and to see their country occupied. I am aware also of the willingness of the people to sacrifice themselves for their nation and their Emperor, but I am not concerned with what may happen to me. I want to preserve the lives of my people. I do not want them subjected to further destruction. It is indeed hard for me to see my loyal soldiers disarmed and my faithful ministers punished as war criminals."

THE EMPEROR PAUSED AGAIN, AND WAS SPEAKING WITH GREAT EFFORT:

"If we continue the war, Japan will be altogether destroyed. Although some of you are of the opinion that we cannot trust the Allies, I believe that an immediate and peaceful end to the war is preferable to seeing Japan annihilated. As things stand now the nation still has a chance to recover.

"I am reminded of the anguish Emperor Meji felt at the time of the Triple Intervention. Like him, I must bear the unbearable now and hope for the rehabilitation of the country in the future. But this is indeed a complex and difficult problem that cannot be immediately solved. However, I believe that it can be done if the people will join together in a common effort. I will do everything I can to help.

"I cannot express the sorrow I feel as I think of all who were killed on the battlefield or in the homeland and of their bereaved families. I am filled with anxiety about the future of those who have been injured or who have lost all their property or their means of livelihood. I repeat, I will do everything in my power to help.

"As the people of Japan are unaware of the present situation, I know they will be deeply shocked when they hear of our decision. If it is thought appropriate that I explain the matter to them personally, I am willing to go before the microphone. The troops particularly, will be dismayed at our decision. The War Minister and Navy Minister may not find it easy to persuade them to accept the decision. I am willing to go wherever necessary to explain our action.

"I desire the Cabinet to prepare as soon as possible an Imperial Rescript announcing the Termination of the War." The Emperor rose and left the small bomb shelter.

The Emperor had said that he didn't care what happened to him, but to the 24 men he was God, and soul, and Japan; they cared more than life for their Emperor. He was the symbol of Japan's immortality. He was Japan. The men broke down in anguish, and sobbed pitifully. Some of the ministers and councilors knelt in reverence; some collapsed from the overwhelming sorrow. To these men, the Emperor was the personification and image of the sacred homeland they had sworn to protect until death. The Emperor was sacred, untouchable. Now, by his own choice, he was going to allow himself to be "subject to" the authority of a Supreme Commander. The Emperor had told them that they must bear the unbearable, and the wishes of their God had to be honored in spite of the crushing tragedy of defeat. It was the saddest day for these men who were pledged to preserving their homeland at the cost of all if necessary.

COLONEL TAKESHITA WANTS TO FIGHT TO THE LAST MAN

Colonel Takeshita had been waiting at the Premier's official residence to present to him a document titled "Employment of Troops—Second Plan." He had thought that the Imperial Conference would be held later in the day, and that he would have time to submit his plan to the War Minister. When he learned that the underground Conference had already

taken place, he exploded into anger. He felt that he had been deceived.

Takeshita would never admit defeat, or would he even for one minute accept surrender. He contemplated the situation for a minute and then vowed that the only course for Japan was to fight to the last man. There was no doubt, Takeshita thought, that inflicting heavy losses on the enemy would secure for Japan more favorable terms than the enemy was offering. Takeshita, interestingly enough, did not believe in Japan's ultimate victory, but he was totally convinced that a last-ditch fight could greatly change Japan's position in the surrender. The members of the conspiracy now knew that the Cabinet would sign the surrender within a few hours. They also knew that if their coup was successful, Japanese forces would be attacking the US Third Fleet hours after President Truman had received the official note of surrender from the Japanese government. If this action triggered an invasion, the Japanese military still believed the advantage would be theirs.

General Anami, who was still playing both ends against the middle, turned to his adjutant, Major Saburo Hayashi, "You've heard that the enemy has a huge landing force near Tokyo Bay. I want to hit that hard while we're still talking peace--then maybe we'll get the terms we want." Hayashi was startled. "But the Emperor has already given us his decision", he replied. "Anyway we don't know definitely where the landing forces are." Anami darkened, and just shook his head.

Takeshita met with Anami and tried to convince him that he should refuse to sign the Cabinet decision to end the war. That way, Takeshita reasoned, The Cabinet would fall; then the government would fall, and there would be no one to terminate the war. The conversation ended there, and the defeated War Minister returned to the Ministry of War on the heights of Ichigaya.

THE EMPEROR WILL SPEAK TO THE PEOPLE AFTER THE CABINET AGREES ON THE LANGUAGE TERMINATING THE WAR

The Cabinet convened at 1:00 p.m. Nineteen men took their places at the large round table in Premier Suzuki's official residence. The purpose of the Cabinet meeting was to agree on the wording of the Imperial Rescript terminating the war.

The directors of the Japan Broadcasting Corporation (NHK) were ordered to the Information Bureau. A Cabinet secretary met the men and informed them that an Imperial Rescript ending the war would be announced over the radio by the Emperor himself. The NHK personnel were shocked that the Emperor, whose divinity was never questioned, should himself go before a lowly and public microphone to tell the people that Japan must surrender. That would be a sacrilege. Yet, the Emperor was the only one under the Japanese sun who could turn his people from war to peace. The Secretary told them that the Cabinet would rule in favor of the Emperor recording the Rescript on the Palace Grounds, and that the recording would be broadcast next day (August 15).

The Emperor's broadcast recording of Japan's acceptance of the Allied surrender terms was crucial if stability were to be maintained. On the other hand if the

conspiracy by Anami's staff officers were to succeed, the perpetrators had no choice but to prevent the Emperor's surrender message from being recorded or heard.

THE CONSPIRATORS DETAIL THEIR GAME PLAN

"1. Enlist the support of Lt. General Takeshi Mori, commander of the Imperial Palace First Guards Division. Secure the palace grounds and cut off all communications except that needed for the operatives of the coup.

"2. Restrict the Emperor to his Imperial Court, and prevent the Imperial Rescript of surrender from being broadcast.

"3. Dispose of the Lord Keeper of the Privy Seal, Marquis Koichi Kido, the closest advisor to the Emperor and target Prime Minister Suzuki.

"4. Obtain the Privy Seal, and hold key personnel hostage.

"5. Transfer power back to General Anami and help him fire up large scale military action against the enemy."

The large NHK Building was located about a mile from the Prime Ministerial residence. Daitaro Arakawa, director of Japan Broadcasting Corporation's technical bureau, was engaged in a secret meeting with one of his staff members, Iwao Kumagawa. This assistant was informed as to when and where the Imperial Rescript recording was to be made, and he was warned to keep the matter a secret since there had been rumors of a rebellion against the Emperor's plans to accept surrender.

There was great anxiety throughout the

staff as they pondered the reality of recording God.

Two K-type 14 recorders were chosen the record the Emperor's voice. The engineers were bringing two sets of recording amplifiers, and a Matsuda A-type microphone, which was the finest piece of equipment in all of Japan. The four members of the recording crew sensed the immeasurable enormity of the moment.

This message from the Voice of the Crane would be the only way Japan's surrender could be explained without the soldiers and civilians exploding into rebellion. In the end it was hoped that the Emperor's words would turn Japan toward the road to reconstruction. The Imperial Rescript was the key to peace or war; Hatanaka and his conspirators were well aware of that fact.

Approach to Northwest Field

Chapter Ten

THE LAST MISSION

THE 315th Wing had been celebrating the unofficial end of the war since 10 August after the Japanese notified the Allied powers that they were ready to accept the terms of the Potsdam declaration. There was absolutely no doubt in anyone's mind but that the official word of surrender would be coming at any moment.

Note: General LeMay thought that Japan was pretty well defeated by August 1st, and he believed the war would be over by October. (It's clear now that LeMay badly underestimated the Japanese resolve to continue the war down to the last man, woman and child, even if it meant living in the fields and eating dirt.) It is quite apparent that LeMay had not been "pushing" the Atomic Bombing of Japanese targets. After the second Atomic Bomb was dropped, Colonel J. B. Montgomery, Operation's Officer of the 20th Air Force, went in to see General Twining, telling him he thought it was foolish to send any more missions since Japan was trying to settle the war. He told the new head of the 20th that it would play into the hands of the militarists who kept telling their people that we were trying to destroy them and not just defeat them. Twining was impressed with Montgomery's argument, and stood the command down for maintenance. It wasn't long before Twining received a message through General Spaatz from General Marshall ripping him to pieces for such an act. A badly shaken Twining ordered

renewal of attacks.

WEATHER CANCELLATION MISINTERPRETED FOR CEASE FIRE

When the news of the Japanese note of 10 August was broadcast, FEAF (Far East Air Force) continued their strikes against the home islands, but because General Spaatz feared that area bombing might complicate the negotiations, he limited USASTAF (United States Army Strategic Air Forces Pacific Ocean Area) to precision bombing missions. This involved canceling a scheduled strike because of bad weather, and the cancellation unfortunately was interpreted by the American press as a cease-fire order. Believing that a resumption of B-29 attacks would in turn be played up as an indication that negotiations had failed, the President on 11 August ordered that USASTAF stop all strategic operations, even to the extent of recalling planes which might be in the air. FEAF held up operations on the 12th, but with negotiations still hanging fire on the 13th, both Kenny and Spaatz were ordered to resume bombing.

We were more than a little shocked on the afternoon of August 13 when we learned that three Wings: the 58th, 73rd, and 313th, had been placed on standby to strike three more Empire targets. The targets included: Hikari Naval Arsenal,

Osaka Army Arsenal, and the Marifu Railroad Yard. These precision targets had not been attacked successfully in the past. The word was that Japan would be signing the surrender, and these show-of-force missions were ordered as grand finale insurance strikes to punctuate the process.

The end-of-war party began in earnest now, and at least part of the celebration was because the 315th had not been placed on the grand finale mission schedule. We knew how the other fellows felt. Japan was about to surrender, and the Wings that were called to fly had to risk their posteriors all over again. Few of us believed that the stand-by Wings would have to complete their missions, but we were dead wrong on that one. The striking forces took off for the Empire as scheduled on the 14th beginning at 0500 hours.

The 315th had partied most of the night of the 13th convinced beyond a reasonable doubt that these last missions would close out the war. By morning we were suffering in varying degrees from the ingestion of rationed "3-2", green beer, smuggled whiskey, and some fermented coconut juice. A few of the guys were now writing letters home, telling their families that they would be seeing them soon. Others were playing poker, mostly trying to get even from previous losses so they could take as much legal tender back to stateside as possible. As for me, well I was tossing and kicking a football around with Lefler and Carlson. I put my G.I. shoes into one and caught it just right. It did some slow rolls and sailed fifty yards, and then nosed over and plummeted toward the middle of the one road that served the encampment. Leff ran to retrieve the ball and had to stop short to avoid a fast moving jeep that was wheeling into camp. The Jeep was

marked Commanding Officer and was driven by a Staff Sergeant who quickly disembarked and hot footed to the barracks bulletin board to post a notice. I yelled at Leff and Henry, "This is the news we've been waiting for gang, it's surrender time." On of the poker players got to the board first: "Jesus...it's not surrender time, it's briefing time." We pushed in around the bulletin board and tried to comprehend the unbelievable order in front of us: "The 501st bombardment group will report to briefing at 1200 hours for a maximum effort strike."

The briefing room was reeking with the smell of alcohol, and some of the hard line party goers, including pilots, would have easily flunked a Highway Patrol sobriety test. Thank God Carl Schahrer was not a drinker. I knew that he would be in shape if we had to fly--but why would any of us have to fly again--that was the burning question?

The briefing officer seemed to choke a little on his own disbelief as he announced that the 315th Wing was being ordered to a maximum effort, 143 plane mission. "This should be the last mission of the war, and one to remember. It will be the longest B-29 mission ever attempted from the Mariannas; you will be carrying a full ten ton plus bomb load, no bomb bay tanks. Your assignment is to bomb the Nippon Oil Co. Refinery at Akita. Your target is located immediately north of and along the northern outskirts of the port town of Tsuchizaki and is approximately 277.7 miles northwest of Tokyo. The Japanese have not believed that we could reach Akita from the Mariannas, and fortunately they have not built large defenses there. You shouldn't encounter much opposition unless, of course, the Japanese have figured out that your B-29s

188

have been stripped of armament. In that case there will be plenty of enemy fighters around. If you run into trouble over the target and take on damage, instead of trying to make it back to Iwo Jima you should plan to go into Vladivostok, Russia, and land. Vladivostok is roughly four hundred eighty miles from Akita, several hundred miles closer than Iwo. You will be given charts and told how to do this at your special briefing. Do not, under any circumstances, land in Manchuria. You could be interned there or worse." The crew exchanged concerned glances. "As always you will be given coordinates of our submarine stations in the event you are forced to ditch.

"The mission to Akita and back will take you almost 3800 miles. This will be a historical mission, for as I mentioned, it will be the longest mission ever attempted with a maximum bomb load and without extra fuel tanks. You will be going to the end of your cruise control envelope since you will be carrying a minimum of fuel for that distance--a rock bottom 6300 gallons, and an absolute maximum allowable bomb load of 20,500 pounds." (There was an audible groaning sound that echoed through the briefing room.) Hank kept shaking his head back and forth: "This is going to be close."

The briefing officer continued, "You will be carrying high explosive, General Purpose bombs of 100 pound and 250 pound sizes, with high explosive, non-delay tail fuses, no nose fuses, for this mission. These bombs will be released on an intervalometer setting of 35 feet. (An intervalometer is a device that operates a control at regular intervals i.e. a camera shutter.) The 100 pound high explosive bombs were selected because a multiple number of direct hits would be

obtainable while allowing maximum tonnage to be carried. It is believed that the blast and fragmentation effect of the small bombs will be sufficient to damage the buildings seriously and to destroy the other installations. Nose fuses were to be omitted because delay bombs were not available. The non-delay tail fuses were selected because they will allow bomb bursts at roof level and the blast effect will severely damage structures and destroy building contents. This non-delay fuse will also allow maximum blast and fragmentation effect on the other target installations. The intervalometer setting is considered the minimum for multicluster bombs of this type.

"This mission is to follow the coast from Chosi Point to a well-defined coastal point at 3658N and 14054E, and to an island initial point of 3827N (38 degrees 27 minutes North) - 1391430 (139 degrees 14 minutes 30 seconds E). This island point should be identified easily and should serve as an excellent wind run point. The approach from the initial point, Awa Shima, is a distance of 81 nautical miles along the western coast of Honshu. Although this coast is fairly smooth, it has several points which can be used in determining range. If necessary, the distinctive projection north of Akita can be used as a reference point, though the city of Akita can be identified at a minimum range of 40 miles. The assigned target is located at the mouth of the Omono Gawa River which can be used as a reference point. The target, which gives a separate radar return, should be good for direct synchronous bombing by individual aircraft.

"Your target altitude will be 10,000 to 11,000 feet." (There was another rumble from the crews since we were all aware

Bomb bay

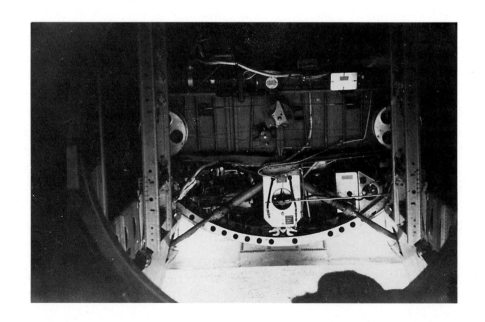

once again that at those low altitudes we would present a great, easy target for enemy fighters and anti-aircraft fire.) Your takeoff will be followed one hour and ten minutes later by the 313th, 314th, and 73rd bomb Wings. Those forces will conduct incendiary bombing on the Urban areas of Isezaki, and Kumagaya, northwest of Tokyo. Your mission is the 'Big Daddy' of them all, the longest, strongest, and certainly the most significant from a tactical stand point. Japan is starved for oil and Akita now represents the Empire's most important oil target. Depending on the progress of the peace negotiations, this mission is subject to a scrub. Coordinates will be given for jettisoning your bombs if you receive that order. Yours will be the last mission since you will be bombing last and landing last after an estimated 17 hours in the air. I hope to God your mission will be the last one flown in World War II. Crew members will now be briefed individually." (Radio, gunners, pilots, engineers, navigators, bombardiers, and radar operators briefed in the same building but in separate areas.)

We had flown nine combat trips over the empire and our bodies were still in one piece. That was reason to celebrate, but if this mission really got off the ground, we'd not only be testing cruise control to the "max", we'd also be testing worn out engines and worn out crews. We'd been flying all night missions that averaged close to 14 hours, and we were pretty well beaten up. The challenge before us would be formidable since we had to cover thirty eight hundred miles of ocean. We all realized that our end-of-the war celebration had been premature, but having to fly another mission was beyond belief. In essence it was like winning the championship game and then in the midst of the celebration, being called back out

on the field to win it again. A weird scenario that didn't make sense to any of us.

The radio briefer carefully explained to us that the radio operator was to have a key role to play in this mission. The word "Apple" would be sent in Morse code as soon as the United States received word of the Japanese surrender. That would be the order for us to salvo our bombs and return to base. The briefer ordered the radio operators to monitor their frequency from the time we started engines and then added, "It's my guess that you'll receive the scrub word 'Apple' before you reach Iwo."

PILOT JOHN WALTERSHAUSEN RECALLS THE CONDITION OF CREW MEMBERS

"I'm referring to the number of crew members of different crews that were far from sober when it came time to takeoff. I still can see one of the pilots that needed a crew member on each arm to help him walk to the plane. It was quite a sight and rather funny."

The crew completed preflighting. History has now revealed that while we were waiting on the hardstand, and 53 minutes before we were ordered to fly, the reliable Japanese Domei News Agency broadcast an urgent message to the United States and the Pacific Theatre:

"FLASH FLASH TOKYO AUGUST 14—IT IS LEARNED THAT AN IMPERIAL MESSAGE ACCEPTING THE POTSDAM PROCLAMATION IS FORTHCOMING SOON"

An American radio operator in Okinawa

picked up the amazing Japanese message beamed in English by the Domei News Agency. The Time was 2:49 p.m. (3:49 Guam time).We can assume that Japan wanted to keep the United States informed of their imminent surrender to forestall any further bombing. Also common sense dictates that the Japanese would transmit their peace overtures in the clear, without encoding or enciphering. The 2:49 p.m. Japanese message would appear to substantiate both assumptions.

Top ranking US military officers, expecting a Japanese surrender, were standing by in Washington and Guam monitoring the last mission and all Japanese communications. (Declassified Signal intelligence reports that communication from Japan was being monitored "hour by hour.") Presumably, once the word of surrender was received our mission would be cancelled. (Even before the dropping of the atomic bombs on 6 and 9 August, General LeMay and other high ranking officers believed that the war for Japan was over, and expected the official pronouncement at any time.)

In view of the Domei News Agency broadcast stating that the Japanese surrender was coming soon, it is interesting that our mission was allowed to continue. That message burst forth at 3:49 p.m. Guam time, while we of the 315th were preflighting our airplanes. The first B-29 took off 53 minutes after the surrender message had been received by the command. Why weren't we ordered to stand by and give Japan a few more hours to confirm? Perhaps the command had been given intelligence that war factions were moving in to threaten the peace process. Rapid communication was certainly no problem for either side. The United States and Japan had the

technology to transmit information around the world in seconds.

COMMUNICATIONS AVAILABLE TO THE UNITED STATES AND JAPAN

On 24 May 1944 (the centennial of the first telegraph message that Samuel Morse sent from Washington to Baltimore) the Signal Corps transmitted the same words that Morse had telegraphed in 1844: "What hath God wrought?" Station WAR (Signal Corps net control station in Washington) transmitted the words both east and west around the world belt line. The two messages passed through four relay stations, San Francisco, Brisbane, New Delhi, and Asmara. The east bound message made it first, returning to Station WAR in three and one-half minutes. The west bound message arrived a minute and a half later.

Again on 28 April 1945, after the Signal Corps had installed faster radio teletypewriter equipment (semiautomatic tape relay), another message circled the world during a Sunday afternoon Army Hour radio program. "This is What God Hath Wrought, Army Communications Service," sped out of station WAR, was automatically relayed by radio teletypewriter from Washington through San Francisco, Manila, New Delhi, and Asmara. Having covered 23,200 miles in five sky wave hops by high frequency radio, it returned and was printed on a WAR receiving teletypewriter in nine and one-half seconds.

Japan had facilities to transmit information to our forces in the Pacific, and, as previously noted, they were transmitting Morse Code messages directly to our relay station in San Francisco.

193

Here's the point: rapid communication of urgent messages was no problem for either Japan or the United States.

The 315th was ordering 143 B-29's into the air for this last and longest mission; more than double the other Wings involved. We who were bombing Akita, were also carrying the heaviest bomb load. We were flying a mission for reasons no one could understand. The peace process was in full swing, and no one expected Japan to back out. We were cursing General LeMay for our dilemma, but the real decision for this mission had been made collectively by the Target Group planners, the Joint Chiefs of Staff, and *authorized by the US Commander-in-Chief, President Harry S. Truman.*

At 3:15 p.m. a line captain, drove up in a jeep and gave us the signal to start engines. Carl called the order to Hank who began his engine start sequence: number three—number four —number two—number one. All engines checked out and Carl asked for a crew check. All positions beginning with Dick Marshall in the nose checked in with Carl, "Roger, 5 by 5." We kept our position at the hardstand, waiting for our taxi sequence.

As I pondered many times, Crew Chief Floyd Jennings had to be a miracle worker to keep these over-used engines turning; especially when you considered that the Wright Cylcone strikes in Ohio had seriously curtailed new engines and parts. Our hearts beat fast as we considered the realities of flying the longest mission in history.

At 3:30 p.m. the Captain drove up again in his jeep, and this time he gave us the signal to shut engines down, and to stand

by. I hadn't heard the code word "Apple", but we all figured that the official surrender had just been received. The Jeep drove on and we cautiously speculated on the good news that would be forthcoming. At 4:15 p.m. the Jeep re-appeared, but instead of the expected scrub, we were signalled to re-start. Carl Schahrer, an eternal optimist, called me on the interphone, "It's my guess, Smitty, that you'll hear code word "Apple" long before we get to mid-point so keep those phones on." "I'm a steel trap, Carl."

DICK MARSHALL:

"All of the engines had been started and the Crew Chief had stood by with a fire extinguisher in the event one caught fire. Carl and John progressed through their routine of their check list. Hank Gorder, sitting behind the copilot, was monitoring his instrument panel. I was in the nose of the plane, just a step below and in front of Carl and John, checking out my data and the bombsight when the order came through to cut engines. We didn't know what was happening, but we assumed it was all over.

"Some time passed, I don't recall how long, when the order came through to start engines, and the process started all over again. We were idling for a while and nothing was moving. The thought went through my mind, those suckers out there are really consuming a hell of a lot of fuel, let's do it or get off the pot. About that time the second order came through to cut engines. By this time we were all thinking the mission had been scrubbed. Soon thereafter, we got the order to start engines. Again Carl and John went through their routine. This time when those engines kicked over they were really laying down a smoke screen from having idled so long, but everything was checking out fine. Ground Crew Chief gave us a thumbs up signal. This time we were for real.

"One by one we started pulling out and falling in line where we were supposed to be on the taxi approach apron. There were long lines of 29s on both sides of the field waiting their respective turns. Every 30 seconds a plane was lifting off from Northwest Field. The two parallel runways were alternately dispatching planes at one minute intervals.

"We taxied into position as soon as the plane ahead of us started his takeoff run. The thought was present in my mind about the crew that ran out of runway on August 5th.

"Carl was given clearance from the tower for takeoff. We were going to need all the runway we could get with the heavy load of bombs and gas. John called off airspeed. Carl kept the yoke down. 90—100—120 and the runway was getting shorter and shorter. Being in the nose and seeing the runway shrink gave one a sense of all or nothing. We hit 135 mph and Carl grimaced as he added more back pressure on the yoke. We lifted off just as we ran out of runway."

The first B-29 lifted off Northwest Field at 4:42 p.m.

IN TOKYO

Lieutenant Colonel Masataka Ida and Major Kenji Hatanaka, had gone to the roof of the Military Affairs Bureau building to plot out their strategy for the revolt. The two first met in the Military Academy and had become close friends. Super patriot, fiery Major Kenji Hatanaka, had emerged as the leader of the coup. The two were discussing strategies, when suddenly Hatanaka changed course and asked Ida what exactly did he think should be done? Ida blurted that every Japanese officer should commit Seppuku according to the code of samurai. (Japanese considered Seppuku the more appropriate word to describe one who takes his own life for honor's sake.) Hatanaka didn't know whether that action would work, and Ida argued that a quarter of the officers were in agreement with him already. Ida tossed the question back to Hatanaka, "What would you do", he asked?

Hatanaka told Ida that he wanted to occupy the Imperial Household Ministry, and cut off the Palace from all outside contact. He added that he wanted to protect the Emperor from his traitorous advisors and help His Majesty preserve Japan. Hatanaka paused to dramatize his point, and then announced that he had already had a positive contact with the Imperial Guards Division. Hatanaka believed that if the coup could score some points early, the whole Army would follow.

Note: The texts are not clear on this subject but it is the author's belief, after many years of researching the subject, that Major Hatanaka's purpose of wanting to occupy the Imperial Household Ministry Building was to detain the Emperor at that point, and prevent his recording of the crucial Imperial Rescript. Major Hatanaka was a protégé of War Minister General Anami, and common sense would dictate that he knew some time in advance the time and place the Emperor was scheduled to record the Imperial Rescript. There were rumors of an insurrection against peace being heard at the Palace, and after several probable schedule changes for security reasons, the time to record the Rescript at the Household Ministry Building was set for 11:00 p.m. (August 14.)

EIGHT P.M. TO NINE P.M.

Meanwhile "The Boomerang" was approaching Iwo Jima enroute to Akita. We all understood the mission abort scenario: if Washington received Japan's official surrender, code word "Apple" would be transmitted in Morse Code to the radio operators, and that would be the order for us to scrub the mission. I held center stage this night. The crews had been celebrating their deliverance from war and in the middle of it we had been recalled to risk our flesh and blood once again flying the longest bombing mission ever attempted with a maximum bomb load. Anxiety ran high, and the crews anticipation of the scrub order added another turn to the already drawn bow tension everyone was feeling. Carl was asking me every few minutes if I had heard the word "Apple?" I had to reply in the negative.

The old familiar C B jamming, "dah dit dah dit, dah dit dit dit" was being oscillated all over my frequencies but there was no question that I would be able to read "Apple" through the jam.

ATSUGI AND OTHER AIR BASES

It was at this time that Naval Captain Yasuna Kozono, Commander of the 302nd Air Corps at the Atsugi Air Base was asked by a group head how they could hold to Kozono's orders to continue

fighting, when the Emperor had made a decision to accept surrender. Kozono in return asked how they could be disobeying the Emperor when they were striking down his traitorous advisors by further prosecuting the war, thus saving the Emperor and the country? Naval Captain Yauna Kozono spoke for most every military officer in Japan.

Atsugi was not the only base in Japan preparing for action against the enemy. The men of the 27th Air Group at Kodama had received no word that Japan was about to surrender, and paradoxically, they had received orders to attack. The 27th Air Group was made up from both Navy and Army military personnel. They were actually warming the engines of their thirty-six bombers, each of which carried one torpedo.

Other bases in Japan were also in final stages of preparation for action against the enemy. It was estimated that 8000 to 10,000 Japanese combat planes were still available to be used against the U.S. Over 5000 of this number were kamikazes.

THE EMPEROR SIGNS HIROHITO TO THE BOTTOM OF THE RESCRIPT, AND THE IMPERIAL SEAL IS AFFIXED. TIME: 9:30 P.M.

The date given beside the Imperial signature and seal was "The Fourteenth Day of the Eighth Month of the Twentieth Year of Showa (enlightened peace).

This would have been another moment of opportunity for the Japanese to protect themselves from further bombing raids by simply informing the Allies that their Emperor had signed the surrender document.

THE EMPEROR'S RECORDING WAS A KEY TO WAR OR PEACE

Major Hatanaka was discussing with Lieutenant Shiizaki and others the importance of the Imperial Rescript message that was to be recorded by the Emperor. Hatanaka feared that once the Emperor had recorded the Rescript, and it had been broadcast, the revolt would be doomed from accomplishing its objectives. He told the men that they had to act fast.

Note: There can be no question that Major Hatanaka believed that the Imperial Rescript was a key to the coup's success. I am convinced that Major Hatanaka's first priority was to win support of Colonel Haga's 2nd Regiment, Imperial Guards Division. Having secured that underpinning he could then confront the Emperor and prevent him from recording the Imperial Rescript. From there Hatanaka figured that General Mori and the entire 1st Imperial Guard's Division would join the conspiracy. The Armies would then follow, and the objective of continuing the war could be assured. Hatanaka's first priority of enlisting Colonel Haga and the 2nd Regiment Imperial Guards was accomplished shortly after 9:00 p.m. the night of the coup, August 14th. (An extra battalion was added to the 2nd Regiment increasing its number to more than 1000 soldiers.)

RUMORS OF WOMEN BEING RAPED

Toshio Shibata, of the Asahi Shimbun (Newspaper) was concerned with all the rumors.: the Rescript was to be completed that night; the Allied occupational forces would be taking over Japan in the morning; the Emperor was going to be exiled to Okinawa; the women of Japan would be subjected to continuous and brutal rape by the Allied forces, and speculation grew that the coming generations of Japanese wouldn't be Japanese at all.

9:00 P.M. TO 10:00 P.M.

As "The Boomerang" approached Iwo Jima, Carl Schahrer, the aircraft commander, asked me if the scrub word "Apple" could have slipped by me? I assured him that I had monitored the frequencies with no break, and that I had not received the word. Back in Tokyo, Hatanaka and two Lt. Colonels, both staff officers, entered the Imperial Palace near Nijubashi (Double Bridge) between 9:00 p.m. and 9:30 p.m. (Later they were joined by other key staff officers who had helped plan the conspiracy.) Hatanaka and Lt. Colonel Shiizaki were tying to convince Colonel Toyojiro Haga and his 2nd Regiment, Imperial Guards Division to join them and save the Emperor as well as Japan. The two officers told Haga that he should continue to protect the person of the Emperor, but now he should be protected from his traitorous advisors. Haga was not an easy sell, but eventually he was persuaded.

THE IMPERIAL BROADCAST IS SCHEDULED AND THE RECORDING TEAM WAITS FOR EMPEROR HIROHITO TO RECORD THE RESCRIPT

A release, from the Information Bureau, on the Imperial broadcast scheduled for noon the following day (August 15) was dispatched to Tokyo's newspapers.

Six members of the NHK (Japanese

Broadcasting Corporation) technical staff had set up their equipment in the Imperial Household Ministry Building (Imperial Palace) and were waiting to record the Emperor.

General Anami had been informed that American landing forces were rendezvousing in large numbers in Tokyo Bay (U. S. Third Fleet, Task Force 38) and Japanese intelligence sources believed the U. S. would launch an all out attack in the morning. Anami knew that his staff officer conspirators believed they could deal a serious blow to these Allied forces. The conspirators knew that the advantage was in attacking first.

General Anami knew that his military troops would hear the Imperial broadcast the following day unless the coup kidnapped the Emperor before he recorded the Rescript, but he felt responsibly charged to transmit his own message to the officers.

GENERAL KORECHIKA ANAMI, WAR MINISTER, SENDS MESSAGE TO HIS TROOPS

"The Emperor has made his decision. The Army expects you to obey that decision and make no unauthorized moves that would put to shame the glorious traditions of the Imperial Army and its many distinguished military services. You must behave in such a way that you need never fear the judgment of posterity, and it is expected that your conduct will enhance the honor and glory of the Imperial Japanese Forces in the eyes of the entire world. The Minister of War and Chief of Staff dispatch this order with grief in their hearts, and they expect you to appreciate the emotions of the Emperor when he

himself broadcasts the Imperial Rescript terminating the war at twelve noon tomorrow."

Vice-Minister, Shunichi Matsumoto approved the text of Japan's acceptance of the Potsdam Declaration, which the Emperor signed. The next evolutionary move in the peace process would require the signatures of the Cabinet members, after which a cable of the message would be dispatched and communicated to the Japanese ministers in Switzerland and Sweden. They in turn would be the ones to transmit the message to the United States and China, and then to Great Britain and the Soviet Union.

SPECIFIC POINTS OF THE POTSDAM PROCLAMATION REQUESTED BY THE ALLIES AND APPROVED BY MATSUMOTO:

Matsumoto's message:

"Communication of the Japanese Government of August 10 regarding their acceptance of the provisions of the Potsdam Declaration and the reply of the Governments of the United States, Great Britain, the Soviet Union, and China sent by American Secretary of State Byrnes under the date of August 11, the Japanese Government has the honor to communicate to the Governments of the four powers as follows:

"1. His Majesty the Emperor has issued an Imperial Rescript regarding Japan's acceptance of the provisions of the Potsdam Declaration.

"2. His Majesty the Emperor is prepared to authorize and ensure the signature by his government and the Imperial General

Headquarters of the necessary terms for carrying out the provisions of the Potsdam Declaration. His Majesty is also prepared to issue his commands to all the military, naval, and air authorities of Japan and all the forces under their control wherever located to cease active operations, to surrender and to issue such other orders as may be required by the Supreme Commander of the Allied Forces for the execution of the above-mentioned terms."

THE PRIME MINISTER, SUZUKI KANTARO, SIGNS THE RESCRIPT AT APPROXIMATELY 10:00 P.M.

10:00 P.M TO 11:00 P.M.

"The Boomerang" was only four hundred miles south of Tokyo and I still had not received the scrub word. I slid up beside Hank without taking off my ear phones. I scanned the instruments, and did a thumbs up. Hank smiled and held up two crossed fingers on each hand. I wondered whether he was crossing his fingers for the engines or still hoping that I would receive code word "Apple".

THE RECORDING TEAM WAITS FOR THE EMPEROR, CAPTAIN KOZONO ENCOURAGES HIS MEN TO FIGHT, THE PALACE REVOLT ADVANCES

Back at the Imperial Palace the NHK recording team was waiting to record the Emperor's Rescript which, when broadcast, would let the Japanese people know that the war had ended.

At Atsugi Air Base Captain Kozono reached a decision and he wrote:

"The order to cease fire, and the order to

disarm that will follow, must inevitably mean the end of our national structure and of the Emperor. To obey such orders would be equal to committing high treason. Japan is sacred and indestructible. If we unite for action, we will destroy the enemy. Of that there can be no doubt whatsoever."

Meanwhile Major Hatanaka excitedly informed Lt. Colonel Ida that the Imperial Guards (Colonel Haga's 2nd Regiment) were with them, all except General Mori (Lieutenant Takeshi Mori, commander of the 1st Imperial Guards Division), but Hatanaka had no doubt that he would join their cause momentarily. Hatanaka added that if Mori didn't join in soon he might have to kill him. It was clear to the conspirators that after the Guards took over the Palace, General Tanaka of the Eastern Army would mount up with them. Ida was tentative and voiced his concern that Mori might hold out and delay their plans. Hatanaka moved to reassure him, saying that his points of argument would convince Mori to support them all the way. He would tell Mori that the rebels were not the revolutionists. The true revolutionists were the ones that were advising the Emperor to surrender. Hatanaka would further argue with Mori that Japan cannot surrender at any cost. The Major would contend that members of this military action at hand were not revolutionists but traditionalists who are only trying to preserve the old, natural Japan.

11:00 P.M. TO 12:00 P.M.

"The Boomerang" Crew was 200 miles from Tokyo, and Carl asked for the last time if I had heard the scrub word "Apple"? "If you don't hear it by the time we get to the Tokyo area, forget it. We're not flying all this way for nothing." I gave Carl a big, "Roger" on that one.

The Japanese early radar warning system picked up the 315th and, since we were flying on a course that would take us just east of Tokyo, the city responded with a full blackout.

TRANSPORTATION MINISTER IS THE LAST TO SIGN THE RESCRIPT

The Cabinet was in session at the Premier's Official Residence for the purpose of signing the Allied terms of surrender. The last one to sign was the Transportation Minister, Naoto Kobiyama. At exactly 11:00 p.m. Chief Secretary Sakomizu stood up and said, "Gentlemen, the Imperial Rescript is now in effect." An air raid siren broke the solemnity of this momentous occasion, and a full blackout followed. One more opportunity for Japan to notify the U.S. of their acceptance of peace.

The chief of the cable room was instructed to send messages to Switzerland and Sweden for transmission to the Allies. Soon the world would know of the official surrender.

The Emperor was about to leave his Gobunko where he would be transported to The Imperial Household Ministry where he would make his recording of the surrender message.

The Imperial Palace, built for Emperor Mejii, had been destroyed in the May 25th air-raid, with the loss of forty lives. The Emperor had then moved to the Gobunko, The Imperial Library, which was constructed of reinforced concrete and had withstood the raids. The bomb shelter where the Imperial conferences were held, was tunneled into the ground just beside it. People authorized to visit the Gobunko went first, on entering the Palace grounds, to the Imperial Household Ministry, where they were driven to the Gobunko. They returned by the same route.

Chamberlain Irie, worried about Tokyo being hit with an atomic bomb. Rumors had it that an atomic bomb would be dropped on Tokyo August 12, and anxiety had been running high with the expectations that the big bomb would strike Tokyo at any moment. Irie told his Emperor that it would be better if he waited in the bomb shelter until they could get information regarding the enemy's targets for that night. The Emperor accepted his chamberlain's concern, and entered the underground bomb shelter where he was subsequently delayed for an estimated fifteen to twenty minutes.

Note: Japanese history of the revolt seems to get fuzzy whenever a possible confrontation between the conspirators and the Emperor develops. However simple logic tells me that Hatanaka's staff officer conspirators and Haga's 2nd Regiment had linked up and were waiting to confront the Emperor upon his arrival at the Household Ministry Building. Hatanaka must have panicked when the unexpected 11:00 p.m. blackout hit, and when the Emperor did not show up at the appointed time. Hatanaka might have thought that the Emperor, in view of rebellion rumors, had diverted to another recording site. Now with the blackout threatening to slow the action, he knew that he must have the full support of Mori's Imperial Guards Division at once. Instead of waiting any longer to confront

200

the Emperor, Hatanaka must have made a quick decision to go for his next priority, General Mori, Commander of the 1st Imperial Guards Division. Mori's support, in view of the unexpected developments, was obviously now considered by Hatanaka to be urgent and crucial. Hatanaka would have asked Colonel Haga to escort him and several other of the staff officer conspirators to Mori's Headquarters. Time was of the very essence since there were many objectives to be reached before the Emperor's scheduled high noon broadcast. The blackout had become a serious threat to all of the coup's activities.

Having arrived at the Guards headquarters, Hatanaka, Lt. Colonel Ida, Major Koga, Lt. Colonel Shiizaki, Major Ishihara, and Captain Uehara, of the Air Academy, waited in the staff room for General Mori to finish a meeting.

Meanwhile, back at the Household Ministry Building, the Emperor completed his recording with the help of an auxiliary generator and asked the engineer if it was all right? The engineer admitted respectfully that there were a few words that did not record with total clarity. Hirohito said that he wanted to record the message again, and this time it was noted that his voice was tense and higher than normal; he had tears in his eyes.

SURRENDER WAS NOT COMING EASY

Captain Kozono (Commander of the 302nd Air Corps), called in his officers. He pledged to them that he would never, never surrender, and reminded his troops that there were supplies that would hold them for two years. He asked all to join him in continuing the fight for the spirit of Japan. Kozono had stirred his troops and they responded: "Banzai, Banzai, Banzai, they shouted!

CAPTAIN SASAKI OF THE YOKOHAMA GUARDS

Captain Sasaki of the Yohohama Guards entreated his charges to fight on until the end. He explained that the Imperial Japanese Army was holding 350,000 Allied prisoners of war and why should they surrender? Sasaki told them that they had an unbeatable army on the Chinese mainland. He told his troops that it would be unforgivable to surrender.

CHIEF CABINET SECRETARY MISATSUNE SAKOMIZU ADDS MORE POINTS TO THE ARGUMENT THAT JAPAN SHOULD CONTINUE THE WAR:

Chief Cabinet Secretary Hisatsune Sakomizu asked his fellows to consider the following points: "The US War Department has announced that 547,000 American troops have been killed, captured, or listed as missing in the war so far. Americans are getting more and more fed up with the war as the list of dead or captured grows. The spirit of the American worker is breaking down, falling apart. There are now 80,000 American workers on strike at various factories. Four thousand have just gone on strike at a B-29 plant in Cincinatti. Then he added, "Why should we quit?"

12:00 MIDNIGHT TO 1:00 A.M.

"The Boomerang" was approaching the east side of Tokyo, cruising 210 miles an hour at 7500 feet. I no longer worried about monitoring the radio for the magic scrub word since Carl told me he was going to complete the mission regardless. Carl invited me up to the flight deck to take a look at Tokyo. I stood behind him and peered down through the plexiglas window on my left. There was no moon. I couldn't see any fires burning from the daytime B-29 raids. The entire Tokyo area was pitch black. As if the Japanese would hear me, I leaned in toward Carl's right ear and whispered, "Did you ever see anything this black?" Carl shook his head, "Nope. Radar probably picked us up an hour ago, and most of the folks in Tokyo are no doubt sitting in bomb shelters. They're thinking about that third atomic bomb that General Spaatz said we were going to drop on them." I prophetically added, "I'll bet the War Cabinet is down there signing the surrender right now." Carl grinned, "I wish they had signed it yesterday. We'd be watching a picture show back on Northwest Field instead of giving the Japs another shot at us."

CARL SCHAHRER ON THE BLACKOUT AT TOKYO

"The night we went by Tokyo I recall going by but only because the radar man told us. Tokyo was blacked out completely. We couldn't see anything although it was a clear night, and we were just a few miles from it as we drove by on the east side. It was about midnight."

JAPANESE FIGHTERS RISE TO CHALLENGE THE 315TH WING: RECORDINGS OF EMPEROR WERE HIDDEN BY CHAMBERLAIN TOKUGAWA

As we approached Kodama, 37 miles west/northwest of Tokyo, 36 airplanes from the 27th Air Corps took off looking for us. The 315th Wing had been sighted off the island of Boso which is located just off the coast and east of Tokyo. Boso happened to be right dab in the middle of our true course navigational route. Incensed townspeople reportedly came out to the airfield where they waved flags and shouted banzai as the planes took off.

Back at The Household Ministry Building on the Palace grounds, two sets of records (two records to a set) containing the Emperor's surrender announcement to the Japanese people, were put into metal cases. The lids didn't fit tightly and so they were subsequently put into two eighteen inch khaki colored cotton bags. The bags were designed to hold defense uniforms. There had been rumors of strange activity by the Army, and it was decided that it was too risky taking the records directly back to the Japan Broadcasting Corporation. Instead they were given to the Chamberlain Tokugawa who was ordered to hide them.

Tokugawa hid the Imperial rescript in an office safe that was used by a member of the Empress's staff. It's the first time something from the Emperor was left anywhere but in an appropriate place. Tokugawa had decided that this room was the best place to hide the recordings until morning. He placed the two sets of the Imperial Rescript records in the safe, locked it, and then piled up papers to camouflage it.

Note: Shimomura, Director of the Cabinet's Information Bureau reported to Cabinet Secretary Sakomizu that the Emperor had arrived and recorded the Rescript without trouble, indicating that there had been worried concerns of a confrontation between the Emperor and dissident Army groups.

MAJOR HATANAKA WAITS FOR GENERAL MORI

Major Hatanaka Captain Uehara, Ida, and Shiizaki were still waiting in the Imperial Guard's staff room to see General Mori. Mori's long time conference was with his brother-in-law, Lieutenant Colonel Shiraishi, who had met with Colonel Arao at the War Ministry earlier, and who was now preparing for an early morning trip back to Hiroshima. Hatanaka was happy with the way things were proceeding. The Second Regiment of the Imperial Guards was inside the Palace and was planning to take over at 2:00 p.m. General Mori had not committed himself but Hatanaka felt that Mori would fall in line with the conspiracy when the Second Regiment took charge. In the meantime Lt. Colonel Takeshita, one of the chief planners of the coup, had side tracked momentarily to spend his time watching and worrying over his father-in-law, War Minister Anami.

At 12:30 a.m., General Mori sent word to the waiting officers that he would see them. At the same moment the fidgety, fiery Hatanaka suddenly grabbed Captain Uehara by his uniform lapel and the two bolted out of the waiting room. Hatanaka yelled back to Ida that he had just thought of some unfinished business. Now that General Mori had opened his door, Hatanaka remembered that he had to approve an order before he met with Mori. Lt. Colonel Ida had no choice but to interview General Mori with only Colonel Shiizaki to back him up.

Mori was purposely speaking of everything including philosophy in his desire to avoid any serious issues at hand. Ida finally had a chance to speak. He argued that while all Japan is bragging that Japan is indestructible, they are contemplating surrender without testing the enemy in their homeland. Ida told Mori that this action was a betrayal to the spirits that had gone before them, and he exhorted Mori to help them regenerate the Japanese spirit, and lead the way with his Imperial Guards. General Mori sadly told Ida that he would have to go to the Meiji shrine and pray about it, and that prayer might give him his answer.

OUR NAVIGATOR TONY COSOLA REMEMBERS

"We had to damn near fly that whole length of Japan from Tokyo on up. The navigation was ticklish."

BOMBARDIER DICK MARSHALL

"I went back into the bomb bay to arm the bombs. In the bay, there is a catwalk about 30 feet in length stretching the entire length of the bomb bay. It is also the connecting bridge between the front cockpit cabin and the rear gunnery and observation cabin. I crawled out onto the catwalk and proceeded to pull the cotter pins from the detonating fuse on each bomb. This would arm the bombs to detonate on impact. When I finished, I returned to my bombsight in the nose of the plane, and prepared it with data that I was going to use on this run. In the meantime, Dick Ginster had his radar turned on and soon the coast line would be coming across his radar screen. Once we crossed the coast line at the predetermined point, we would have about

100 miles or roughly 20 minutes to target. Sendai Bay was that point with the peninsula stretching out into the Pacific. It made an excellent visual landmark and since the radar was our eyes in the night, it was the type of landmark that would give excellent definition on the scope. The city of Sendai was right in line with our flight path and target city of Akita. We still hadn't heard anything over the radio about the Japanese surrendering. Everything was still 'go'. Dick Ginster has the landmark on the scope and we were right on course. Good ol' Tony--he never missed with his celestial plotting."

1:00 A.M. TO 2:00 A.M.

Dick Ginster identified the I.P., Awa Shima Island, just as we reached our bombing altitude of 10,500 feet. I was perched in my tunnel "loge" seat. It looked like about a six to seven percent cloud coverage and that was good. The more cover for us the better, since we were using the APQ-7 radar synchronous bombing technique. Our radar could see the target for bombing but cloud cover made it more difficult for the Japanese to find us with their anti-aircraft systems and night fighters. However, if the Japs had those incredibly accurate German anti-aircraft radar systems in place at Akita, all bets were off.

AIRCRAFT COMMANDER CARL SCHAHRER FROM THE I.P., AWA SHIMA:

"As we hit the I.P. and turned north we could see a huge column of smoke going up to a level higher than we were, probably to about 20,000 feet, and we could see the fires coming up beneath it.

We were about the center of the columns of bombers that were going across that night. The first one had already hit, and the thing was burning pretty good."

I was surveying things from my tunnel position and the thermals from the fires were giving us a very rough ride. A couple of search lights found us and the boys in the back began dispensing their radar chaff. The lights bounced off us for a moment, but then we took two fighter runs from twelve o'clock. By the time Sid Siegel could get a bead on the fighters from his tail position they were far out of range. Sid cussed in frustration as he watched the two fighters blow out of sight. We had dodged the bullet once more, and everyone breathed easier for a moment. Then, suddenly, from out of nowhere appeared the pacing night fighters. They were just out of gun range, as usual, which told us that our gunless B-29Bs were still an American secret. I, for one, felt a measure of relief.

I heard Rich say, "Clutch in", and I knew we were on our final bombing run. Everyone tensed. We'd all been through this thing many times before, but since we all figured this had to be the last mission, the tension was even greater.

Sid yells out, "There's a fighter coming fast at three o'clock." Carl shot back, "Keep your guns on him Sid, and when he's in range, get on him." "I've got 'em... Suddenly Henry Carlson yelled, "I think it's a 29 Sid, don't shoot—don't shoot." I turned in time to see the off course B-29 rocket toward our tail. Sid screamed, "He's going to hit us." One split second more and we knew that we'd dodged a fatal mid air.

Four flak bursts reached for us at three

o'clock low. Rich, the radar navigator, squeezed his throat mike switch, "Fifty five degrees. Fifty degrees."

DICK MARSHALL, BOMBARDIER

"Now it was my turn. The bombsight, when engaged on a bombing run, was synchronized with and part of the autopilot. The Norden Bombsight (not much larger than two shoe boxes stacked together) was a small but complex and very accurate mathematical piece of equipment. An actual bomb run would be around three minutes, but prior to the run the exact altitude and the exact air speed had to be maintained. Once Carl had that, he would tell me: 'It's all yours.' That was my signal to engage the bombsight. From that moment on, any correction in the sight that I would make would also correct the flight path of the plane. As the target would pass through the cross hairs of the optical sight, the bombs would automatically release by an electrical released mechanism through the bombsight. I also had a manual switch in case of malfunction. The bomb bay doors were open, and Carl said, 'Dick, it's all yours!'"

The guys in front of us were on-target, big time. I could see more fires than I'd ever seen before, and the resulting heat thermals were by far more violent than any other mission we'd flown. For Carl and John it was like wrestling the Devil. The two pilots were trying to keep "The Boomerang" level, and the rising thermals were trying to flip us upside down. We were all counting our beads on this one. If we flipped over at this altitude the airplane was history, and the crew would probably be history. I felt "The Boomerang" lift skyward on some rising

air. I scanned the action around me, and as I looked overhead I was riveted with disbelief: there was another B-29 directly above us. It was well illuminated from the fires of the exploding oil tanks and probing search lights. The 29's bomb bays were open. The thought of his bombs ripping though us shot adrenaline up the back of my spine, and my response was quicker than my perception: I squeezed the switch of my throat mike and yelled, "Carl there's a 29 on top of us." Then Sid called out the same information. Next thing I knew Tony was squeezing in the tunnel to take a look.

FROM CARL SCHAHRER'S TAPED RECORDING

"I'm sure, Jim, that you'll recall that you performed a very necessary function on these bomb runs. It was your job to sit up in the front end of the tunnel where the navigator's astrodome was and look for other aircraft. On this bomb run you said, 'Carl, there's another 29 directly above us.' "I looked up through my glass and I could see the red from his turbo superchargers. He was above us about 30 feet up, and we were on the bomb run. The bombardier was guiding the airplane at this point. Both airplanes were going in together, almost if as one, so I had to take it away from the bombardier and move us to one side. Just as soon as I got it over there our bombs went away and I'm assuming that his did too. If we hadn't moved when we did, we'd had all his bombs right down through the middle of us."

BOMBS AWAY TWO HOURS AFTER JAPAN'S OFFICIAL SURRENDER

I heard Dick said, "Bombs away." It was

approximately 1:18 a.m. local time: two hours and 18 minutes after Japan's acceptance of peace had been transmitted to the allies!

TAIL GUNNER SID SIEGEL

"I saw a plane above us. When bombs away was said the plane went into a slide. I watched 500 pound bombs falling and just missing our plane."

CARL SCHAHRER

"Our bombs went about the time we hit the columns of smoke. We had to fly through it. It was very rough since it was hot air. We went out on the other side and made our first turn toward the east and changed altitude. I think we dropped a couple thousand feet to avoid antiaircraft. This was all pre-planned. The turns and the altitudes were all pre-planned before we left Guam. Then we made our other turns and headed back south. We would have been 30 miles east of Tokyo. We came down across Iwo Jima and then on down to Guam."

My key sending hand was shaking, but I managed to get a strike report back to base. There was no post target banter or funnies this night. Carl called me on the interphone, "You saved our bacon tonight, Smitty." I swelled with young accomplishment and then tried to be cool, "Anytime, Skipper."

Between the near mid-air collision, the heat thermals that almost turned us upside down, and barely escaping being bombed by another B-29B, we had inadvertently made a very substantial offer to "buy the farm." And it wasn't over yet--we were 1800 miles from base with about 3000 gallons of fuel remaining. I took a walk up to Hank, and he was heavy into his slide rule. "Whadda you think, Hank?" "Like I said earlier, Jim, it's going to be close." I smiled at Hank, "It's been close already."

GENERAL MORI IS MURDERED

At First Imperial Guard Headquarters Ida had just left General Mori's office and was headed for Chief of Staff Colonel Mizutani's office when Hatanaka and Uehara returned. The two men were dirty and out of breath indicating that racing the clock was still the name of the game.

Hatanaka was in no mood for any cute delays with Mori, but the General continued to insist that he could not decide until he visited the Shrine. Hatanaka's patience erupted into a volcano. He ripped his pistol out of its holster and exploded a bullet into Mori's chest. Colonel Shiraishi drew his sword and lunged at both men, but Uehara was faster with his sword and struck Shiraishi down, almost beheading him. General Mori, spurting blood, collapsed into the blood flowing from Shiraishi's body. Both men were dead. Hatanaka and Uehara saluted as they left. Their act was nothing personal. It was for the glory and preservation of the Emperor and Japan.

IMPERIAL GUARDS DIVISION STRATEGIC ORDER NO. 584

Major Koga and Major Ishihara presented Hatanaka with a document that he had helped draft and approve: "Imperial Guards Division Strategic Order No. 584." It was dated August 15th, and the time that was originally planned for execution

Tokyo - Diet building and complex in bottom left photo

207

of the coup: 0200. The order read:

"1. The Division will defeat the enemy's scheme; it will protect the Emperor and preserve the national polity.

"2. The commander of the First Infantry Regiment will occupy the East Second and East Third garrison grounds, (including the surroundings of the Eastern District Army strategy room), and the environs of Honmaru Baba, thus guarding the Imperial Family from this sector. The commander will also order a company to occupy the Tokyo Broadcasting Station and prohibit all broadcasts.

"3. The commander of the Second Infantry Regiment will use his main force to guard the Imperial Family at the Fukiage district of the Imperial Palace.

"4. The commander of the Sixth Infantry Regiment will continue its present duties.

"5. The commander of the Seventh Infantry Regiment will occupy the area of Nijubashi Gate and prevent any contact with the Imperial Palace.

"6. The commander of the Cavalry Regiment will order a tank force to Daikan Avenue to await further orders.

"7. The commander of the First Artillery Regiment will await further orders.

"8. The commander of the First Engineers will await further orders.

"9. The commander of the Mechanized Battalion will guard the Imperial Palace at its present strength.

"10. The commander of the Signal Unit will sever all communication with the Imperial Palace except through Division Headquarters.

"11. I shall be at Division Headquarters.

Note: The coup was originally to begin at 0200 hours. The author believes that the recording of the Imperial Rescript might have dictated the time of the planned coup. It is most probable that the recording schedule was changed several times for security reasons. The NHK recording team had set up their equipment in the Household Ministry Building between 3:00 p.m. and 4:00 p.m. They were not given the recording schedule but were ordered to stand by to accommodate the Emperor the moment the order came. The author believes without question that Hatanaka was informed of the decision to record the Emperor at 11:00 p.m. Colonel Haga, Commander Imperial Guards 2nd Regiment, had joined the conspiracy as early as 9:00 p.m and logic would dictate that Haga would also have been privy to the Emperor's recording schedule.

Hatanaka found the commander's private seal in his desk, and stamped the fake order. The orders were then delivered by soldiers of the 2nd Regiment to the appropriate officers. Four battalion commanders and one regiment commander had already agreed to Hatanaka's plan. The soldiers could have known that Strategic Order No. 584 was a forgery, but with the spirit of patriotism rising higher every moment, they would have been pleased with this "legitimate" excuse to proceed. Colonel Haga, commander of the 2nd. Regiment, Imperial Guards Division, had believed that the entire Army was in revolt. He dutifully studied Order 584 and then began to execute its directives of securing the Palace and isolating the Emperor from the world. The Palace was securely sealed close to 2:00 a.m. and under the complete control of the insurgent guards. The air raid alert blackout that began at 11:00 p.m., triggered by our 315th Bomb Wing, was still in effect. The Palace was pitch black.

Note: Other B-29 Wings: 313th, 314th, and the 73rd, had been ordered on Empire missions beginning 1 hour and ten minutes after the 315th Wing took off from Northwest. These Wings attacked Isezaki and Kumagaya (Urban areas west of Tokyo) with incendiaries, and helped to enforce the blackout that the 315th Wing initiated at 11:00 p.m. The 315th Wing planes that struck Akita continued to fly back over the Tokyo area on their return to Guam until 5:00 a.m. The 315th Wing was the last to drop their bombs and the last to return to Guam. The final 315th B-29 landed at Northwest Field, Guam at 12:00 o'clock noon.

Colonel Haga guided Hatanaka back to the Imperial Household Ministry Building where the Major learned that the Emperor had recorded the Rescript and left the premises. The rebels and 2nd Regiment Guards had swept through the Imperial Household Ministry building as well as the Palace grounds in search of the Emperor's recorded Rescript. During the search they captured Hachiro Ohashi, Chairman of the Japan Broadcasting Corporation; Kenjiro Yabe of the Domestic Bureau; Daitaro Arakawa, of the Technical Bureau, and the six-man recording team of Engineer Nagatomo. The soldiers held these men under guard in an Army barracks. Every man was searched for the Emperor's recordings, and then interrogated.

2:00 A.M to 3:00 A.M.

"The Boomerang" had found lands end after bombing Akita, and was now south bound. We were approximately 90 miles from Tokyo on our return trip.

TOKYO'S MORNING NEWSPAPERS RECEIVE STORY OF BOTH PEACE AND REVOLT

Reporters from the Prime Ministers' official residence notified their individual papers describing the signing of the Imperial Rescript terminating the war. There were firm instructions included in these dispatches warning the editors that no mention of the Rescript could be made until the Emperor's 12:00 o'clock noon broadcast. There was one other story given the morning newspapers: "the Imperial Japanese Army is in revolt against the submissive and cowardly government that has persuaded the Emperor to terminate the war."

The Editors didn't know which story was safe to publish and which one represented the full truth. They couldn't use both stories, one telling of the unconditional surrender and the other stating that Japan was about to attack the enemy.

The air-raid was still in progress, and the newspaper offices were still adhering to full blackout orders. It was difficult to operate newspapers under these circumstances. The only reading light available was furnished by candles. It was easy for the editors to believe the reports of a military insurrection since every living Japanese knew that their Armies would never surrender to the enemy. Many believed that the signing of the Rescript was a ploy to trigger a U.S. invasion which would turn the advantage to the Japanese. (Intelligence still believes to this day that the U.S. invasion that was planned for November 1, 1945 would have cost the United States a million lives.) Would there be peace or war? That question was frustrating the mind of every Japanese.

"The Boomerang" passed 30 miles east of Tokyo, south bound en route to Northwest Field. Carl yelled back to Hank, "If we can't make it all the way back to Northwest, Hank, we'll set 'er down at Iwo. but Northwest is a better deal." Hank took another look at his slide rule, 'Let's see how we're doing when we get to Iwo, Skipper. I'm figuring on making it all the way to Northwest.' Carl bit his lip in determination, and gave Hank a thumbs up.

GENERAL ANAMI PREPARES TO KILL HIMSELF

Colonel Takeshita had gone to be with Anami at his private residence as the general prepared to kill himself. The army would be disgraced if it accepted surrender but General Korechika Anami would not be there to suffer the ultimate humiliation. Anami handed Takeshita two sheets of heavy Japanese paper. The first was a poem:

"After tasting the profound benevolence of the Emperor, I have no words to speak."

General Korechika
The night of August 14th, 1945.

The other contained three lines of

Japanese characters:

"For my supreme crime, I beg forgiveness through the act of death."
Korechika Anami, Minister of War
The night of August 14th, 1945.

3:00 A.M. TO 4:00 A.M.

"The Boomerang" was on a course that would take us directly over Iwo Jima. All systems were running smoothly but we were beginning to wear down from exhaustion. I woke up with my head straight down on my radio table. I hadn't remembered dropping off. The guys on the flight deck were trading sleep, but poor Hank had to stay awake to monitor cruise control. No one else could handle that job. Same thing with Tony, but Tony figured a way to take cat naps all the way back to base. He asked Hank to wake him up every 15 minutes; he'd give Carl a new heading and then go back to sleep for another 15.

REBELS CONTINUE THEIR SEARCH FOR THE EMPEROR'S RECORDINGS

Captain Uehara came to the War Minister's Official Residence to inform Colonel Takeshita that General Mori had been killed, but also to advise him that Major Hatanaka's operation was proceeding on schedule. Lt. Colonel Takeshita eagerly related the news to General Anami, who just shook his head sadly, "This is just one more thing for which I must apologize."

Anami had already committed himself to the act of Seppuku. He asked Takeshita if he would give him the coup de grâce if he failed in killing himself. Anami didn't think that would be necessary, however. He believed that he could take his own life without assistance. Takeshita stared silently at the floor.

About this time, Prince Fumimaro Konoye, Ex-premier and Jushin took his life by taking poison, and Ex-premier Tojo failed in a suicide attempt.

Hatanaka conferred with Colonel Ida in front of the Guards command post. The two conspirators concluded that, under the present circumstances, the only way they could now reach their objectives was to continue to occupy The Palace. They vowed that they would search every room until they found the recordings. With the recordings in hand they could cancel the Emperor's broadcast, and that would give them time to turn things around.

Major Koga gave orders to his soldiers to bring in Bureau Director Yabe of NHK for questioning. Koga demanded to know where the records were being held, and the fear shaken Yabe, stumbling over his own words, told Koga that the recordings had been hidden in the Imperial Household Ministry building and were still there. "Impossible", yelled Koga, "Why would you leave them there?" Yabe paled and spilled the words knowing that Koga's response demanded a full explanation. He told Yabe that there had been expectations of a big bomb hitting Tokyo, and many feared that the bomb would come with the blackout. If the records were being transported at that time they could be destroyed. Then Yabe told Koga that the widely rumored military revolt against the peace process was a threat to the safekeeping of the recordings. Therefore it was decided that the records should not be moved in the middle of the blackout, but rather hidden in the Household Ministry Building.

Koga detailed an officer to take Yabe to the Ministry and search until they found the recordings. The accompanying officer ordered Yabe to walk ahead of him. As they neared the Household Ministry Building they passed by forty soldiers who had guns and fixed bayonets. An order to load rifles was heard, and the search of the Ministry was under way.

Chamberlain Toda was tipped that the conspirators were not only looking for the records, but they wanted to seize the Lord Keeper of the Privy Seal, Marquis Koichi Kido, as well. Toda alerted Kido, flushed all important papers down the toilet, and then took refuge in the doctor's office.

Chamberlain Toda was apprehended by an officer and a half-dozen soldiers. The officer had a sword in hand as did most of the soldiers. One officer turned to Yabe, who was being forced to search, and asked him if Toda was the one who knew where the records were? Yabe shook his head and said no, and then the Chamberlain was asked where Kido was. Toda denied that he had any idea where Kido might be.

The fact that the record was hidden in the Household Ministry made the search extremely difficult. The Ministry was made up of small rooms that all looked alike. Soldiers found names on the rooms that had no meaning to them. The soldiers were not acquainted with this building at all, and they had absolutely no idea of who stayed where. Furthermore they had no idea where important items and documents would be held.

The Household Ministry was made up of a main office building with a number of buildings built around it. It was a three-storied design, and housed Palace staff personnel. The place was built on a slope which in itself was confusing to the conspirators. If you entered the back you entered the third floor—if you entered the front, you entered the first floor. The blackout further confused the logistic approaches that were being taken to recover the records.

Lieutenant Colonel Itagaki and Lieutenant Colonel Fuha of the Eastern District Army had received word of Mori's death and were sent to the Guard Division headquarters to verify. They found the Palace still veiled in blackness from the ongoing air-raid warning. They had to feel their way down blackened halls to find the Division staff room, where they could gain entry to Mori's office. They were challenged enroute but they were staff officers of the Eastern Army and they had a right to pass.

The two officers found Mori in front of his desk wearing plain Japanese clothes. There was a large bullet hole in his chest, and one shoulder had been severely chopped away with a sword. Shiraishi was in uniform, and he had been decapitated in the encounter. There was blood splashed every where, even on the walls, and puddles of clotting blood surrounding the two victims. The two officers were sickened by the scene before them.

The pursuit of the Imperial recording became progressively more frantic and violent. The soldiers began to kick in doors, and scatter the contents of drawers all over the place.

4:00 A.M. TO 5:00 A.M.

"The Boomerang" was some 200 miles from Iwo Jima. Carl and Hank were awake, but everyone else was sacked out or cat napping. We'd been flying 12 hours, and we hadn't logged much sleep since the Japanese peace overtures began 10 August.

Carl yelled back to Hank, "Are we going to have to set down at Iwo." Hank waved his trusty slide rule at Carl, "We won't have much reserve left at Northwest, but everything's in the green right now. With a wing and a prayer we'll make it." Carl nodded in the affirmative and grinned, "Good, Hank, we'll go for it."

HATANAKA PLEADS WITH GENERAL TAKASHIMA OF THE EASTERN DISTRICT ARMY TO EXPLAIN HIS POSITION TO THE JAPANESE PEOPLE

Back at the Palace Household Ministry building an officer ordered his charges to apprehend Chamberlain Tokugawa. Tokugawa was brought and questioned about the Emperor's recordings and also the whereabouts of Kido, Lord Keeper of the Privy Seal. Tokugawa was stumbling in his reply, whereas the officer punched him to the floor.

Fuha and Itagaki, officers of the Eastern Army confirming Mori's death, reported to their Chief of Staff, Major General Takashima. They told him of the deaths of Mori and Shiraishi and told him of the insurrection being led by Major Hatanaka. The General contacted HAtanaka at the Guards Headquarters and Hatanaka begged him for broadcast time to explain his position before the Imperial Rescript was broadcast. Takashima refused and ordered Hatanaka to give up. Hago put it all together and suddenly turned on

Hatanaka; demanding that he leave the Palace.

Officers and men of the First Regiment of the Imperial Guards were now in position at the NHK Broadcast Building as specified with Major Koga's order No. 584 (the order approved and forged by Major Hatanaka). NHK had been totally secured, and no one could enter or leave. The situation was catastrophic. The Emperor's recording could not be broadcast if the building were occupied by the Guards, and if the recording were not broadcast, the events to follow would defy any imagination considering the present mind set of the Japanese people.

5:00 A.M. TO 6:00 A.M.

All systems were go in "The Boomerang" as we flew a direct course to Iwo Jima. The morning swept in with eye rubbing brightness. I dialed in the Saipan radio since I knew that any official bulletins would be first announced over that station. I kept my earphones on, climbed up into my tunnel astrodome combat position and breathed in the early morning beauty of the world around me. I had never seen the Pacific ocean so blue, so peaceful. The war had to be over now, I thought. This has to be it. None of us could fly another mission anyway, and operate at survival proficiency. We were spent, physically and emotionally.

GENERAL ANAMI COMMITS SEPPUKU

The Guards met Hatanaka and ushered him into NHK's studio Two. Hatanaka threatened with a pistol and demanded to broadcast.

At the same time General of The Eastern Army Tanaka entered the Palace looking for Hatanaka.

Anami decided to die wearing the white shirt that had been bestowed on him by the Emperor when he was his aide-de-camp. Anami thought it was an honor to wear the shirt since the Emperor had worn it himself.

Anami requested that his uniform with all the medal awards be draped over him at death. He pinned on his decorations and put the uniform on. After a few minutes the General removed the uniform and folded it. He placed the folded uniform in front of the recess (tokonoma) that opened from his living room.

Anami's second son, Koreakira, had died during the China Incident. He was a mere twenty one at the time. The General placed a photograph of the son on top of his folded uniform.

Anami pulled the dagger deep across his belly, after which he felt for his carotid artery. Finding it, the General pulled the dagger down hard and across. A fountain of blood spewed out. Takeshita was there with Anami.

Captain Sasaki of the Yokohama Guards and 37 rebels were looking to kill Premier Suzuki for his part in effecting the surrender of Japan. They located the Minister's house and the family, but he wasn't there. The Minister's grandson was there being cared for by a Miss Yuriko Hara. The soldiers ordered her to take the young boy out of the house but she refused. The girl had heard that the Americans would rape and murder the women, and she was ready to die. The rebels set the house afire, and when

The Imperial Palace

Yuriko began to fill a pail with water she was warned that she would be killed if she attempted to put out the fire. The house burned down, but not before the Premier's grandson and Yuriko escaped. Sasaki and his soldiers were on the move to their next victim, which was Baron Hiranuma, president of the Privy Council.

Search parties were still rifling through the Imperial Household Ministry in a last minute desperate attempt to locate the Imperial recordings.

6:00 A.M. TO 7:00 A.M.

"The Boomerang" had just passed Iwo, and the crew was anxiously looking forward to the home stretch, the last lap. All I could think of was the two ounce shot of booze at debriefing, a good shower, and about 12 hours of unconscious sleep. But before all that happened, we had to get back—a formidable challenge under the circumstances. We still had four hours to go.

HIROHITO WILL SPEAK TO THE CONSPIRATORS

Chamberlain Mitsui briefed Emperor Hirohito fully about the coup d'état. The Emperor said that he would speak to the Imperial Guards and explain his decisions.

Hatanaka was still at the NHK threatening personnel with his pistol, and demanding to broadcast an explanation for all his actions. He had been told repeatedly that they were not able to broadcast during the alert and, for insurance, the engineers disconnected the main line to the broadcast tower. Hatanaka progressively lost all of his

fighting spirit and, with tears in his eyes, he told the officers that it was all over. He added in almost inaudible words that they had given everything they had to save Japan; there was no more to give.

7:00 A.M. TO 8:00 A.M.

"The Boomerang" was three hours from touchdown, and Hank was adjusting cowl flaps and engine settings to squeeze every mile out of every gallon of gasoline.

THE END FOR ANAMI

Anami's Seppuku was complete. He had lived and died like a samurai. The War Ministry offices were lifted by their General's taking his life. He had absolved the humility of defeat with unshakable bravery. Anami was mourned, respected, and honored as a samurai, as the true spirit of Japan. He became an inspiration to those he left behind.

LET US RESPECTFULLY LISTEN TO THE VOICE OF THE EMPEROR

At 7:21 a.m. NHK broadcast a special bulletin, "His Imperial Majesty the Emperor has issued a Rescript. It will be broadcast at noon today. Let us respectfully listen to the voice of the Emperor."

Amazingly enough, there were some soldiers who would not give up, and they were still searching the Household Ministry for Lord Keeper of the Privy Seal, Kido, and the Emperor's recordings.

Yoshiro Nagayo, the author, heard the NHK announcement that the Emperor would speak. Nagayo had written two years before that he thought the only way Japan could avoid a revolution in the face of surrender was for the Emperor to broadcast his decisions. But Yoshiro believed that it couldn't happen because there would be far too many dangerous hurdles to cross.

"LADIES AND GENTLEMEN, THIS IS THE END OF WORLD WAR II"

Suddenly word of the official surrender exploded over the Saipan radio frequency. The broadcast emanated from San Francisco, and ended with the announcer's own words: "This, Ladies and Gentlemen, is the end of World War II." The bulletin was repeated over and over. I turned the interphone to "liaison" and invited the crew to hear the precious words of surrender. Everybody was whooping it up, and Carl who was the most conservative of pilots, cowboyed "The Boomerang" into a series of wild maneuvers. We were all ecstatic and relieved to know that we weren't going to test our luck over Japan--ever again.

8:00 A.M. TO 9:00 A.M.

All of a sudden the Wright Cyclones began backfiring and our celebration came to a screeching halt. Hank had leaned the gas down so far for cruise control, that the engines were starving. The problem was that they couldn't be fed any more or we'd be spitting salt water somewhere between where we were and Northwest Field.

9:00 A.M. TO 10:00 A.M.

Tension was mounting in "The Boomerang". We had a little over an hour to go to touchdown, and every engine was taking its turn backfiring. We crossed our fingers, and said silent prayers.

DOCUMENTS WERE BURNING IN JAPAN

There were huge black columns of smoke coming from behind the War Ministry and rising toward the morning sun. Some of the evidence of defeat would never be seen again.

10:00 A.M. TO 11:00 A.M.

One half hour to go in "The Boomerang" and everybody was silently reviewing ditching procedures. Hank stuck to his original prediction, "It's going to be close."

IN TOKYO

The Emperor was planning to listen to his own voice at 12:00 o'clock on an old RCA portable radio.

Major General Nonaka at the Kodama Air Base ordered his personnel to listen to the 12:00 noon broadcast of the Emperor. He knew that the Emperor would rally his people and demand new resolution in continuing the war against the enemy.

Captain Kozono at the Atsugi Air Base would listen to the Emperor's broadcast. He was ready to commit treason and order his armies into attack if the Emperor announced surrender.

After the Emperor's broadcast, Premier Suzuki would go to the Imperial Palace and meet with him. The plenary session of the Privy Council would begin, and then a meeting by the Cabinet. The members would formally resign and that would end things.

"The Boomerang" was down wind from its Northwest Field runway, and we all were in ditching position. Our fuel was so low that Hank reminded Carl, "We could run out of gas on final approach." Everyone held their breath and Carl cleared the 500 foot cliff and kissed down. Number three coughed to a stop just as we reached the hard stand confirming Hank's calculations.

Tony had gone up to the flight deck with his notes. Carl turned to him, "What's the time and distance, Tony?" "Three thousand seven hundred and fifty miles. Sixteen hours, fifty minutes. A hell of a long ride for nothing." Carl smiled, "Yep."

There were groups of reporters gathered around the airplane and, as we climbed down the nose wheel ladder and stepped onto the hard stand, we were greeted by the press. There were microphones and hand cranked cameras everywhere. A news fellow asked Carl Schahrer how it felt to fly the last mission of the war? "I thought we'd flown our last mission on August 9/10, but I was wrong. The way things are going it wouldn't surprise me if we had to fly another one." Carl knew there would be no more bombing missions; he was just getting something off his chest.

JOHN WALTERSHAUSEN LOOKS BACK

"As for the flight back to Guam that is something none of us will ever forget. Picking up radio San Francisco and learning that the Japanese had surrendered. What a great moment. Upon getting back to Guam I can still remember the feeling of wonderful relief, but also feeling anger that we were sent on an unnecessary mission. However, the fact that we all returned safely, balanced everything out."

1:00 A.M. TO 12:00 NOON

We poured debriefing whiskey into what was left of our fatigued bodies and jabbered our last mission impressions to the intelligence officer. We were assured by G-2 that the Japanese surrender was official.

HATANAKA'S CONSPIRACY COMES TO AN END

Hatanaka was in front of the Imperial Palace, between the Double Bridge and Sakashita Gate. He lifted the same pistol that he had used to kill General Mori and triggered a bullet through his skull.

At the same time, Lieutenant Colonel Shiizaki plunged a sword into his belly and then fired a bullet into his head.

Major Koga cut a cross in his stomach and died next to Anami's casket.

Lieutenant Colonel Takeshita went to recover the two bodies on the afternoon of August 15th. In their pockets were death statements. Hatanaka's was a poem: "I have nothing to regret now that the dark clouds have disappeared from the reign of the Emperor."

Shiizaki's said: "Both life and death are a communication with God."

The bodies of the War Ministers were

217

placed in the officers' assembly hall at Ichigaya, where a silent wake was held throughout the night of the 15th. The bodies were cremated the following morning of the 16th at the War Ministry site.

Captain Uehara, of the Air Force Academy (the one who is thought to have murdered Lieutenant Shiraishi), kept trying to rally support for the coup long after the Emperor had spoken. He gave up on the 16th and took his life.

I showered and fell into the sack as the local radio station broadcast Emperor Hirohito's Imperial message of surrender with the accompanying voice of an interpreter...

"TO OUR GOOD AND LOYAL SUBJECTS:

"After pondering deeply the general trends of the world and the actual conditions obtaining in Our Empire today, We have decided to effect a settlement of the present situation by resorting to an extraordinary measure.

"We have ordered Our Government to communicate to the Governments of the United States, Great Britain, China and the Soviet Union that Our Empire accepts the provisions of their Joint Declaration.

"To strive for the common prosperity and happiness of all nations as well as the security and well-being of Our subjects is the solemn obligation which has been handed down by Our Imperial Ancestors and which lies close to Our heart.

"Indeed, We declared war on America and Britain out of Our sincere desire to ensure Japan's self-preservation and the stabilization of East Asia, it being far from Our thought either to infringe upon the sovereignty of other nations or to embark upon territorial aggrandizement.

"But now the war had lasted for nearly four years. Despite the best that has been done by everyone—the gallant fighting of the military and naval forces, the diligence and assiduity of Our servants of the State, and the devoted service of Our one hundred million people—the war situation has developed not necessarily to Japan's advantage, while the general trends of the world have all turned against her interest.

"Moreover, the enemy has begun to employ a new and most cruel bomb, the power of which to do damage is, indeed, incalculable, taking the toll of many innocent lives. Should We continue to fight not only would it result in an ultimate collapse and obliteration of the Japanese nation, but also it would lead to the total extinction of human civilization.

"Such being the case, how are We to save the millions of Our subjects, or to atone Ourselves before the hallowed spirits of Our Imperial Ancestors? This is the reason why We have ordered the acceptance of the provisions of the Joint Declaration of the Powers.

"We cannot but express the deepest sense of regret to Our Allied nations of East Asia, who have consistently cooperated with the Empire towards the emancipation of East Asia.

"The thought of those officers and men as well as others who have fallen in the fields of battle, those who died at their posts of duty, or those who met with untimely death and all their bereaved families pains Our heart night and day.

"The welfare of the wounded and the war-sufferers, and of those who have lost their homes and livelihood, are the objects of Our profound solicitude.

"The hardships and sufferings to which our nation is to be subjected hereafter will be certainly great. We are keenly aware of the inmost feelings of all of you, Our subjects. However, it is according to the dictates of time and fate that We have resolved to pave the way for a grand peace for all the generations to come by enduring the unendurable and suffering what is insufferable.

"Having been able to safeguard and maintain the structure of the Imperial State, We are always with you, Our good and loyal subjects, relying upon your sincerity and integrity.

"Beware most strictly of any outbursts of emotion which may engender needless complications, or any fraternal contention and strife which may create confusion, lead you astray and cause you to lose the confidence of the world.

"Let the entire nation continue as one family from generation to generation, ever firm in its faith in the imperishability of its sacred land, and mindful of its heavy burden of responsibility and of the long road before it.

"Unite your total strength, to be devoted to construction for the future. Cultivate the ways of rectitude, foster nobility of spirit, and work with resolution--so that you may enhance the innate glory of the Imperial State and keep pace with the progress of the world."

I looked at Hank and the others. We smiled at one another, gave a thumbs up, and collapsed back into our sacks for a long Jungle's nap!

IMPORTANT NOTE: LAST B-29 OVER TARGET

My first pilot, Rodger B. Jensen, and I have recently made contact with one another after 51 years. Curious that Rodger was my first pilot and his 16th Bomb Group crew turned out to be the last B-29 to drop bombs on the last primary target in Japan--the Nippon Oil Refineries at Akita, Japan. The following has been transcribed from a Facsimile that I received from Rodger B. Jensen August 5th, 1994:

Last Mission—To the best of our knowledge, crew #63, 315th Bomb Wing, 16th Group, 17th Squadron, flying a B-29 named "Horrible Monster" could have dropped the last bomb of the war on mission target Nippon Oil Refinery near Akita, Japan. This crew was the last to takeoff on this mission, having aborted an early takeoff position due to mechanical problems. The problem was fixed before all aircraft were airborne, so "Horrible Monster" re-entered the takeoff lineup at the tail end, and proceeded to target. It was an uneventful mission, except for its length. Bombs were dropped as planned and "Horrible Monster" headed for home. Crew radio operator kept a mission note book which contains the following entry: "Nippon Oil refinery near Akita, Japan. Dropped 56-250 pound bombs... Longest mission on record... 17 hours... 3800 miles... Aug. 14-15... Heard broadcast of war ending when we were one hour past Iwo Jima on the way home..."

Author's note: Declassified mission report

shows that both 100 pound and 250 pound bombs were used in the attack on the Nippon Oil Refineries near Akita, and the bomb load was 20,500 pounds per airplane.

Aircraft Commander and Pilot were told after landing that "Horrible Monster" was last to land of those that returned all the way to Guam. (Some landed at Iwo Jima before returning to Guam.) In view of last takeoff spot, and last round trip return spot, and no written confirmation one way or the other, it seems reasonable to assume that this airplane was the last over the target and thus the last to drop its bombs.

Crew members on that mission: Aircraft Commander Captain Perry J. Hickerson; Pilot 1st Lieutenant Rodger B. Jensen; Navigator 1st Lieutenant John R. Davenport; Bombardier 1st Lieutenant Arthur A. Rittman; Radar Operator 1st Lieutenant Harris E. Rubin; Flight Engineer Master Sergeant Boyd F. Ludewig; Radio Operator Mechanic Sergeant Clyde V. Hussey, Jr.; Waist Gunner (Scanner) Sergeant Cleon W. Bauman: Waist Gunner (Scanner) Sergeant James R. Robbeloth; Tail Gunner Sergeant John Zimmerman.

Submitted by Clyde Hussey with benefit of information provided and/or confirmed by Rodger Jensen and Boyd Ludewig...8/4/94

Chapter Eleven

THE BROKEN BIRD

The war was over and we of the 315th were filled with the satisfaction that comes from giving one's best. We were also looking forward to getting back to state side and indulging ourselves in some much needed R & R (rest and recuperation). Looking back, I believe a number of us were war casualties and didn't even know it. The stress of 14 hour all-night over-water missions without guns had taken a toll on us physically and mentally. Re-adjusting to a peaceful world would take a little time.

B-29 flying had once been a glamorous privilege, but now we were used up, burned out. None of us wanted any more rides in the Big Bird unless it was the ride home. The airplanes had done an incredible job, but the Birds were tired and ragged at the edges, the same as the crews who flew them. The great B-29 Superfortress had been stretched beyond the limits of safety. Problems with the engines continued to multiply as they were patched up again and again. Even the patches were beginning to come apart, and there was serious concern about whether or not our trusty War Chariots could get us back to the States in one piece. The continuing Wright/Cyclone engine strikes in Ohio didn't help matters at all. If the war had lasted any longer, it's certain that an increasing number of 29's would have bit the Pacific "salt", downed by operational problems.

Despite our burning desire to re-acquaint ourselves with good old terra-firma, the military seemed to have other ideas. They ordered us to a curious assortment of air adventures which included: prisoner-of-war drops over the home islands; "snooper missions" (sight seeing missions for ground personnel); air-sea rescue searches, engine slow-timing (checking out engines that had been overhauled or rebuilt); instrument transition, instrument calibration, formation flying, and general island hopping flights. No one complained about the prisoner-of-war missions in which we dropped food and supplies to our captured buddies, but the other flights seemed to be risking men and equipment for no solid reason. Every post-war flight brought with it increasing anxiety. It was "Russian Roulette" with worn out engines, and I promise that no one liked the game.

Tony recalls that he and Carl and a skeleton crew were ordered to an instrument calibration flight right after the war:

THE B-29 CARRIER ATTACK ACCORDING TO TONY COSOLA:

"Periodically we had to check the instruments on the airplane. We had to up and swing the compass to get all the errors calibrated so we could make the adjustment for the navigation aspect of the flight. Then we had to go down off the southeast corner of Guam to a marked place out there in the water on the south shore over a measured course, and calibrate our airspeed reading. We'd go down there at low altitudes and calibrate our airspeed and do all the other things, and sometime those navy antiaircraft guys would lay a few bursts off your wing tip. Nowhere close enough to hurt you but they'd lay it out there, track you along and shoot somewhere out of dangerous range. But it was damn annoying. Carl had about all he could of that and as we came back, they fired at us. We came around the west side of the island and got up there around Apra Harbor; there was this big aircraft carrier in the harbor. Carl instructed me to fire off a red flare, and he feathered up an engine, dropped his gear and flaps. I fired off another flare and he made like he was going to do an emergency landing on that aircraft carrier with that B-29. He took it right on down and the aircraft carrier signal officer was going out of his mind. Then he cut the feathered engine back in, pulled up the gear, and put the coal to 'er and we peeled off and went home. I think Carl got his posterior chewed out pretty good for that one. It was kinda of a humorous situation; this B-29 making and emergency landing on an aircraft carrier."

I wasn't aboard but I heard the "Carrier" story while I was still on Guam. I never had a chance to verify it with Carl until just recently. He just grinned, "That doesn't sound like me does it, Jim?" I chuckled knowingly, and didn't press the issue any further.

As soon as the end of the war sounded, we began hearing rumors that all the refineries we bombed had been mostly empty from day one. If that were true, our efforts in the war had been largely wasted. Although everyone in service knew that there was a big difference between free flying opinions and official facts, the scuttle of empty oil refineries wasn't exactly a morale booster.

A POST-WAR REPORT ON THE JAPANESE OIL SITUATION AS OF JUNE 1945

By the time we began our missions Japan's oil output had been reduced to only 4 percent of its normal refinery yields. Little fuel was being produced domestically, and no supplies were arriving from Southeast Asia.

TONY COSOLA'S RECENT COMMENTS ON THE EMPTY OIL REFINERY RUMORS

"I viewed that with some amusement because we worked so hard and trained so hard, and really did so well considering the novel nature of the tactical approach we took in dropping our bombs. I feel disappointed that we didn't provide a more significant boost to the end of the war, but as you know, Japan was practically on its knees by the time we got over there anyway."

Note: Tony's views were generally shared by all of us at that time. None of us knew how much the 315th Bomb Wing had effected the end of the war. The revelations of the last days came long after the end of fighting, and the last mission was not declassified until 1985! It would seem that the participants of military history know the least about it at the time the events are taking place.

On 28 August we flew from Guam to Isley Field, Saipan to pick up supplies for a 30 August P. O. W. drop in the Tokyo area. Isley Field, which was located on the southern part of Saipan, was formerly "Aslito". It was built in 1935 by the Japanese which had been granted the island by the League of Nations. Isley was completed late in 1944, and was 8,500 feet in length.

The island of Saipan, is 72 square miles in area; it was green, and lush looking when we landed there in August 1945. Saipan had been considered at the time of capture, the most strategic island in the Marianas. It was the first site from which massive B-29 bombing raids could be launched to the heart of the Japanese Empire. It became the home of the 73rd Bomb Wing.

The place was honeycombed with pillboxes and caves and we were amazed to see the thick, solid, construction of the Japanese mortar emplacements. All of them had been scorched by flame throwers, which gave close-up visual evidence of the horrendous battles that had raged there. Talk about the Japanese being dug in, no wonder the U.S. military had their hands full in taking that island.

According to the correspondent, Robert Sherrod, a large segment of the Japanese civilian population, realizing that capture was imminent, calmly and deliberately committed suicide by walking into the sea. That report had given us further insight into Japanese fanaticism long before we reached Guam. The enemy would rather die than surrender. The propaganda characterized the Americans as white devils, and that message was obviously embraced by many Japanese.

THE TAKING OF SAIPAN AND TINIAN

Saipan and Tinian (three miles southwest of Saipan), were struck June 11, 1944. The U.S. Marines landed on Saipan June 15th, 71,000 strong, and Admiral Turner announced that the island was secure 9 July after 25 days of ferocious fighting. On July 6-7 came the biggest attack of the war; a suicide mission ordered by the Japanese military commander, Lt. General Youshitsugu Saito. He ordered his soldiers to take 10 American lives before taking their own life. The Japanese soldiers charged the American troops screaming Banzai! Banzai! Almost all of the Japanese garrison of 30,000 men were killed: 23,811 dead, and 200 taken prisoner. 3,426 Americans were killed, and 13,000 wounded. 22,000 Japanese civilians, or 2 out of 3, perished.

Tinian was invaded by a garrison of 9000 Marines: the 4th Division landed 24 July; the 2nd Marine Division landed July 26th, and the island was secured 1 August 1944. 390 Americans were killed, 1,800 wounded. The Japanese lost 6000 men, and 250 were taken prisoner.

Note: North Field, Tinian, became home base for the 313th Bomb Wing. West Field, Tinian, became the operational base of the 58th Bomb Wing after the Wing left the China-Burma-India theatre.

P.O.W. DROP

Wooden platforms were fitted into the bomb bays providing a loading bed for the P.O.W supplies which were rigged to parachutes. There were a number of 50 gallon drums filled with provisions, and an assortment of medical supplies, food

223

Aerial views of POW camp. Note "Pappy Boyington Here" written on roof
in upper photo

staples, and clothing. The clothing included some large bundles of G.I. shorts and "T" shirts. Some of us figured that the prisoner of war guys couldn't use all those shorts and "T" shirts, and so we diverted some of those items back to our personal use. We couldn't wait to get back to the barracks and try on our ill gotten gains. We discovered, much to our chagrin, that the "no free lunch" law was in effect even on Saipan: the shorts and shirts all turned out to be extra large sizes, and we had to tie knots in the waist to keep from tripping on them. It was a ridiculous sight seeing all those G.I.'s modeling the pilfered oversized skivvys. It made the laugh of the day, but that was about the only reward that came from the requisition. There weren't many fat prisoners of war and I often wondered what the quartermaster was thinking of to send these olive drab "tents" to those skinny P.O.W.'s. Just another example of military SNAFU I suppose.

"The Boomerang" was down for a 300 hour inspection, and so we had to fly a another war weary B-29 on our 30 August Tokyo P.O.W. mission. Hank complained that there was a problem with every single engine on this back-up Bird, but, unfortunately, nothing big enough to warrant a scrub. One thing I remember is that the prop on number three was less than true and caused a vibration that we never could quite eliminate. I peered out Hank's window and I could actually see the displacement of the propeller. My radio gear was pretty well beaten up also, but it did the job. It was sort of amusing how everyone complained about our back-up airplane. We had obviously developed an umbilical attachment to "The Boomerang". And why not; it had certainly lived up to its name during our ten missions over Japan. We all gave the

"Boom" everything we had, and it repaid us by always bringing us back.

I believed that "The Boomerang" was one of the very best Birds in the Wing, and my conviction was supported by the maintenance records. Compared to most of the other airplanes we suffered far less mechanical problems. "The Boomerang" had drawn Technical Sergeant Floyd Jennings, of course, and according to his peers, ol' Jennings was one of the best crew chiefs in the Wing. Much of the credit for our smooth running airplane belonged to Floyd and his crew. They treated "The Boomerang" like a motherless child. Like I've said before, we could never get Floyd to fly with us, and that gave some of us pause. We wondered if there was something that he wasn't telling us. Through the years, though, I've met a lot of airplane mechanics whom you couldn't pry off the ground. Apparently working on them and flying them are two different strokes.

Flying to the Empire in the daytime and in peacetime was an unprecedented experience for us. To see Japan in the light of day for the first time, was an unbelievably exciting prospect. It was 1200 hundred hours, and Dick Marshall yelled, "Land Ahoy". We were all eyes, and if someone had been looking in on us, I'm sure we would have appeared somewhat like kids pressed against the windows of a candy store. The coastline reminded me of California, and then we saw the awesome and beautifully majestic Mt. Fuji. Bomb damage was evident everywhere. In sharp contrast to the war destruction, I could make out acres of untouched rice paddies, trees and green hills. The houses that I saw were without paint; they looked drab and uninviting. To me it was a beautiful but strange land.

We did some dead reckoning (navigating by using ground references) and found our target just west of Tokyo. The P. O. W. camp (which was later identified as Camp Omori) was larger than I had imagined with at least 6 large barracks housing the U. S. prisoners. The following words were printed on the roof of one building: OMORI CAMP WE-THANK-YOU. On the roof of another were large colored letters that read: "PAPPY BOYINGTON HERE!"

PAPPY BOYINGTON

Major Gregory (Pappy Boyington) was truly a legend in his own time. He earned the Medal of Honor, and also the Navy Cross.

Major Boyington was one of the wildest, most colorful and unconventional fighter pilots in history. A native of Coeur d' Alene, Idaho, Marine pilot Major Gregory Boyington joined the American Volunteer Group (AVG) in 1941 and ended up in China where he became a P-40 Flying Tiger pilot under the command of retired Army Air Corps Captain Claire Chennault. In China Boyington began gathering kills and much respect from his comrades for being a top fighter pilot.

In 1943 Boyington later took over a squadron of physical rejects called the Black Sheep Squadron and directed operations against the Japanese out of the Central Solomon Islands. The squadron flew F4U Corsairs and made military history with their successful combat flights against the enemy. Pappy Boyington was credited with 26 kills (two more kills were confirmed subsequently, making the number 28) before he was shot down in St. George Channel, and taken prisoner

January 1944, in Rabaul Harbor, New Britain Island. (New Britain Island is in the Bismark, Archipelago, New Guinea area).

Boyington had taken off from Bougainville January 3, 1944 to lead a fighter sweep over Rabaul, the large Japanese Navy base, which meant two hundred miles over enemy water and terrain. Pappy and his wing man were jumped by some twenty enemy planes. The wingman's plane burst into flame and crashed into the water. Seconds later Pappy and his Corsair both were shot full of holes. The Corsair's main gas tank exploded while Boyington was only a hundred feet above the water. He couldn't climb to bail-out since he would be fried alive. Instinctively he jammed both of his feet onto the stick kicking it all the way forward. He pulled a ton of centrifugal G's and at the same time pulled his rip cord. Miraculously he ejected some way and the chute opened just seconds before he slammed into the water. Boyington, severely wounded, survived 8 hours in and out of a raft, dodging multiple strafing runs, and was finally picked up by a Japanese submarine which took him into Rabaul harbor, the large Japanese Navy facility.

Pappy, now a Prisoner of War, spent 6 terrible weeks of captivity and interrogation in Rabaul, and then was transferred to Truk Island where six of the prisoners were confined to a dark wooden cell and given hellish treatment. Boyington described his new cell like this: "Our quarters at Truk were unique. The cell was neat and clean, and looked as if it had been built recently by a carpenter who knew his business, for there wasn't a single joint through which we were able to see light from out of doors. Of course, I had no way of knowing but I rather imagined that the builder had merely one prisoner in mind when he measured the boards, not six." After weeks of suffering unmercifully from his untreated infected wounds, beatings, diarrhea, and spoiled rice, Pappy and the other prisoners were moved to some island thought to be Saipan, and then in March 1944 they were moved to an intimidation site named Camp Ofuna near Yokahama and finally to Camp Omori in the Tokyo area.

THE MUSIC

Pappy Boyington, in his book Baa Baa Blacksheep stated: "Great hordes of silver B-29s were coming over in the daylight and also at night. The prisoners called them, 'The Music'. We watched them in the daylight, and those great silver airplanes were a beautiful sight. Occasionally we would see some lone Japanese fighter plane try to tangle with them. It would come streaking down in flames, and we could hear it crash to the ground. Then the 29s would start releasing their eggs, and the ground would shake along with the windows, and the sills on the doors would creak back and forth. Yet this was not so bothersome as at night, when the B-29s came over low, at around four to six thousand feet. We could hear them swoop down and dive, the engines roaring. We didn't know where they were, didn't know when to duck. We could just put our faces down into four cotton blankets and hope."

WHO PAINTED "PAPPY BOYINGTON HERE"

Pappy explained in his book, Baa Baa Blacksheep: "A few days after the war was over, some of the boys decided to paint my name on one of the buildings. They used Japanese tooth powder for paint, mixing it with water. They used rags for brushes."

Note: A large number of B-29 crew members were P O Ws being held in this camp.

Dick Marshall manned the Norden Bomb Sight for our mission-of-mercy drop, and had no trouble eye-balling the target which was an open area next to the building that featured Pappy's sign. The one thing no one apparently considered was how the platforms would react aerodynamically. Well they sailed and tumbled and dived, and bounced all over the place. One 29 reported that a platform sailed into traffic and creamed a Japanese dump truck. I tucked a note in one of the packages, and gave my mother's California address, but no one ever responded. I always wonder whether or not the package found the target. Maybe it was picked up in a Japanese dump truck.

Tony Cosola's assessment of the action: "It appeared as if we were trying to kill the P.O.Ws with kindness--literally."

PAPPY BOYINGTON'S COMMENTS ON THE MISSION OF MERCY

Pappy Boyington on the B-29's dropping supplies: "The prisoners went wild. They were running all over the place, and when the B-29s started dropping fifty-gallon drums packed solid with concentrated foods by parachute, I took to an air raid shelter." One prisoner said: "Why don't you stay out here and get some of this stuff? You can watch these things come down and they won't hit you." "Nuts to that," said Pappy, "after living through all

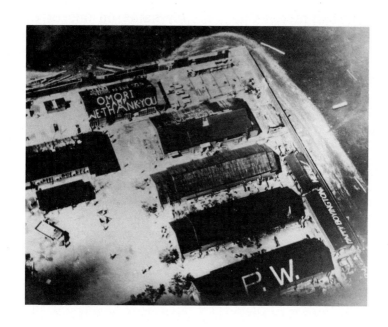

POW supply drops - upper photo is where Marine Ace Greg "Pappy" Boyington was being held

I have, I'm damned if I'm going to be killed by being hit on the head by a crate of peaches."

We left Pappy's Camp after our drop and flew low around downtown Tokyo. I remember seeing dozens of people leaning out of street cars and waving their fists at us. I yelled back just to let off steam, "You started it, Nips, and now we're finishing it." Then we flew towards the Emperor's Palace to the northwest, and the view below was incomprehensible. There was no city at all—just rubble left from the bombing. I thought what a terrible price this war—for both sides. There was a sense of victory here, but also a pervading sadness at seeing the utter devastation of an Empire.

We landed back on Northwest with all engines showing more problems than when we left. We vowed that if we ever had to fly again, we'd take our chances with our old friend, "The Boomerang".

THE CRASH OF CREW #1714

The military kept pushing us skyward in spite of oil leaks, runaway props, engines swallowing valves, fires, turbo malfunctions, and the list went on... It all caught up with some of my buddies a few days later. These fellows (Crew 1714, 16th Bomb Group) and I had gone through the Fairmont, Nebraska training program together. I shared the same barracks with the enlisted men of that crew: radio operator Leonard V. Steveson, engineer John S. Rogers, tail gunner Mevin B. Berkey, waist scanners, Jim A. Humbird, and Davis R Flynt, Jr.

Steveson bunked above me, and we became quite close. Steve was from Colorado, married, and a total gentleman. I got on Steve's case one day for something that was so important I don't even remember what it was; I challenged him to a fight. The encounter quickly blew over but I felt terrible about the incident. Whatever it was, it was my fault, and I later apologized to Steve--not once, but several times.

Steve and his crew had been ordered to Guam about the same time as our crew, and their group encamped just across the road to the northeast. I used to visit the enlisted guys regularly, and, like all soldiers, we'd exchange anecdotes, gripes, and then talk about home. I knew Steve's code hand so well that I could always recognize his transmissions, and he, in turn, could spot mine. Every code sender has a little different style just as everyone has a different personality, and with experience, you could identify the sender.

On 2 September Steve and his crew took off for a P.O.W. mercy mission to Osaka. After a few hours his aircraft commander, Lieutenant George Hutchison, radioed the tower that they had engine trouble and were returning to base. The crew circled until they burned up a good amount of their gasoline (standard operating procedure), and then let down to land.

Hank Gorder and I had just finished another miserable Australian breakfast at the Mess Hall and were walking back to quarters when we spotted a column of black smoke rising to the west. It looked as if it could be coming from Northwest Field. The smoke was mixed with red and orange fire balls. "That could be an airplane", I said, hoping against hope that Hank would come up with a better explanation. "I think it is an airplane" Hank said, and we both took off down the road leading to the field. An enlisted fellow drove up behind us in a Jeep and gave us the signal to jump in. We jeeped up to the Wing's favorite vantage point, mounds of piled-up coral left by the Seabees after they had finished constructing the runways. The "Rock Pile", as we called it, was on the south east perimeter of the field and was a great place for viewing the field. A bunch of us guys, including Steveson, would often go to the site and watch the Birds takeoff when we weren't scheduled to fly. A bus man's holiday it would seem, but none of us ever grew tired watching the B-29s lift off, nose down the cliff to pick up flying speed, and then reach for altitude. A truly beautiful sight.

The scene that was now below us was gut wrenching. We could see a mass of tangled, twisted, broken, metal that was almost fully engulfed in a raging white, orange and red fire. The fire was burning hotter around the flight deck and engine areas. The fuselage of the bird was upside down with a twisted and partially broken off tail that was almost right side up.

We looked for a name on the B-29, but the fire had charred and blackened most of the metal surfaces at that point, making identification impossible. Fire fighting teams moved from the tail to the flight deck area, as several ambulances pulled in closer. The fire teams were now directing all of their efforts to the nose section. Personnel from all over the base began arriving, and everyone was trying to find out what crew was involved.

Suddenly someone in the group, yelled, "That's George Hutchison's crew". I blurted something like, "My God, that's Steve and the guys." The fire fighters were getting the fire around the flight deck under control, and the ambulance attendants were moving in with gurneys. I turned to Hank without taking my eyes off the activity that was taking place, "Do you suppose that some of the guys are still alive?" Hank's reply was barely audible, "There's no way."

Then we saw gurneys being carried from the nose area; it looked like someone had shoveled coal on the stretchers. My innards turned and twisted inside me. It was all over for my buddies. By now a small crowd had gathered and everyone was asking questions. An ambulance that had been positioned just back of the tail drove off, and I wondered out loud whether anyone hadn't gotten out. One of the ground crew guys said that he saw three crew members taken out of the tail. "One guy's clothing was still on fire, but the other two looked to be in pretty good shape." I wheeled around to Hank, "Berkey, Flynt, and Humbird. It looks like they got out." Hank mumbled, "God, I hope so." We both stared blankly and silently at the burned out hulk in front of us. I was thinking of Steve, the engineer, John Rogers, and the others. I was trying to grasp the reality of it all. In a matter of seconds this awful accident had translated the magic of life into the ugliness of death and destruction. I could feel the guilt of wrongly challenging Steve back at Fairmont, and I was reminded of how the mistakes in your life come back to haunt you.

GROUND CREW CHIEF CLAUDE F. WHITEHEAD WAS AN EYEWITNESS

Claude F. Whitehead, a ground crew chief who knew our Floyd Jennings, told me recently that he had witnessed Hutchison's B-29 on it's approach to land: "I couldn't see anything wrong with the engines as they came in on final. They were lined up perfectly with the runway during the first part of their let down, and then suddenly they swerved to the left, heading for that old tree that was left standing between the north and south runway. It looked as though the left wing was going to make contact with the tree; the pilot tried apparently tried to "horse" the Bird over it. It looked like the airplane stalled out; it went in on the nose, twisted upside down and exploded into an inferno. The tail section broke half in two."

Hank and I walked in numbed silence back to camp, and in my silence I pondered the inequities of life. The word back at the barracks was that Berkey, Flynt, and Humbird did get out of the back alive, but Berkey was badly burned and might not live. The three had been taken to Army Hospital 373 south of us; Hank and I agreed that we would visit the fellows first thing in the morning.

I left the barracks to walk off some of the shock I was feeling, and to stop by Steve's quarters to talk to some of the guys. Everyone had heard that the crew reported engine trouble, but they didn't know anything beyond that. I moved over to Steve's cot. There was the depression of Steve's body where he had been resting before the flight. He had left a pack of Lucky Strike cigarettes in the middle of the bed. I looked up to the right where his gear was stored, and there was a picture of his wife and family. A heavy sadness filled me. It just didn't seem right that something like this would happen to such good men.

I sensed someone standing behind me and when I turned around I looked into the face of John S. Rogers, the engineer. The shock at seeing John almost took my tongue--just two words came out: "I thought..." John smiled, "I'm no ghost, Jim. I had to go on sick call this morning for a sore throat. This is the very first time I've ever missed a flight with this crew." John looked down at the floor and then looked at me,"It wasn't meant for me to fly with the crew today. The guys up front, including ol' Steve didn't have a chance. But by the Grace of God, I would've been there too. I'm alive because of a sore throat. It doesn't make sense does it?" I couldn't answer. John pondered it all and then shook his head back and forth slowly, "I don't understand what happened, I just don't understand it." John struggled to find his composure and then went on, "I just came back from the hospital. Berkey is in bad shape, and I don't think he's going to make it. Jim and Davis have minor burns on their arms--that's all. They can't tell me exactly what went wrong. Just that they had trouble with an engine on the right side, and George decided as a precaution to return to base. Besides the back up engineer, they had two extra officers on board." I put my arm around him, "Thank God you're all right, John; there's got to be a reason man; keep the faith, and keep your chin up. You and I know that the guys would want that from you." "Yeah, I know." I told John that I was going to visit Flynt and Humbird, and then I would check in on him later. There was an overpowering emptiness in that barracks. I was glad to leave.

THE ACCIDENT VICTIMS - 16TH BOMB GROUP

1. Aircraft Commander, 1st Lt Hutchison, George R. 0799404
2. Pilot, 2nd Lt Strait, Carl W 0824284
3. Navigator, 2nd Lt Nahouse, Lester R

0702479

4. Bombardier, 2nd Lt Bradley, William E Jr. 0702479

5. Radio Sgt Steveson, Leonard V 36439992

6. Tail Gunner Sgt Berkey, Melvin E 33767117

7. Radar Operator, 2nd, Lt Weber, Rudolph E 02069170

8. Flight Engineer, S/sgt Rogers, John S. was not aboard.

9. Replacement Flight Engineer, Flight Officer T.G. Passarello T-65636

1. Gunner/E, Sgt Humbird, James A 191133841

2. Gunner/E, Sgt Flynt, Davis R Jr. 34832205

Hank and I arrived at Army Hospital 373 at 8:00 a.m. The hospital was built on high ground and the view was quite beautiful from there. We explained to the receiving nurse that we were there to see Davis Flynt, Jim Humbird, and Melvin Berkey, "The crew members that were injured in the B-29 accident at Northwest Field." The nurse asked us to follow her.

Flynt and Humbird had been assigned to beds that were next to one another. They were sitting up, and the arms of both boys had been lightly bandaged. Hank and I greeted the two with some apprehension, but they both were alert and happy to see us. We asked them how they were feeling and they said almost in unison, "We're fine." The two had suffered slight second degree burns to the arms, but otherwise they were unmarked. I sensed that both guys needed to talk about the accident. Jim Humbird explained that they were about two hours into a flight to Osaka when an engine on the right side began running rough. "We circled a few hours to

burn off fuel, and then began our let down. Everything seemed to be normal, but all of a sudden we veered off to the left of the runway. #1 or 2 could have swallowed a valve I guess." Jim choked with emotion. Flynt continued Jim's story, "All of a sudden it felt like we stalled out, and then it was like going over Niagara Falls in a barrel. The nose went in with a terrific impact. The noise was deafening. We were suddenly upside down, then twisted and thrown right side up. The tail ripped apart and we could see daylight through the huge gap. Tail ammo was exploding, and there was fire everywhere. Berkey came out of his tail turret and yelled for us to jump. We hit the ground and both of our flight suits were on fire above the waist. The tail was full of fire by the time Berkey jumped; it was too late. He was a human torch by the time he got out. Berkey was burned bad." Jim looked up at us, "He's in an oxygen tent in the other wing, the nurse said that he might not make it." If he's conscious, you guys tell him that everybody in the crew is okay." Hank and I both nodded.

Jim bowed his head, and wiped his eyes with his fist, vainly trying to keep the tears from cascading down his cheeks. "I don't understand this life at all. Everyone in the crew was the best kind of person except Davis and me. We're the bad guys, always have been, the full-time screw ups, and we're the ones that got out of that airplane in one piece. Berkey's the greatest guy in the world. He would never have jumped out of that Bird until Davis and I got out. He would have stayed in there forever. That's the kind of guy he is. He put me and Davis first. He saved our lives, and what's his reward for saving us? He's going to die just like the other guys; I know it. Nothing makes any sense. And the worse thing... you and Hank have

Crew 58, 16th Bomb Group
Back row: Yost, Bradley Jr., Nahouse, Strait, Hutchison AC, Flynt Jr.
Front row: Rogers Jr., Humbird, Berkey, Steveson

1ST LT. GEORGE K. HUTCHISON 17th

2ND LT. LESTER R. NAHOUSE 17th SQ

2ND LT. WILLIAM E BRADLEY JR 17th

2ND LT. CARL W. STRAIT 17th SQ

234

heard it just like we have. They're saying that every bombing mission the 315th flew was a waste. The rumor is that all the oil storage tanks we bombed were empty." Hank and I nodded our heads in agreement. "All these good men die, and for what? For what... the 315th never even counted in this war--we never even counted. The joke was on us. We didn't do a damned thing to the Japs." No one had any answers. We told the guys that we were glad that they were okay, and we promised to come back and see them.

I signalled the young nurse who had brought us in, and she took us to Berkey. "Don't stay too long, he's pretty weak." Berkey was enclosed in an oxygen tent and wrapped in bandages from head to foot. The only body parts visible were his swollen burned lips, and the big toes of each foot. Hank and I were sick. I started with a quiet, "Hi, Berkey, Jim Smith and Hank Gorder." I watched Berkey's lips form Jim and Hank, his voice was weak but distinct. "How's my crew. Are they all right? " I tried to be upbeat, "Everybody's in good shape, Berkey. They're asking about you. I'll tell them that you're going to be just fine and you will be." "Everybody's okay?", Berkey asked again. Again I lied, "Everyone's fine, Berkey, everybody got out okay." Berk whispered through his burned, swollen lips, "That's good. Tell them I'll see em' soon." "I'll tell them, Berkey. Now you just get well, young man." Berkey didn't answer me. He was wearing out, and I nodded to Hank that is was time for us to leave. Hank leaned in above the oxygen tent so that Berkey would hear him, "We'll be back tomorrow Berkey". "Hang in there Berk"; I added, "We'll see you tomorrow." Berkey was too spent to answer us, he wiggled the big toe on his right foot for his good bye. Hank and I put an arm around the young nurse as we left, and thanked her for everything. She was crying. I guess we all were. Berkey died a few hours later.

I know that there are millions of unsung heroes, but when I think of a hero, I think of an always giving, sandy haired, freckled face kid from California, Melvin E. Berkey. I think of the gentle sweet spirit of a great guy, Leonard "Steve" Steveson. I will always honor those men and their sacrifice.

Note: After almost 50 years I made contact with Steve Steveson's brother, Leo Steveson. He was gracious enough to send the memorial information to me.

MEMORIAL POEM

IN FLANDERS FIELDS by John McCrae

In Flanders Fields the poppies grow
between the crosses (and stars of David), row by row
That mark our place; and in the sky
The larks still bravely singing fly
Scarce heard amid the guns below
We are the Dead. Short days ago
We lived, felt dawn, saw sunset glow
Loved and were loved: and now we lie
In Flanders Field.
Take up our quarrel with the foe;
To you from failing hands we throw
The torch: be yours to hold it high.
If ye break faith with us who die
We shall not sleep, though poppies grow
In Flanders Fields

236

A SHARING BY CHAPLAIN GOLDBURG

A PRAYER

> The young Airmen and Airwomen
>   do not speak
> Nevertheless, they are heard in the
>   still houses: who has not
>   heard them?
> They have a silence that speaks for
>   them at night and when the
>   clock counts.
> They say: We are young. We have
>   died. Remember us.
> They say: We have done what we
>   could but until it is finished
>   it is not done.
> They say: We have given our lives
>   but until it is finished no
>   one can know what our lives
>   gave.
> They say: Our deaths are not ours;
>   they are yours; they will
>   mean what you make them.
> They say; Whether our lives and
>   our deaths are for peace
>   and a new hope or for
>   nothing we cannot say; it is
>   you who must say this.
> They say: We leave you our
>   deaths. Give them their
>   meaning.
> We were young, they say. We have
>   died. Remember us.
>   Oct. 25, 1945

Commanding Officer Tells of Sgt. Leonard V. Steveson's Death

5 Sept. 1945
Re: Leonard V. Steveson
36439992, Sgt.
17th Bomb Sq. 16th Bomb Group

Dear Mrs. Steveson:

By the time this reaches you, you will have received official notification from the Adjutant General concerning your husband's death in line of duty. It is my wish herein to extend to you, in my own name and in that of the entire 16th Bombardment Group, our deepest sympathy on your sorrow.

On Sunday morning, Sept. 2, Sgt. Steveson and his crew took off for a destination in the Japanese Empire, carrying vitally needed supplies to the prisoners of war in a camp there. Before they had gone far they must have run into some sort of trouble for the airplane commander decided to return to this field and make an emergency landing. In making the landing something went wrong; the plane missed the runway, hit two trees, crashed, and burst into flames.

The crash crews were upon the scene at once, battling the flames and cutting through to get the men out. But the plane had broken up badly; all nine men in the forward compartment were killed instantly. They could not have lived to suffer. Only the three men in the rear of the plane got out alive. Of these two sustained only minor injuries; Sgt. Davis R. Flynt Jr., and PFC James A. Humbird. The other, Sgt. Melvin E. Berkey, died of injuries three days later.

The funeral of the nine was conducted from our own chapel on Monday afternoon, Sept. 3rd. Appropriate services were held by the chaplains. Your husband's chaplain is writing you further details concerning the funeral.

Internment was at Army Navy Marine Cemetery No. 2, village of Agat, Island of

Guam. Sgt. Steveson is buried in Grave No. 10, Row 37, Plot 4. A fellow member of his crew is buried on his right; Flight Officer Thomas G. Passarello. No burial has as yet been made in the grave on his left.

The accident occurred about an hour before the signing of the peace terms in Japan; just another stunning circumstance of the whole tragedy. However, may it be some consolation in your grief that your husband died in the performance of a mission of mercy rather than one of destruction.

The supplies that were being flown in to the prisoners of war in Japan are saving lives. It was in this noble service that he gave his life. We are proud of his courage and sacrifice.

Very respectfully yours,
Andre F. Castellotti, Lt. Colonel, Air Corps, Commanding Officer

Headquarters 16th Bombardment Group

Office of the Chaplain
APO 182 c/o Postmaster, San Francisco, Calif.
6 September 1945

Mrs. Betty L. Steveson
N. Menard Street
Mason City, Illinois

RE: Steveson, Leonard V.
36439992, Sgt.
17th Bomb Sqdn.

Dear Mrs. Steveson,

I want to add my word of sympathy to the other messages which you have received relative to the death of you husband, Sergeant Leonard V. Steveson, 36439992. I have not been with the organization long enough to know him intimately but I did see him frequently, especially while he was getting the ship ready for their missions. He was a good member of a good crew, you can be sure of that--and proud.

The entire crew was eager to be a part of the "prisoner-of-war mission" because they were eager to serve their fellow-men who had a tougher break than their own. It must be a source of considerable comfort to know that your husband gave his life while engaged in a mission of mercy, seeking to lift the burden from suffering mankind.

We had services for the nine men who were killed in the crash in the Briefing Room which we use for a Chapel. It was beautified by a palm platform built by his fellow soldiers. The nine flag-covered caskets were in a row, side by side. Pall-bearers were fellow radio operators from his squadron.

Three of the men were Roman Catholic. Father Gannon said Mass for them, following our Protestant service. It really gave the effect of being one service.

Our service opened with "I am the resurrection and the life; he that believeth in me, though he were dead, yet shall he live; and whosoever liveth and believeth in me shall never die." Then followed the Invocation and Lord's Prayer after which we read the 90th Psalm and the 23rd.

Lt. Richard G. Kunel, a baritone soloist from the 73rd Air Service Group, sang Geoffrey O'Hara's "There Is No Death".

I tell you they have not died,
They live and breathe with you;
They walk here at your side
They tell you things are true.
Why dream of poppied sod
When flow'r and soul and God
Knows there is no death!

--Gordon Johnstone.

The New Testament lesson was John 14;1-3, 15-20, 25-27 and Romans 8:14-19; 22-25; 28; 31-35; 37-39. It seemed to me that these passages had messages of hope and confidence which all of us needed to be reminded of at that time. I pray that they shall speak words of courage to you as you read them.

The service ended with a prayer and the benediction. The organist, Corporal Earl L. Tintle, played "Consolation" by Mendelssohn for a prelude and "A Hymn to the Setting Sun" by Lacey for an interlude between the Protestant and Catholic services.

The cemetery is in a lovely spot overlooking the Pacific. There are men at work constantly to keep it neat and to beautify it with native shrubbery and grasses.

Eventually it will be a garden where the heroes of Guam lie at rest. At the committal service full military honors were accorded your husband. We are proud of him and we know you are too. May God bless you in your hour of sorrow. May He grant you peace.

If at any time we can be of assistance to you, please do not hesitate to let us know. In deep sympathy,

Donald W. Zimmerman
Chaplain (Capt.) USA

Aircraft Commander at work

Navigation Station

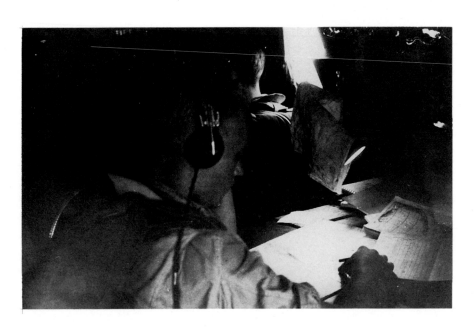

Chapter Twelve

PROJECT SUNSET

General MacArthur conducted the signing of the instruments of peace aboard the U.S.S. Missouri on September 3, 1945. Japanese Foreign Minister Mamori Shigamitzua, Imperial Army General Yoshijiro Umezu represented the Japanese. With the actual signing of peace by the Allies and Japan, we were pawing ground to get back Stateside. However, moving troops out of Guam was a frustratingly slow process.

In the meantime the Air Corps kept us defying gravity. On 5 September we experienced a frightening dé-jà vu. Our crew had been scheduled to fly to the Philippines. We used a B-29 with the tail number 3654. "The Boomerang" was still down for its 300 hour inspection. Two hours out of Northwest Field a left side engine began to run rough. We decided to feather it, and go back to base. We circled for hours to get rid of fuel, and then we began our let down sequence. I can guarantee you that every man aboard 3654 was thinking about the George Hutchison crew accident. Carl greased the Bird in as we all held our breath.

"THE BOOMERANG" CREW VISITS IWO AFTER THE WAR

In the Command's apparent obsession to keep us in the air, we were ordered to fly Iwo Jima military personnel to the Empire on "Snooper" missions. These flights were actually sight seeing missions honoring soldiers who had served on Iwo Jima. During the operation "The Boomerang" crew R.O.N.'d (rested over night) on Iwo and toured the island, an experience that no one would ever forget.

A strange island, Iwo Jima. Almost everywhere you looked, you could see steam rising from the volcanic ash soil. I enjoyed a hot shave and shower without the benefit of a hot water system. The volcanic ground was just naturally hot, and it was enough to heat the plumbing.

The roads sparkled brilliantly in the bright sunlight, looking as though they had been sprinkled with diamonds. The "diamonds" turned out to be shrapnel. The rain of enormous firepower on Iwo has been well documented, but you had to see it to believe it. Japanese live rifle shells were all over the place. I picked up as many as I could carry.

We climbed Mt. Suribachi and stood at a raised U.S. flag, the same spot where Lieutenant Schrier and five men, including an Indian, Ira Hayes, raised the Stars and Stripes for the Fifth Marine Division. It was a solemn moment of reflection and appreciation for our Marine buddies.

Part of the volcanic symmetry of Mt. Suribachi was missing on the ocean side, and when I asked about the strange formation, I was told that the ocean side of Suribachi had been blown away so that further eruptions would flow out to sea. These engineers are pretty crafty guys, I thought.

THE PLACE WHERE YOUNG DREAMS DIED

The crew climbed back down Suribachi and walked to the American cemetery. Thousands of head stones dotted the area. A good number of the stones showed memorials and mementos left there by fighting buddies: personal effects i.e. rosaries, pictures, combat knives, notes, poems, statements of love and Bible verses. We were all numbed by the evidence of ultimate sacrifice. No one spoke as we studied the individual head stones. Thousands of young men and their young dreams died here. An overwhelming sadness fell on all of us. We all gave silent thanks to the fallen American heroes, and went on our way.

As the long post-war days wore on, those empty oil refinery rumors persisted. The history of the Japanese oil dilemma during World War II was being explained this way: In spite of their conquest of Borneo, Sumatra, and Burma, and the severe restrictions imposed on civilian consumption, fuel supplies for the Imperial Armed Forces were by no means fully assured. The British and Dutch refineries had been sabotaged, but the Japanese did not restore them. They instead shipped the crude oil to Japan for refining, then sent the oil and petrol out again to their combat areas, thus incurring heavy expense in freight and fuel itself. When Japan lost the Philippines they no longer could control the sea lanes to the Netherlands, or the tin and rubber from Malaysia. By 1 April, 1945 the Allied

surface and air attacks together with submarine attacks and mines had cut off all oil from Japan.

Military analysts had concluded that all of Japan's hope of any military success depended on her remaining oil.

NO FUEL FOR THE DEAD

By January 1945, the Imperial Navy was forced to fuel some of its ships with alcohol. Navigational training was eliminated for pilots. Although the military controlled all fuels, it was helpless to find additional supplies. The civilian population simply could not sacrifice any more. Japanese who lived through the winter of 1944-1945 remember forty-five consecutive days of below-freezing temperatures. It was the coldest winter in twenty years. Fuel and food scarcities reduced the Japanese to near starvation. A campaign of Yase-gaman ("strength through slimness") designed to cloak deprivation in the spirit of patriotism was instituted. There was insufficient fuel to cremate the dead in the last days of the war, and funerals were delayed several days.

LOTS OF FIRE

All I knew is that I saw lots of fire at every refinery target, and I never bought the "empty storage tank" rumors in their entirety. I reasoned that if the "empty storage tanks" still contained enough fuel to make huge fires, each raid was slowing down Japanese hardware, and we were actually driving Japan closer to surrender with each hit. We set off an inferno at Akita, creating thermals that almost turned us upside down, and it was hard for me to believe that Akita was even close to being empty, as some rumors had it.

One irrefutable fact: we were highly qualified and we gave everything we had. The 315th did one hell of a job. The crews were always at high risk since we flew great distances over water with increasingly problematic engines, and carried no armament except a modest tail turret. Two fifties and a next to useless 20 millimeter cannon represented our total fire power. We weren't much of a threat in air to air combat, that's for sure.

Late in October the command began implementing Project Sunset which was the name of the operation for airlifting of personnel back to the States. The crews began to break up as each member became a stand-by replacement for the troop deployment process. It was a great feeling to be going home, but it was sad to see the Old Boomerang crew dissolve. There was no question that experiencing life and death situations with others had a permanent, and strong bonding effect. We would all miss one another.

I was assigned to a crew in the 314th Bomb Wing for my flight back to the States. The B-29 we were flying was equipped with the 5 standard turrets, and it had seen a lot of day light action over Japan, it was pretty well thrashed. Number three engine had an oil leak (in my experience there were more engine malfunctions on the right side than there were on the left) and wouldn't produce full power. The crew chief said that it might take several more days to correct the problem, and none of us could handle any more delays. The aircraft commander told the chief that we'd chance it, and asked him not to report the problem. The flight crew was more than ready to accept the risk in order to get home.

GOOD-BYE GUAM, HELLO LIEUTENANT JIM SMITH

October 23, 1945 I said farewell to Guam and flew to Kwajalein on the first leg of our trip back to Stateside. It was weird operating the radio in this strange turret Bird. The central fire control system turned my "dance floor" into a claustrophobic cubicle, and that took all the fun out of things.

The navigator was First Lieutenant Jarvis. His accent told me that he was from New Jersey, before he did. Jarvis was a terrific guy, and he and I hit it off from the first handshake. When we arrived at Kwajalein he invited me to the Officer's Club with him, but I had to remind Jarvis that I was only a Sergeant and the brass certainly wouldn't cotton to a non-commission officer drinking at their bar. "The hell with them," fumed Jarvis. He dug into his gear and found a pair of silver lieutenant bars, "Pin these things on your flight suit and they'll never know the difference."

About ten minutes after we entered the "O" Club I recognized a Major on the other side of the bar. I whispered to Jarvis while trying to hide my face with my hand, "I know that Major, I'm dead in the water." Jarvis tried to reassure me, but I was sweating "bullets." I could see my present status being blown away with an untimely court martial. I tried to disappear like Houdini by slinking low on the bar stool, but it didn't work. The Major spotted me and set a true course for our position. I started to disembark but Jarvis put a hook on my arm. The Major sat down on my left and I froze. Jarvis pipes up, "Hi Major, I understand you know

Lieutenant Smith." As I stared into my glass pondering my court martial I heard the Major reply, "Sure I know Lieutenant Smith, welcome aboard Smith." I made a hesitant, mechanical turn to the Major then with great relief I blurted out three "Thank-you-sirs" before I could stop. The Major and Jarvis howled; I finally found the humor of my own dilemma and began laughing with them. The Major ordered a drink for us; then we for him; then him for us, and we soon lost count. It wasn't long until we were slapping one another on the back, and the party was on. My reprieve was living proof that the war was indeed over in every aspect.

Number 3 was still leaking oil but we pressed on for Hawaii. Carl Schahrer had been assigned a relief pilot on a mixed crew and I was amazed to hear his tail numbers while I was monitoring my assigned frequency. His 29 was having engine trouble, and they were being forced down at Johnston Island. (As it turned out Carl didn't touch down at Sacramento's Mather Field until 9 November. I beat him there by a week.)

NUMBER FOUR RUNS AWAY

We lifted off from John Rogers Field, Oahu, after sundown, and it was a takeoff that would burn forever in the minds of all who were present. We rotated and climbed to about two hundred feet. I sensed some high speed RPM's and my experience told me that we had a runaway prop. I peered around the Central Fire Control turret and yelled to my new friend Jarvis, "Feels like we've got a runaway." Jarvis waved a hand at me, "Nothing's wrong, you're gettin' paranoid, Smith!" I shot back, "Could be but we definitely have an r.p.m. problem." Jarvis took a step

up toward the engineer, and then slammed back down into his position: "It's number 4, we've got a runaway!" I remembered that we hadn't been able to get full power on the oil leaking number 3, and now with number 4 gone, we were in the worst trouble imaginable. Number 4 feathered, and a minute later the aircraft commander was fighting for his life. The commander ordered the engineer to restart. By a miracle the governor held this time. We were still in the ball game but just handing this side of a stall. We skimmed low over the highway clearing a truck by less than 50 feet. I scrambled into my ditching position; the Bird stabilized some, and then agonizingly, little by little, we clawed our way back up to altitude. We eventually reached our cruise altitude of 10,000 feet; the engineer pulled the power systems back to cruise, and everything checked in the green. Jarvis gave a heading to the Aircraft Commander and we continued toward Mather Field, Sacramento. No one had ever heard of a B-29 lifting off, losing inboard power, having the outboard run away, and still making it. I realized that I had used up all my luck, and I vowed that if we made it back to Mather, I'd kiss the Superfortress stuff good bye forever. Court-martial or not, I resolved that I would never leave the good earth again in a B-29 (I didn't).

"C U"

My last Morse code contact was with a military radio station at Hamilton Field, San Franciso. At the end of my transmission the guy sent a happy dah dit dah dit, dit dit dah (C.U.). I returned the metaphor, and closed it out with a "R" "AR" (Roger-Out). That was the last time I ever touched the key.

After landing at Mather, the hard bitten,

seasoned combat Aircraft Commander confessed that he didn't think we were going to make it on that Hickam Field takeoff. I walked over to aft section by myself, gently kissed the airplane, and patted her, "You brought me back alive. I'll always be grateful to you Big Bird-- good luck."

I was shipped back to Fort Leavensworth, Kansas on a troop train to begin a 60 day Terminal Leave before being mustered out of service in Santa Ana, California. All of us were adding our two cents about the war we had just fought, the airplanes, the anecdotes. One guy spoke for all of us when he said, "Towards the end, every time we got airborne some system failed on the damned airplane, and it was progressively getting worse. A B-29 is going to kill me yet--I know it." I chuckled, "How's a B-29 going to kill you now; you'll never fly in one again?" "Then one will fall on me, man; I promise you. Yeah, I'll just be walking down the street, and one will fall on me." The way the guy said it cracked all of us up.

TERMINAL LEAVE

I went back to see my Dad and Step-mother while I was on my terminal leave, and it was all sort of depressing. There were times when friends and even family would say things that hurt: "Well, you oil refinery guys didn't do much good or we wouldn't have had to drop the big bombs." The atom put em' away real fast." Others would ask: "Why didn't you make it as an officer and fly those big birds instead of playing around with dits and dahs on your radio? You guys never had the action that those B-17s had. What the hell, you flew 10 missions over Japan. I know guys in the 8th in England that flew

fifty missions." Some people, of course, were supportive, but it's amazing how quickly some forgot the military sacrifices when the threat of war had subsided.

THE OLD KING COLE ROOM

Of course I had to check out the King Cole Room in Omaha one more time. All the gung ho war mentality that was always a hallmark there seemed to be gone. I remember sitting at the bar and this time I felt out of place, like a total stranger. I had been there when I was attending Creighton as a Cadet, and then again as a B-29 crewman from Fairmont Army Air Base. It was just one big party then and everybody seemed like family, but now all those parts were missing.

Since I was still in uniform and sporting a 20th Air Force patch and ribbons, someone would occasionally ask a question or two about my role in the Pacific. There were no raised eyebrows of curiosity, and no more interest when I explained that we had bombed oil refineries exclusively. It was abundantly evident that the only subject that held any interest for the public was the atomic bomb. We of the 315th were just "also rans" for sure. The challenges, danger, and national purpose were gone and so was the excitement and fulfillment that came with being one of the participating players. This was understandable but it didn't make the transition from war to peace any easier.

TONY COSOLA, IN HIS MEMOIRS, SAID IT THIS WAY

"It was a terrible let down after the war. I felt that it was productive, challenging, exciting. When the risks were gone there was a great sense of loss because the purpose that had inflamed me for the last couple of years no longer existed. I had a terrible conflict with that."

SANTA ANA REVISITED

I had to report to Santa Ana, California for separation. Just the sight of that place brought back dark memories of my Cadet wash out. Some things had changed: the mess halls were serving up great chow including quart bottles of milk; we were being catered to by German prisoners of war. The prisoners also cleaned the barracks and latrines. One morning one of the prisoners was sweeping in front of my bunk and I smiled at him in a gesture of friendliness. Moments later I saw him pick up a fifty cent piece that someone had dropped. The guy studied it for a moment, and then I guess he remembered my friendly smile cause' he brought the piece over and tried to give it to me. He couldn't speak any English nor I any German; I just put my arm around him and slipped the coin into his pocket. The guy had tears in his eyes, and so did I.

There was an orientation lecture at Santa Ana where we were given a letter from President Truman thanking us for our service in the Armed Forces. I had made my way to the foyer of the building after the lecture where a four star General approached me. I snapped to stiff attention thinking that I had done something wrong, but the General smiled and said, "At ease Sergeant. I just wanted to ask you a couple of questions." (I just couldn't seem to comprehend that I was almost a civilian again and that the war was really over.) I answered a few of the General's questions about the 315th, and

then told him that we flew the last mission on August 14/15. I wondered what he meant when he said, "That mission might be more significant than you know." In any case he dropped it at that and then congratulated me on my Air Medal that I had received. I thanked the General and then went on my way. I thought, if all generals were like this guy, I might stay in service, but I knew better than that.

On January 16, 1946 the military counted my separation points at Santa Ana and decided that I qualified to be mustered out of service. A first lieutenant gave me the pitch to stay in and held up the officers' candidate school pitch. I just shook my head, "I was promised that carrot so many times, and I'm still a buck Sergeant." I forced a weak smile, "The military will have to press on without me. I pass."

America had fought a two ocean war since December 1941, and everybody was shifting into a peacetime mentality as fast as they had geared up for war. The subjects of war were being pushed aside and replaced by happy thoughts of getting back to civilian life. However there was still a considerable amount of chatter and speculation about the atomic bomb: its past, present and future role in the world scene. We didn't trust Russia although they had joined us as an ally, and it was generally thought that Russia would pose our next military threat. In that sense, the atomic bomb was a real comfort to us.

I was a ship without a rudder at this point, and I didn't know what I was going to do with my life. If I had been able obtain a commission I would have stayed in service, but as a non-commissioned officer, no way. Most of us guys had missed college because of service and the majority of us were considering that option. Interestingly enough, Russia had an influence on the numbers that entered college: I and many others were wondering about the sense of sweating a higher education when we probably would have to go back into service after a year or so and fight Russia.

Aircraft graveyard, Guam

Chapter Thirteen

REVELATIONS AND SPECULATIONS

The strange on-off-on last mission that we were ordered to fly August 14/15 was, in its self, enough to keep me searching for "why" answers throughout the years. Moreover I was driven to challenge the allegations that the 315th Bomb Wing had bombed mostly empty oil facilities, and in that context was somewhat less effective than first believed.

"The Joint Target Group (previously called the Committee of Operation Analysts [COA]), was set up in the Joint Chiefs of Staff organization to provide recommendations on Twentieth Air Force targets, and began functioning in 1944. The Joint Target Group based its recommendations on the assumption that the principal function of air attack was to pave the way for an invasion of the home islands. But after studying the results of the March fire raids, General LeMay came to the conclusion that with proper logistic support, air power alone could force the Japanese to surrender. LeMay's view was shared privately by some members of General Arnold's (General "Hap" Arnold, Commanding General Of U. S. Army Air forces) staff, and by some members of the Navy Air Force Staff. The selection of strategic bombing objectives was being argued back and forth in the Joint Target Group in Washington, but more and more selection of such objectives was being evaluated in terms of influence upon the proposed invasion of Japan. "

"By April, 1945 Army Air Force intelligence had come to the opinion that the petroleum industry in Japan was in such a critical state that the destruction of facilities and stores would react immediately upon the tactical situation. General Curtis LeMay, Commander of the XXIst Bomber Command, and Lt. General Barney M. Giles who came to Guam as a deputy commander of the 20th Air force, decided that the 315th Wing would devote its efforts exclusively to oil targets. This decision was enthusiastically endorsed by General Carl Spaatz who was slated to command all B-29's under USASTAF POA (United States Army Strategic Air Forces Pacific Ocean Area) beginning in July 1945."

LeMay ordered the 315th Wing to bomb oil refineries exclusively, thinking that we would cripple Japan's fuel producing capability and end the war. What LeMay and the Allies did not know was that Japan's oil potential had been reduced to only 3 or 4% of its normal refinery yields by the time the 315th began its operation.

DESPITE ASSERTIONS THAT THE 315TH WING'S OPERATION HAD BEEN LESS DAMAGING TO THE ENEMY THAN PREVIOUS ESTIMATES, THERE ARE FACTS THAT PROVE OTHERWISE

Whatever Japan's oil capacity figured by

June 1945, we reduced it even more. Due to the fact that most oil production was confined to a relatively few modern facilities, by concentrating on 11 of Japan's newest refineries, we of the 315th Wing reduced overall oil output by 30 percent in little more than a month of operations. Synthetic production was cut down to 44 percent, which represented an actual loss of 265,000 barrels. The 315th flew fifteen missions against 10 oil refineries in Japan between 26 June and 15 August. The missions were conducted by streams of single aircraft flying at night and bombing from 10,000 feet to 15,000 feet. The Wing dispatched 1,200 planes, of which 1,095 bombed primary targets, dropping 9,084 tons of bombs. The very heavy bomb loads were possible because our B-29Bs had been stripped of all armament except the tail turret. We increased the bomb load from 14,631 on the first mission to Yokkaichi to 20,684 pounds on the August 9 mission to Amagasaki.

The 20th Air Force estimated that B-29 attacks had destroyed about 6,000,000 barrels of tank-storage capacity; we had reduced Japan's refining capacity from 90,000 barrels a day (December 1941) to about 17,000 barrels.

UBE, AUGUST 5/6

The 315th Bomb Wing attacked the Ube liquefaction plant (the largest synthetic plant in Japan proper), for the second time August 5/6. The target was built on reclaimed land and we sank it!

OUR BOMBING MISSION TO UBE CREATED A DIVERSION WHICH PROTECTED THE "ENOLA GAY"

The "Enola Gay" dropped the atomic bomb on Hiroshima at 8:16 a.m., August 6th. "The Boomerang" bombed Ube, just 73 miles south of Hiroshima, less than 7 hours before. The 315th Wing mission to Ube created an effective diversion protecting the "Enola Gay" and her two accompanying B-29s.

LeMAY HAD IT FIGURED

In the Iron Eagle Narrative written by General Curtis E. LeMay: LeMay, after asking a few questions about the atomic bomb prior to bombing Hiroshima 6 August announced that he would want to send a single, unescorted plane on the bombing mission (as we know the "Enola Gay" was accompanied by two B-29s, one a photo plane and the other an instrument plane). A large fleet of bombers, all protecting one queen bomber somewhere in their midst, would attract attention and perhaps resistance. But one bomber alone, flying at a high altitude, would undoubtedly be taken for a weather or reconnaissance plane, and ignored.

JAPANESE RADAR OPERATORS CONFUSE THE "ENOLA GAY" FOR PHOTO RECONNAISSANCE

The Japanese believed the "Enola Gay" and her two sister aircraft were harmless photo reconnaissance B-29s enroute to assess the damage that we had inflicted on Ube.

From Japan's Longest Day: "At eight o'clock Hiroshima radar operators detected two B-29's (there were actually 3 B-29s). A warning was sounded. The planes mounted to an extremely high altitude; the radio announced that they

Pilot Fred Williams, Jr., Crew 62

Radar and Engineer's Station

251

were on a reconnaissance flight. Most of the city's quarter of a million people didn't bother to seek shelter, anticipating no bombing. Many gazed up into the sky to watch the maneuver."

"A" BOMBING OF NAGASAKI, 9 AUGUST

At 11:00 a.m., 9 August, the second and last atomic bomb decimated 42.2% of Nagasaki (Northern Kyushu facing the East China Sea).

"The Boomerang" and 94 other crews bombed the Nippon Oil Refinery at Amagasaki that same night (August 9). Photo reports showed that Amagasaki was almost completely destroyed. Damage was well distributed. In the tank area, only two tanks remained undamaged. Synthetic oil plants showed damage to a gasometer, four buildings, and a sulphur removal unit. In the refinery area, four refining units and 30 tanks were destroyed. In addition, nine other tanks and 25 buildings were damaged.

THE JAPANESE WERE SPLIT IN THEIR VIEWS OF PEACE AND WAR

Even after the second atomic bomb fell on Nagasaki the Supreme Council for the Direction of War was still split in its peace/war deliberations. War Minister Anami, and the two Chiefs of Staff, Umezu for the Army and Toyoda for the Navy, vowed to continue the war. The military message to the Japanese people after the atomic bombings was this: "We have but one choice; we must fight on, even if we have to chew grass and eat earth and live in the fields, for in our

death there is a chance for our country's survival. The hero Kusunoki pledged to live and die seven times in order to save Japan from disaster. We can do no less..." Prime Minister Suzuki had taken the Supreme Council's resolution into the cabinet and described the "secret weapon" Japan would use in the final battle. The weapon was to be suicide: suicide planes, suicide submarines, crash boats, human torpedoes, mines, and antitank bombs. The cabinet endorsed the resolution as a Fundamental Policy paper. Major Hatanaka and his fellow War Ministry staff officers moved to take things a giant step further.

THE AMAZING MISSION TO AKITA, AUGUST 14/15

Despite rumors of immediate cessation of hostilities following Japan's peace overture on 10 August, and even though Japan's Domei News Agency notified the Allies 53 minutes before the Akita mission August 14th, that acceptance of the Potsdam Declaration was coming soon, "The Boomerang" and the 315th Wing were ordered to fly the longest bombing mission ever attempted with a full bomb load. The target was Akita which was 277.7 statute miles northwest of Tokyo.

In view of General LeMay's assessment that Japan was defeated even before the atomic bombs were dropped, it's curious that the 315th was ordered to fly an extremely high risk bombing mission to Akita, 9 days after the atomic bombing of Hiroshima, and 53 minutes after the Allies had received Japan's message that "surrender was coming soon." It has been established that the top brass was monitoring the Last Mission from Washington. The Signal Corps had a communication network that could transmit information around the globe in less than four minutes. (We were briefed that code word "Apple" sent to us in international Morse code would be the order for us to scrub our mission and return to base.) There could be no military excuse that there wasn't time or technology to abort the mission before it was airborne or anywhere along its route.

We were ordered to start engines, stop engines, start engines, and then go. Apparently, during this scenario, there was last minute information being received by the command that was crucial to the mission status. The fact that a scrub had been set in place with the code word "Apple" was proof that a Japanese surrender was anticipated at any time, but why the last minute confusion? Now that we know the unofficial surrender was beamed to the command 53 minutes before we took off for Akita, the last mission takes on even more intrigue.

THE PALACE REVOLT HAD ITS BEGINNING AND END IN THE SAME TIME FRAME AS THE LAST MISSION, AUGUST 14/15, 1945

Major Kenji Hatanaka, War Minister Anami's protégé, led the Ministry of War staff officers in a Palace Revolt. The insurrection was designed to destroy the peace initiatives and extend the war. To accomplish this goal the conspirators planned to prevent Hirohito from recording his surrender message, and then "protect" the Emperor from his traitorous advisors by kidnapping him and holding him incommunicado at his quarters. Orders would then be issued to the armies to attack the U.S. Naval forces lying just outside Tokyo Bay. The revolt began

moving at the same time "The Boomerang" and the 315th were rolling for takeoff on Northwest Field enroute to Akita.

Whether anyone in the military or the President of the United States, Harry S. Truman, had any knowledge of a revolt against the Emperor, we may never know. The United States did not have intelligence operatives in the Home Islands, and most intelligence information from within Japan came from communication intercepts. There was one known official contact in Japan referred to by the Office of Strategic Services only as agent 673. Agent 673 was in touch with Admiral Fujimura, believed to be a high officer of the Japanese intelligence service in Europe. He was supposed to be in direct and secret cable contact with the Japanese Minister of Marine and believed to have the confidence of the Japanese government. Sonovan, head of the O.S.S. explained privately to Truman that 673 was a German national who had been taken prisoner by the Japanese in World War I and upon his release had remained in Japan and established important commercial relations there, and gained the confidence of high Japanese circles, particularly the Navy. Perhaps 673 had passed along specific word of the Revolt or suggested that a revolt was developing against the Emperor. One thing is without argument or contention: The United States was aware of peace and war factions in Japan, and the command knew that certain elements of the Japanese military posed a major threat to the peace process. President Truman cautioned his commanders to watch for treachery following Japan's peace overture on 10 August. By 14 August, war and peace forces in Japan were balanced on the razor's edge.

WAR FACTIONS WERE READY

Major Hatanaka and members of the conspiracy were convinced that if they could hold the Emperor incommunicado, impound the surrender recordings, and prevent the broadcast of the Imperial Rescript, the war factions would fall into line like dominos. It has since been revealed that Admiral Onishi wanted to sacrifice twenty million Japanese in kamikaze strikes, and Naval Captain Kozono of the 302nd Air Corps in Atsugi was eagerly standing by for orders to attack the U.S. Third Fleet which was lying outside of Tokyo Bay, and operating up and down the Japanese Home Islands. Five thousand, five hundred Kamikaze's were ready, and another five thousand conventional Japanese fighters were poised to strike. The Emperor's recorded Imperial message of surrender was the pivotal key to peace or war.

THE LAST MISSION AND THE PALACE REVOLT COLLIDE

"The Boomerang" and the 315th Bomb Wing punched out the lights of the Palace Revolt at 11:00 p.m. By all accounts, the blackout that ensued slowed down the coup, and threw the operation off rhythm. If the military dissidents were to reach their ultimate goal of extending the war, they had to intercept the Emperor, prevent him from recording the surrender message, and then hold the Emperor incommunicado while they issued their own military orders for the armies to continue the war. Time became an ever increasing factor.

Major Hatanaka and some of his fellow conspirators had entered the Palace grounds at 9:30 p.m. August 14th.

Japanese historians, who may have been embarrassed by the fact that General Anami's Staff members planned to kidnap their Emperor, have left some curious gaps in their accounting of the revolt between the time the conspirators entered the Palace at 9:30 p.m. and their murderous confrontation with General Mori between 12:00 midnight and 1:00 a.m. The probable action that took place during that three hour plus interval would appear self-evident to anyone who has studied the Palace Revolt. The conspirators knew that the Emperor would begin his recording of the Imperial Rescript message at the Household Ministry Building at approximately 11:00 p.m. (the same time the War Cabinet would conclude signing the Potsdam Declaration of surrender). Hatanaka, speaking with Colonel Ida during the initial planning of the coup between 4:00 p.m. to 5:00 p.m., August 14th: "I want to occupy the Imperial Household Ministry Building." Without question reason would suggest that the rebels would be waiting close to the Household Ministry Building to intercept the Emperor. The 11:00 p.m. blackout forced the Emperor into his bomb shelter and delayed his expected arrival at the Household Ministry Building. I believe these unforeseen developments panicked Hatanaka, and with time working against him, he knew that he must enlist the support of General Mori's 1st Imperial Guards Division immediately. (Although there is not a direct mention that Colonel Haga and his 2nd Regiment Guards escorted the conspirators to General Mori's headquarters where Hatanaka and Uehara confronted Mori, I believe logic demands that conclusion.) Major Hatanaka then murdered Mori in his quarters, and his accompanying officer conspirator, Captain Uehara, slashed to death Lt. Colonel

Shiraishi. (Haga did not learn of the murders until later.) In diverting to Mori's headquarters, the conspirators missed their chance to intercept the Emperor outside the Imperial Household Ministry Building, and prevent him from recording the Imperial Rescript.

After murdering the reluctant Mori and his brother-in-law Lt. Colonel Shiraishi, staff officer of the general army, the rebels returned to the Household Ministry Building but it was too late. The Emperor had already recorded his message and returned to his Imperial quarters. The conspirators searched frantically all night in the blacked out catacombs of the Household Ministry Building, but they failed to find the recorded Rescript. The revolt subsequently unraveled.

I believe that the 11:00 p.m. blackout that sent the Emperor to his bomb shelter, delaying his arrival at the Household Ministry Building, spared him from falling into the hands of the conspirators and cleared the way for Hirohito to record the vital Imperial Rescript. At the very least, the blackout permitted the recordings to be safely hidden away by Tokugawa where they remained undetected throughout the blackened night.

In his book, The Two-Ocean War, Samuel Eliot Morison states: "It was a very near thing. That night a military plot to seize the Emperor and impound his recording of the Imperial Rescript (which was to be broadcast the 15th) was narrowly averted. Attempts were made to assassinate Suzuki and others. But the Emperor's message to his people went out in the morning... If these elements had had their way, the war would have been resumed with the Allies feeling that the Japanese were hopelessly treacherous, and with a savagery that is painful to contemplate."

Note: There has been speculation as to the significance of the Palace Revolt. Some argue that the conspirators were chasing the wind, and didn't really pose a serious threat to the peace process. The arguments could go on throughout eternity, but there are several facts that cannot be ignored: the conspirators who planned the coup against the Emperor's peace moves were not a bunch of half-baked diehards off the street. They were the proud "Young Tigers", the highly esteemed crack staff officers of War Minister General Anami. In 1945 General Anami, and Army Chief of Staff, General Umezu were the two most powerful men in Japan. Hirohito then was a figurehead even though a figurehead of vital importance. He was the moral and spiritual leader whose signature was mandatory on all important state documents.

Although some contend that the revolt could never have reached its objectives, the leaders of the coup were betting their very lives that they would prevail.

AND WHAT ABOUT THE LAST MISSION ITSELF

Intelligence knew by August that Japan was pitifully low on oil reserves and oil production. The evidence suggests that the Joint Chiefs of Staff ordered the last mission to drive the stake into the heart of any further Japanese war effort. Our tentative on/off/on last mission indicated that there was some high level maneuvering taking place. Whatever the subjects of discussion, our mission was allowed to continue, and the commanders' discussions of our last mission are curiously missing from U.S. historical records.

WHAT WAS THE SIGNIFICANCE OF AKITA?

If Akita was just another dry oil refinery, as rumored after the war, why would its destruction have made any strategic impact on those elements who were committed to extending the war?

If intelligence had miscalculated oil refining capabilities and storage capacities in previous targets, they were right on the money with Akita.

THE LAST MISSION TO AKITA, 14/15 AUGUST WAS DECLASSIFIED IN 1985. THE FOLLOWING IS TRANSCRIBED FROM THE TACTICAL MISSION REPORT:

Target 90.6-1066

NIPPON OIL CO. REFINERY, AKITA
Latitude: 39 degrees 45 minutes North
Longitude: 140 degrees 04 minutes East
Elevation: Approximately 50 feet
IMPORTANCE: It is one of the most important targets in the Japanese Petroleum Industry. Processes crude oil from the oil fields around Akita, which are the largest natural petroleum producers in Japan proper. The annual crude capacity was estimated in late 1944 at 1,320,000 barrels annually, representing 37 per cent of the Inner Zone oil refined. Cracking capacity was estimated as lower than that necessary to refine the crude oil available. Capacity has increased in importance since it is not dependent on imported petroleum as are most existing refineries in Japan proper. The plant is believed to have tankage capacity in excess of operating requirements.

AKITA ACTUALLY REPRESENTED MORE THAN 67 PERCENT OF OIL REFINED CRACKING CAPACITY

The 37 percent figure given above, representing Akita's contribution to the Inner Zone Oil refined, was calculated late in 1944 at 1,320,000 barrels annually. That estimate was made before our operations began. The 315th, according to the historical statistics, destroyed 30 per cent of the Japanese oil production the first month. So, by the time we bombed Akita, those facilities represented much more than 37 percent of oil contributed to the Inner Zone Oil refined--perhaps as much as 67 percent.

UNIT HISTORY 315TH BOMBARDMENT WING MICROFILM ROLL #C0154 EXCERPTS

"The last mission of the 315th Wing took off on 14 August after having been delayed because of peace negotiations. Because of the possibility of cancellation of this mission due to negotiations, all crews were thoroughly briefed to jettison bombs and return to base when properly notified. (As you know, we were not recalled.) This mission was believed to be the longest flown by any type aircraft without bomb bay fuel tanks. Total distance was 3239 nautical miles (3724.85 statute miles), and the planned elapsed time was 16:30 hours. ("The Boomerang" flew 3740 miles and logged 16 hours 50 minutes.) This target was of extreme importance to the enemy as it processed crude oil from the fields around Akita, the largest natural source in Japan proper."

THE 1985 DECLASSIFIED MISSION REPORT CONTINUED

"1. LOCATION AND IDENTIFICATION: The target is located immediately north of and along the northern back of the mouth of the Omono River and on the northwestern outskirts of the port town of Tshuchizaki. It is five miles northwest of the city of Akita and fourteen miles southeast of a peninsula of land jutting out from the west coast of Honshu into the Sea of Japan.

"2. PLANT DESCRIPTION: The target area roughly describes a rectangle measuring 2250 feet northeast to southwest and 2000 feet northwest to southeast. Facilities for refining are confined to the southern part of the area. Tankage occupies the northern portion of the area. Railroad spur running through southern limits of the compound connects the plant with the mainline Railroad to Aomori. Bunkering facilities are believed to exist. "

The 315th Wing scheduled 143 airplanes for this mission.

Bomb Loading:

"Mission number 328 (315th Wing) Expected Bomb load 20,500 pounds.

"Time of first take off: 0642 Z (4:42 p.m.)

"Time of last take off: 0858 Z (6:58 p.m.)

"Altitudes:

"(a) Enroute to target: 5,000--5,800 feet; 7,000--7,800 feet.

"(b) Attack: 10,000 feet to 11,000 feet.

"Bomb Load:

"(a) 100 pound GP's using T-19 adapters to extent available, remainder 250 pound GP's.

"(b) Fusing: No nose fuse and non-delay tail.

"(c) Intervalometer Setting: 35 feet.

"The night precision attack of the 315th Wing against the Nippon Oil Refinery at Tshuchizaki, was expected to include approximately 140 aircraft carrying a total gross tonnage of about 1400 tons. Direct radar synchronous bombing was to be used."

"Mission Number 328 (315th Wing)

"This mission is to follow the coast from Chosi Point to a well-defined coastal point at 36 degrees 58 minutes N--140 degrees 54 minutes E and to an island initial point at 38 degrees 27 minutes N--139 degrees 14 minutes 30 seconds E. This island point should be identified easily and should serve as an excellent wind run point. The approach from the initial point, Awa Shima, is a distance of 81 nautical miles along the western coast of Honshu. Although this coast is fairly smooth, it has several points which can be used in determining range. If necessary, the distinctive projection north of Akita can be used as a reference point; though the city of Akita can be identified at a minimum range of 40 miles. The assigned target is located at the mouth of the Omono Gawa which can be used as a reference point. The target, which gives a separate radar return, should be good for direct synchronous bombing by individual aircraft."

"Mission Number 328--Nippon Oil Refinery, Akita:

"a. The primary target was bombed by 132 aircraft of the 315th Wing between 0048 K (local time) and 0339 K (local time) August 15th. The axis of attack was 27 degrees. Weather over the target was reported as 7/10--10/10 clouds with winds of 17 knots from 330 degrees.

"First to land: 2307 Z (9:07 a.m.) August 15

"Last to land: 0200 Z (12:00 noon) August 15

"143 airplanes dispatched, 132 effective, non-effective

"Landing at Iwo Jima: 13 aircraft

C. I. U.
TWENTIETH AIR FORCE
APO 234, C/O POSTMASTER
SAN FRANCISCO, CALIFORNIA

"10 September 1945

"DAMAGE ASSESSMENT REPORT NO. 205
"TARGET 90.6--1066
"N I P P O N   O I L   R E F I N E R Y, TSHUCHIZAKI

"20th AF Mission No. 328   315th Wing Date Flown: 14/15 August, 1945

"Mission Results

"Akita's total oil storage facilities were 70% destroyed. The buildings of the refinery were 98% affected, 87% destroyed and 11% gutted and seriously damaged. Damage was most concentrated in the south and east portions of the target. Area VII containing storage buildings and transportation facilities was 100% destroyed. (Photos revealed that no part of the target was untouched.)

"Railway sidings in this are indicated by T on attached annotated blow-up were dislocated and rail cars thrown off the tracks or destroyed. Piles of open stores in this area were affected to an indeterminate extent.

"Area IV containing refining units and two cracking towers at "C" is probably inoperative, oil storage facilities adjacent to the cracking towers were destroyed. All structures in Area III, administrative area were destroyed.

"Facilities in area VI were 82% destroyed and gutted. The northwest corner of the refinery containing crude storage tanks, area I. Six of the original eight tanks or 73% were destroyed.

MISSION REPORT DATE: 5 SEPTEMBER 1945.
WHY WASN'T AKITA BOMBED BEFORE

Akita was bombed approximately one hour and forty eight minutes after the Japanese had cabled their official surrender to the Allies. The 315th Wing received a Distinguished Unit Citation for this last B-29 mission.

The question arises: "If Akita was so important why wasn't it bombed before?" The answers seem simple:
1. Akita was nearly beyond the B-29s range capability, and why risk men and equipment unnecessarily when we were already crippling Japan by systematically blowing up all of her oil reserves?

2. Why destroy the richest oil fields in Japan when our occupation troops were about to take over the home islands. The U.S. troops could certainly use that oil since the facilities represented 67% of Japan's annual refining capability at the time we destroyed it.

3. Our mission was conducted 53 minutes after the command heard that Japan was surrendering. The scrub capability ("Apple" in Morse code) was built into the mission. We were ordered to start engines, then shut engines down and stand by, finally we were given the signal to start engines and fly the mission. We were never given the order to scrub. Certainly the command was weighing our occupational need for Akita against the threat it posed in supplying petrol to the military diehards. There is a body of evidence out there that indicates the United States wanted to get the war over before Russia could get further involved and claim some of the spoils. Perhaps the U.S. wanted to make certain the Russians didn't benefit in any way from Akita's oil resources. Whatever the reason, our on-off-go mission to Akita was obviously viewed by the command as an action of extreme military importance.

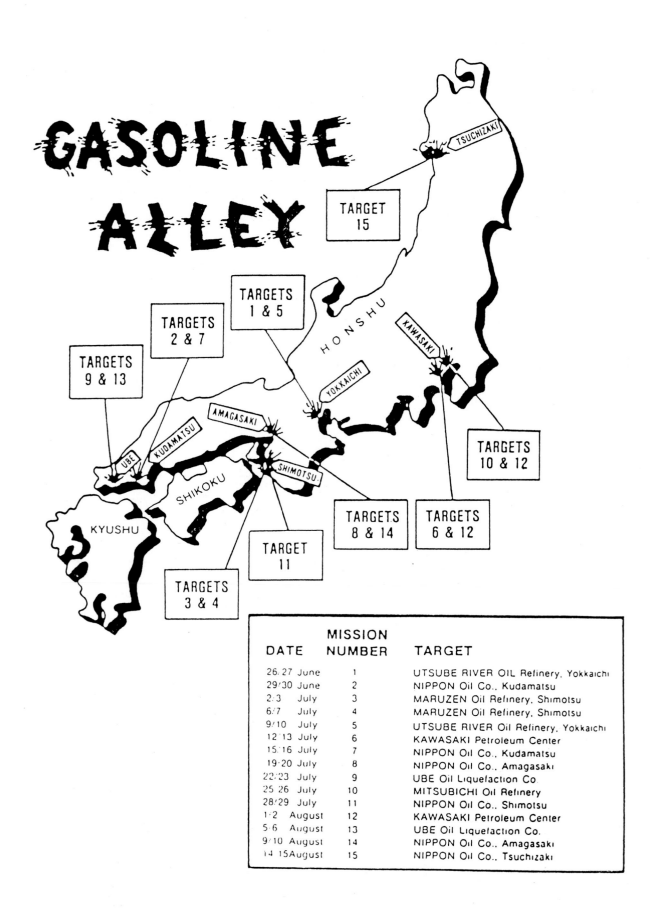

GASOLINE ALLEY

TARGET 15

TARGETS 1 & 5

TARGETS 2 & 7

TARGETS 9 & 13

TSUCHIZAKI

KAWASAKI

HONSHU

YOKKAICHI

AMAGASAKI

KUDAMATSU

UBE

SHIMOTSU

SHIKOKU

KYUSHU

TARGETS 10 & 12

TARGETS 8 & 14

TARGETS 6 & 12

TARGET 11

TARGETS 3 & 4

DATE	MISSION NUMBER	TARGET
26/27 June	1	UTSUBE RIVER OIL Refinery, Yokkaichi
29/30 June	2	NIPPON Oil Co., Kudamatsu
2/3 July	3	MARUZEN Oil Refinery, Shimotsu
6/7 July	4	MARUZEN Oil Refinery, Shimotsu
9/10 July	5	UTSUBE RIVER Oil Refinery, Yokkaichi
12/13 July	6	KAWASAKI Petroleum Center
15/16 July	7	NIPPON Oil Co., Kudamatsu
19/20 July	8	NIPPON Oil Co., Amagasaki
22/23 July	9	UBE Oil Liquefaction Co.
25/26 July	10	MITSUBICHI Oil Refinery
28/29 July	11	NIPPON Oil Co., Shimotsu
1/2 August	12	KAWASAKI Petroleum Center
5/6 August	13	UBE Oil Liquefaction Co.
9/10 August	14	NIPPON Oil Co., Amagasaki
14/15 August	15	NIPPON Oil Co., Tsuchizaki

260

Chapter Fourteen

EPILOGUE

ADMIRAL CHESTER W. NIMITZ (COMMANDER-IN-CHIEF U.S. PACIFIC FLEET AND PACIFIC OCEAN AREA) AND ATTACHED FAST CARRIER FORCE, TASK FORCE 38 UNDER COMMAND OF ADMIRAL WILLIAM (BULL) HALSEY

On 1 July, Task Force 38 sortied from Leyte Gulf to operate close to Japan, and there it stayed until Japan surrendered. T F 38 roamed up and down the Japanese coast striking Japanese navy vessels, and for the first time, a naval gunfire force bombarded a major installation within the home islands of Japan, the iron works at Kamaishi. The battleships South Dakota, Indiana, and Massachusetts, two heavy cruisers and nine destroyers were used. On July 16 a task unit under Rear Admiral Oscar Badger, comprising the battleships Iowa, Missouri, and Wisconsin, two light cruisers and eight destroyers, bombarded the Nihon Steel Company and the Wanishi Ironworks at Muroran, Hokkaido. At the war's end Task Force 38, along with other naval units, had positioned two aircraft carriers outside Tokyo Bay.

At 11:00 p.m. August 14 (time of the Palace blackout), "The Boomerang" was 200 miles south of Tokyo enroute to Akita, and Admiral Nimitz was sending a message to all naval units:

"Cease offensive operation against Japanese forces. Search and patrol.

Maintain defensive and internal security measures at highest level and beware of treachery or last moment attacks by enemy forces or individuals." (That last statement shows that the U.S. Forces were bowstring ready for any false moves from the Japanese.)

IF THE CONSPIRACY AGAINST THE EMPEROR HAD REACHED ITS GOALS

If the palace revolt had succeeded, our naval forces would most certainly have come under attack some hours after President Truman had received the official Japanese note of surrender. A third atomic bomb was being readied to be shipped to Tinian, and could have been dropped on Japan on the first good weather day after August 17 or 18. Truman told Navy Secretary James Forrestal and Secretary of War Henry L. Stimson that he would suspend further atomic missions unless Tokyo's reply was unsatisfactory. This statement by Truman adds credence to the speculation that another atomic bomb could have been dropped on Japan if the conspiracy had upset the peace initiatives.

Other retaliatory options included an Allied invasion which would have inflicted awful losses on both sides. Those of us who remember President Harry S. Truman know that he would have responded

261

promptly to any Japanese military action coming after Japan's cabled surrender. (Truman said that he would not order any more atomic bombs to be dropped unless Japan's reply was unsatisfactory.)

Any hitch in the peace process would have placed both sides at great risk. For anyone who is acquainted with the Japanese tenacity and discipline, it would seem clear that the Japanese would have indeed fought to the last man, woman and child if they had not been asked to accept surrender by their Emperor God.

Major Hatanaka and his co-conspirators believed that a U.S. invasion would give Japan the greatest advantage, and even though some believed that the U.S. would eventually prevail, all of the conspirators believed that any extension of the war, would result in a favorable revision of the unconditional surrender terms. They were dedicated to this end.

IF THE OPTION OF INVASION HAD BEEN IMPLEMENTED, THE COST IN LIVES WOULD HAVE BEEN EXTREMELY HIGH ON BOTH SIDES

The United States was set to invade Kyushu November 1, 1945 (Olympic), and Honshu March 1, 1946 (Coronet). The Japanese still had significant military capability including ammunition. 5,350 Kamikaze's were left, and another 5000 for orthodox use. Aircraft were to be readied on small grass strips in Kyushu, Shikoku, and western Honshu, and in underground hangars and caves, to be used for Kamikaze operation against the Allied amphibious forces invading Kyushu. There would have been massive losses to the Allies even before they landed on shore. Japan had two million home island soldiers, and they were well prepared

against an invasion. U.S. intelligence told us in 1945, and they tell us now, that we would have lost upward of 800,000 men in the invasions; the Japanese would have lost millions.

FROM OIL & WAR, ROBERT GORAISKI AND RUSSELL W. FREEBURG:

"Japan was at wit's end to provide the barest needs to its military. The major oil shipping ports of Balikpapan and Surabaja had been abandoned in December 1944, and by January 1945 the Imperial Navy was forced to fuel some of its ships with alcohol. Navigational training was eliminated for pilots.

"Although the military controlled all fuels, it was helpless to find additional supplies. Combat units were reduced to impotence. The civilian population could not be called upon to sacrifice further; it had already sacrificed all. Coal, charcoal, and firewood were in short supply. Propane was not available at all. Yoshio Yamada, a retired Tokyo contractor, recalled there was insufficient fuel to cremate the dead in the last days of the war."

It was a war begun as a fight for oil and ended by the lack of it -- Asahi Shimbun (Newspaper)

God was on the side of the nation that had the oil -- Professor Wakimura, Tokyo Imperial University, in postwar interrogation.

THE 315TH BOMB WING

1. We of the 315th Bomb Wing reduced Japan's over-all output of oil by 30

percent in a little more than a month of operation. We reduced the synthetic production to 44 percent. The 315th Wing was awarded a Distinguished Unit Citation for attacks on the Maruzen oil refinery at Shimotsu, the Utsubo oil refinery at Yokkaichi, and the petroleum center at Kawasaki in July 1945.

2. The 315th Bomb Wing sank the Ube Liquefaction Company on our second mission to the target 5/6 August, and in so doing, we set up a deception that cleared the way for the "Enola Gay" and the atomic bomb. The 315th received a D.U.C. for the mission.

3. At 11:00 a.m., August 9, an atomic bomb exploded on Nagasaki. On the same night (9/10 August) we nearly erased the Nippon Oil Company at Amagaski. The 315th Wing received a D.U.C. for this mission.

4. August 14/15 we flew the longest mission from the Mariannas with a full bomb load, and without bomb bay tanks. Our overflight produced a Tokyo blackout that interfered with the incredible palace revolt against the Emperor's peace initiatives. The mission went on to destroy the Nippon Oil Company Refinery at Akita. That refinery represented 67 percent of Japan's annual inner zone oil production at the time we destroyed it.

Note: From the Unit history microfilm: "This target was of extreme importance to the enemy as it processed crude oil from the fields around Akita, the largest natural source in Japan proper." The damage assessment on all structures averaged 86%. Photos revealed that no part of the target was untouched. Once again the 315th received D.U.C. for its excellence of operation.

THE SIGNIFICANCE OF AKITA

By destroying the Akita oil fields and its refineries, we further discouraged Japan's military diehards, thus taking Japan further away from at least three terrible U.S. options that remained: invasion of the Japanese Home Islands, further decimation of Japan by bombing, or dropping another atomic bomb.

The bizarre, false start, last mission which was ordered 53 minutes after the Domei News Agency announced: "IMPERIAL MESSAGE ACCEPTING THE POTSDAM PROCLAMATION IS FORTHCOMING SOON", jiggled out of focus simply because it was upstaged by the two Atomic bombs that decimated Hiroshima and Nagasaki. The daring Palace Revolt did not come to light until some years later, and the connection between the last mission and the revolt was never considered until now.

Ask anyone who has memory of the Pacific War, excepting members of the 315th Bomb Wing. They will tell you that the atomic bombs ended the war. Actually the war wasn't over until the last B-29 missions were flown 6 days after Nagasaki.

The great on-the- scene historian, Samuel Eliot Morison, states in The Two-Ocean War: "When these facts and events of the Japanese surrender are known and weighed, it will become evident that the atomic bomb was the keystone of a very fragile arch. Certainly the war would have gone on, and God knows for how long, if the bomb had not been dropped. It has been argued that the maritime blockade would have strangled Japanese economy, and that the B-29s and naval bombardment would have destroyed her principal cities and forced a surrender without benefit of atomic fission. I do not think that anyone acquainted with the admirable discipline and tenacity of the Japanese people can believe this. If the Emperor had told them to fight to the last man, they would have fought to the last man, suffering far, far greater losses and injuries than those inflicted by the atomic bombs."

AUGUST 15, 1945

"The Boomerang" and the 315th Bomb Wing were returning to base when the official announcement of surrender came.

THE FACTS ARE NOW CLEAR

The last mission closed the curtain on the Pacific War. The palace revolt with all its speculations, and the elements of the last mission to Akita are finally known. These actions made a difference, and history has the obligation to report them with honesty and clarity.

PRESIDENT TRUMAN

"It's the small events unnoticed at the time that later are discovered to have changed history."

LETTER FROM PRESIDENT HARRY S. TRUMAN

"To you who answered the call of your country and served in its Armed Forces to bring about the total defeat of the enemy, I extend the heartfelt thanks of a grateful Nation. As one of the Nation's finest, you undertook the most severe task one can be called upon to perform. Because you demonstrated the fortitude, resourcefulness and calm judgment necessary to carry out that task, we now look to you for leadership and example in further exalting our country in peace."

THE WAR WAS OVER!

A true B-29/Pacific War story has been told from start to finish. In so doing the missing links between Nagasaki and the signing of peace topside of the Missouri have been set back in place!

MISSION ACCOMPLISHED!

TARGET INFORMATION SHEET
TARGET 90.6-1066 - NIPPON OIL CO. REFINERY, AKITA

This, along with other materials, would be distributed at the pre-mission briefing.

TARGET: 9016-1066

OBJECTIVE AREA: 90.6-AKITA

T A R G E T   I N F O R M A T I O N   S H E E T

TARGET 90.6-1066

NIPPON OIL CO. REFINERY, AKITA

Latitude: 39° 45' N
Longitude: 140° 04' E
Elevation: Approx. 50'

1. **LOCATION AND IDENTIFICATION:** The target is located immediately north of and along the northern bank of the mouth of the Omono River and on the northwestern outskirts of the port town of Tsuchizaki. It is five miles northwest of the city of Akita and fourteen miles southeast of a peninsula of land jutting out from the west coast of Honshu into the Sea of Japan.

2. **PLANT DESCRIPTION:** The target area roughly describes a rectangle measuring 2250 ft. northeast to southwest and 2000 ft. northwest to southeast. Facilities for refining are confined to the southern part of the area. Tankage occupies the northern portion of the area. Railroad spur running through southern limits of the compound connects the plant with the mainline Railroad to Aomori. Bunkering facilities are believed to exist.

3. **IMPORTANCE:** It is one of the most important targets in the Japanese Petroleum Industry. Processes crude oil from the oil fields around Akita, which are the largest natural petroleum producers in Japan proper. The annual crude capacity was estimated in late 1944 at 1,320,000 bbls. annually, representing 37 per cent of the Inner Zone oil refined. Cracking capacity was estimated as lower than that necessary to refine the crude oil available. Capacity has increased in importance since it is not dependent on imported petroleum as are most existing refineries in Japan proper. The plant is believed to have tankage capacity in excess of operating requirements.

5 September 1945.

TARGET SECTION, A-2
TWENTIETH AIR FORCE

267

315 WING FIELD ORDER #49
TARGET 1-77 - NIPPON OIL CO. REFINERY, AKITA

The field orders contain all information pertinent to the mission, including navigation aids and locations of ships and aircraft assigned to rescue duty.

315 WING FIELD ORDER # 49

1066   TARGET

CREW NO. 62

AIRPLANE COMMANDER   Eckhart

AIRPLANE NUMBER   62

TIME AT STATIONS   1744   K

TIME TO START ENGINES   1754   K

TIME OF TAKE OFF   1809   K

After take off, climb straight ahead at 200 CAS for 4 minutes on North runway and 5 minutes on South runway from beginning of take off roll, then left turn on course to Iwo.

Climb from base at   200   CAS to Altitude 7200

Cruise to Iwo at 203   CAS

Cruise from Iwo to climbing point at   199   CAS

Climb at 200   CAS to bombing altitude

Cruise at bombing altitude   205 CAS.   Bombing Altitude 10800

Axis of attack: 27 deg   true

IP.

MPI:

Breakaway as briefed

Return_____ **Max range cruise - 10000'**

**Running lights off when within 200 miles of Empire and IFF off 50 miles of Empire

Altimeter set at 29.92 throughout mission except for landing.
                +IFF
**All lights off 150 miles before reaching IP and on again 150 miles after passing IP

271

Kinkasan Light   38° 16'N - 141° 35'E

Inubo Saki Light 35° 42'N - 140° 52'E

Hachijo-Jima 33° 02'N - 139° 50'E

Sofu Gan 29° 49'N - 140° 21'E

Before 2200K (1200Z)	Little Lulu	Abie 565	Airdale 71
After 2200K (1200Z)	Saltlick	(565V6)	(71V135)
			After 01:05K

Before 2200K (1200Z)	Chlorinated	Abie 613	Playmate 72
After 2200K (1200Z)	Palm Reader	(613V6)	(72V180)
			After 01:45K
			35° 00'N - 141° 10'E

Before 2200K (1200Z)	O'Reillys Daughter	Abie 604	Playmate 73
After 2200K (1200Z)	Salome	(604V6)	(73V180)
			After 0230K
			32° 30'N - 141° 10'E

Before 2200K (1200Z)	Ball and Chain	Abie 592	Playmate 74
After 2200K (1200Z)	Hiram Walker	(592V6)	(74V180)
			After 03:15K
			30° 00'N - 141° 10'E

	Bird Dog 65	Playmate 65
	65 (X087)	(65V180)
	28° 00'N -	After 02:50K
	140° 45'E	28° 00'N - 140° 45'E

	Bird Dog 66	Playmate 66
	66 (X087)	(66V180)
	26° 30'N-	After 03:20K
	141° 00'E	26° 30'N - 140° 00'E

	Playmate 20
	(20 x 550)
	20° 00'N - 143° 30'E
	During Return

Solid Jack	Playmate 18
18° 00'N -	(18 xx 550)
144° 30'E	18° 00'N - 144° 30'E
	During Return

	Playmate 16
	(16 xx 550)
	16° 000'N - 145° 20'E
	During Return

Appendix III

315TH BOMB WING OPERATIONS FORECAST FOR 14-15 AUGUST '45

Detailed weather forecasts and a weather map would be provided for each aircraft prior to a mission.

TARGET: AKITA

315TH BOMB WING OPERATIONAL FORECAST FOR: 14 - 15 August '45

ZONES	to 19 N 143 E	to Iwo	to 34 N 134 E	to 40 N 149 E	TARGET	to 38 N 141	Guam
30,000							
25,000	5.0						
20,000							
15,000							
10,000							
5,000							
SURFACE							
WEATHER	OVERCAST	SHOWERS	SHOWERS	BROKEN	BROKEN	BROKEN	OVERCAST
VISIBILITY	18	18 - 2½	20 - 12	18 - 6	15 - 6	15 - 6	18 - 12
ALTIMETER	29.90	29.80	29.89	29.92	29.75	29.81	29.84
TURBULENCE			Light				
FREEZING LEVEL	16,000	16,000	16,000	15,000	15,000	15,000	16,000
ICING	---	---	---	---	---	---	---

NO MOON DATA
MEAN TIDE RANGE : .5 ft.

MISSION #10
LAST MISSION
14-15 Aug 45
TSUHU SAKI

277

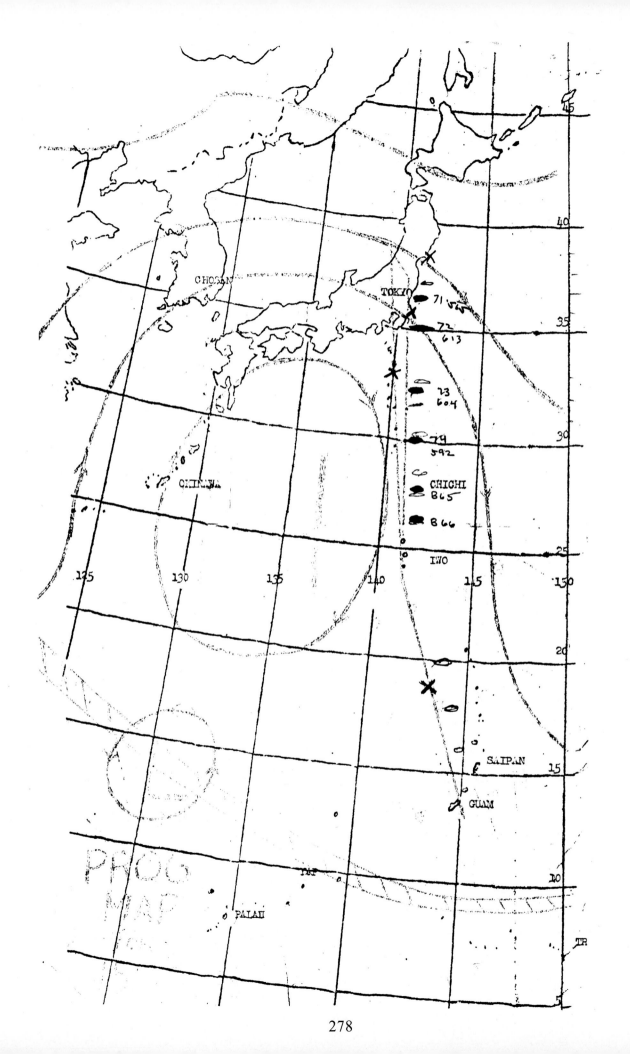

Appendix IV

PHOTO INTELLIGENCE TARGET 90.6-1066
NIPPON OIL REFINERY CO. - AKITA

Photo intelligence would be utilized both prior to and after a mission. Pre-raid photos would be used to familiarize the crews taking part in the mission with target layout and setting. Post- raid photos would provide information for damage assessment.

Photos RR2 and RR5 are APQ-7 Radar Scope pictures of the Nippon Oil Refinery target area taken on 8 Aug 1945.

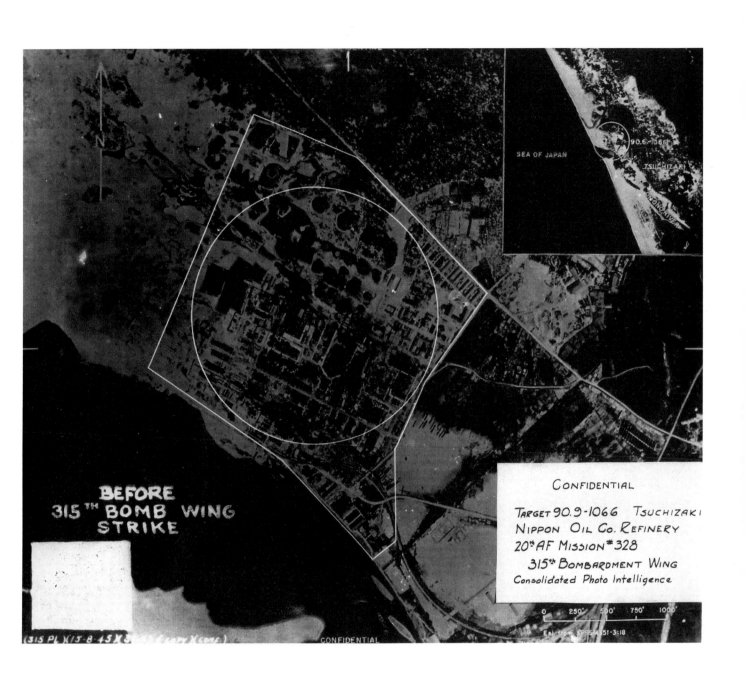

BEFORE
315ᵀᴴ BOMB WING
STRIKE

CONFIDENTIAL

TARGET 90.9-1066 TSUCHIZAKI
NIPPON OIL Co. REFINERY
20ᵗʰ AF MISSION #328
315ᵗʰ BOMBARDMENT WING
Consolidated Photo Intelligence

SEA OF JAPAN

TSUCHIZAKI

CONFIDENTIAL

"AFTER"

315TH MISSION NO 15, AF 328

TARGET 90.6 -1066 NIPPON OIL REF

PHOTO INTELLIGENCE

(315 PL) (6 SEPT. 45) (57

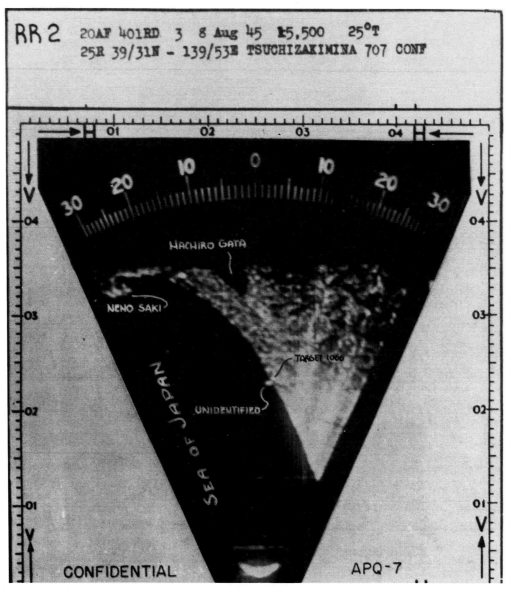

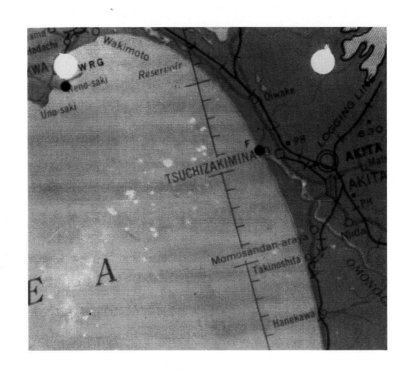

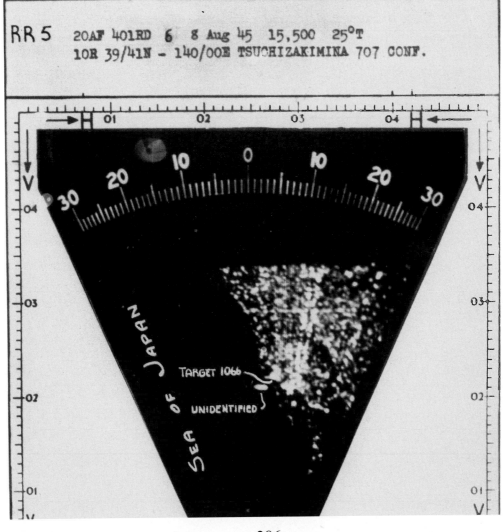

RR5 20AF 401RD 6 8 Aug 45 15,500 25°T
10R 39/41N - 140/00E TSUCHIZAKIMINA 707 CONF.

Appendix V

DAMAGE ASSESSMENT REPORT NO. 205
TARGET 90.6-1066
NIPPON OIL CO. REFINERY - TAUCHIZAKI (AKITA)

C. I. U.
TWENTIETH AIR FORCE
APO 234, c/o POSTMASTER
SAN FRANCISCO, CALIFORNIA

10 September 1945

DAMAGE ASSESSMENT REPORT NO. 205
TARGET 90.6 - 1066
NIPPON OIL REFINERY, TSUCHIZAKI

20th AF Mission No.: 328   Date Flown: 14 August 1945

315th Wing

SUMMARY

The targets total oil storage facilities were 70%
destroyed. The buildings of the refinery were 98% affected, 87% destroyed and 11% gutted and seriously damaged.
Damage was most concentrated in the south and east portions of the target. Area VII containing storage buildings and transportation facilities was 100% destroyed.
Railway sidings in this area indicated by T on attached annotated blow-up were dislocated and rail cars
thrown off the tracks or destroyed. Piles of open stores
in this area were affected to an indeterminate extent.
Area IV containing refining units and two cracking
towers at C is probably inoperative, oil storage facilities adjacent to the cracking towers were destroyed.
All structures in Area III, administrative area were
destroyed.
Facilities in area VI were 82% destroyed and gutted.
The north west corner of the refinery containing crude
storage tanks, area I. Six of the original eight tanks
or 73% were destroyed.

SUMMARY OF DAMAGE TO TANKAGE

| | | TYPE OR STORAGE | | |
	CRUDE	INTERMEDIATE	REFINED PRODUCTS	TOTAL
Orig.*Capacity - bbls.	300,000	107,800	287,780	695,580
New Damage - bbls.	218,000	70,640	197,080	485,720
- %	73	65	69	70
Total damage and Removal- bbls.	218,000	70,640	197,080	485,720
- %	73	65	69	70

*Original means capacity visible on first coverage, unless new tankage
has been added.

ITEMIZATION OF DAMAGE

Annot No.	IDENTIFICATION	DESCRIPTION OF DAMAGE	
		Original	destroyed and gutted
I	Crude storage tanks structures	300,000 bbls 800 sq.ft	218,000 bbls 800 sq.ft.
II	Finished products tanks no structures	174,400 bbls	133,400 bbls.
III	Finished products tanks no structures	580 bbls.	580 bbls

289

D/A Report No. 205 - Cont'd.

ANNOT NO.	IDENTIFICATION	DESCRIPTION OF DAMAGE	
		Original	Destroyed and gutted
IV	Intermediate storage tanks	53,900 bbls	45,140 bbls
	gasometers	87,300 cu.ft.	58,240 cu.ft.
	structures	155,600 sq.ft.	57,600 sq.ft.
	Finished products tanks no structures	111,000 bbls	97,300 bbls.
VI	Intermediate storage	53,900 bbls	25,500 bbls
	structures	77,780 sq.ft.	74,900 sq.ft.
VII	Finished products tanks	1,800 bbls	1,800 bbls
	structures	248,000 sq.ft.	248,000 sq.ft.

References:

      A. AOF 90.6
      B. Strike attack report 143, CIU 20th AF 18 August 1945

Photography:

      Pre-strike:3PR5M351 3: 19 24 July 1945   Alt. 25,500'
      Post-strike:3PR5M413 2: 13-16 scale 1/4000 30 August 1945
                3PR5M417 2: 6-8 scale 1/5000   2 September 1945

Inclosures:

      1. Annotated and attached:

          Blow up from 3PR5M351 3:19

Approved.................... _V. Shidak Capt AC_
            HAMILTON D. DARBY
            MAJOR, AC

DISTRIBUTION "B"

CONSOLIDATED STATISTICAL SUMMARY
OF COMBAT OPERATIONS
MISSION 14 AUG 1945

Excerpts of strike report pertaining to The Last Mission #328 (#1066) by the 315 Bomb Wing, Nippon Oil Refinery Co., Akita.

TWENTIETH AIR FORCE

CONSOLIDATED STATISTICAL SUMMARY OF COMBAT OPERATIONS

FORM 34

MISSION NO. 325 – 330

22 August 1945

Field Order No. 20

Mission #325 – 58th Wing – Maximum Effort – Hikari Naval Arsenal (#671)
Mission #326 – 73rd Wing – Maximum Effort – Osaka Army Arsenal (#382)
Mission #327 – 313th Wing – Maximum Effort(3 Groups) – Marifu Railroad Yards (#2202)
Mission #328 – 315th Wing – Maximum Effort – Nippon Oil Refinery, Tsuchizaki (#1066)
Mission #329 – 313th & 314th Wings – Maximum Effort (2 Groups) – Kumagaya Urban Area
Mission #330 – 73rd & 314th Wings – Maximum Effort (2 Groups) – Isezaki Urban Area

EFFECTIVENESS OF MISSIONS

Aircraft Airborne. 779
Percent Of Aircraft On Hand 90.9%

Aircraft Bombing Primary Targets. . 709
Percent Of Bombing Aircraft Airborne. 92.6%

Bombs Dropped On Primary Targets. . . . . 4463 Tons

Bombs Dropped On Other Targets. . . . . . 65 Tons

Bombing Results – No post strike reconnaissance made, data
unavailable.

COST OF MISSIONS

Aircraft Lost. . . . . None

Aircraft Damaged. 33
Percent Of Aircraft Airborne. 4.2%

Crew Member Casualties. . . . . None

Aircraft Landing at Iwo Jima & Okinawa . . . 89

DATE OF ISSUE
22 August 1945

33RD STATISTICAL CONTROL UNIT

35PTU 7-11-58

HEADQUARTERS
TWENTIETH AIR FORCE
APO 234

SUBJECT: Report of 4 Precision Attacks and 2 Incendiary Strikes
Against Targets on Honshu on 14-15 August, 1945

TO   : Commanding General, U.S. Army Strategic Air Forces,
APO 234, San Francisco, California

1. IDENTIFICATION OF REPORT:

        a. Major Operations on this Date: Field Order Number 20,
dated 13 August 1945, Headquarters Twentieth Air Force, directed the
58th, 73rd, 313th, 314th and 315th Bombardment Wings to attack 4 precision targets and 2 urban areas on Honshu with maximum effort. Field
Order Number 121, Headquarters 313th Bombardment Wing, dated 14 August
1945, also directed the 313th Wing to attack 4 Japanese mine fields.

        b. Operations Reported Herein: This Tactical Mission Report
includes the following maximum-effort missions:

Mission Number	Wing	Force Assigned	Target
325	58th	4 Groups	*Hikari Naval Arsenal (90.32-671) Tokuyama, Honshu
326	73rd	4 Groups	**Osaka Army Arsenal (90.25-382) Osaka, Honshu
327	313th	3 Groups	**Marifu Railroad Yards (90.30-2202) Iwakuni, Honshu
328	315th	4 Groups	*Nippon Oil Refinery (90.6-1066) Tsuchisaki, Honshu
329	314th	2 Groups	*Kumagaya (Honshu) Urban Area
330	314th	2 Groups	*Isesaki (Honshu) Urban Area

        *Primary visual and radar targets
       **Primary visual targets

        (1) The Fuji Textile Mill (90.24 - 2140/1141) was a
secondary visual target for the 73rd Wing and the Nakajima Aircraft
Company (90.25 - 1635) was designated as a primary radar target. The
Otake Army Depot (90.30) was a secondary visual and primary radar target
for the 313th Wing. No last resort targets were specified.

        c. Operations Reported Separately: The attack by the 313th
Wing against 4 Japanese mine fields is included in a separate Tactical
Mission Report covering Twentieth Air Force mining operations for July
and August of 1945.

294

2. MISSION PLANNING:

    a. Selection of Targets:

        (1) Targets Considered: The most important precision targets that had not been attacked successfully and the remainder of the 180 designated small urban areas that had not been bombed successfully were considered in the selection of the targets for these missions.

        (2) Targets Selected and Reasons: The above-mentioned targets were selected in order to take advantage of the weather and yet compress the attacks in the minimum possible time. The precision targets (Hikari Naval Arsenal, Osaka Army Arsenal, and Marifu Railroad Yards) were planned for attack during the day with attacks by night on the urban areas and the Nippon Oil Refinery precision target. In the event that weather was unfavorable on the date for the day missions they were to be postponed until the following day with no change in the night attacks. This would allow a one-day leeway to make a weather decision.

    b. Importance of Targets:

        (1) Mission Number 325 - Hikari Naval Arsenal: Located on the northern shore of the Inland Sea, 10 miles southeast of Tokuyama, this target is one of the enemy's 4 or 5 most important naval arsenals and one of the 10 most important arsenals in all Japan. It has a ground area of 28,700,000 square feet, a roof area of 4,450,000 square feet, 268 large buildings and countless small buildings. Of the target construction, 15.5 per cent is of steel and light material construction. This arsenal produces all types of ordnance.

        (2) Mission Number 326 - Osaka Army Arsenal: This target, located in the eastern part of the city of Osaka, 7 miles from Osaka Harbor, is one of Japan's most important arsenals. It manufactures all types of ammunition, shells, bombs, primers, propellants and fuzes. Although the small area of explosives storage indicates relatively little shell loading, the 100-acre extension to the east has increased the importance of the arsenal and it is reported to be manufacturing guns up to 16 inches in size. There are 183 buildings in the target area.

        (3) Mission Number 327 - Marifu Railroad Yards: The Marifu Railroad Yards at Iwakuni, on the Sanyo main line, are 8 to 10 tracks wide and approximately 3000 feet long. These yards have no repair facilities or roundhouses.

        (4) Mission Number 328 - Nippon Oil Refinery: This target is located immediately north of and along the bank of the Omono River on the northwestern outskirts of the port town of Tsuchisaki, 5 miles northwest of the city of Akita. It is one of the most important targets in the Japanese petroleum industry, processing crude oil from the fields around Akita, the largest natural petroleum producers in the Japanese homeland. The annual crude capacity was estimated in 1944 at 1,320,000 barrels. This capacity has increased in importance since, unlike most existing refineries in Japan proper, it is not dependent on imported petroleum. The tankage capacity of the plant is believed to be in excess of operating requirements.

        (5) Mission Number 329 - Kumagaya Urban Area: Kumagaya, located about 40 miles northwest of the Imperial Palace of Tokyo and 8 miles southeast of Koizuma, is a center of aircraft parts (airframe and engine) production for the Nakajima Aircraft Company. It is also one of

distinct radar points at Hiburi-Misaki and Murozumi. The best reference point is a very small island, 3 miles south of the target, which can be seen at very long range. Radar operators could obtain excellent results if blind bombing were necessary.

(c) <u>Mission Number 326 - Osaka Army Arsenal</u>: The initial point for this mission, 3416N - 13504E, located on the peninsula at Kada, has been used successfully on most previous Air Force missions into Osaka. The arsenal in Osaka cannot be identified by radar and area radar bombing was believed to have little value because of the bombed-out areas surrounding the target. Offset bombing at high altitudes was not recommended because of the lack of distinct offset aiming points. The assigned primary radar target is the Nakajima Aircraft Company at Handa. This target does not resolve itself as a single radar return but its location, between Handa and Narawa, which smear together in a separate signal, makes it a fair target for blind bombing.

(d) <u>Mission Number 327 - Marifu Railroad Yards</u>: The initial point for this mission is the most southern island in the Seto-Nai-Kai and should be good for a radar check point as well as for a wind run point. The radar navigation from the departure point is along the distinctive shore line which each operator could use for wind checks or position fixes. The target is only fair for radar bombing but using Otake Army Depot as secondary visual target this mission would have an excellent radar target. The Otake Army Depot is located on a prominent coastal projection and radar operators could use the coast line as reference point in locating the target.

(e) <u>Mission Number 328 - Nippon Oil Refinery</u>: This mission was to follow the coast from Chosi Point to a well-defined coastal point at 3658N - 14054E and to an island initial point at 3827N - 1391430E. This island point should be identified easily and should serve as an excellent wind run point. The approach from the initial point, Awa Shima, is a distance of 81 nautical miles along the western coast of Honshu. Although this coast is fairly smooth, it has several points which can be used in determining range. If necessary, the distinctive projection north of Akita can be used as a reference point, though the city of Akita can be identified at a minimum range of 40 miles. The assigned target is located at the mouth of the Omono Gawa which can be used as a reference point. The target, which gives a separate radar return, should be good for direct synchronous bombing by individual aircraft.

(f) <u>Missions Number 329 and 330 - Kumagaya and Isesaki</u>:

Both these incendiary missions were to use a common initial point. This point, 3609N - 14019E, is the northermost corner of the "Y" shaped Kasumiga Ko, which gives a well-defined radar shore line. The initial point can be easily identified at the landfall point. Although Isesaki is a good radar target, radar navigation from the initial point to the target may prove difficult. Isesaki is located 75 nautical miles inland with only one good radar axis from the southeast which avoids all mountainous terrain. The scheduled run is upwind and difficulty from heat thermals may be expected at the release point. For these reasons the altitude was to be 15,000 feet, thus providing good radar navigation, good rate checks in synchronous bombing, and avoiding heat thermals as much as possible. A river with several outstanding bridges runs parallel to the scheduled route and by following this river the radar operators could find the triangle of cities, Isesaki, Maebashi and Takasaki. All three cities have excellent returns and could be identified from a range of 15 to 20 nautical miles. The same radar and navigational factors were applied in planning the miss-

1. **Bomb Selection:** Bombs, fuzing and interval-ometer setting for this mission were the same as for the mission against Kumagaya.

2. **Reason for Selection:** The reasons for selection of the bombs, fuzing and intervalometer setting for this mission were the same as those for Mission Number 329. The force assigned was believed sufficient to achieve a minimum density of 225 tons of bombs per square mile.

(2) **Bomb Loading:**

a. Bomb load estimates were as follows:

Mission Number	Wing	Target	Expected Bomb Load (pounds)
325	58th	Hikari Arsenal	12,000
326	73rd	Osaka Arsenal	14,000
327	313th	Marifu Railroad Yards	12,000
328	315th	Nippon Oil Refinery	20,500
329	314th	Kumagaya	16,000
330	314th	Isesaki	16,000

b. **Ammunition Loading:** Ammunition loading for these missions was in accordance with established policy.

c. **Gasoline Loading:** Fuel load estimates were as follows: 58th and 313th Wings, 7100 gallons; 73rd and 314th Wing 6700 gallons; and 315th Wing, 6300 gallons.

d. **Flight Planning:**

(1) **Routes:**

(a) **Mission Number 325 - Hikari Naval Arsenal:**

Route	Reason for Choice
Base to Iwo Jima	Iwo Jima was the first assembly.
to	
3243N - 13233E	This was a reassembly point at I Shima.
to	
3256N - 1320530E	This was the point of Tsurima Saki, an easily identified departure point on the northeast side of Kyushu.
to	
3324N - 1314230E	This initial point was Tsukuishi Bana on the northern shore of Beppu Wan, easily identified for a good approach to the target.
to	
Target	
to	
Iwo Jima to Base	Tactical Doctrine

(b) **Mission Number 326 - Osaka Army Arsenal:**

	Reason for Choice
Base to Iwo Jima	Iwo Jima was the first assembly.

altitude of 15,000 feet was specified.

(d) Mission Number 328 - Nippon Oil Refinery: Photographs revealed 10 heavy antiaircraft guns, 6 medium weapons and 1 searchlight in the Akita area. This was a very poor night defense and only meager and inaccurate flak was expected. Medium weapons would have little effect on aircraft at the planned base altitude of 10,000 feet. The planned route avoided other flak areas.

(e) Mission Number 329 - Kumagaya: No antiaircraft defenses were apparent on photographs of the Kumagaya area. The 60 heavy guns at nearby Ota were avoided on the planned axis of attack. Little or no flak was expected at the planned altitude of 14,000 feet and the route was to avoid other flak areas.

(f) Mission Number 330 - Isesaki: Although no flak defenses had been observed in the Isesaki area the only possible radar approach would bring the aircraft within the effective range of the 60 heavy guns of the Ota defenses. A previous mission (Mission Number 313 to Maebashi) using the same approach, however, had encountered only meager and inaccurate flak. Only meager and inaccurate flak was expected from the Ota area at the planned base altitude of 15,000 feet and the route was to avoid other defended areas.

(5) Assembly Points: Assembly points were to be as listed under Flight Planning, Part (1), of this section.

(6) Departure Points: Departure points were to be as listed under Flight Planning, Part (1), of this section.

(7) Initial Points: Initial points were to be as listed under Flight Planning, Part (1), of this section.

(8) Rally Points: No rally points were specified for these missions.

(9) Route Back: The return routes were to be as listed under Flight Planning, Part (1) of this section.

e. Bombing Factors:

(1) Bombing Altitudes, Axes of Attack, Length and Time of Bomb Runs, Drift and Forces:

Mission Number	Wing	Force (Group)	Axis of Attack (Degrees)	Bomb Run (Miles)	Time of Bomb Run (Minutes)	Bombing Altitude (Feet)	Drift (Degrees)
325	58th	4	20	41½	8 3/4	15,000	7 R
326	73rd	4	43	43	8 3/4	20,000	5½ R
327	313th	3	9	31	6 3/4	15,000	8 R
328	315th	4	28	87	21	10,000-11,000	4 R
329	314th	2	270	53	14 3/4	14,000-14,800	1 L
330	314th	2	281	65	18	15,000-15,800	3 R

b. Routes Out: (See Annex A, Part I, for navigation track chart). No navigational deficiencies were reported on these missions. Individual aircraft accomplished long range navigation to the assembly points in the case of the daylight strikes and to the target areas in the case of the night missions. Radar was used as a navigational aid and for wind determination, for the daylight strikes and for wind determination, navigation and bombing on the night attacks.

c. Assemblies: Assemblies for the daylight missions were effected as planned.

d. Targets:

(1) Primary: A total of 713 aircraft, including 23 pathfinder aircraft, bombed the primary visual and primary visual and radar targets from 140255Z to 141739Z at altitudes of from 10,200 to 25,100 feet. A total of 4462.7 tons of bombs were dropped.

(2) Targets of Opportunity: Ten aircraft dropped 65.4 tons of bombs on targets of opportunity as follows: Saeki, Nakamura, Shimizu, Nobeoka, Nagahama, Matsumaru, Wakayama, Kiwasa, Saganoseki, Sendai and Koizumi. Four of these aircraft also bombed their primary targets.

(3) Remainder of Force: Forty-seven aircraft were non-effective on these missions.

(4) Route Back: The return route was flown as briefed. Eighty-nine aircraft landed at Iwo Jima.

(5) Landing: Aircraft landed as follows:

Mission Number	Wing	First Landing	Last Landing
325	58th	141035Z	141345Z
326	73rd	140953Z	141211Z
327	313th	140904Z	141056Z
328	315th	142307Z	150200Z
329	314th	142133Z	142314Z
	313th	142109Z	142240Z
330	314th	142254Z	150041Z
	73rd	142100Z	142250Z
Twentieth Air Force Total:		140904Z	150200Z

(6) Fighter Escort and Sweeps: (See Annex A, Part VIII, for details on fighter activities for these missions) A total of 151 fighters of the Seventh Fighter Command were airborne for these missions, 2 Groups escorting the B-29 mission to Osaka and 2 Groups attacking the Nagoya area.

(7) Loss and Damage:

(a) Enemy Aircraft: No claims were made by B-29s or escorting fighters on these missions.

(3) Altitudes:

    (a) Enroute to target: 6,000 - 6,800 feet; 8,000 - 8,800 feet.

    (b) Attack: Force (1) 15,000 feet to 15,800 feet
                   Force (2) 14,000 feet to 14,800 feet.

(4) Bomb Load: M-47IB's; M-17 IC's; and E-46 IC's.
                     All clusters fused to open 5,000 feet above target.

(5) Each force will send out 12 pathfinders to strike target first.

(6) Force (1) will dispatch two special jamming airplanes to orbit the point 3615N - 13923E with a ten mile radius at altitudes of 18,000 feet and 18,500 feet. These airplanes will be equipped to barrage the 72-84 Mc and 190-210 Mc regions and to spot jam any gunlaying or searchlight radars appearing outside the barrage. Additional quantities of rope will be carried by these airplanes.

(7) Bombing Airspeed: 215 MPH CIAS

(8) Take-off: 141730K.

315th Wing:

(1) Primary Visual and Radar Target: 1066-NIPPON OIL CO. REFINERY

    LPI   FORCE REQUIRED

    074126   4 Groups - Maximum

    LPI Reference: Twentieth Air Force Litho-Mosaic TSUCHIZAKE AREA, 90.6 URBAN.

(2) Route:

    Base
    IWO JIMA
    3658N - 14054E
    3827N - 139143OE (I.P.)
    Target (3945N - 14004E)
    3816N - 14131E
    IWO JIMA
    Base

(3) Altitudes:

    (a) Enroute to target: 5,000 - 5,800 feet; 7,000 - 7,800 feet.

    (b) Attack: 10,000 feet to 11,000 feet.

(4) Bomb Load:

    (a) 100 lb GP's using T-19 adapters to extent available, remainder 250 lb GP's.

    (b) Fusing: No nose fuse and non-delay tail.

    (c) Intervalometer Setting: 55 feet.

(5) Take-off: 141630K.

An examination of the above data reveals the following:

(1) There is some indication of saturation of the
defenses; i.e., the third squadron of the 498th Group was only one-half
minute behind the second squadron. Damage is second squadron--5 aircraft;
damage in third squadron--0 aircraft. The third and fourth squadrons of
the 499th Group were over simultaneously, but only one squadron received
damage from moderate, accurate flak. The other squadron received only
meager, accurate flak.

(2) The 497th Group (last group in) was 6½ minutes
behind the 500th Group--a sufficient interval to permit the defenses
to get set. However, flak was moderate and in general inaccurate
(1 aircraft hit). Possible reasons for this were the factors of crew
fatigue, tube overheating, or guns getting out of level due to pro-
longed firing.

d. On withdrawal, following a right breakaway, several aircraft encountered meager, inaccurate, heavy flak from Nara (East of
Osaka).

e. No aircraft were lost to flak on this mission, and of
145 aircraft bombing, 28 or 19.3%, sustained flak damage. This figure is
significantly lower than the 61.0% damage inflicted by these same defenses on Mission Number 284 (cloud cover--0-3/10). An explanation of this
fact is somewhat obscured since the conditions of attack were the same in
each case--weather conditions were actually more favorable to flak operations for Mission Number 326.

3. Mission Number 327 - Marifu Railroad Yards - Iwakuni:

a. The primary target was bombed by 108 aircraft of the 313th
Wing between 0255Z-0318Z from 15,000-17,900 feet. Axis of attack varied
from 9° - 170°.. Weather was reported as CAVU-3/10 undercast.

b. The only flak encountered during the entire mission was two
inaccurate, heavy bursts over the target.

c. No aircraft were lost or damaged as a result of flak on
this mission.

4. Mission Number 328 - Nippon Oil Refinery, Akita: *NIGHT*

a. The primary target was bombed by 134 aircraft of the 315th
Wing between 1413 43Z-1417 21Z from 10,000-15,200 feet. Axis of attack
was 27° T. Secondary target, Sendai, was attacked by one aircraft.
Weather over the target was reported as 7/10-10/10 clouds with winds
of 17 knots from 330°.

b. Flak en route to the target was reported as follows:

Location	Coordinates	Remarks
Hitachi	36 36 N - 140 41 E	Gun flashes.
Sukagawa	37 18 N - 140 22 E	Meager and inaccurate, heavy.
Niigata	37 57 N - 139 05 E	Meager and inaccurate, heavy (seen at a dist-ance).

301

c. Flak in the target area was nil to meager and inaccurate, heavy. Two ineffective searchlights were reported at the target area.

d. On withdrawal from target there was no flak reported.

e. No aircraft were lost or damaged due to flak.

f. Searchlights were ineffective as follows:

Location	Coordinates	Number
Hitachi	36 35 N - 140 40 E	14
Koriyama	37 28 N - 140 21 E	1
Takada	37 28 N - 139 50 E	10-12
Nugata	37 57 N - 139 05 E	11-15
Gatsugi	38 30 N - 139 30 E	6

g. Blackout of target was effective.

5. Mission Number 329 - Kumagawa Urban Area:

a. The primary target was bombed by eleven aircraft of the 313th Wing and 70 aircraft of the 314th Wing between 1521Z-1639Z from 14,000-19,000 feet. Axis of attack varied from 270°-292°. Weather was reported as 1/10-10/10 undercast.

b. En route to the target flak was nil.

c. Over the target flak was nil to meager, inaccurate, heavy and medium. Two to 4 ineffective searchlights were seen in the target area.

d. On withdrawal flak was nil.

e. No aircraft were lost or damaged as a result of flak on this mission.

6. Mission Number 330 - Isesaki Urban Area: NIGHT

a. The primary target was bombed by eight aircraft of the 73d Wing and 79 aircraft of the 314th Wing between 1508Z-1715Z from 15,000-16,000 feet. Axis of attack varied from 283°-302°. Weather was reported as 7/10-10/10 undercast.

b. En route to the target meager, inaccurate, heavy and medium flak was encountered at Ota. Two to 4 searchlights were observed in this area.

c. Over the target flak was nil.

d. On withdrawal flak was nil.

e. No aircraft were lost or damaged as a result of flak on this mission.

f. Ineffective searchlights were seen at: Tachikawa, Hachioji, Atsugi and Hiratsuka.

OUR MISSION (#328) LONGEST MISSION 16:50 MIN

MISSION ____325 – 330____

DATE ____14 August 1945____

AIRCRAFT PARTICIPATING

UNIT	NUMBER OF AIRCRAFT ON HAND	SCHEDULED	FAILING TO TAKEOFF	AIRBORNE	TIME OF TAKE OFF DATE	FIRST	LAST	TIME OF RETURN DATE	FIRST	LAST	BOMBING PRIMARY TARGET	BOMBING SECONDARY TARGET	BOMBING OTHER TARGETS	COMPLETING AUXILIARY MISSIONS	EFFECTIVE	NON-EFFECTIVE	LANDING AT IWO JIMA
58WG	181	170 / 1a	3 / 1	167 / 1	13 Aug.	2010Z	2217 Z	14 Aug.	Mission #325 1035 Z	1345 Z	157 / –	– / –	4 / –	– / 1	161 / 1	6 / –	20 / –
73WG	191	165 / 4b	4 / –	161 / 4	13 Aug.	2015Z	2147 Z	14 Aug.	Mission #326 0953 Z	1211 Z	145 / –	– / –	2 / –	– / 4	147 / 4	14 / –	4 / –
313WG	136	120 / 1a	5 / –	115 / 1	13 Aug.	1900Z	2021 Z	14 Aug.	Mission #327 0904 Z	1056 Z	108 / –	– / –	2 / –	– / 1	110 / 1	5 / –	41 c / –
315WG	166	(143) / 2d	2 / –	141 / 2	14 Aug.	(0642Z)	0858 Z	14 – 15 August	Mission #728 2307 Z	(0200 Z)	132 / –	– / –	– / –	– / 2	132 / 2	9 / –	(13) / –
313WG / 314WG	* – / 90	16 / 65 / 12e	2 / 2 / –	14 / 63 / 12	14 Aug. / 14 Aug.	0815Z / 0752Z	0916 Z / 0839 Z	14 Aug.	Mission #329 2109 Z / 2133 Z	2240 Z / 2314 Z	11 / 59 / 11	– / –	– / –	– / – / 2	11 / 59 / 11	3 / 4 / 1	2 / 3 / –
TOTAL #329		(81) / 12e / 2	4 / – / –	77 / 12 / 2	14 Aug.	0752Z	0916 Z		2109 Z	2314 Z	70 / 11	– / –	– / –	2 / –	70 / 11 / 2	7 / 1 / –	5 / –
73WG / 314WG	** 93	13 / 71 / 12 e	3 / – / –	10 / 71 / 12	14 Aug. / 14 Aug.	0802Z / 0845Z	0835 Z / 1005 Z	14 Aug. / 14-15 August	Mission #330 2100 Z / 2254 Z	2250 Z / 0041 Z	8 / 66 / 12	– / –	1 / 1 / –	– / –	9 / 67 / 12	4 / –	6 / –
		3 g	1	3							–			3			

25 PIW – 7-13-52

303

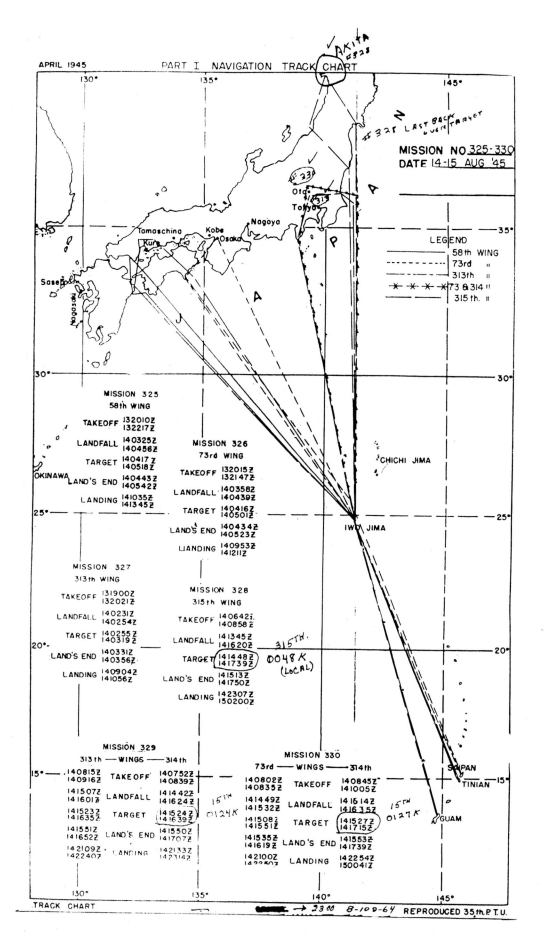

AKITA
#325

#325 LAST BACK OVER TARGET

MISSION NO. 325-330
DATE 14-15 AUG '45

#323

Otd
#313
Tokyo

Nagoya
Kobe
Tomaschina   Osaka
Kure
Sasebo
Nagasaki

LEGEND
——————— 58th WING
- - - - - - 73rd "
————————— 313th "
——*—*—* 73 & 314 "
————————— 315th "

J   A   P   A   N

CHICHI JIMA

MISSION 325
58th WING

TAKEOFF	132010Z / 132217Z
LANDFALL	140325Z / 140456Z
TARGET	140417Z / 140518Z
LAND'S END	140443Z / 140542Z
LANDING	141035Z / 141345Z

OKINAWA

MISSION 326
73rd WING

TAKEOFF	132015Z / 132147Z
LANDFALL	140358Z / 140439Z
TARGET	140416Z / 140501Z
LAND'S END	140434Z / 140523Z
LANDING	140953Z / 141211Z

IWO JIMA

MISSION 327
313th WING

TAKEOFF	131900Z / 132021Z
LANDFALL	140231Z / 140254Z
TARGET	140255Z / 140319Z
LAND'S END	140331Z / 140356Z
LANDING	140904Z / 141056Z

MISSION 328
315th WING

TAKEOFF	140642Z / 140858Z
LANDFALL	141345Z / 141620Z
TARGET	141448Z / 141739Z
LAND'S END	141513Z / 141750Z
LANDING	142307Z / 150200Z

315TH.
0048K
(LOCAL)

MISSION 329

	313th ── WINGS ── 314th	
TAKEOFF	140815Z / 140916Z	140752Z / 140839Z
LANDFALL	141507Z / 141601Z	141442Z / 141624Z
TARGET	141523Z / 141635Z	141524Z / 141639Z
LAND'S END	141551Z / 141652Z	141550Z / 141707Z
LANDING	142109Z / 142240Z	142133Z / 142314Z

15TH
0124K

MISSION 330

	73rd ── WINGS ── 314th	
TAKEOFF	140802Z / 140835Z	140845Z / 141005Z
LANDFALL	141449Z / 141532Z	141614Z / 141635Z
TARGET	141508Z / 141551Z	141527Z / 141715Z
LAND'S END	141535Z / 141619Z	141553Z / 141739Z
LANDING	142100Z / 142250Z	142254Z / 150041Z

15TH
0127K

SAIPAN
TINIAN

GUAM

Appendix VII

EXCERPT OF LETTER BY GEN. CURTIS LEMAY, C.O., 21ST BOMBER COMMAND

Extracted from Jim B. Smith's journal. This letter deals with the contributions to the war effort made by the 315th Bomb Wing.

- LETTER EXTRACT FROM Gen. Curtis Lemay -
21st Bomber Command C.O.

In the short time of its operation,
the 315th Wing revolutionized heavy bombardment by proving that it is possible
to knock out small difficult targets
through the use of APQ-7 radar. This pioneer
organization blazed a new path in aerial
warfare, accomplishing the task with
the lowest combat losses on record.

The primary target was found
and attacked on every mission flown,
with an extremely high percentage of
airborne aircraft dropping bombs on
the assigned objectives.

No estimate is available at this
time, but is believed that the blasting
of nine refineries and storage areas
seriously crippled Japan's oil production
capacity and that had the attacks

307

continued much longer the Nipponese production would have been cut to a trickle, seriously handicapping their ability to wage war, thus materially shortening the length of the war and saving countless American lives.

DISTINGUISHED UNIT CITATION - 501ST BOMBARDMENT GROUP
23 JANUARY 1946

Distinguished Unit Citation being presented to 501 Bomb Group, 23 January 1946

HEADQUARTERS TWENTIETH AIR FORCE
APO 234, c/o Postmaster
San Francisco, California

GENERAL ORDERS)
            :   23 January 1946
NO.........13)

SECTION V

DISTINGUISHED UNIT CITATION   As authorized by Executive
Order 9396 (Sec I, WD, Bull 22, 1943), superceding Executive
Order 9075 (Sec III, WD Bull 11, 1942), and under the provisions
of paragraph 2d (1), Section IV, Circular No 333 WD 1943, and
letter, Headquarters United States Army Strategic Air Forces,
file AG 200.6, subject:"Distinguished Unit Badge", dated 11
October 1945, and paragraph 4 Section I, General Orders 1,
Pacific Air Command, United States Army, 25 December 1945,
(Classified), the following units are cited for outstanding
performance of duty in action against the enemy:

The 501st Bombardment Group (VH) is cited for outstanding
performance of duty in armed conflict with the enemy. During the
period 6 July 1945 to 13 July 1945 that organization delivered
devastating attacks against Japanese petroleum installations on
the island of Honshu to demonstrate the revolutionary
capabilities of a new radar bombing instrument which was
undergoing its first test under battle conditions. Personnel of
the 501st Bombardment Group (VH) demonstrated efficiency, courage
and devotion to duty in long flights over enemy water and through
adverse weather conditions which often cut off all visibility.
B-29 aircraft of this unit had sacrificed defensive fire power
for speed and bomb-carrying capacity by stripping the planes of
all armament except three .50-caliber tail guns. With this bare
protection, aircraft were more than usually vulnerable to enemy
fighter attack and anti-aircraft defenses. On the night of 6
July 1945, the 501st Bombardment Group (VH) attacked the Maruzon
Oil Refinery at Shimotsu, considered one of the most important
refineries and oil storage points for the enemy navy in its home
islands. Flying more than 1500 miles from their home base,
aircraft of this Group attacked the target in single bombing runs
without defensive escort.

Despite an undercast which completely obscured the refinery, 95
percent of the installation was destroyed. On the night of 9
July 1945, the 501st Bombardment Group (VH) attacked the Utsubo
Oil Refinery at Yokkaiehi, one of the three most important oil
refineries in Japan. This installation produced a significant
portion of the aviation gasoline used by the enemy's air forces,
and while it had undergone previous attacks, it was still capable
of production. Radar photograph plots showed that 100 percent of
the group aircraft had passed directly over the target against
enemy anti-aircraft fire and unfavorable weather conditions. the
refinery was left in reins. On the night of 12 July, the 501st
Bombardment Group (VH) attacked the Kawasaki Petroleum Center
located in the heart of Japans most important and most heavily
defended industrial district. This target comprised the
facilities of four leading oil companies and had a combined daily
refining capacity of 7,000 barrels. Despite intense and accurate
anti-aircraft fire, 82 percent of the Group aircraft that were
plotted passed directly over the target, and smashed warehouse,
tanks, pipe stills, furnaces and other vital equipment, thus
delivering a serious blow to the enemy's ability to produce
petroleum products. On all of these missions, ground personnel
of the 501st Bombardment Group (VH) displayed outstanding
ability, willingness, and ingenuity in carrying out their
assigned tasks, under extreme handicaps. The improvised
equipment and methods of work while maintaining aircraft on a
base still under construction and lacking many facilities. The
achievements of the 501st Bombardment Group during this period
contributed greatly to the destruction of the major oil refining
and storage capacity of Japan and drastically reduced the power
and ability of the enemy to continue the war, thereby bringing
honor to the United States Army Air Forces and to the entire
military service.

311

BY COMMAND OF MAJOR GENERAL PARKER:

                                    L H RODIECK
                                    Colonel, GSC
                                    Chief of Staff

OFFICIAL:

            GUSTAV A NEUBERG
            Lt Col, AGD
            Adjutant General

DISTRIBUTION: A AND D
        Plus 2 - PACUSA SCU APC 925
              5 - Ea Organ

                        A CERTIFIED TRUE COPY:

                        RICHARD W. FLURY,
                        Captain, Air Corps

Appendix IX

MISSION NOTES

These notes were kept by Jim B. Smith while serving aboard "The Boomerang" and contain information pertaining to "missions" flown by that aircraft and her crew with the 315th Bomb Wing.

My Diary of combat missions count began with Turk Island which explains the discrepancy between the diary count and the mission count over the Japanese Empire.

MISSION TO ROTA AND TO PARAJAMIS ARENT
RECORDED BECAUSE THEY DIDNT OFFER ANY
OPPOSITION. THEY WERE MILK RUNS.

COMBAT MISSION NO. 1
TRUK ATOLL   JUNE 16 1945
        MISSION TIME 7:30 HR.
TOOK OFF AT 12:00 MIDNIGHT AND BOMBED
AT 4:00 A.M. TARGET WAS MOEN AIRSTRIP IN
CENTER OF ATOLL. WEATHER VERY BAD ALL THE
WAY. ENCOUNTERED MODERATE TURBULENCE-
HEAVY RAINS - ICING AT BOMBING ALTITUDE OF
16000' AND ST. ELMO'S FIRE.
        TARGET BOMBED BY RADAR.
OPPOSITION MEAGER TO NILL.

Above not shown page 260

315

COMBAT MISSION NO. 2

TARGET - MITSUBI RIVER OIL REFINERY -
YOKKAICHI JAPAN (HONSHU ISLAND).

DATE: JUNE 26 1945

BOMB LOAD - 27 × 500 G.P.   35 PLANES

GAS LOAD - 6780 GAL.

TAKE OFF TIME - 1700

MISSION TIME - 14:00 HRS.

WEATHER - GENERALLY GOOD TO EMPIRE.

10/10 COVERAGE OVER TARGET AT BOMBING ALT.

15, 400 ft.

BOMBING - RADAR

RESULTS - TARGET 20% DISTROYED

OPPOSITION - SEVERAL SEARCHLIGHTS.:

INACCURATE FLAK. SEVERAL FIGHTERS

PACING US BUT DID NOT ATTACK.

COMBAT MISSION NO. 2

TARGET - NIPPON OIL REFINERY - KUDAMATON
JAPAN (HONSHU)

DATE - JUNE 29, 1945

BOMB LOAD - 27 X 500 G.P. (60 PLANES)

GAS LOAD - 6780 GAL.

TAKE-OFF - 1700

MISSION TIME - 15 HRS.

WEATHER - GENERALLY GOOD TO EMPIRE.
    LOW UNDER CAST + 5/10 COVERAGE AT BOMBING
    ALTITUDE OVER TARGET.

BOMBING - RADAR SYNCHRONOUS RUN AT 15,400

RESULTS - REFINERY SLIGHTLY DAMAGED.
LOCOMOTIVE WORKS ALONG SIDE 50% DAMAGED.

OPPOSITION: FLAK MEAGER. FIGHTERS PACING
    US. SEVERAL SEARCH LIGHTS.

COMBAT MISSION NO. 4.

TARGET - MARUZEN OIL REFINERY

WAKAYAMA JAPAN (HONSHU)

DATE - JULY 2, 1945

BOMBLOAD: 32 X 500 G.P.   60 PLANES

GAS LOAD: 6780 GAL

TAKE-OFF - 1730

MISS TIME - 14 HRS.

WEATHER - GENERALLY GOOD TO EMPIRE.

LOW UNDERCAST OVER TARGET 3/4 MOON

BOMBING : RADAR

RESULTS - TARGET 95% DESTROYED

OPPOSITION - USUAL FLAK AND PACING

FIGHTERS.

COMBAT MISSION 5

TARGET - MITSUBI RIVER OIL REFINERY
YOKKAICHI, JAPAN (HONSHU).

DATE - JULY 9, 1945

BOMB LOAD - 32 X 500 G.P. (60 Planes)

GAS LOAD - 6480 GAL.

TAKE-OFF 1830

MISSION TIME - 13:45 HRS.

WEATHER - BAD TO 1/10.

BOMBING: RADAR

RESULTS - TARGET 30% DESTROYED

OPPOSITION - NUMBER OF SEARCHLIGHTS.

MODERATE FLAK. SEVERAL SHIPS CONED.

ONE SHIP OBSERVED TO RECEIVE FIGHTER

ATTACK.

COMBAT MISSION NO. 6

TARGET - NIPPON OIL REFINERY, AMAGASAKI
(OSAKA, KOBE AREA) JAPAN (HONSHU)

DATE - JULY 19, 1945

BOMB LOAD- 36 x 500 G.P.   80 PLANES

GAS LOAD - 6280 GAL

TAKE OFF - 1730

MISSION TIME - 1400 HRS.

WEATHER - BAD TO TWO - 3/10 LOW AND

3/10 HIGH OVER TARGET 1/4 MOON

BOMBING - RADAR.

RESULTS - TARGET 35% DESTROYED

OPPOSITION - THIRTY SEARCHLIGHTS OBSERVED

USED R.C.M. ROPE AND WAS NOT CONED.

SHIPS RECEIVED MODERATE FLAK

RESULTING IN BATTLE DAMAGE.

REMARKS: LANDED IN HEAVY RAIN ON

RETURN TO BASE.

COMBAT MISSION NO. 7

TARGET - UBE COAL LIQUEFACTION COMPANY
                    UBE JAPAN (HONSHU)

DATE : JULY 22, 1945

BOMB LOAD - 36 X 500 G.P.   80 PLANES

GAS LOAD - 6780

TAKE OFF - 1730

MISSION TIME - 15:30 HR.

WEATHER - GENERALLY GOOD NORTH OF IWO

MILD FRONT 50 MI. SOUTH OF EMPIRE.

TARGET AREA CLEAR. LOW UNDERCAST IN

AREA. FULL MOON. INTENSE FRONT ENCOUNTERED

50 MI SOUTH OF EMPIRE FOR 200 MILES

EXTREMELY TURBULENT.

BOMBING - RADAR

RESULTS - 50% DESTROYED.

OPPOSITION - SLIGHT ALTHOUGH TARGET

IN CENTER OF MAIN NITE FIGHTER DEFENSES

OF EMPIRE AND 150 MILE RUN OVER

LAND AND FULL MOON.

COMBAT MISSION NO. 8

TARGET: SHIMOTSU OIL REFINERY

SHIMOTSU, JAPAN (HONSHU)

DATE - 28 JULY 1945

BOMB LOAD - 36 × 500 G.P.

GAS LOAD - 6480 GAL.

TAKE OFF - 1630

MISSION TIME - 14 HR.

WEATHER - MOD. TURBULENCE TO TWO. 3/4 MOON

TO TARGET

BOMBING: RADAR AT 10,200'

RESULTS - 80% DESTROYED

OPPOSITION - RADAR CONTROLED AUTO WEAPON

AT AIMING POINT. FIRE ACCURATE. RECEIVED

40 BURSTS WHICH SHOOK HP SHIP BUT

CAUSED NO DAMAGE. NO SEARCHLIGHTS.

COMBAT MISSION NO. 9

TARGET: UBE COAL LIQUEFACTION CO.
UBE JAPAN (HONSHU)

DATE: 5 AUGUST 1945

BOMB LOAD - 36 X 500 G.P.   (110 PLANES)

GAS LOAD - 6480

TAKE-OFF - 1630

MISSION TIME - 15:30 HRS.

WEATHER: GENERALLY GOOD. 5/10 COVER

    AT TARGET.

BOMBING - RADAR AT 10,000'

RESULTS: TARGET SUNK.

OPPOSITION: SLIGHT.

REMARKS: FIRST MISSION WITH BOTTOM

PAINTED. SHIP 5-8 M.P.H. SLOW.

323

MISSION 10

TARGET: NIPPON OIL REFINERY AMAGASAKI (HONSHU),

DATE - 9 AUGUST 1945
BOMB LOAD: 40 X 500 G.P.
GAS LOAD: 6280 GAL.
TAKE-OFF - 18:30
MISSION TIME - 14:30 HRS.
WEATHER: TROPICAL TYPHOON BETWEEN GUAM
& IWO. USED RADAR TO MISS MOST OF IT
TARGET AREA CLEAR.
BOMBING: RADAR AT 15,200'
RESULTS - TARGET COMPLETELY DESTROYED
OPPOSITION - 75 SEARCH LIGHTS. SHIP
   BLOWN UP IN FRONT OF US. OUR SHIP
   RECEIVED HOLE IN NOSE SECTION AND
RADIO ANTENNA BLOWN OFF. USED ROPE.

COMBAT MISSION NO. 11

TARGET - NIPPON OIL REFINERY
AKITTA, JAPAN (NORTH HONSHU)

DATE: AUGUST 14, 1945

BOMB LOAD - 164 X 100 G.P.   (150 PLANES).

GAS LOAD - 6780 GAL.

TAKE OFF - 1630

MISSION TIME - 17 HRS.

WEATHER - MOD. BUILD UP - 8/10 COVERAGE.

BOMBING - RADAR (10,400')

RESULTS - TARGET COMPLETELY DESTROYED

OPPOSITION - SLIGHT

REMARKS - LONGEST MISSION EVER ATTEMPTED
WITH FULL LOAD AND NO BAY TANKS. 3800
MILES. HUGE FIRES AND SMOKE UP TO 20,000
FEET. GREATEST TONNAGE CARRIED BY
SINGLE ~~~~ WING. NEWS OF ~~ END OF WAR
RECEIVED 1 HR. FROM BASE ON RETURN.

P.W MISSION — NO. 12

TARGET — P.W. CAMP IN TOKYO

DATE — AUGUST 30

BOMB LOAD — P.W — FOOD — MEDICAL EQUIP —
          CLOTHES

GAS LOAD — 6780 GAL.
TAKE-OFF — 0400 HRS.
MISSION TIME — 17 HRS.

WEATHER — GENERALLY GOOD

BOMBING — DROPPED SUPPLIES BY CHUTE
          AT 300'

OPPOSITION — NONE

REMARKS — NO. 2 PROP ABOUT TO SPIN
          OFF AND NO. 1 BACKFIRING BADLY
          OVER TOKYO.

Appendix X

PILOT'S LOG - BOOMERANG AIRCRAFT COMMANDER
CARL W. SCHAHRER

DATE 1945	MAKE OF AIRCRAFT	AIRCRAFT FLOWN CLASS	TYPE	CERTIFICATE NUMBER	MAKE OF ENGINE	H.P.	REMARKS OR INSPECTOR'S SIGNATURE CERTIFICATION NUMBER AND RATING	CROSS COUNTRY FROM	TO	INSTRUMENT RADIO OR HOOD	TIME DUAL CO-PILOT	AS STUDENT	AS INSTRUCTOR	SOLO DAY	NIGHT
April 6	B-17			Navy	4-Pratt	1200	Gunnery (Camera) Fighter								
20								Sharpshooter		4 00				1 30	
21								Interception		1 00				4 00	
May 15	B-29			Army 3640	4-Wright	2200	Shake Down - Kearney Neb.	Radio Compassnova						8 15	
20	B-29			Army 2660	4-Wright	2200	Kearney Nob. To Mather F.P. Calif.	Furgate Cal - AirSpeed Cal.		1 0				4 20	6 00
29	B-29			Army 3640	4-Wright	2200	Mather Cal. To NAS Holdenu	(BAF)		4 00				10 40	
June 1	B-29			Army 3148	4-Wright	2200	NAS Honlulu H.I. to Kwajalein	M.I.						7 00	
June 2	B-29			Army 3148	4-Wright	2200	Kwajalein to Guam							7 15	
June 7	B-29			Army 3640	4-Wright	2200	A.S.Kaplan Chug - Executrey - Bend	Reid & Kwarn Air Raids						18	1 30
8	B-29			Army 3640	4-Wright	2200	Air Attack To Kawanier Locantea	Leproning		8 00				2 55	
14	B-29			Army 3148	4-Wright	2200	Launch At Anna Harbor N.W.							2 25	4 00
16	B-29			Army 3648	4-Wright	2200	Combat Mission - Track - Nova	Jepan		1 00				4 15	
23	B-29			Army 2660	4-Wright	2200	Guam - Indiana Guam Bonaire	At Patroys Island						5 00	8 00
16	B-29			Army 3640	4-Wright	2200	Combat - Aircraft Fired On Highway	Yukaicu Japan		1 00				5 00	8 45
17	B-29			Army 3148	4-Wright	2200	Combat - Nippo On Railway Kwanatsu	Japan		1 00				5 00	7 30
Nov 2	B-29			Army 3642	4-Wright	2200	Combat - Maribenor Railway	Chalayama Shog		1 00				7 45	35 45

Pilot's flight log book page. Columns (left portion): DATE 1945, AIRCRAFT FLOWN (MAKE OF AIRCRAFT, CLASS, TYPE, CERTIFICATE NUMBER, MAKE OF ENGINE, H.P.), REMARKS OR INSPECTOR'S SIGNATURE CERTIFICATION NUMBER AND RATING. Right portion: CROSS COUNTRY (FROM, TO), INSTRUMENT RADIO OR HOOD, DUAL (AS INSTRUCTOR, AS STUDENT), TIME SOLO (DAY, NIGHT).

DATE 1945	MAKE OF AIRCRAFT	CERT. NUMBER	MAKE OF ENGINE	H.P.	REMARKS	FROM	TO	INSTR. RADIO/HOOD	DUAL AS INSTR	TIME SOLO DAY	NIGHT
11 July	B-29	42-3040	4-Wright	2200	Condr - Mitsubishi Oil Refinery	Yontan	Japan	Gunn 1.00		7.00	8.35
14 July	B-29	3640	4-Wright	2200	#6 Condr - Nippon Oil Refinery	Ogasawara	Japan			5.00	4.00
21 July	B-29	3640	4-Wright	2200	#7 Condr - Ube Liquefaction Coal		Ube Japan	Actual 2.00		6.15	7.00
24 July	B-29	3640	4-Wright	2200	Condr - Shimotsu Oil Refinery	Shimotsu	Japan	Actual 2.00		5.00	6.40
1 Aug	B-29	3640	4-Wright	2200	Agst from Tokyo Oil Field	(early morning return)			R.J. Comm	1.10	
7 Aug	B-29	3640	4-Wright	2200	Antioped American Congress				4.00 Comm	2.15	4.30
5 Aug	B-29	3640	4-Wright	2200	Condr - Ube Liquefaction Company	Ube Japan		Actual 1.00	4.00 Comm	6.00	7.25
9 Aug	B-29	3640	4-Wright	2200	Condr - Nippon Oil Refinery	Amagasaki	Japan	Actual 2.00	4.00 Comm	7.00	5.00
17 Aug	J-17	5540	4-Wright	1730	Condr - Nippon Oil Refinery	Akita Japan		Actual 1.00	R.J. Comm	5.30	1.00
25 Aug	J-29	3640	4-Wright	2200	Emergency Equipment and Cargo	Or of Transport Crew		Actual 40		4.00	10
23 Aug	B-29	42-63710 (Tojo)	4-Wright	2200	Air Guard - Evac Silver Stream	Japan		Action 40	R.J. Comm	1.00	
30 Aug	B-29	3640	4-Wright	2200	Air Survey Mission to Tokyo Area	(Yokohama Harbor)			7.00	6.10	7.00
31 Aug	B-29		4-Wright	2200	Air Survey Mission N-Sissy Sagar	(Sasebo)			A.J. Comm	1.30	
5 Sept	B-29	42-64655	4-Wright	2200	Non Standard Formation Flight	3rd Wing			4.0 Comm	.15	2.00
8 Sept	B-29	42-63613	4-Wright	2200	Japanese Surrender Flight				40 Comm	1.30	
1 Sept	B-29	42-6340	4-Wright	2200	Tactical Drill Tactical Area 30 Min Exercise				AC Comm	1.30	

TOTAL: 9.40 2.7 mS | 55.25 49.25

I CERTIFY THAT THE FOREGOING ENTRIES ARE TRUE AND CORRECT

(signature) 1st Lt AC
0-78451

330

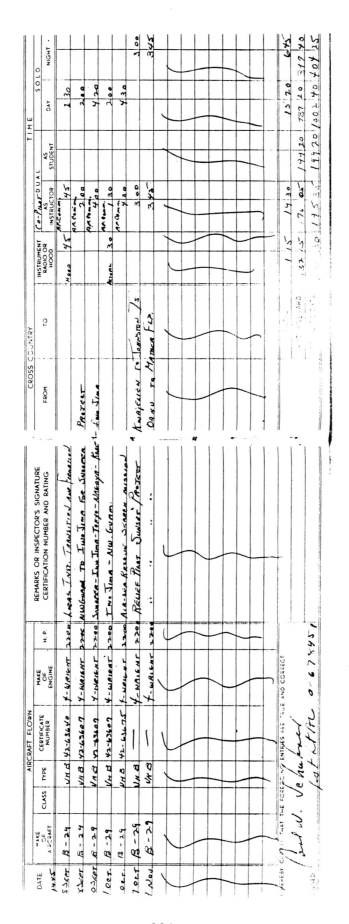

DATE	AIRCRAFT FLOWN						REMARKS OR INSPECTOR'S SIGNATURE CERTIFICATION NUMBER AND RATING	CROSS COUNTRY		TIME				
1945	MAKE OF AIRCRAFT	CLASS	TYPE	CERTIFICATE NUMBER	MAKE OF ENGINE	H.P.		FROM	TO	INSTRUMENT RADIO OR HOOD	Co-Pilot DUAL AS INSTRUCTOR	AS STUDENT	SOLO DAY	NIGHT
5 Sept	B-24		VHB	42-63640	4-Wright	2200	Local Inst. Transition and formation			Hood 45	McCombs 45		1:30	
8 Sept	B-24		VHB	42-23609	4-Wright	2200	Millington to Iwa Jima for Service	Pratser			RR Cooper 2:00		2:00	
02 Sept	B-29		VHB	42-23609	4-Wright	2200	Sumakra-Iwo Jima-Tokyo-Nagoya-back-Iwo Jima		Iwo Jima		RR Cooper 4:00		4:20	
1 Oct	B-29		VHB	42-23609	4-Wright	2200	Iwo Jima - NW Guam			Night 30	McCombs 1:30		2:00	
Oct	B-29		VHB	42-63625	4-Wright	2200	Air-Sea Rescue Search mission				McCombs 4:20		4:30	
7 Oct	B-29		VHB	—	4-Wright	2200	Relief Flight Sunset Project	Kwajalein to Johnston Is.			3:00			1:00
1 Nov	B-29		VHB	—	4-Wright	2200	" "	Oahu to Mather Fld.			3:45			3:45

I hereby certify that the foregoing entries are true and correct

Robert W. Vehmeier

Cert. No. 0-6784511

	1:15	19:30		13:20	6:45
	:32:15	:76:05	199:20	787:20	312:40
	:30:119:55	199:20	1302:40	709:25	

RECORD OF COMBAT DUTY
JIMMIE B. SMITH

ARMY AIR FORCES CERTIFICATE OF APPRECIATION
TO: JIMMIE B. SMITH

_opy FROM THIS

Record of Combat Duty

GROUP _____ 501st _____ CREW NO. __29__

SQUADRON _____ 21st _____ POSITION __RD__

NAME ___Smith_____Jimmie_____B.___Cpl-SGT_39699665__27.L__
      (LAST)   (FIRST)   (M.I.)   (GRADE)   (ASN)   (MOS)

Awards-Decorations Granted _1 a Mtdal, S.O.13, SEC.XI, 28 JUL.45 A.P.O.45_

Date Left Continental U.S. ___20 MAY 45___ AUTH: _O.PVA. o 27.21 ALPHABER FUL_

DATE OF EACH COMBAT MISSION	GEOGRA-PHIC LO-CATION OF TARGET	COMBAT FLYING HOURS	NUMBER CREW CREDIT SORTIES	Cumulative Totals			INITIAL MONTHS ON	INITIAL BY CREW MEMBER
				COMBAT FLYING HOURS	CREW CREDIT SORTIES	MONTHS ON DUTY	ENTRY	
16 JUN 45	TRUK	7:05	0	7:05	0		44	Cuz
26 JUN 45	YOKKAICHN	14:00	1	21:05	1	1		LxS
29 JUN 45	KUDOMATSU	14:45	1	35:50	2	1		luf
2 JUL 45	SHIMOTZSU	13:30	1	49:20	3	1		CuS
9 JUL 45	YOKKAKHI	13:35	1	62:55	4	1		Cuz
19 JUL 45	AMAGASAKI	14:00	1	76:55	5	1		lub
22 JUL 45	UBE	15:15	1	92:10	6	2		Cuz
28 JUL 45	SHIMATSU	13:40	1	105:50	7	2		luS
1 AUG 45	ABORT	1:10	0	107:00	7	2		lu.45
5 AUG 45	UBE	15:30	1	122:30	8	2		
8 AUG 45	AMAGASAKI	14:25	1	136:55	9	2		R.S
14 AUG 45	TSUCHIZAKI	16:50	1	153:45	10	2		
30 AUG 45	TOKYO	16:55	1	168:55	11	3		lube
		13.10						

335

ARMY AIR FORCES
Certificate of Appreciation
FOR WAR SERVICE

TO

JIMMIE B. SMITH

I CANNOT *meet you personally to thank you for a job well done; nor can I hope to put in written words the great hope I have for your success in future life.*

Together we built the striking force that swept the Luftwaffe from the skies and broke the German power to resist. The total might of that striking force was then unleashed upon the Japanese. Although you no longer play an active military part, the contribution you made to the Air Forces was essential in making us the greatest team in the world.

The ties that bound us under stress of combat must not be broken in peacetime. Together we share the responsibility for guarding our country in the air. We who stay will never forget the part you have played while in uniform. We know you will continue to play a comparable role as a civilian. As our ways part, let me wish you God speed and the best of luck on your road in life. Our gratitude and respect go with you.

COMMANDING GENERAL
ARMY AIR FORCES

336

Appendix XII

THE B-29B

On December 17, 1944, 315th Wing Headquarters was directed to carry out special modifications on all B-29 aircraft in its inventory. These included the removal of all armament and the central fire-control system, replacement of the plexiglass gunners' blisters on the sides of the aircraft with smooth ports, replacement of the existing tail turret with the new radar-directed APG-15 turret, and the installation of the new APQ-7 Eagle Radar in place of the current APQ-13 unit. These modifications, which became standard on the B-29B, came about as a result of a special study carried out at Alamogordo AAF, NM. This study, designed to test the vulnerability of the B-29 to fighter attack, showed that the heavily-laden bomber was not only difficult to control at 30,000 ft, but that a steep bank or sudden control movement could cause the aircraft to stall.

Lt. Col. Paul Tibbets, who was assigned to carry out the test, discovered the superior handling characteristics of the stripped aircraft by accident. When his test ship was down for repairs, Tibbets decided to continue the test with an available B-29 which was equipped with only the tail guns. Not only was the ship's rate of climb significantly greater, it could also fly well above 30,000 ft and at speeds higher than those of many fighters. In subsequent tests it was discovered that the stripped bomber could turn in a smaller radius than attacking fighters. The removal of all armament also meant that these aircraft could carry a greater bomb load over a longer distance than the standard B-29.

As a result of this study, the 315th was chosen to test the tactical value of the lighter B-29s in combat. The stripped ships would be used until the specially built B-29B became available.

The new B models were built by the Bell Aircraft Corporation in Atlanta, GA, and were manufactured in batches along with standard A models. Bell built 311 B-29Bs which included other modifications in addition to the new radar and the lack of main armament. Among these were modified engine baffles to increase engine cooling, and both landing gear and bomb-bay doors were converted to pneumatics to reduce system cycling times.

The following table gives specifications for the B-29B-60-BA. All data not listed is the same as the B-29A.

Powerplant:	Wright R-3350-23, 2200 hp at takeoff	
Weight:	Empty:	69,000 lbs
	Gross:	110,000 lbs
	Maximum:	137,500 lbs
Performance Speed:	Maximum: 364 mph at 25,000 ft	
	Cruising:	228 mph
	Landing:	105 mph
Service Ceiling:	32,000 ft	
Climb:	20,000 ft/38 min	
Range:	3875 miles/18,000 lbs bombs	
	5725 miles ferry	

B-29B PRODUCTION
BELL AIRCRAFT, ATLANTA, GEORGIA

AAF Serial Numbers

B-29B-30-BA	42-63581		42-63621
B-29B-35-BA	42-63622		42-63691
B-29B-40-BA	42-63692	through	42-63736
	42-63738	through	42-63743
	42-63745	through	42-63749
	42-63751		
	44-83890	through	44-83893
	44-83895		
B-29B-45-BA	44-83896	through	44-83899
	44-83901	through	44-83903
	44-83905	through	44-83907
	44-83909		44-83910
	44-83912		44-83913
	44-83915		44-83916
	44-83918		44-83919
	44-83921		44-83922
	44-83924		44-83925
	44-83927		44-83929
	44-83931		44-83933
	44-83935		44-83937
	44-83939		
	44-83941	through	44-83943
	44-83945		44-83947
	44-83949		44-83951
	44-83953		44-83955
	44-83957		44-83959
	44-83961		
B-29B-50-BA	44-83963		44-83965
	44-83967		44-83969
	44-83971		44-83973
	44-83975		44-83977
	44-83979		44-83981
	44-83983		44-83985

	44-83987	44-83989
	44-83991	44-83993
	44-83995	44-83997
	44-83999	44-84001
	44-84003	44-84005
	44-84007	
B-29B-55-BA	44-84009	44-84011
	44-84013	44-84015
	44-84017	44-84019
	44-84021	44-84023
	44-84025	44-84027
	44-84029	44-84031
	44-84033	44-84035
	44-84037	44-84039
	44-84041	44-84043
	44-84045	44-84047
	44-84049	44-84051
	44-84053	44-84055
B-29B-60-BA	44-84057	44-84059
	44-84061	44-84063
	44-84065	44-84067
	44-84069	44-84071
	44-84073	44-84075
	44-84077	44-84079
	44-84081	44-84083
	44-84085	44-84087
	44-84089	44-84091
	44-84093	44-84095
	44-84097	44-84099
	44-84101	44-84103
B-29B-65-BA	44-84105	44-84107
	44-84109	44-84111
	44-84113	44-84115
	44-84117	44-84119
	44-84121	44-84123
	44-84125	44-84127
	44-84129	44-84131
	44-84133	44-84135
	44-84137	44-84139
	44-84141	44-84143
	44-84145	44-84147
	44-84149	44-84151

Appendix XIII

AVAILABILITY OF A THIRD ATOMIC BOMB

For 50 years there has been a growing and often bitter controversy surrounding the availability of a third atomic bomb in the closing days of World War II. Was another atomic weapon ready for immediate use, or would it have taken several months to assemble, as some have suggested? Highly regarded references on the subject, such as The Decision to Drop The Bomb by Giovannitti and Freed, Rising Sun by Toland, and Day One by Peter Wyden suggest that the third atomic bomb would have been ready by mid-August. In Day One, Wyden states on page 294 "General Groves factories were still producing plutonium and uranium, and in Los Alamos Oppenheimer was still assembling more bombs, but shortly after the Nagasaki bomb drop, Groves and General Marshall decided to hold up further shipments to Tinian. Reports from Tokyo were beginning to suggest that the Japanese were considering surrender. But unless they gave up by August 13, the deliveries were to resume."

From this one would conclude that the bomb would then have been ready for use on the first day with favorable weather conditions after August 17 or 18, 1945.

Appendix XIV

501ST BOMB GROUP
CREW PORTRAITS

Crew Y-33 "For The Luvva Mike". Miller AC, Nav, Cogut, Ham
Nightingale, Krawetz, Van Driel, Vios, Edscorn, Tiffany

Crew Y-1 "Fleet Admiral Nimitz": Commanding Officer 501st Bomb
Group Col. Boyd Hubbard

Crew Y-20: Preston AC

Crew Y-23: Tone AC

Crew Y-24: LeBlank AC

350

Crew Y-25: Braun AC, French, James, Lenzner, Thomas, Henne, Schreiber, Tiffany, Tower, Rogers, Allsburg

Crew Y-26 "Dark Angel": Byrne AC, Hauser, Klopper, Schroeder, Allen, Uptegrove, Saccents, Fowler, Gearhart, Gillespie

351

Crew Y-28 "Ol' Mathusalem": Garrett AC

Crew Y-29 "Boomerang": Schahrer AC, Cosala, Waltershausen, Ginster, Marshall, Smith, Leffler, Gorder, Siegel, Carlson

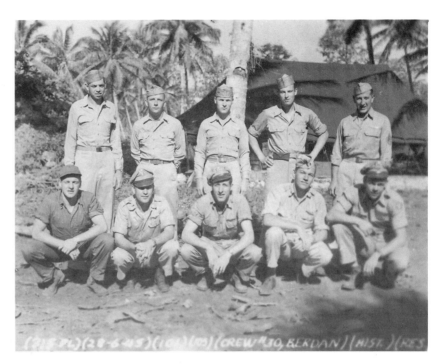

Crew Y-30: Berdan AC, Cotterill, Cohn, Willard, Tipps, Oxendine, Haley, Christopher, Johnson, Lowery

Crew Y-31 "Sweet Chariot": Norton AC, Gamble, Schauer, Galbraith, Moylan, Crusse, Haworth, Ronat, Mangione, Armstrong

Crew Y-33 "For The Luvva Mike": Miller AC

Crew Y-34: Conger AC

354

Crew Y-35: Leche AC

Crew Y-63 "Late Date": Mitchell AC, Nield, Martin, Boone, Zinns, Powell,
Totty, Boyle, Baer, Womack

355

Crew 62, 16th Bomb Group: Eckhart AC, Nelson, Carlson, Williams Jr.,
Ried, Wadsworth, Kechele, Richmond, Humbert

Crew 63, 16th Bomb Group: Hickerson AC, Jensen, Davenport, Rittman,
Rubin, Ludewig, Hussey Jr., Bauman, Robbeloth, Zimmerman

BIBLIOGRAPHY

The Army Air Forces in World War II, (Craven/Cate 1945)

Air Command and Staff College Student Report, Major Ralph L. Swann

Air Force Combat Units of World War II, Department of the Air Force, USAF Historical Division Air University (Maurer and Maurer)

Air Force History, Washington D.C.

Behind Japan's Surrender, (Lester Brooks)

Baa Baa Blacksheep, (Pappy Boyington)

Combat Chronology 1941/1945, The U.S. Army Air Forces in World War II

Day One, Peter Wyden

Declassified Mission Reports: Hiroshima, Ube, Akita

Declassified Base Facilities, Volume 1, National Archives, U.S. Army Forces, Middle Pacific, J. E. Hull, Lieutenant General Commanding

Foreign Relations of U.S. 1945

Handbook Flight Operating Instructions U.S.A.F. Series B-29, B-29A, B-29B, And B-29 Receiver Aircraft

Hirohito, Emperor of Japan, Mosley 1966

Historical Times Inc., Harrisburg, Pennsylvania, 17105

Impact the Army Air Forces Confidential Picture History of World War II

Imperial Tragedy, Thomas M. Coffee

Japan's Imperial Conspiracy, Berganini

Japan's Longest Day, Kodansha International (The Pacific War Research Society)

Library of Congress, Washington D.C.

National Archives Military Reference Branch

Oil & War, Robert Goraiski and Russell W. Freeburg

Personal Papers and Documents

Silent Victory, Clay Blair Jr.

Strategic Air War Against Japan by Major General Haywood S. Hansell Jr.

Tapes and notes from the crew

The Making of The Atomic Bomb, Richard Rhodes

The Shadow Warriors, Bradley Smith

The Two-Ocean War, Samuel Eliot Morison

The Iron Eagle, Curtis LeMay

The Decision To Drop The Bomb, Giovannitti and Freed

The Rising Sun, John Toland

The Signal Corps: The Outcome, G. R. Thompson and Dixie R. Harris

The War--A Concise History 1939-1945, Louis L. Snyder

Total War, Galvocoressi and Wint

Truman, (David McClullough 1922)

The Marshall Cavendish Illustrated Encyclopedia of World War II, 1944-1945

U.S. Army in World War II, The Technical Services,

Wild Bill Donovan, the Last Hero, (Anthony, Cave and Brown)

JIMMIE B. SMITH

To you who answered the call of your country and served in its Armed Forces to bring about the total defeat of the enemy, I extend the heartfelt thanks of a grateful Nation. As one of the Nation's finest, you undertook the most severe task one can be called upon to perform. Because you demonstrated the fortitude, resourcefulness and calm judgment necessary to carry out that task, we now look to you for leadership and example in further exalting our country in peace.

Harry Truman

THE WHITE HOUSE